P9-DTB-422

Elaine

Happy B-Day
This is to get you
in the S.A. mood.

Brian

LOST CITIES
& ANCIENT
MYSTERIES OF
SOUTH AMERICA

by David Hatcher Childress
Lost Cities Series author

Adventures Unlimited Press
Box 22
Stelle, Illinois 60919

Thanks to Dave Millman and Co., More thanks to Mark Segal, who took the cover photo; Janet and Kim, who made the cover so beautiful. And to Carole Gerardo, Linda, Nancy, Gregory Deyermenjian, Rene Chabbert, Herbert Sawinsky, Bill, and a host of other people, without your help this book would not have been possible.

Other titles in David Hatcher Childress' <u>Lost Cities Series</u>:

Lost Cities of China, Central Asia, & India
Lost Cities of Ancient Lemuria & the Pacific
Lost Cities & Ancient Mysteries of Africa & Arabia
Lost Cities of North & Central America (avail. late 89)

About the Author:

David Hatcher Childress was born in France, and raised in the mountains of Colorado and Montana. At nineteen, he left the United States on a six-year journey across Asia and Africa. For the lat six years David has been exploring in South America. An ardent student of history, archaeology, philosophy, and comparative religion, he has authored numerous articles, which have appeared in publications around the world, as well as seven books, including *Lost Cities of China, Central Asia, & India, Lost Cities of Ancient Lemuria and the Pacific* and *Anti-Gravity and the World Grid* .

Currently, he travels the globe in search of lost cities and ancient mysteries. He also leads small groups of similarly interested individuals to some of these sites, including many mentioned in this book. David and Adventures Unlimited are currently searching for the lost cities of Paititi and Yanantin Orco in Peru. For a complete catalogue of Mr. Childress' and other unusual books or more information on his expeditions–

Please write or call
Today:

Adventures Unlimited
Box 22
Stelle, IL 60919-9989 USA

815 253 6390

Adventure Unlimited welcomes correspondence from anyone, anywhere, anytime. Please direct all correspondence to Mr. Childress to the above address.

This book is dedicated to the great explorers that continue to uncover the many mysteries and lost cities that still exist in the fantastic continent of South America.

Library of Congress Number: 86-070411

Lost Cities and Ancient Mysteries of South America.

Cover photo by Mark Segal
Cover photo © 1985 by Mark Segal Photography

© 1986 by David Hatcher Childress
All rights reserved.*
Printed in United States of America.
First Edition.
First Printing: September 1986
Second Printing: January 1989

ISBN 0-932813-02-X

Published by Adventures Unlimited Press
Box 22, Stelle, IL 60919-9989 USA
815 253 6390

Distributed Internationally
by Publishers Network

Adventures Unlimited gives permission for a limited use of material contained in this book. We just ask you to give credit to Adventures Unlimited Press and David Hatcher Childress and send us a copy of the publication. If you have any questions regarding the reuse of this material please call or write to Adventures Unlimited at the above address.

TABLE OF CONTENTS

LOST CITIES AND ANCIENT MYSTERIES OF... SOUTH AMERICA

Lost Cities still await explorers in the jungles of South America.
Drawing by Brian Fawcett, courtesy of the Lima Times.

Chapter One

On the Road in South America: Ancient Continent of Mystery

*"Why not strike out and go to Mexico or
South America and explore for lost cities
as you've always wanted to do?" I asked myself.
-Gene Savoy, South America's
greatest living explorer*

I have always loved a good mystery. Most of my life I have spent searching for mysteries: ancient lost cities buried deep in jungles and deserts, remote temples and monasteries at the far reaches of the earth. At the age of nineteen, I had set off from my parents' home in Montana to roam the hinterlands of Central Asia. Now many years, and many more countries and adventures later, I was on the road again.

As the plane slowly descended into Lima International Airport, early that January morning in 1985, I looked out the window and took a deep breath. I was arriving in South America for the first time, but this trip was already the culmination of a lifetime of intriguing research.

No other continent on earth is as shrouded in controversy and mystery as South America. Historians, archaeologists, anthropologists, geologists and other experts are simply unable to come to any kind of consensus on the who, what, when, why, and how of ancient civilization and technology in South America. Theories of what transpired during the last twenty-five thousand years on this continent range from the horribly conservative and mundane, to the blatantly ridiculous. In fact, the more one looks into the facts, the stranger and more mysterious the story becomes.

3

Yet, some things about South America cannot be doubted, simply because they are so undeniably present: giant cities built out of 100-ton stone blocks; vast complexes of tunnels and caves that extend beyond measure; spectacular gold treasure beyond one's wildest imagination; ancient cities and pyramids, barely discernible through the dense jungle growth; anachronistic and geographically impossible artifacts which defy rational explanation; and colorful legends that make the most outrageous science-fiction sound like docile children's stories.

These were just a few of the things that had brought me to South America. Others were far more ordinary: the famous Carnival of Río de Janiero; the vineyards of Chile; the beautiful waterfalls of Iguazu; the splendid mountains of the Andes; and the charming women of Brazil—to name a few.

South America is a vast, unexplored playground for a crazy adventurer with a lust for life, and I had bought my ticket for a long, dizzy ride. Like so many newcomers to a slightly jaded and devious amusement park, I didn't know quite what I was getting into. South America is a land of danger—of bandits and desperados, untamed Indians who treasure a blond shrunken head on the end of their spear, and police who frame tourists, making them pay to get out of jail. Crime runs rampant throughout the continent, violence is common-place, and simply riding a bus through the mountains may give the traveler occasion to think he is spending his last day on earth.

I was no newcomer to adventure and danger, however. As a rogue archaeologist who has traveled the world, I have lived the last ten years like a beer commercial, grabbing for all the excitement and action I could—and loving it! Whether crossing a pass high in the Himalayas, hitchhiking through a remote desert in Africa, or trying to keep alive in a war-torn, third-world country, I continually wore my perpetual foolish grin of delight, eagerly lapping up the last few drops of excitement. That is not to say that I was not frightened from time to time, nor miserable on many occasions—the beer commercials always end long before the going gets bad. But, once back home comfortable again at some friend's house, or restlessly working a job, I would look back at even the most un-comfortable times with a certain amount of yearning and wistful remembrance. Perhaps you know the feeling.

How should I describe myself? Maybe the way I would like others to perceive me: youthful, with a healthy shock of blond hair and an eager smile. I am no movie star, but I'm told I have a certain amount of charm. And I like people. Meeting people is one of the great joys of travel, so it does not pay to be shy when traveling in foreign countries. I am fond of believing that I am invisible, although my blond hair and gold wire-frame glasses often have the natives of Africa, Mongolia, or the Amazon giving me a good look-over.

My previous expeditions had taken me throughout Asia and Africa. After a year of college, I left Montana to travel and study in the Far East. I lived and worked in India and the Middle East for a year, then went on to Africa. There, I worked and traveled my way for two-and- a-half years around the continent before hitching my way on yachts back across the Indian Ocean. I lived, worked and studied on the Indian sub-continent for another year or two before going on to China, where by sheer luck I became one of the first hitchhikers ever to vagabond around China.

When I returned to the United States at the age of twenty-five, I had been gone for almost six years. After re-entering the workforce for a short time, I took another long trip back to Egypt, Israel, and Europe, then returned again. Yet somewhere inside I knew my longing for adventure, my research into history, and my search for lost cities would all eventually lead me to South America—a land, I sensed, where some of the answers I sought about the origins of civilization might be found.

I had not come to South America unprepared. As on all of my trips, I was traveling light, but equipped with the essentials I would need for my sojourn. In my trusty, green backpack—which less ambitious travelers have called my bag of tricks—I carried:

1 down-filled sleeping bag (warm enough for chilly nights high in the Andes, also good for the South American deserts, or anywhere in Patagonia. In the hot jungles, I either slept on top of the bag, beneath mosquito netting, or inside the sleeping bag with the side zipped all the way down. In the Amazon, you may also want to carry a hammock, but these are readily available.)

1 light, down vest

1 wool sweater

1 nylon/cotton parka with hood (When worn with the down vest, wool sweater and a couple of shirts, this parka was sufficient to keep me warm on even the most freezing night in the Andes. If one plans much climbing at high altitudes, especially above 17,000 feet, a down jacket with hood plus long underwear and wind pants should be standard gear.)

1 ground sheet/poncho (This could be used underneath the

5

sleeping bag for sleeping outside, or rigged into a makeshift tent. The combination of this sheet with my sleeping bag and other gear enabled me to spend the night outdoors in almost any weather.)

1 backpack (Mine is an internal frame type with one large main compartment, which can also be used as a "bivouac sack.")

1 large, plastic water bottle

1 bottle of water purification tablets

1 Swiss-Army knife (with can opener, scissors, and plenty of other gadgets. My knife had a key ring, which allowed it to be attached to my belt with a length of nylon cord.)

2 pairs of long pants (one a pair of jeans for rough traveling, plus one pair of respectable-looking tan khakis for dining at a nice restaurant or getting a permit at a government office.)

1 leather belt with a secret zipper pocket (inside, folded American bills of various denominations can be stashed.)

1 nylon valuables packet (large enough for a passport, travelers cheques and documents, worn inside the clothes.)

1 leg document pouch . (This can be made by removing the foam from a basketball-type knee pad. First, cut off the top, remove the foam pad, then use velcro to seal up the opening. This creates a pouch worn on the inside of the calf or thigh, held up by its own elastic.)

2 cotton T-shirts

1 permanent-press shirt (for looking sharp when dealing with officials or border guards, or for going out in the evening.)

1 khaki safari shirt with many pockets

1 pair of walking shorts

2 pairs of shoes (one pair of comfortable sports shoes, another pair of leather walking shoes or hiking boots. Today, nylon and leather "super-sports" shoes can be purchased which are much lighter than boots, and much more comfortable as well. Unless you are planning some major mountaineering or hacking your way for two weeks through the jungle, heavy boots are usually unnecessary.)

4 pairs of socks, some cotton, some wool

1 pair of rubber thongs, "flip-flops" (wearable in the shower or on the street.)

1 small first-aid kit and toiletries (Carry disinfectant, band-aids, aspirin, gauze, needle and thread, plus other medicaments, including lomotil or Pepto-bismol. Medicine is cheap and easily available throughout South America, but be prepared with your own supply for long sojourns into the jungles and mountains.)

1 flashlight, compass, and a length of nylon cord
5 boxes of matches and a butane lighter
2 candles
1 small deck of cards and a pocket chess set
5 or 6 assorted books (including at least one guide to South America, a blank journal, *Mysteries of Ancient South America* by Harold Wilkins, *The Ultimate Frontier* by Eklal Kueshana, and various other books which I read and traded as I traveled.)
1 map of South America
1 single-lens reflex camera with a 30-80mm zoom lens
10 rolls of color slide film
5 rolls of black and white print film
1 pair of sunglasses
1 wool ski hat
1 pair of wool gloves with nylon mitten shell
A large assortment of souvenirs, knicknacks, postcards, snacks, etc. (It is important to carry food with you in certain areas, especially when you are on an unfamiliar road with an unknown distance to the next town.)

Thieves in South America are as clever and active as anywhere in the world. Normal money belts will often not suffice. So, it behooves the traveler to conceal valuables by distributing them all over his body. Another trick is to first wrap small things of value in an elastic, Ace-type bandage, then wrap and secure this packet around the inside of your calf with a safety pin. This method is used by many South Americans. I prefer to spread my money around my body: in my normal-looking leather money belt, in the valuables packet inside my shirt, some local currency in my front pocket, and the rest in the elastic pouch on the inside of my thigh!

Traveling light is a key to real adventure travel. Be sure that you can fit everything compactly into your backpack. Make sure also that you can carry your backpack comfortably, as well. You may be walking down a road for quite some time before a truck or bus comes along, therefore never carry more than you can handle.

§§§

Landing in Lima, Peru at six-thirty in the morning was a real zoo. I had met some other Americans—Mark, Bob and Steve—on the plane. We had fought our way together through customs, reported a stolen camera, and made it outside to the waiting horde of taxi drivers who shouted at us, vying to take us into the central area of the city.

The airport is a fair distance from Lima, located in one of the worst suburbs. The ride from the airport into town isn't likely to give you a very good impression of Lima, Peru's largest city and the first Spanish-founded city in South America. In the bright, cloudless morning, we passed block after block of mud-brick shanties, unpaved streets, and the unmistakable signs of poverty everywhere. It was dismal.

Mark looked out the window and said, "Where's the green? Doesn't anything grow around here?"

To the east the brown desert hills quietly pushed Lima into the Pacific Ocean. The whole coast of Peru is desert. Continuing south, well into Chile, this arid strip becomes the driest desert on earth, the Atacama.

South America is the world's fourth-largest continent, after Asia, Africa and North America. Covering an area nearly the size of Alaska of 496,222 square miles (1,285,216 square kilometers), Peru is the third-largest country in South America, after Brazil and Argentina. With five million people, Lima ranks as the largest city in Peru by far. The country itself has a population of only nineteen million; approximately half are Indian, the other half a mixture of European and Mestizo, or half-caste.

Only a portion of Peru is desert. The arid coastal region extends 50 to 100 miles (80 to 160 km.) inland. Beyond it are the central mountains, with their lofty plateaus, deep valleys, snowy peaks and green terraced farms. The Andes *Cordillera* , or mountain range, divides the country roughly in half, from north to south. On the eastern side of the these rugged peaks are the heavily-forested slopes leading down to the Amazon basin. These mountains not only divide Peru, but are also the source of the Amazon River, the longest and largest river in the world.

After the unimpressive ride from the airport, we arrived at the San Sebastián Hostel, a few blocks west of the Plaza San Martín. The Youth Hostel in Miraflores, an upperclass suburb south of Lima, is less expensive, but we were eager to stay in the heart of the city.

There are a number of popular hotels around the center of Lima, including the Hotel Roma and Hotel Savoy on Jirón Ica, near the San Sebastián. The Hotel Europa, Hotel Comercio and Hotel Pacifico can be found around the Plaza de Armas, while the Richmond Hotel, Gran Hotel and Hotel Universio are located near Jirón Carabaya, the main street between the Plaza de Armas and the Plaza San Martín. All of these hotels can be enjoyed for the equivalent of $3 or $4 U.S. dollars a night for a single room, $5 or $6 for a double. For the most part, you take your chances with these hotels. They are often full, and are invariably in various states of repair and cleanliness.

For a nicer neighborhood which costs more money, try some of the other moderate hotels in Miraflores, which are near the beach. These hotels, such as the Gran Hotel, will all have pools and will cost about $20 a night. This is definitely the nicest area in Lima. Ask at the tourist office at Jirón Union, just south of the Plaza San Martín, for help with hotels and other advice. If the hotels are full, ask their advice on places to stay nearby.

§§§

As soon as we had found our rooms, we were back out on the streets, heading for Lima's main plaza, the Plaza de Armas. Located on the east side of this wide square is the imposing *Cathedral* , where the Pope spoke to the people of Lima in 1985. Here, children were selling ice cream, while a nonchalant soldier absentmindedly twirled his submachine gun in front of the Palacio de Gobierno to the north.

Bordering the square was also a small café and a statue of Francisco Pizarro, the ruthless conquistador who conquered an empire of millions with just a few hundred soldiers. We passed beneath Pizarro astride his horse, his sword majestically drawn, his face wearing an expression appropriate for one readied to loot and pillage a nation. We decided to have lunch at the café, and took a table on the terrace outside.

Looking out at Pizarro and the Plaza de Armas, I couldn't help thinking about the great moment when the first Europeans set foot on South America. But then, who were the first?

It is only within the last few hundred years that the Archbishop of Ulster proclaimed that, based on his analysis of the Bible, the world was created in 4004 BC. I think he decided that it must have happened on a Tuesday. While historians concede that the earth probably got its start many years before this, they still maintain 4000 BC as the popularly accepted date for the beginning of civilization, portraying humans living as "cave men" for a few hundred thousand years prior to that time.

Many experts now agree that civilization at Jericho in Jordan and other cities in Turkey can be pushed back to about 7,000 BC. But Sumeria is still generally taught in schools as being the first civilization, going back about seven thousand years to 5,000 BC.

However, the "experts" throughout history have continually been proven wrong. With the discovery of bronze artifacts in

9

Thailand which are hundreds and even thousands of years older than those found in Sumeria (traditionally where bronze work and metallurgy are thought to have originated), it has been proven that advanced cultures predate Sumeria. But when certain pieces do not fit into the historical puzzle, what do we do? Throw them away? Fortunately not, in the case of some scholars, who have been demonstrating that South America has ruins and other evidence of civilization which may far predate those found elsewhere. This continent is rapidly becoming the most controversial area in the world, when it comes to prehistory and civilization, as readers of this book will soon discover.

According to many of the so-called experts, mankind came to North America via a land bridge across the Bering Sea into Alaska and Canada a few thousand years ago. Conservative "experts" place this crossing at about 12,000 BC. Other more radical "experts" date it to about 28,000 BC.[1] And yet, human bones found in California, Arizona, Alberta, and Ecuador have all shown by carbon-dating techniques that man was present in the Western Hemisphere by about 30,000 years BC.[2] A skull found at the Otavalo archeological site in Ecuador was radio-carbon dated at 30,000+ BC.

In the early seventies, a new method of dating bones was developed at the San Diego Museum. Known as Aspartic Acid Racemization (AAR) dating, this technique tagged skeletal remains found in the Americas at 38,000+, 40,000+, 45,000+, 50,000+ BC. Incredibly, one human bone found in Sunnyvale, California, was pinpointed at 70,000 years and possibly older! It was so old, no radio-carbon was left in the skeleton! [2]

However, it was discovered in 1985 that these figures were erroneous, having been based on calibration skeletons which had been erroneously dated by radioactive methods. AAR dating requires an accurately dated reference skeleton, and once these had been recalibrated, the skeleton originally dated at 38,000 BC was redated to 5,100 BC. Dr. Jeffrey Bada, a leading proponent of AAR, announced the mistakes in *American Antiquity* magazine in 1985.

This does not necessarily destroy those theories that would place original occupation of the Americas before 30,000 BC. Artifacts that cannot be carbon- or AAR-dated have been found in geological strata that date thousands of years earlier. Some artifacts, isolated at 70,000 BC, have been found at El Bosque, Nicaragua; Old Crow, Yukon; Crown Point and Texas Street, San Diego; and Santa Barbara, California. A Mission Valley, California artifact was dated at 100,000 BC, and artifacts found at a famous Flagstaff, Arizona dig have been dated at 100,000 to 170,000 years old. To raise eyebrows even higher, dates of 250,000 BC have been assigned to El Horno and Hueyatlaco, two sites in Mexico, while excavations at Calico Hills, California have been given dates of 500,000 BC! [2]

Frankly, dating arrowheads and stone tools is quite tricky. One must guess the age by dating the geological strata where the tool is found. Given the possibility that our whole understanding of geological change could be totally erroneous, our current usage of geological dating may be way, way off. If this is true, things are probably younger. However, radio carbon dating is still a fairly accurate method for tagging organic objects. Yet, when dating bones older than about 30,000 years old, radio-carbon dating becomes grossly inaccurate.

As Dr. Goodman points out in his book, *American Genesis* , dates for human bones and artifacts found in North and South America are generally twice the age of those found in Europe. For instance, the oldest human skulls in Europe carry dates of 35,000 years, compared with 70,000 years in America. However, Goodman is referring to AAR dates, now known to be inaccurate, ironically, because of inaccurate carbon dating. Artifacts such as projectile points and bone tools have been dated at 20,000 years in Europe, but 40,000 years, if not more, in the Americas.

Yet, these startling finds point to a conclusion that humans lived in South America long before crossing a Bering Straits land bridge during the last ice-age. There seems to be little doubt that such a land bridge existed between Alaska and Siberia, but it may be unnecessary. In the winter of 1985 a young American wandered across the frozen Bering Strait to the Soviet Union, where he was arrested, detained, then flown back to Alaska by helicopter. In fact, rather than ask if it was possible to cross the strait at all, maybe we should ask which way early man crossed it! To quote the archaeologist, C. W. Ceram: "Instead of assuming that the Indians came from the Old World, he (a European freethinker) could have decided that they represented the primitive human race from which he himself was descended." [3] Ceram, at least, felt it possible that the migration across the Bering Strait may have proceeded from the Americas to Asia.

But why do we limit our explorations of the past, by requiring our ancestors to cross oceans using land bridges? Vast oceans have not been much of a barrier to people over the last few thousand years. The Polynesians and Micronesians navigated vast expanses of oceans in outrigger canoes, sailing more than three times the distance between Africa and South

America. If the Polynesians and other cultures could sail vast oceanic distances thousands of years ago, then why could not more advanced cultures sailing larger ships in the Mediterranean do the same thing at the same time?

Most people have heard speculation that the Vikings sailed their long ships to Greenland and Labrador about a thousand years ago. But can we take seriously more radical proposals of Irish monks sailing up and down North America, as well as Portuguese and Basque fishermen, Roman, Greek and Phoenician explorers, Hebrew gold miners, and Egyptian traders?

Impossible? Why? Is the Atlantic so impassable? Hardly. People have crossed the Atlantic in rowboats, kayaks, and simple rafts. The ancient sailors of the Mediterranean sailed ships far superior to those in which Columbus sailed across the Atlantic. In fact, on Columbus' second voyage to the New World, he wrote about finding the wreckage of a European ship on the Island of Guadeloupe in the French West Indies.[4]

Many historians find the evidence of visitation to the Americas by ancient explorers and traders overwhelming. In 1976, a Brazilian diver named Jose Roberto Teixeira was spearfishing around a rock off Ilha de Gobernador in the Baia de Guananbara near Río de Janeiro, when he found three intact Roman *amphorae* (clay vessels used to hold wine), in an area with several shipwrecks, some dating from the sixteenth century AD. He reported that the area of his find is littered with pottery shards and large pieces of other amphorae.

The Brazilian Institute of Archaeology was extremely interested in these amphorae and sent photos to the Smithsonian Institute, which identified them as Roman. Later, Dr. Elizabeth Lyding Will of the Department of Classics at the University of Massachusetts, Amherst, identified the amphorae as Second to First Century BC, "... apparently manufactured at Kouass, the ancient port of Zilis (Dchar Jedid) on the Atlantic coast of Morocco, southwest of Tangiers." Dr. Michel Ponsich, the archaeologist who had conducted excavations at Kouass, agrees with Dr. Will on the place of manufacture, and gives the amphorae a date of Second Century BC.[4]

An American archaeologist who specializes in underwater digs, Robert Marx, investigating the site near Río de Janeiro where the amphorae were found, located a wooden structure in the muddy bottom of the bay. Using sonar, Marx discovered that there were actually two wrecks at the site, one a sixteenth century ship, and another which was presumably a more ancient ship, the source of the amphorae.

But before Marx could dive to the site, trouble started.

Brazilian authorities did not savor the idea of a Roman ship-wreck off their coast, and Spain and Portugal are still disputing who first discovered Brazil. Marx was even accused of being an Italian agent sent out to drum up publicity for Rome! Under pressure, the Brazilian authorities refused to grant permission for Marx to keep diving; and later permanently banned him from entering Brazil.

Marx felt that the ship might have been blown off course in a storm. Wrecks thought to be Roman have been found off the Azores. Indeed, many modern sailing ships make the Atlantic crossings in only 18 days. In the last century alone, over 600 forced crossings of the Atlantic have occurred as ships and rafts were blown to the Americas by storms. Yet, I do not personally believe that the Romans were accidently showing up to sunbathe on the Copacabana Beach near Río de Janeiro. More than likely, they were deliberately sailing to the New World!

Many other Roman artifacts have been found in Latin America. A large hoard of Roman jewelry was found in graves near Mexico City by Dr. Garcia Payón of the University of Jalapa in 1961. Roman *fibula* (a clip used to hold together a Roman toga), as well as Roman coins have frequently been found. In fact, a ceramic jar containing several hundred Roman coins, bearing dates ranging from the reign of Augustus down to 350 AD and every intervening period, was found on a beach in Venezuela. This cache is now in the Smithsonian Institution. Experts there have stated that the coins are not a misplaced collection belonging to an ancient numismatist, but probably a Roman sailor's ready cash, either concealed in the sand or washed ashore from a shipwreck.[4]

The Romans are not as often associated with world travel as another great ancient power: their deadly rivals, the Carthaginians. In the first century BC, Greek geographer, Strabo wrote, "...far famed are the voyages of the Phoenicians (who were also known as Carthaginians, from their two main colonies, Phoenicia and Carthage), who, a short time after the Trojan War (circa 1200 BC), explored the regions beyond the Pillars of Hercules, founding cities there and in the central Libyan (African) seaboard. Once, while exploring the coast along the shore of Libya, they were driven by strong winds for a great distance out into the ocean. After being tossed for many days, they were carried ashore on an island of considerable size, situated at a great distance to the west of Libya."[4]

In 1872, near Paraiba, Brazil, a stone bearing a Phoenician inscription was discovered. It was thought to be a forgery for almost a century, when in 1968, Dr. Cyrus Gordon, Chairman of the Department of Mediterranean Studies at Brandeis University, announced that the inscription was genuine. Copies of the Paraiba inscription speak of a Phoenician ship circumnavigating Africa until it was blown to the shores of Brazil.[5,6] Indeed, the discoverer of Brazil, Portugese explorer Pedro Alvares Cabral, was attempting to round Africa in AD 1500 when he was blown off course and landed in Brazil. It is believed that he named Brazil after after the legendary Irish Island of Hy-Brazil.

A Carthaginian shipwreck containing a cargo of amphorae was discovered in 1972 off the coast of Honduras, according to Dr. Elizabeth Will.[4] Some scholars believe that the Toltec Indians were in fact Carthaginians, who, after being defeated by Rome in the Punic Wars, left the Mediterranean for West Africa. From there they migrated to the Yucatan Peninsula of Mexico, where they re-established their civilization. The Aztecs later destroyed them, and Carthaginian gold bars fell into the hands of the Aztecs, later surfacing in the United States as part of Montezuma's gold and the "Seven Gold Cities of Cibola."

Even the Jews may have reached South America. King Solomon's mines have been attributed by some as being located in New Mexico or at the mouth of the Amazon. Inscriptions in archaic Hebrew near Las Lunas, New Mexico, supposedly tell of their voyage and establishment of their city. However, there is a great deal of debate about what the inscription actually says, even by those who believe it genuine. Even as late as 734 AD, Jews seeking refuge from persecution sailed from Rome "... to Calalus, an unknown land." This land is now believed to be Las Lunas.[7,8]

If the ardent celebrator of Columbus Day finds this a bit beyond his or her paradigm, there's more. Just a few years earlier, seven bishops and a reported 5000 followers fleeing from the Moors in Spain sailed from Porto Cale, Portugal, for the island of Antillia. They landed on the west coast of Florida, according to some historians, and made their way inland to found the new city of Cale, which later may have become modern Ocala. The Jews from Rome could have learned of this Portugese exodus, gone to Porto Cale, hoping for exact sailing directions. Once in America, they called the new land Calalus, a sort of latinized Cale. The Portugese voyage was certainly known to Columbus, who thought he would find their decendants on an island. Perhaps he thought that the European wreck he found on his second voyage was from this expedition.[7]

The point is that crossing oceans is not very difficult—not now, not in ancient times. Not only could the Portugese and

Christopher Columbus have crossed the Atlantic in the Middle-Ages, but just about anyone in an earlier time with a seaworthy ship could have done so as well. In fact, we have the famous Piri Reis map at the Topkapi Museum in Istanbul to testify that the Atlantic was being navigated long before the European Dark Ages "experts" declared that the world was flat. The Piri Reis map shows the entirety of the west coast of North and South America, plus a good portion of Antartica, just a few years after Columbus made his first voyage to the New World. Put together from older maps, Columbus himself probably carried an earlier copy with him. This map's strangest aspect is that it accurately shows details of Antarctica's land mass which which are today covered with ice, which we have only known were accurate for the last few years!

The subject of ancient voyagers to the Americas could easily take up an entire book, and has many times. There appears to be a strong connection between these ancient voyagers and South American lost cities. This background information on possible voyages to the new world is necessary for any complete discussion of pre-Columbian civilization, lost cities and ancient mysteries of South America.

§§§

"Shoeshine, señor?" asked an eager young voice. I looked down from the statue of Pizarro into the hopeful brown eyes of a hard-working kid who should have been in school, a ragged street urchin of about ten.

Checking my white canvas tennis shoes, I decided that there was just no way in the world they could be shined. "No, sorry," I apologized, but I glanced over at the other guys anyway, to check their shoes.

It turned out we were all wearing tennis shoes, but that didn't deter this enterprising young man. He wanted to shine shoes, and wouldn't take "no" for an answer. Meanwhile, Mark had met a young Peruvian nurse who was pleased to practice her English on us. Just as the waiter came over to shoo away the shoe-shiner, the nurse, Esther, offered to show us the way to the Plaza de San Martín. Attractive and energetic, she looked like she had been through some tough times. Her dark hair fell limp around a long face, her brown eyes looking at us hopefully, perhaps fantasizing that one of us would take her back to America.

Mark was tall and lively, with hair as dark as Esther's. Sometimes boisterous, he was definitely out of character now

15

as he generously paid our entire bill, probably trying to impress Esther. Quieter and older than Mark, Steve was of medium build with a thick red mustache, which made up somewhat for his receding hairline. He helped Esther out of her chair, while Bob and I distracted the shoeshine boy in order to get our group past him. In his fifties, Bob was older and more worldly than the rest of us, his blond hair still thick beneath his straw hat. An extremely well-read man, he became the unofficial story-teller of the group, often regaling us with wildly speculative tales of the "real" history of whatever area we were visiting at the time.

Shortly the four of us gringos and Esther made it to the street, moving quickly past the shoeshine boy and Francisco Pizarro, Esther in the lead. Soon we were engulfed in the great crowd that seems to flow endlessly between the Plaza des Armas and the Plaza San Martín on the Jirón de la Unión. The Jirón de la Unión is the Broadway of Lima, the main shopping street. It has been turned into a pedestrian mall, and is quite a circus. At any one time there are hundreds, if not thousands, of people meandering up either side of the street, window shop-ping, or just checking out the other shoppers. One may catch a juggler or magician on the street, a band of musicians playing old Inca songs, or possibly even a pickpocket.

As Esther led us through the crowd, Mark and I got caught in a tight press of spectators. When we got to the other side, Mark noticed that the outside pocket on his walking shorts had been slashed! "Damn!" he exclaimed. "I'm glad I wasn't keep-ing anything in there."

Esther seemed concerned. "Be careful! There are many thieves about!" she admonished, casting a quick glance around the crowd. It was a lesson well learned.

We spent the next few days wandering about Lima, and there was much to do. Among the many museums to visit are the Gold Museum at Museo Miguel Mujica Gallo in the Mon-terrico suburb. Here you'll find an incredible collection of pre-Columbian gold, and even Pizarro's sword in the arms collection upstairs. The Museum of Anthropology and Archae-ology on Avenida Sucre in the Pueblo Libre suburb, with plenty of pre-Spanish exhibits, and the Museum of Natural History on Avenida Arenales, are both worth a visit. Other things to see are the Museo de Arte, the Cathedral at the Plaza de Armas, and the street market nearby.

The very best place for night life and restaurants is the Miraflores area, and we spent most of our evenings there, dining at a sidewalk cafe and drinking the local beer, Cerveza

Cristal. After one evening out on the town, Steve, Mark, and I headed back to the hotel, while Bob stayed out partying.

It was after three in the morning when Bob got back to the hotel. "Do you know what happened to me tonight?" he burst out, waking everyone up.

We sat up in our beds in this four-bed room on the terrace of the San Sebastián Hostel, wondering if the army was hot on Bob's tail. "What happened, man?" someone finally asked, turning on the naked bulb in the center of the room

"Well, I was out at this disco," said Bob, his voice calm but strained, "and I met this Peruvian guy and a couple of girls. They invited me to sit with them, and I ended up buying them some drinks, since they were out of money. After a couple of hours, he invited me up to his apartment, to get money to pay me back. This was about an hour and a half ago. I waited outside while he went to his apartment, and when he came back, he said he had a gift for me, and pulled out a little piece of paper. Well, I guessed what it was—cocaine! I told him, 'No thanks,' but just then two guys in black suits and machine guns stepped out of the shadows and arrested us both!"

"No kidding!" exclaimed Steve, "What did you do then?"

"They took me into a police station just around the corner, strip searched me, and found my money belt and traveler's cheques, plus the cash I had brought with me. They threw me in a cell, and the policemen kept telling me that I would spend the rest of my life in prison, unless I opted for 'la solución'!"

"I can guess what that was," I said, getting up to get a drink of water from the bathroom down the hall.

"You got it! They wanted a bribe, basically all the cash I had on me, which was $300! Son-of-a-bitch! I didn't know what to do, they wouldn't let me make a phone call—I wanted to call the American Embassy. So I paid up and they let me out. What else could I do?"

It was a sad story, and I had certainly heard of such things before; we wondered if it had been a set-up from the very beginning. $300 is a lot of money in Peru. Incredibly, the same thing happened the next night with Mark. He was out by himself in Miraflores, met a couple of guys in a café, and was walking down the street with them toward the beach. Just then, two policemen came along and arrested them all on drug charges. They forced Mark to cash a $50 traveler's cheque and to pay them a total of $130 to get out of jail.

"What can you do when someone has a machine gun in your face?" he reflected. Really! Apparently, this game is played by the Peruvian Intelligence Police (PIP), who routinely arrest tourists in the Miraflores area on trumped-up drug charges (and sometimes not-so-trumped-up drug charges), then extort money from them. We called the American Embassy after this happened the second time to find out what was going on, and whether there was any way to get some money back. The friendly American assistant consul said that this was quite common, and that unfortunately there was nothing that she could do about it.

We were about ready to escape Lima at this point. We had had enough of the big city, and it was time to see some more of the country. I was growing restless to find some lost cities and explore the many mysteries of South America. We would be damned if the PIP were going to catch us again!

Francisco Pizarro and a facsimile of two of his signatures.

Chapter Two

South of Lima to Nazca:
Candlestick of the Andes

Someday, after we have mastered
the winds, the waves, the tides and gravity,
we shall harness for God the energies of Love.
Then for the second time in the history of the world
man will have discovered fire.
-Teilhard de Chardin

We caught a bus from the "Arequipa Express" bus station, close to the Plaza San Martín. About a dozen bus companies operate from Lima, fanning out to all parts of the country. Buses, though, travel primarily either south or north along the coast. To get to Cuzco from Lima, you can either fly or go by bus south to Arequipa, then take a train. We planned the latter.

The bus took about five hours to get to Ica, center of the Peruvian wine-growing area, some two hundred miles south of Lima. The drive is along the Pan American Highway, a two-lane road that winds along the desolate coast all the way down to Chile. (The Pan American Highway actually starts in Alaska, extending all the way to Patagonia. Were it not for a small section missing in the Darien Gap in Panama, it would be possible to drive down the entire west coast of North and South America). We just relaxed in our seats watching the desert slide past, marveling at the occasional fertile valley. Though it very rarely rains along this coastal desert (certain portions of the Atacama Desert further south in Chile have never had rain as long as records have been kept), melting Andean snow forms rivers which flow down from the Andes about a hundred miles inland. Irrigation water flowing from these rivers into the valleys makes habitation and farming possible.

We stopped at the Bay of Pisco and checked into the Paracas Hotel. This is the most expensive hotel in the Paracas area, but we decided to splurge. Other hotels can be had for $3 to $6 a night, including the Progreso Hotel, the Embassy Hotel, and the Portofino Hotel. The Paracas area is especially well-known for the wine liqueur created there known as *pisco* , which is the basis for the most popular drink in Peru, the Pisco Sour.

Near Paracas are found Nazca and Ica, both areas incredibly rich with archaeological artifacts. Paracas has yielded beautiful ancient pottery that is famous throughout Peru, and is also home to a great number of caves in use for thousands of years. These caves were once used as burial chambers by an ancient people, and an amazing number of preserved mummies have been discovered in them recently. Indeed, a labyrinth of caves is found around Paracas, most of them never having been explored. Many of these caves which start at the ocean and go deep underground have been used over the centuries by pirates to hide treasure.[10]

But the reason we had come here was to examine the famous "Candlestick of the Andes." We had just enough time left in the afternoon to take a boat out on the bay and observe this striking artifact from its best vantage point. Over 800 feet long, carved directly into the rock of the towering cliffs facing the sea, this ancient signal of unknown purpose is clearly visible from as far as twelve miles out to sea. Resembling a candelabra or trident, it appears to be pointing inland toward the Nazca Plain. That it forms some kind of enormous marker is clearly evident. When the Spanish conquistadors first discovered the carving, they took it as a sign from heaven, the Holy Trinity, and interpreted it as a signal for them to conquer, Christianize, and literally enslave the local population.[9]

When the Spaniards finally examined the markings, they found a rope of tremendous thickness attached to the central fork, and remains of other ropes that had once been attached to the other two forks. Speculating on the purpose of these ropes, it has been suggested that the Candlestick may have been used as a tidal calculator. But more likely is Peruvian investigator Beltran Garcia's theory that it formed a gigantic seismograph, and that at one time it was equipped with counterweights, graded ladders, and ropes sliding on pulleys that could measure earthquakes throughout South America.[9] If it was a seismograph, it must have been made to measure some pretty colossal shocks, but South America gets them!

French investigator Robert Charroux thinks that the area has been placed under a taboo, making it off limits to local Indians, and that the Candlestick is a marker proclaiming this taboo. In fact, Charroux claims to be the first person to step on the sands around the marker during this century! He feels the taboo was placed to protect a vast treasure hidden in the area, possibly near the marker. Indeed, he suggests that perhaps the lost treasure of the Incas themselves, including the mummified remains of Inca Kings, might be found nearby.[10]

What purpose did the Candlestick serve? A gigantic seismometer makes a lot of sense, but it would also seem to have the secondary purpose of a highly visible "sign post," signaling ships far out in the Pacific. Erich Von Daniken goes so far as to suggest that it was a marker signaling space ships and directing them to Nazca.[11] This seems highly unlikely, and hardly necessary—anyone traveling though space would hardly need such a marker to point their way!

Another explanation of the Candlestick of the Andes is told in L. Taylor Hansen's book, *He Walked the Americas* . She researched Peruvian, Mexican, and Pacific islander legends of a man known variously as Wakea, Viracocha and Quetzal Coatl. According to New Zealand and Peruvian legend, Hansen wrote, Wakea sailed from New Zealand to the Polynesian Islands, and then landed on the coast of Peru, sometime in the first century AD. Known in Peru as Viracocha (possibly one of several legendary Viracochas), he was a tall man in a robe, with long hair and a flowing beard. He gained his reputation preaching and telling strange stories of distant lands, often in the form of parables. He encouraged people to be loving and to help one another, abhorred war and violence, and was a man of great personal power. He was even reported to have been able to heal the sick!

While at Paracas, Viracocha stood near the ocean and told the story of a man who was persecuted by his enemies, then nailed to a cross on a hill with two other persons likewise punished. With its resemblance to the story of Christ in the New Testament, this story continues to evoke strange theories and explanations. If you haven't guessed already, Hansen suggests that Viracocha may well have been Jesus himself! She also relates the rest of the legend, that while Viracocha told the story, a shadow appeared on the hill behind him of three men on a cross. After Viracocha had finished his tale and left, the shadow remained. His moved followers then went up the hill and scraped out the shadow, creating the Candlestick of the Andes that we see today.[24]

We didn't have time to explore the Candlestick itself, but

made it back to the hotel just before dark, where we had a good swim before dinner. We rose early the next morning, boarding a bus to Nazca, some 100 miles south of Paracas. Our plan for the day was to charter a small plane to fly over the fabulous markings on the flat, barren Nazca plain.

These markings were first noted from the ground, not the air as many writers have suggested. A Peruvian archaeological expedition in 1926, headed by the father of modern Peruvian archaeology, Julio C. Tello, was digging at Cantallo, near Nazca. When two members of his team climbed a hill in the late afternoon to look for more possible ruins, they noticed large "lines" on the ground, seemingly man-made, and recorded them.[22]

However, what they could not see were the fantastic portrayals of birds, reptiles and insects that cover the plain, nor the full extent of the many trapezoidal markings. By 1930, the lines and the shapes they formed were well known to the Peruvian Air Force. In June, 1941, Dr. Paul Kosok, a professor of history at Long Island University, was investigating pre-Columbian irrigation systems when he spotted the lines on some aerial photos. He was joined in researching their origin in 1948 by Maria Reiche, a German mathematician and astronomer. Reiche has become a sort of patron saint of Nazca, living in an adobe hut on the edge of the desert, devoting her life to discovering the significance of the lines, which she believes is largely astronomical.

The system of markings was once mistakenly described as "Inca roads." Unlike authentic Inca roads, these trapezoids, triangles, squares, and other geometrical markings do not lead anywhere, but form a maze with no discernible pattern. In an interview in 1984, Felicia Murray, who accompanied aerial photographer Marilyn Bridges to Nazca, said that, "...walking the lines is a way to change one's state of everyday consciousness." Traversing one large triangle from apex to base, she said, made her and Bridges, "...feel like we were growing smaller."

Similarly, it has been suggested that the natives would walk the lines of the animals engraved in the plain to take their "power" or attributes. The lines are attributed to the Nazca culture who peopled the south coast of Peru between 2,350 and 1,400 years ago. But archaeologists agree that this was not the first culture to inhabit the area, as dated sites confirm that the central Andes were inhabited starting 9,000 to 12,000 years ago, if not earlier.[12]

Other markings similar to those at Nazca can be found

between Pisco and Nazca, as well as in the central Andes, Chile, and places as far away as California and Wyoming! On the south side of the Nazca River is the lost city of Kahuachi, theoretically a shrine of the Nazcas. It consists of six pyramids, the tallest of which looms up over 65 feet (20 meters), overlooking a large walled court. Also associated with Kahuachi was Estaquería, a strange array of log pillars arranged in twelve rows of twenty. Estaquería has now all but disappeared, its pillars having been used as raw material by local charcoal makers.[12]

We arrived at the airport and had lunch while waiting for our flight over the plain. There are a number of hotels in Nazca, now a popular tourist stop in Peru because of the markings. The least expensive are the San Martín and the Nazca Hotels, for a couple of dollars per night. The Maria Reiche Hostel at the airport goes at $16 for a double, and the Montecarlo Hotel is priced similarly. The most deluxe is the Majoro Hacienda.

After lunch, we took off on our forty-five-minute flight over the lines in a six-seat Aero Condor plane. It was quite a thrill, rumbling down the dirt strip, the whole plane shaking with the force of the engine and rough stones underneath. Suddenly the pilot pulled up on the stick, sending us winging our way over the desert.

We flew at an altitude of 1000 meters (3,300 feet) over the lines, circling clockwise around the plain. The pilot would yell over the deafening sound of the engine that we were now over such-and-such a figure. "There's the spider down there!" he would yell at me, sitting next to him in the co-pilot's seat.

"What?" I would yell back.

"The spider! The spider! The spider is down there!" he repeated.

"Oh, I see!" I would shout back, and then inform the rest of the gang in the back of the plane. It now seemed that it hadn't been such a good idea to have lunch before the trip, as Steve had grabbed a paper sack and was busy returning the hamburger he had eaten. Seemingly unconcerned about this risk to the interior of his plane, the pilot banked again to show us more.

Below us we saw figures of a spider, a condor, a monkey, a lizard, a parrot, and a whale. Also present are mysterious "hands" (now thought to be a bat), as well as a dog, a tree, a hummingbird, and even a figure imaginatively named the "astronaut." Each figure is plainly discernable, and there is a general consensus that they form a Peruvian zodiac of sorts, each figure representing a constellation.

The real mystery consists of the other lines and "runways" which can be made out beneath the figures. Flying over the plain, it is evident that the figures are superimposed over these other lines. We may therefore assume that the lines and "runways" are older.

It is interesting that even the most conservative scholars admit that the trapezoidal shapes look like runways. Looking down from the cockpit of that Aero Condor plane, I had to agree. Through the clever use of perspective, the ancient architect who designed the trapezoids gave them the appearance of great length. The far ends of each side move closer together, much as a modern full-length runway appears to an approaching jet pilot. Yet, what strange runways. They run all over the place, going up and down hills with no regard for obstructions. This would have been a pretty confusing airport!

One thing I did notice, though, was that the trapezoidal markings seemed to radiate from a central point. These runways tapered down into a central hub, while other lines crossed them and took off across the desert. On the other hand, the superimposed figures stood out like a child's scribbling in a gigantic coloring book. This is an enigma that runs in concentric circles: each mystery, solved or unsolved, brings us to another mystery.

Steve was feeling better as we rumbled in to a landing on the very real runway at Nazca airport. I got the feeling it might have been smoother coming in on one of the ancient "runways" out there on the plain as the plane bounced and shook to a stop. For the pilot we were just another plane load of tourists, but for us it had been the ride of a lifetime, back into the mysterious past.

§§§

On the bus back to Ica, where we would spend the night, I reflected on the mystery of Nazca. Sure that my experience with hundreds of other ancient mysteries around the world would give me a unique perspective, I had felt that I would be able to solve the mystery of the Nazca markings. I was wrong.

But I think that I may have some interesting insights into the mystery. First of all, lines like the ones found at Nazca are not unique. Tony Morrison points out in his book, *Pathways to the Gods* , that similar lines stretch into the interior of Peru, all the way to Tiahuanaco in Bolivia. These lines are perfectly straight, just like those at Nazca, even climbing over boulders, rock outcroppings and hills. Nothing, but nothing, interrupts one of these lines, and they literally travel for hundreds of miles through the barren mountains of western Peru! Created in the same manner as those at Nazca, the darker topsoil was removed to reveal the lighter soil beneath.[12]

Some observers at Nazca have suggested that these lines can be equated with "ley lines," Chinese "Spirit Paths" and "Dragon Lines," and with what is postulated to be the earth's "electromagnetic grid." Great Britain is covered with ley lines, running from ancient dolman and stone works to others hundreds of miles away, also in perfectly straight lines![13] Britain also has its share of gigantic figures carved into hills and fields, such as the Long Man of Wilmington, and the Cerne Abbas Giant cut into the chalk of Dorset.

Interestingly, this "world electromagnetic grid" was apparently marked out and used by the ancients for a purpose as yet not completely understood. Such major ancient sites as the Great Pyramid of Egypt, the Great Pyramid of China, and certain pyramids in Mexico seem to be located at key points on this theoretical grid.[15]

We can theorize that the gigantic figures at Nazca are part of a large-scale astronomical or astrological computer, etched into the previously-existing lines at a later date, probably by the Nazca culture that inhabited the area circa 100 AD. The lines themselves most probably date from a time contemporary with Tiahuanaco in Bolivia, since some of the lines point all the way through the Andes to its site near the shores of Lake Titicaca. Unfortunately, we have no real way of dating any of the earth drawings, so this is all speculation.

But we are still left with an enigma: these amazing figures, and the trapezoidal shapes formed by the lines, are only discernible as such from air. Of what use are figures that no one can see? Is it possible that the builders had some capability for flight? Furthermore, there are really three types of markings on the plain of Nazca: the figures, the straight lines that Tony Morrisson thinks point to Tiahuanaco, and the "landing strip" trapezoidal markings that radiate from the hub. Were each from a different, successive culture? Why and how were the markings created?

Frankly, I think we can forget the hypothesis that the Nazca Plain is a landing base for extraterrestrial visitors, which comes largely from sensationalistic book marketing. But the fact that the lines are only visible from the air still remains. Is it possible that people, humans of earthly origin, were somehow taking to the air in ancient times? It has been suggested by some otherwise conservatively-minded scientists that these Nazca folk may have had hot-air balloons in which they rode above the plain. And it was reported by early historians that the Incas used a form of hang glider in the Andes Mountains! Legends from all over the continent tell of gods coming from out of the sky and landing in various places. This recurring theme is one of the most popular in South America, even entering into the mythology of the Incas. Such "gods" were not necessarily from outer space. Isn't it more likely, should these legends be based on fact, that these beings were men?

A gold artifact found in Columbia and exhibited world wide is what appears to be a model of a delta-wing jet airplane. When not on exhibition, this piece is kept in a collection at the State Bank of Bogota. This little gold airplane has been dated as being between 750 and 1000 years old, and possibly older (There is no way to date a gold artifact; its age must be inferred from its style and motif, and the geological strata in which it is found). Different people, on observing it, have described it as a bird, butterfly, or flying fish, though it looks uncannily like an airplane, even displaying what appear to be "instruments" and other mechanical details beneath it and around the cockpit.[15]

As if this weren't startling enough, all kinds of flying vehicles are mentioned in prehistory. According to stories of different sources, King Solomon had an airship, and Alexander the Great's army was attacked by flying shields when he invaded India. Frankly, you can take every "gods from outer space" hypothesis, extract the real evidence presented (not the hoaxes and lies: Erich Von Daniken was convicted of fraud some years ago), and find in that evidence indications of the capability of flight in ancient times. For example, many ancient Indian epics, including those of the Ramayana and Mahabarata, contain references to airships known as *Vimanas* . These Vimanas weren't magic carpets or fiery chariots of the gods. Rather, they were described as having been flying machines similar to zeppelins. And, according to popular Indian legends from around 3,000 BC, but based on older texts, they were flown not by aliens, but by human beings, ancient Indians of the Rama Empire.[16] While we cannot simply read ancient legends as historical record, isn't it possible that at least some part of these stories are based on truth? Of course, there is also the possibility that some sophisticated science-fiction writers were at work in India five thousand years ago.

Interestingly, there is an odd connection between ancient India and ancient South America. The language of the Indus Valley Civilization, Harappan, is derived from the ancient language of the Rama Empire. The now-extinct South-Indian language of Dravidian also seems to have its roots in Harappan and the language of Rama. Harappa is only now being deciphered, using Dravidian as the key. Not only that, but the written script Harappan has a correspondent script half a world away—on Easter Island! The Rongo-Rongo script of Easter Island, still undeciphered is virtually identical to the Harappan script! Links between ancient India and Easter island are the topic of a great deal of discussion, and further links between Easter Island and South America are also well known.

Return for a moment from the realm of wild conjecture, back into the world of hard facts. Could the people of Nazca have created enormous figures on the ground without ever having been able to see them, figures that no one would ever see until the advent of flight, a lapse of a thousand years or more? Maybe the people just wanted to walk the crazy lines like Felicia Murray said, getting dizzy and entering an altered state of consciousness.

According to a *Literary Digest* article on November 12, 1932, Army Air Corps flyers in California photographed shapes similar to those found at Nazca before the Nazca lines were ever discovered. In an area near Blythe, California, just east of Los Angeles, they took photos of giant human and animal figures ranging from 50 to 167 feet in length. Just like the Nazca figures, they were made by removing the topsoil and exposing the lighter soil underneath. George Palmer, who spotted the figures while flying from Hoover Dam to Los Angeles, wrote, "Near two of the human shapes are figures of serpents and four-legged animals with long tails. One giant, or god, appears just to have stepped out of a large dance ring."[17]

Arthur Woodward, ethnologist of the Los Angeles Museum, made "... efforts to find out who made the figures, but to no avail. The Mohave and Chemehuevi Indians who once frequented this area said they had no knowledge of them. But he found new hope upon learning that there was another similar figure near Sacton, Arizona, on the north branch of the Gila River, which the Pima call *Haakvaak* , or 'Hawk-Lying-Down.' "[17]

So, in California we have more mysterious desert markings, nearly identical to those at Nazca, though without the ley lines. Who made these markings all around the world, which can only be understood from the air? Similar giant figures, like huge signals to the sky, can be found in Australia, Britain, Ohio, the Mississippi Valley, Chile, and Wyoming.[17] Is this all just some bizarre coincidence?

An interesting situation exists today in New Guinea and other areas, where airplanes and their pilots ventured into remote mountain and island areas, particularly during World War Two. After they left, the natives, who had never before seen such strange men or machines, worshiped them as gods. Called "Cargo Cults," these natives proceeded to build wood and stone replicas of the aircraft they had seen, to encourage the flyers' return. One can imagine ancient balloons or hang gliders venturing over less advanced areas of South America, encouraging the creation of the ancient gold delta-wing aircraft on display in Colombia.

§§§

"Dave, we're at the Ica Museum. Come on!" urged Mark, already climbings off the bus. Standing up in the isle to follow him, I looked out the windows. We had made it to Ica, the main town between Nazca and Paracas. Compared to the desert that we had been driving through, Ica was cool and shady. Time and my imagination had both flown on the trip here from Nazca. The idea of ancient men flying around South America is pretty fantastic, I must admit. Maybe I was suffering from a combination of the desert heat with the jostling my brain had received on the rough landing at Nazca, but I had to smile as I thought of a Rama Airways flight boarding for Atlantis, Easter Island, and Nazca at gate number nine. "Please have your boarding passes ready," says the Egyptian stewardess in Dravidian, as you glance at the departure signs written in Rongo-Rongo along the concourse...

The last one out of the bus, I meandered into the museum, stopping quickly at a water fountain inside before looking carefully around. My attention was immediately drawn to a case containing some human skulls that were strangely elongated. I was staring at the skulls, wondering what a living person with such a deformed skull would look like, when a stranger next to me spoke.

"Pretty long heads on these fellows, wouldn't you say?" asked a man in his fifties, of medium stature. He took off his brown plastic glasses momentarily and wiped them on a hand-kerchief. "Strange practice."

"Yeah, it is pretty strange," I said, "I wonder how they did that?"

"Who knows?" he replied, turning his attention to the next glass case. It contained some mummies, squatting as if they had been buried in jars. I mentioned to my new companion that I had just come from Nazca, and had been thinking about the possibilities of airships from Atlantis, though I didn't expect him to know anything about it.

"That's funny," he said, nodding to the mummies in the glass case, "these two mummies you see are wearing Atlantean turbans."

"What!" I exclaimed, looking into case. The two male mummies inside were wrapped in a sort of poncho-cloak, and had cloth wrapped around their heads and knotted to the side of the forehead. These turbans were made of a red and black woven wool material. I had never seen any like them before, in the Middle East, India or anywhere.

"Yes," the man went on, "you mentioned Atlantis. I thought you might like to know that this is the type of turban worn in Atlantis thousands of years ago. It's curious that these fellows are wearing the same turban. It's rather distinctive."

"People in Atlantis wore turbans like this?" I asked, too amazed to first ask the obvious question about Atlantis' existence!

"So I understand," he went on. "They also wore shoes with toes that curled up at the end, kind of like the Sultan of Baghdad. Atlantis sank in a cataclysm quite a few years ago, but remnants of their culture can be found in many places, as you see. What's more, look at these mummies over here. Do you see anything strange about them?"

I looked them over carefully. They were in a crouched position, their knees up against their chests, their skin dried and preserved by the arid climate and some sort of mummification process. "Yeah!" I suddenly noticed, "they have blond hair!"

"That's right," said the man. "Their hair is a sort of reddish-blond. These people were came from a different race than the Quechua and Aymara Indians who now live in this area. How do you suppose they got here?"

Well, this was all news to me. I looked hard at the mummies. Sure enough, they had reddish-blond hair, they were wearing those odd turbans, but they weren't wearing shoes that curled up at the toe. If the Atlanteans did have some sort of airships, would they have used Nazca as a supply base and aerodrome? Was the Candlestick of the Andes an aerial marker for airships coming across the Pacific? Once again I found myself daydreaming about the Rama Airways flight from Easter Island, departing for the last time many thousands of years ago. Our own landing at Nazca earlier that day must have been rougher than I thought!

§§§

After leaving the museum, we decided to stop in at the

village of Ocucaje near Ica, where a certain Dr. Cabrera has a private museum. Dr. Cabrera met us as we walked up. He was a friendly man in his fifties with a small dark mustache and black plastic-rimmed glasses. His museum consists of a lot of rocks; but what incredible rocks!

He has two rooms filled with rocks of various sizes, from the size of a baseball up to large boulders. Etched into these rocks are drawings of men wearing feathered headresses and other simple clothing, but they are doing the most incredible things—using magnifying glasses, stethoscopes, and telescopes; performing surgery, blood transfusions, and organ transplants; even attacking dinosaurs!

There are stone carvings of stegasaurus, brontosaurus, pterodactyls, as well as kangaroos. Furthermore, people are riding or attacking these dinosaurs in many of the carvings. Dr. Cabrera has literally thousands of these stones, which he says have been collected from nearby fields where they are just lying about. Locals supposedly pick them up, and he buys them for a small price. The drawings of surgery and "scientific studies" are amazing, but the pictures of people attacking dinosaurs are enough to turn any paleontologist pale. Yet, statuettes known as the Acambaro Figurines have been discovered in Mexico, which also show what appear to be reptiles supposedly extinct in the Mesozoic Era.[17,19]

Talking to Dr. Cabrera, it was obvious that some of his conclusions were pretty wild. Dr. Cabrera estimated the age of these stones at about ten million years, give or take a few thousand. When I asked him why he thought they were so old, he replied with a straight face, "Because that's when these animals became extinct!" Mark rolled his eyes at this one, and I hid my grin by turning away to continue looking through our host's bizarre collection.

Frankly, the explanation that these stones are that old and have lain around the Ica district for that long isn't very plausible. Far more likely, the stones are a few hundred years old, perhaps even a few thousand. In fact, since the discovery a few years ago of a craftsman in a nearby village makes these stones, it is even more likely that they are no older than you or I! This means that many, if not all, of the collection are fakes. But, Dr. Cabrera insists that they are not all fakes, and argues that he could not afford to have bought so many stones if they were, nor could anyone make a living manufacturing them. More convincing were Dr. Cabrera's petrified wooden totem poles with figures carved into them. They at least showed some signs of age, though like the stones, they may have been carved recently.

The Peruvian government recently decided to declassify the stones as antiquities, and merely label them as "made in Peru." However, these undatable stones cannot be dismissed so easily, as there is a report that some of these stones were sent back to Spain by explorers in 1562, indicating that the current supply may not have all been carved by entrepreneurs from a local village.[61] It is quite possible that once the Indians saw the interest which legitimate stones generated, they carved newer ones with more and more startling subject matter. Or, if we want to speculate, is it possible that some of the ancient reptiles depicted on the stones were not extinct, or rather that some were still alive several thousand years ago.

Dr. Cabrera had an interesting story of his own about the Nazca plain. He maintains that the ancient people of Nazca flew in "flying bowls or pots" by using a form of "anti-gravity." According to his story, three gigantic crystal pyramids could be found beneath Nazca, which generated positive "magneto-energy" which repelled the flying machines, nullifying gravity.

Here was another Nazca Plain airship theory, though I personally didn't put much stock in it, considering its source. At least the good doctor believed that the people of Nazca had created this advanced technology themselves, rather than it being the work of extraterrestrials. Were crystal pyramids actually buried beneath the Nazca Plain? Anything was possible on that wild day in the desert, but that was one lost city that I wasn't going to be looking for. Besides, it was almost dinner time!

Perhaps the hot desert sun tended to drive people a bit around the bend. Dr. Cabrera seemed to have suffered from a slight touch of heat stroke. But then, the Nazca plain did appear to bring out some bizzare ideas and theories; perhaps I have succumbed to the sun's effects myself. Whatever the story, Dr. Cabrera's museum is very real, and well worth a visit.

We decided to spend a night in Ica, before heading further south for Arequipa. There are many inexpensive hotels in Ica, as it is the capital of the district. Try the Comfort Hotel, the Jacaranda Hotel, the Colon Ica Hotel, the Luren Hotel or the Presidente Hotel, just to name a few. A room in each can be had for $2 to $5. We chose yet another, the Salvatierra Hotel, and each paid just over $2 to share a four-bed room with our own bath.

The night air was quiet and fresh as I stared up at the stars just before going to bed. Overhead, a modern-day airship flew past, perhaps a Peruvian Air Force plane, buzzing south toward the Nazca Plain. If this were daytime, I reflected, he might have seen the Candlestick of the Andes at Pisco, and used it as directional marker. But with his radio and electronics, he had no need of that. As the sound of his jet faded off into the distance, I wondered how much longer his airship, and all the other airships of South America and the world, would continue to exist. With the world seemingly on the brink of nuclear, economic, and geological disaster, our civilization too could fall. What would the possible survivors think of legends of our very real airships and runways? Would there even be legends?

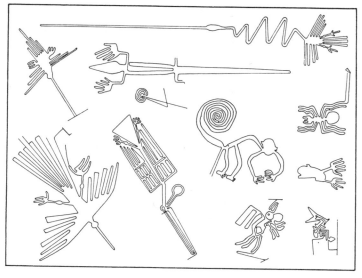

Some of the gigantic figures etched into the plain of Nazca.

South America

For nearly 500 years, tales of lost cities and treasure have lured adventurers to South America. These cities are still being sought today. Do they exist?

During their conquest of South America, the Spanish enslaved many of the natives. Here they are being forced to carry baggage for an expedition in the Andes. Note live volcanoe in the background.

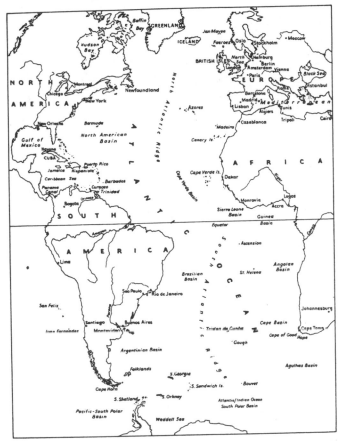

The Atlantic

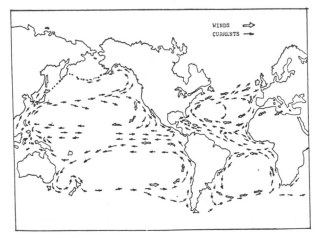

Circular navigation routes using winds and currents

In August, 1498 Columbus made the first landfall on the mainland of South America, at the fulf of Paria opposite Trinidad. The size of the Orinoco river convinced him that he had discovered "a vast continent".

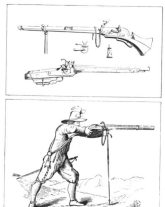

Firearms were used only rarely during the early conquests. Arquebuses were fired by a lighted wick and later by a flintlock mechanism. These early guns were heavy to carry and cumbersome to fire.

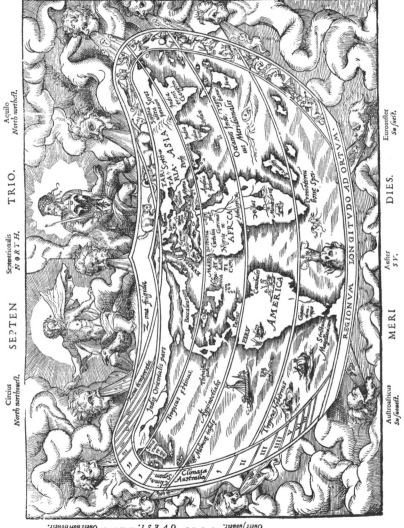

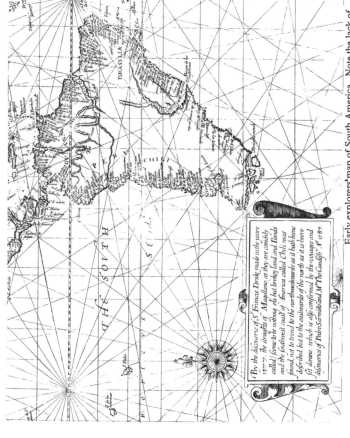

By the diligence of Sr Frimcis Drake made in the yeare 1577. the straights of Magellane as they are cōmōly called, seeme to be nothing els but broken land and Ilands and the southwest coast of America called Chili was found, not to trent to the northwestwards as it hath beene described but to the eastwards of the north as it is here set downe: which is also confirmed by the voyages and discourses of Pedro Surmiēto and Mr The Candish. Aº 1587.

THE SOUTH SEA

TROPICUS

BRASILIA

PERV

CHILI

Early explorers' map of South America. Note the lack of detail in the interior of the continent—surprisingly, the situation has not changed as much as you might think.

(previous page) Ancient map showing an interestingly distorted view of the New World, circa. 1551.

THE PIRI RE'IS MAP OF 1513

IN ALL THE WORLD THERE IS NO OTHER MAP LIKE THIS MAP—PIRI RE'IS

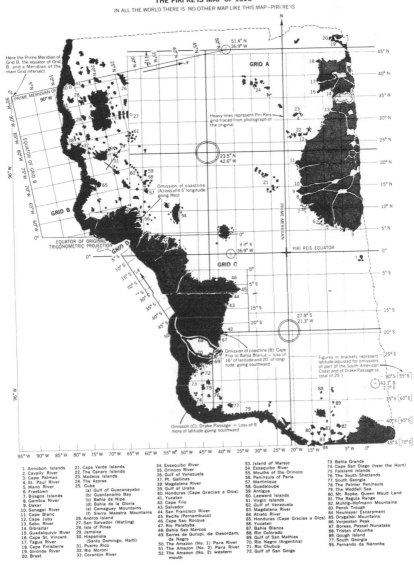

1. Annobon Islands
2. Cavally River
3. Cape Palmas
4. St. Paul River
5. Mano River
6. Freetown
7. Bijagos Islands
8. Gambia River
9. Dakar
10. Senegal River
11. Cape Blanc
12. Cape Juby
13. Sebu River
14. Gibraltar
15. Guadalquivir River
16. Cape St. Vincent
17. Tagus River
18. Cape Finisterre
19. Gironde River
20. Brest

21. Cape Verde Islands
22. The Canary Islands
23. Madeira Islands
24. The Azores
25. Cuba
  (a) Gulf of Guacanayabo
  (b) Guantanamo Bay
  (c) Bahia de Nipe
  (d) Bahia de la Gloria
  (e) Camaguey Mountains
  (f) Sierra Maestra Mountains
26. Andros Island
27. San Salvador (Watling)
28. Isle of Pines
29. Jamaica
30. Hispaniola
  (Santo Domingo, Haiti)
31. Puerto Rico
32. Rio Moroni
33. Corantijn River

34. Essequibo River
35. Orinoco River
36. Gulf of Venezuela
37. Pt. Gallinas
38. Magdalena River
39. Gulf of Uraba
40. Honduras (Cape Gracias a Dios)
41. Yucatan
42. Cape Frio
43. Salvador
44. San Francisco River
45. Recife (Pernambuco)
46. Cape Sao Roque
47. Rio Parahyba
48. Bahia Sao Marcos
49. Serras de Gurupi, de Desordam,
  de Negro
50. The Amazon (No. 1) Para River
51. The Amazon (No. 2) Para River
52. The Amazon (No. 2) western
  mouth

53. Island of Marajo
54. Essequibo River
55. Mouths of the Orinoco
56. Peninsula of Paria
57. Martinique
58. Guadaloupe
59. Antigua
60. Leeward Islands
61. Virgin Islands
62. Gulf of Venezuela
63. Magdalena River
64. Atrato River
65. Honduras (Cape Gracias a Dios)
66. Yucatan
67. Bahia Blanca
68. Rio Colorado
69. Gulf of San Mathias
70. Rio Negro (Argentina)
71. Rio Chubus
72. Gulf of San Gorge

73. Bahia Grande
74. Cape San Diego (near the Horn)
75. Falkland Islands
76. The South Shetlands
77. South Georgia
78. The Palmer Peninsula
79. The Weddell Sea
80. Mt. Ropke, Queen Maud Land
81. The Regula Range
82. Muhlig-Hofmann Mountains
83. Penck Trough
84. Neumeyer Escarpment
85. Drygalski Mountains
86. Vorposten Peak
87. Boreas, Passat Nunataks
88. Tristan d'Acunha
89. Gough Island
77. South Georgia
95. Fernando da Naronha

The Candlestick of the Andes.

A mummy and woven textile, both thousands of years old, found in Paracas.

The author and his pilot, about to fly over Nazca Plain.

Lines at Nazca, as seen from the air. While some lines and figures seem astronomically oriented, others lead far to the interior to Tiahuanaco, while still others resemble landing strips.

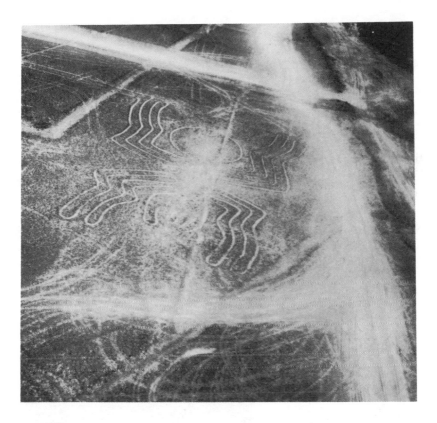

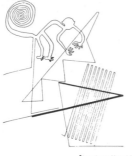

The Nazca plain is thought to be a gigantic astrological calendar by some. Certain figures etched into the plain correspond with constellations and are believed to be alined to the movements of the earth, sun and planets.

SERVICIO AEROFOTOGRAFICO NACIONAL

Above, the hummingbird of Nazca. Below, a large bird aligns with the solstice positions of the sun setting in December and rising in June. Lines leading in other directions cross the tail of the bird and their function is unknown.

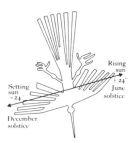

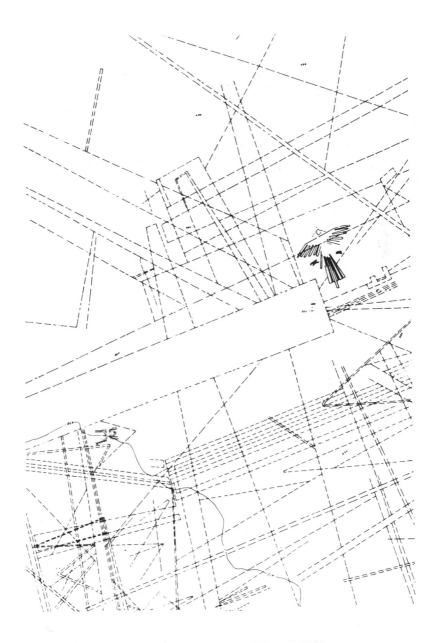

The layout of a portion of the Nazca Plain.

This giant figure, seen from the air is 180 feet long and can be found in the desert near Blythe, California. Its similarity to the drawings at Nazca is startling. Other gigantic etchings on the earth can be found in Chile, Ohio, Britain, Australia and all over the world.

This gold artifact from the collection of the Government of Colombia, said variously to be a bee, flying fish, and other animals, looks astonishingly similar to a modern delta-wing jet.

Dr. Cabrera at his museum in Ica.

A "petrified" totem pole, in front of part of Dr. Cabrera's
large collection of mysterious stones.

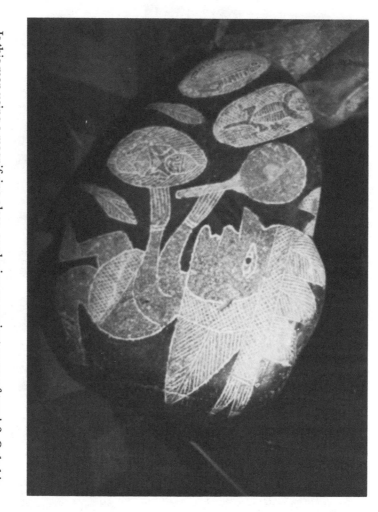

Is this man using a magnifying glass, or playing an ancient game of tennis? Only his hairdresser knows for sure! From Dr. Cabrera's collection.

Kangaroos in South America? From Cabrera's museum.

Some of the carved stones found around Ica seem to depict prehistoric animals. Did forgers carve all of these stones?

Chapter Three

Cuzco and Central Peru:
Lost Treasure of the Incas

Every mystery solved brings us to
the threshold of a greater one.
-Rachel Carson

The next day we took a bus for Arequipa, the second largest city in Peru, and the capital of the Arequipa district. It is located at the foot of the high and beautiful volcano, El Misti. The city itself is largely built from the white volcanic stone found nearby, from which it gets its nickname, the "White City."

We had left in the early morning from Ica, and faced a day-long bus trip south through the now familiar desert, dunes, barren hills, and occasional green valley. We arrived in Arequipa in the late afternoon, and had some time to look around the city before we took a train into the highlands of Peru that night.

Arequipa is a pleasant city, even though it is quite large. It has managed to retain a certain colonial charm, and the area of the central plaza is a nice place to hang out. The main attraction in Arequipa is to see the Saint Catherine Monastery. Once an important convent, it was closed for 400 years, from the sixteenth century until it was reopened in 1970. It is located just a block from the main square, and is a city unto itself, a miniature labyrinth of white walls and alcoves. Inside is a huge library of 20,000 old books, and seemingly endless statues of a bloody Jesus, his face a painful grimace, hanging from a cross.

We took about an hour to wander through the convent, now set up for tourists. Admission is about a dollar. As we passed the fifteenth or so detailed crucifix, Mark commented, "Why do they have to make him look like he's in such pain? With all the blood and suffering on his face, it's a wonder that these people can enjoy themselves at all. Do Catholics always stress that side of the Christ story?"

"Not really," answered Steve. "Most Catholic churches don't make such a big deal of it. Certainly Christ is not usually portrayed so gruesomely!"

That was true, I knew. It is perhaps a particular Spanish view of Jesus that causes them to portray him in such fashion. Did this violent depiction of a "savior" contribute to the Spaniards disregard for human life and liberty? The dreaded Spanish Inquisition, largely administered by Dominican monks, seemed to be driven by a certain pain and gore mentality. And the conquistadors were certainly not known for their compassion.

Other things to see and do in Arequipa include visiting the Archeological Museum and the Cathedral, plus shopping around the main plaza. You'll find the airline and bus offices, as well as the tourist office, located nearby.

As far as accommodation goes, there are quite a few hotels on Calle San Juan de Dios, the second street east and a bit south of the plaza. This is also where the long-distance bus stations are located. You'll find plenty of budget hotels between the many bus companies, including the Hotel Corona, Hostal Royal, Hostal Lira, Hostal Comercio. Others on the cross street of Alta de la Luna include the Hostal Moderno, Hotel Pacifico, and the Hotel Pension Colonial. You take your chances with getting a room in these hotels, but there are scores of inexpensive hotels where you can have a room for a few dollars. One that is popular is the Hostal El Mirador on the Plaza de Armas which has a roof top snack bar and a good view of El Misti.

We boarded the overnight train to Juliaca, located just outside Puno. It was a clear evening, with a bright moon and plenty of stars. We sat in padded seats in second class and chatted with some of the other travelers: Europeans on their way to Cuzco, Peruvians traveling on business, and Bolivians on their way to La Paz from Lima and Arequipa.

Young children wandered the train station, which is at the end of the bus station street on Tacna y Arica. "Candy or gum, señor?" they would ask, looking up. I gave in and bought some eucalyptus tablets for my sore, desert-parched throat, and boarded the train.

The trip between Puno and Arequipa takes all night, the times arranged so you leave in the evening and arrive in the early morning. Watch your luggage and belongings carefully on trains and buses in the Andes, as the notorious thieves are quite clever and active. Many travelers contend that the thieves here are the worst in the world.

Some of my companions kept a keen eye on their luggage all night, but I was soon sleeping like a baby. I have had so many things stolen from me in my many years of travel that losing one more item wouldn't make much difference. While suddenly finding your entire backpack gone can be rather disconcerting, paranoia can spoil a trip. Balance is the key: don't do things that are foolish, but don't spend your trip casting a distrustful eye on everyone you meet. I particularly like one Arab proverb in this regard:

Trust in God,
But tie up your camel at night.

§§§

We arrived in Juliaca bright and early the next morning. It was a different world! Instead of the desert and barren mountains, we were now on the Altiplano of Peru with its green valleys, mountains, and hills. Llamas, alpacas, and vicunas grazed the pastures, and Quechua Indians dressed in colorful alpaca wool wandered the station selling sweaters, scarves, and mittens made from the same material. The air at nearly 13,000 feet was brisk and clear, a sharp contrast to the desert air at sea level from the previous afternoon.

We hustled our luggage out of the carriage, and scrambled for another train that would take us north to Cuzco, ancient capital of the Inca Empire. Only a few miles south was Lake Titicaca and Puno, but we would be coming back this way and would see those places then. Within two hours the train to Cuzco was heading south with its cargo of tourists and their new sweaters. Indeed, Juliaca is an excellent place to buy handmade wool items.

We rumbled by the snowy Andes Mountains as our train headed up toward the pass that would take us down into the Urubamba Valley and Cuzco. As I ate some fruit for breakfast, a thrill ran up my spine: this was lost city country, a land of mystery, adventure, and treasure. Few other areas in the world are as full of both legendary and true lost worlds and empires as this, the highlands of Peru and the dense tropical rain forests of the Amazon River watershed to the east.

The history of the conquest of the Inca Empire by the Spanish makes one of the most bizarre and incredible stories of history. That Francisco Pizarro with only 183 men could conquer a sophisticated empire of several million people is a feat that has never been equalled, and probably never will!

Pizarro made his first expedition down the Pacific Coast from Panama in 1527, attracted by rumors of gold and other treasure. A Greek of his company went alone from the ship into an Inca village on the coast, and was taken to be a returning god by the natives. They brought him to a temple filled with more gold than he had seen in his life. Returning to the ship, he told Pizarro about the fabulous wealth he had had seen. Satisfied that the rumors were true, Pizarro returned to Panama and then to Spain to prepare another expedition. He set out again in 1531, landed on a lonely beach in Ecuador and began marching inland. He was entering the newly united Inca empire, which had just recovered from a civil war.[2] The people of Peru, Bolivia, and rest of the Inca empire were not all true Incas, but largely Quechua and Aymara Indians. Incas were the ruling elite, of a different race, who believed themselves descended from "Manco Capac," a red-haired, bearded messenger from God.

After taking the town of Tumbez and putting quite of few of the people to death, the Spanish conquistadors continued their march south. At Cajamarca, they were received by Inca royalty with great pomp, splendor, and gifts. The ruler of the Incas (or more correctly, "the Inca") Atahualpa was impressed by their beards and white skin, believing them to fulfill a prophecy about the return of Viracocha, the bearded prophet from many hundreds of years before. American Indians have no facial hair, though the first Incas are said to have had reddish-brown hair and beards, like Viracocha. Therefore, Atahualpa believed that the Spanish were Incas themselves, Sons of the Sun, gods in their own right, just as he, the Inca, was a god.

The conquistadors remained in Cajamarca for a time, while the Inca showered them with gifts. In fact, the Incas believed that the horses ridden by the Spaniards were also men, and assumed by the way the horses constantly chewed on their bits that these were the horses' fodder. The Incas would put bars of gold and silver in the horses' feeding troughs, saying, "Eat this, it is much better than iron." The Spaniards found this quite amusing, and encouraged the Indians to keep bringing gold and silver for the horses to eat! [21]

Finally, Atahualpa himself came to the Spaniards from his nearby palace. During this audience inside the walls of Cajamarca, Atahualpa had with him no less than thirty-thousand men, all under strict command not to harm the Spaniards, even if they themselves were attacked. This prohibition proved to be their downfall. The conquistadors kept many of their men in hiding, ready to attack, as Pizarro and his generals with the Dominican friar Vincente de Valverde had their audience with Atahualpa in the town square.

The Inca welcomed them as Viracocha Incas and fellow Sons of the Sun. Then the friar Valverde addressed the Inca, telling him about the one true faith, and the most powerful men on earth, the Pope and King Charles of Spain. After a long speech translated by the Indian Felipe, the Inca asked the source of the friar's material, who responded by handing the Inca a Bible. The Inca placed it to his ear. Hearing nothing, he threw it to the ground.

This rather unpious gesture from Atahualpa was just what the conquistadors wanted. The Spaniards attacked in full force, many from hiding, and began a slaughter of the Incas. They killed literally thousands, many while trying to escape. Not one conquistador was hurt, with the exception of Francisco Pizarro himself, who was wounded by one of his own men as he reached for Atahualpa.

Remember, the Incas had been commanded not to fight! It is said that the morning after the battle, the Spaniards went out for a stroll around Cajamarca and came on many handsome, nude Inca women bathing in the imperial open air baths. Thus began the rape of these women and more, totaling, according to several historians, 5,000 women ravished! [21,22]

And so was Atahualpa kidnaped by a mere 160 gold-crazed conquistadors. Some of the original 183 had died of disease and in earlier battles. To secure his freedom, Atahualpa offered to give the Spaniards gold in exchange for his release. Sensing that they still did not realize the fabulous wealth at his command, Atahualpa stood up in the room in which he was imprisoned and reached as high as he could; he offered to fill the room with gold to that height in return for his release. The Spaniards agreed.

Complicating the story at this point were several intrigues. First, there was a great rivalry between Francisco Pizarro, his brother Ferdinand, and Don Diego de Almagro. Indeed, Francisco Pizarro and de Almagro were bitter enemies. Second, Atahualpa was still at odds with his brother Huascar, who by many accounts was the legitimate heir to the Inca throne. While he was still in captivity, Atahualpa ordered Huascar arrested, believing him to be plotting the take-over of the Empire. It had been the civil war between the two brothers that had weakened the Inca Empire just prior to the arrival of the Spanish. Both Atahualpa and Huascar now took a rather fatalistic attitude to the events taking place, as their father had predicted such a conflict before his death.[21]

Third, most of the subjects of the Inca Empire were not Incas, but common Indians of entirely different races and cultural heritages. Few were loyal to the Incas, and many of them eventually sided with the Spanish. Finally, again from captivity, Atahualpa ordered his brother Huascar killed, thinking this would save the empire from him, believing that the Spaniards may not release him even after the ransom was paid. All of these factors together set the stage for the fall of the greatest civilization extant in the Western Hemisphere at the time.

It took some time for the gold to reach Cajamarca, as it had to be brought from Quito, Cuzco, and other cities that were hundreds of miles away. While the ransom was being gathered, Pizarro sent some of the conquistadors as emissaries to Quito and Cuzco to ensure that Atahualpa had not ordered an assault on Cajamarca. When they returned, they reported that fabulous wealth was to be found in these cities. The Incas did not use gold, silver, and precious stones for currency as Europeans and other cultures did. Instead, they were valued for decoration, and used extensively for religious objects, furnishings, and even utensils. Many buildings had interior gold-lined walls, and exterior gold rain gutters and plumbing. Therefore, when the Inca was ransomed for a room full of gold, to the Incas it was as if they were paying with pots and pans, old plumbing, and rain gutters!

These were sent gladly, though religious objects and those with esthetic value were not. The ransom paid has been estimated to have been 600-650 tons of gold and jewels and 384 million "pesos de oro," the equivalent of $500,000,000 in 1940.[22] Given the rise in the price of gold since then, today that ransom would be worth almost five billion dollars.

Not surprisingly, once the ransom was paid, Atahualpa was not released. The Indian interpreter, Felipe, had fallen in love with one of Atahualpa's wives, and he was keen to see that the Inca did not survive. He spread the rumor that Atahualpa was raising an army to storm Cajamarca. This being the only excuse the Spaniards needed to execute the Inca, he was condemned to death. Spaniards who had befriended Atahualpa advised him to convert to Christianity before his execution, which would allow the Dominical fathers to strangle him as a Christian rather than burn him at the stake as a heretic. He complied, was baptized, then strangled. This was done even though more gold was on its way, as part of a second ransom, worth much more than the first.

Meanwhile, three Spanish emissaries came back from Cuzco, the Inca capital, with even more treasure, looted from the Sun Temple. They brought an immense freight of gold and silver vessels loaded on the backs of 200 staggering, sweating Indians. And, the second ransom train of 11,000 llamas was on its way to Pizarro's camp. Loaded with gold, it had been sent by Atahualpa's queen from Cuzco. But when they heard of the Inca's assassination, the Indians drove the llamas off the road and buried the 100 pounds of gold that each animal carried. Sir Clements Markham, who had a particularly keen knowledge of Peru, believed that the gold was hidden in the mountains behind Azangaro. The Cordillera de Azangaro is a wild sierra little known to foreigners, the name in Quechua meaning, "place farthest away." It is believed that this was the farthest-eastern point in the Andean cordilleras which the old Inca empire dominated. Another version of this story says that the treasure was hidden in a system of tunnels that goes through the Andes.[22,23]

Much gold may have been lost, but each conquistador was still made a multi-millionaire, as John Harris picturesquely describes in his Moral History of the Spanish West Indies. "Nothing was so cheap, so common, so easy to be got as gold and silver...a sheet of paper went for ten Castilians of gold...Debts were paid in wedges of gold, and no Spaniard troubled if a creditor got twice the amount of his debt."

Another fantastic treasure story involves "The Garden of the Sun." Sarmiento, a Spanish historian (1532-1589), wrote that this subterranean garden was located near the Temple of the Sun. "They had a garden in which the lumps of earth were pieces of fine gold. These were cleverly sown with maize—the stalks, leaves and ears of which were all of gold. They were so well planted that nothing would disturb them. Besides all this, they had more than twenty sheep with their young. The shepherds who guarded the sheep were armed with slings and staves made of gold. There were large numbers of jars of gold and silver pots, vases, and every kind of vessel were cast from fine gold."

Shortly after the conquest of Peru, Cieza de Leon, part Inca and part Spanish, wrote, "If all the gold that is buried in Peru...were collected, it would be impossible to coin it, so great the quantity; and yet the Spaniards of the conquest got very little, compared with what remains. The Indians said, 'The treasure is so concealed that even we, ourselves, know not the hiding place!'

"If, when the Spaniards entered Cuzco they had not

committed other tricks, and had not so soon executed their cruelty in putting Atahualpa to death, I know not how many great ships would have been required to bring such treasures to old Spain as is now lost in the bowels of the earth and will remain so because those who buried it are now dead." [22]

What Cieza de Leon did not say was that, although the Indians as a whole did not know where this treasure lay, there were a few among them who did know and closely guarded the secret.

§§§

"Maize, señor?" asked a young woman in wool, from outside the train. She held a straw basket on her left arm, and lifted back the cloth covering it to expose corn cobs that had been roasted over coals. A beautiful Indian woman in her thirties, her cheeks were a deep red, contrasting sharply with the long black hair hanging down in braids on either side of her face.

"Si, uno!" I replied, and inquired the price. It was about five cents a cob. I paid, and rapidly bit off the rows, moving the cob like the roller of my old typewriter back home. Looking around at the poverty of the area, I wondered if I had paid too much.

I took stock of the small town in which we had stopped on the way through the pass to Cuzco. In the distance were the snow-covered peaks of the Andes. Alongside the tracks was a stream, the headwaters of the Urubamba, where some Indian women washed their clothes. It was not much of a town, just a village in the mountains, perfect for grazing the domestic llamas and alpacas.

I realized how deceptive this image could be, this land and people. Was it possible that they knew the secrets and wonders of the lost Inca empire? Are the secrets known to a chosen, initiated few? These Indians live in an area which which is possibly the resting place of many treasures, yet they live their lives simply, in what we might mistakenly call desperate poverty.

A popular fashion for many years in this area has been gold teeth. Dentists have made fortunes here, sometimes pulling good teeth to replace with gold ones. An Indian will come to the dentist wanting a few gold teeth, giving the dentist a lump of gold or a gold artifact. The dentist performs the oral surgery, keeping a portion of the gold for himself as payment. The patient goes back home to live in poverty on his small farm, but with that special glitter in his smile that is so prized.

Where do the Indians get this gold? They will not say. Nor

will they spend it. They will only use it for their teeth.

The woman selling corn came back. The train was about to leave and she wanted to sell the rest of her corn; it was now half price. I bought another cob, paid her and smiled. She smiled back, showing a familiar golden sparkle in her mouth. I laughed and she laughed with me. As the train pulled out, I waved goodbye. She ran after the train, handing me one more cob, her last. "Adios, gringo!" yelled the woman with the golden smile. Did she know the secrets of the Andes?

§§§

Atahualpa's first wife, the queen, had sent the 11,000 llamas to Cajamarca with the second ransom. But Pizarro had demanded, after seeing the previous treasures, that he be shown the source of this fabulous wealth before he would release the Inca. He had heard that the Incas possessed a secret and inexhaustible mine or depository, which lay in a vast, subterranean tunnel running many miles underground. Here was supposedly kept the accumulated riches of the country.

However, legend has it that the queen consulted the Black Mirror at the Temple of the Sun, a sort of magic mirror similar to that in the story of Snow White. In it she saw the fate of her husband, whether she paid the ransom or not. She realized that she must not reveal the secret of the tunnels or wealth to the gold-crazed conquistadors, and that her husband and the empire were doomed.

The horrified queen ordered the entrance to the great tunnel to be closed under the direction of the priests and magicians. A large door into a rocky wall of a cliff gorge near Cuzco, it was sealed by filling its depths with huge masses of rock. Then the disguised entrance was hidden under green grass and bushes; so that not the slightest sign of any fissure was perceptible to the eye.[22]

Conquistadors, adventurers, treasure-hunters, and historians have all wondered about and searched after this legend. What incredible treasure did the Incas seal into these tunnels? And the tunnels themselves, when and how were they made, and where do they go?

Most historians agree that the most precious verifiable piece of this treasure was the great Sun Disc, which was seen by the earliest Spaniards to visit Cuzco. It is said to have been fashioned after a human face of solid gold, radiating shafts of light as it blazed in the sun. It personified the Sun and the one

61

god, the central creator of the cosmos. The ancient Incas worshiped the Sun, much in the same way that the Egyptians at the time of Akhnaton worshipped Aton the Sun, or Ra as he later became known.

The Sun Disc was a massive plate of purest gold, encrusted thickly with emeralds and other gems of superb size and quality. At dawn, the sun's rays fell directly onto this disc in the temple chamber, where it reflected light back onto gold everywhere, on the walls and ceilings. The cornices were made of gold, and a broad gold frieze, worked into the stonework, adorned the whole exterior of the temple. Two other smaller sun discs sat on each side of the main disc, and a second large disc much like the first was hung on the opposite wall, to reflect the light of the setting sun.[22,23,21]

A smaller copy of the disc was at one time in the possession of one of Pizarro's men, Don Marcio Serra de Leguisamo. He had looted it from the Temple of Sun shortly after the kidnapping of Atahualpa. Leguisamo lost his smaller sun disc in an overnight gambling binge, and died poor. The sun disc was probably melted down into a gold bar and sent to Spain, "for the glory of the king."[22]

The legend continues that on either side of the great Sun Disc in the Sun Temple at Cuzco sat the embalmed bodies of thirteen former ruling Incas, in chairs of gold, standing on gold slabs. In these same chairs they had sat in life. The outraged Indians hastily hid these sacred mummies with the rest of the treasure in the tunnels.

Twenty-six years after the hiding of these treasures and mummies, Polo de Ondegardo, a conquistador, accidentally stumbled on the mummies of three kings and two queens, taken from the corresponding Temple of the Moon. All the mummies were stripped of their jewelry and broken into pieces by the treasure-hunters.[22,23]

A movie was even made from the Sun Disc legend in 1954, starring Charlton Heston as an archaeologist with a map to the hiding place. Hollywood named the movie The Secret of the Incas, and, yes, he found it in the end. This has yet to happen in real life, however.

In his book Secret of the Andes, George Hunt Williamson provides a different version of the story. He says that the Sun Disc is actually "the Golden Sun Disc of Mu."[25] It was fashioned thousands of years ago in the fabled Pacific Continent of Mu, and taken to a temple near Lake Titicaca by a Lord Meru just before Mu was submerged in a cataclysm (twelve-thousand years ago, according to Williamson). It was kept in this temple for about eleven-thousand years, until the Incas proved that they were spiritually advanced enough to be its caretakers. They were then allowed to keep the Sun Disc in the Temple of the Sun at Cuzco until the conquistadors came, when it was removed. Again according to Williamson, it is now kept in a secret monastery in a remote valley of the Andes, a sort of South American Shangri-La.

Williamson's book seems to be a mixture of fact and fiction, and I doubt that he would deny this himself. An ancient continent in the Pacific may well have existed. That the Golden Sun Disc of the Incas was from Mu, there is not much evidence. But there is indeed some independent evidence that a monastery such as Williamson describes does exist.

So where is this system of tunnels beneath Cuzco and the Andes? And just what is the extent of these tunnels? The mummies of the Incas and much of the treasure are believed to still be hidden in the tunnels that run under Cuzco and the ruins of a megalithic fortress called Sacsayhuaman. The old chroniclers say the tunnels were connected with the Coricancha, a name given to a sacred area of old Cuzco.

Coricancha contained many ancient temples, including the Temples of the Sun and the Moon, and all of these buildings were believed to be connected with Sacsayhuaman by underground tunnels. The place where these tunnels started was known as the Chincana, or "the place where one gets lost." This entrance was known up until the mid-1800's, when it was walled up. In his book Jungle Paths and Inca Ruins, Dr William Montgomery McGovern states:

"Near this fortress (Sacsayhuaman) are several strange caverns reaching far into the earth. Here altars to the Gods of the Deep were carved out of the living rock, and the many bones scattered about tell of the sacrifices which were offered up here. The end of one of these caverns, Chincana, has never been found. It is supposed to communicate by a long under-ground passage with the Temple of the Sun in the heart of Cuzco. In this cavern is supposed, and with good reason, to be hidden a large part of the golden treasure of the Inca Emperors which was stored away lest it fall into the hands of the Spaniards. But the cavern is so huge, so complicated, and its passages are so manifold, that its secret has never been discovered.

"One man, indeed, is said to have found his way underground to the Sun Temple, and when he emerged, to have had two golden bars in his hand. But his mind had been affected by days of blind wandering in the subterranean caves, and he died almost immediately afterwards. Since that time many have gone into the cavern—never to return again. Only a month or two before my arrival the disappearance of three prominent people in this Inca cave caused the Prefect of the Province of Cuzco to wall in the mouth of the cavern, so that the secret and the treasures of the Incas seem likely to remain forever undiscovered."

Another story, which may well be derived from the same source, tells of a treasure-hunter who went into the tunnels and wandered through the maze of tunnels for several days. One morning, about a week after the adventurer had vanished, a priest was conducting mass in the church of Santo Domingo. The priest and his congregation were suddenly astonished to hear sharp rappings from beneath the church's stone floor. Several worshippers crossed themselves and murmured about the devil. The priest quieted his congregation, then directed the removal of large stone slab from the floor (this was the converted Temple of the Sun!) The group was astonished to see the treasure-hunter emerge with a bar of gold in each hand.[23]

Even the Peruvian government got into the act of exploring these Cuzco tunnels, ostensibly for scientific purposes. The Peruvian Seria Documental del Peru describes an expedition undertaken by staff from Lima University in 1923. Accompanied by experienced speleologist, the party penetrated the trapezoid-shaped tunnels starting from a tunnel entrance at Cuzco.

They took measurements of the subterranean aperture and advanced in the direction of the coast. After a few days, members of the expedition at the entrance of the tunnel lost contact with the explorers inside, and no communication came for twelve days. Then a solitary explorer returned to the entrance, starving. His reports of an under-ground labyrinth of tunnels and deadly obstacles would make an Indiana Jones movie seem tame by comparison. His tale was so incredible that his colleagues declared him mad. To prevent further loss of life in the tunnels, the police dynamited the entrance.[54]

More recently, the big Lima earthquake of 1972 brought to light a tunnel system beneath that coastal city. During their salvage work, workers found long passages no one had ever known existed. The following systematic examination of Lima's foundations led to the astonishing discovery that large parts of the city were undercut by tunnels, all leading into the mountains. But their terminal points could no longer be ascertained because they had collapsed during the course of the centuries.[54] Did the Cuzco tunnels explored in 1923 lead to Lima? As far back as the 1940's, Harold Wilkins, in his book Mys-

teries of Ancient South America, wrote that they did. And what
of the rumored tunnels near the Candlestick of the Andes? [22]

Stories of these treasures and tunnels abound in Peru and
other areas of South America. Many researchers believe that
these tunnels run for hundreds of miles through the mountains,
as far south as Chile, as far north as Ecuador or Columbia, as
far to the east as the Amazon jungles! Rumors of tunnels,
treasures, and hidden entrances are so numerous that I ran into
them in nearly every country I visited.

Sometime around the year 1844, a Catholic priest was called
to absolve a dying Quechua Indian. Whispering quietly to the
priest, the old Indian told an amazing story about a labyrinth
and a series of tunnels going back far beyond the days of the
Inca emperors of the Sun. It was told under the inviolable seal
of the confessional, and could not be divulged by the priest
under pain of death. This story would probably never have been
told, except that the priest, while traveling to Lima, met with a
"sinister Italian." The priest let out a hint of great treasure, and
was later supposedly hypnotized by the Italian to get him tell
the story! [26,22]

"I will reveal to thee what no White man, be he Spaniard, or
American, or English, knows," the dying Indian had said to the
priest. He then told of the queen's closing of the tunnels when
the Inca Atahualpa was being held captive by Pizarro. The
priest added under hypnosis that the Peruvian government, in
about 1830, had heard rumors of these tunnels and sent an
expedition out to find and explore them. They were
unsuccessful.

In another similar story, the Father Pedro del Sancho tells in
his Relacion that in the early period of the conquest of Peru,
another dying Indian made a confession. Father del Sancho
wrote "...my informant was a subject of the Incan Emperor. He
was held in high esteem by those in power at Cuzco. He had
been a chieftain of his tribe and made a yearly pilgrimage to
Cuzco to worship his idolistic gods. It was a custom of the
Incas to conquer a tribe or nation and take their idols to Cuzco.
Those who wished to worship their ancient idols were forced to
travel to the Incan capital. They brought gifts to their heathen
idols. They were also expected to pay homage to the Incan
emperor during these journeys." [23]

Del Sancho continues, "These treasures were placed in
ancient tunnels that were in the land when the Incas arrived.
Also placed in these subterranean repositories were artifacts and
statues deemed sacred to the Incas. When the hoard had been

placed in the tunnels, there was a ceremony conducted by the high priest. Following these rites, the entrance to the tunnels was sealed in such a manner that one could walk within a few feet and never be aware of the entrance."

"...My informant said that the entrance lay in his land, the territory which he ruled. It was under his direction and by his subjects that the openings were sealed. All who were in attendance were sworn to silence under the penalty of death. Although I requested more information on the exact location of the entrance, my informant refused to divulge more than what has been written down here." [23]

Another interesting story of the tunnels around Cuzco and the incredible treasure they contain is about Carlos Inca, a descendant of an Inca emperor, who had married a Spanish lady, Dona Maria Esquivel. His Castillian wife thought that he was not ambitious enough, and that he did not keep her in the style she deemed befitting her rank, or his descent.

Poor Carlos was plagued night and day by his wife's nagging, until late one night, he blindfolded her, and lead her out into the patio of the hacienda. Under the cold light of the stars, when all around were asleep, and no unseen eye was on the watch, he began to lead her by the shoulders. Although he was exposing himself to death at the hands of the Quechuas, torture, and other risks, he twirled her around three times. Then, assuming her disorientated, he led her down some steps into a concealed vault in or under Sacsayhuaman Fortress. When he removed her blinds, her tongue was finally silenced. She stood on the dusty, stone floor of an ancient vault, cluttered with gold and silver ingots, exquisite jewelery, and temple ornaments. Around the walls, ranged in fine gold, were life-size statues of long dead Inca kings. Only the golden Disk of the Sun, which the old Incas treasured most, was missing. [22]

Carlos Inca was supposedly one of the custodians of the secret hiding place of Inca treasure that eluded the Spanish and other treasure seekers for centuries. The U.S. Commissioner to Peru in 1870 commented on this episode, "All I can say is if that secret chamber which she had entered has not been found and despoiled, it has not been for want of digging...Three-hundred years have not sufficed to eradicate the notion that enormous treasures are concealed within the fortress of Cuzco. Nor have three-hundred years of excavation, more or less constant, entirely discouraged the searchers for tapadas, or treasure mounds." [22]

There certainly appears to be some repetition and borrowing between some of these stories. Yet most historians and archaeologists believe that they are based on some fact. That tunnels and lost treasure exist, there seems to be no doubt. But the real questions are, where are they? And, who made them?

Indeed, some historians believe that a similar set of tunnels exists in Arizona. At the turn of the last century, the American army was pursuing Geronimo around Arizona; he and his braves would ride into box canyons with the calvary in hot pursuit. The Indians would then literally vanish, and the U.S. Army was totally mystified. Later the same day, it would be reported, Geronimo and his troops would suddenly turn up in Mexico, hundreds of miles distant! This happened not once, but several times. Is it possible that Geronimo was aware of, and using, a system of ancient tunnels that exist in the American southwest? Navaho Indians in New Mexico and Arizona have told me the same story, and that certain members of their tribes know about these tunnels, but keep them secret.

Similarly, Christopher Columbus wrote that when he landed on the the Caribbean island of Martinique, a story of tunnels was brought to his attention. The Carib Indians told the Spaniards about the Amazon women who lived without men. Columbus and his crew were informed that these women warriors would hide in ancient subterranean tunnels if they were bothered by men. If their persistent suitors followed them into the tunnels, the Amazons cooled their passions with a flurry of arrows from their strong bows.[22,23]

Other tunnels are said to exist in India, Tibet and other parts of Central Asia, in the Ahaggar Mountains of Algeria, and even in Europe and Britain.[16,26,27] What the truth is, we may never really know. But, I was to find myself coming into contact with these legends repeatedly, and, at one point in my South American journey, with the tunnels themselves.

§§§

Are the stories of Inca treasure true? I wondered as we pulled into Cuzco in the late afternoon. Outside, clouds gathered on the northern edge of Cuzco valley. Orange tiled roofs of homes filled the high, green capital of the ancient Inca Empire.

A Peruvian we had met on the train, a small, middle aged man who spoke broken English, warned us of thieves and pickpockets at the station. "Careful, gringos," he said, looking around at the many taxi drivers, children, and vendors who lurked anxiously outside the station. "This is Cuzco, the tourist capital of Peru, and the criminal capital of Peru as well. Stay together, and we will all take a taxi down to the Plaza de

Armas."

The five of us piled into a rusty, barely running Ford. It looked like it had driven the Pan American Highway several times already, and through the Darien Gap as well, where there is no road! Our driver was a hook-nosed, wild-looking Meztiso with a wool cap and an old sport coat. Blasting his horn, he wound his way through ancient Cuzco, down cobblestone streets, and past ancient stone buildings until he coasted to a stop in the Plaza de Armas, in the center of old Cuzco. We grabbed our luggage and pitched in a hundred soles each, paying him 500 soles, about two dollars.

Most of the inexpensive hotels in Cuzco can be found within a couple of blocks of the main square. If you arrive early enough, you can stop in at the tourist office, where they will find you a hotel for your budget. If you arrive at the airport, taxi drivers and pitch men will rave about their hotels, offering you free rides, though you will probably end up paying for the ride with an increased room rate.

There are literally dozens of hotels around the Plaza de Armas, many of them right on the square. You have to take your chances, as they are often full, and their rates seem to change almost daily. Ask other travelers for advice on where to stay. Around the square are located the Plaza, Panamericano, Arentina, Royal, Inca, Central, Bolivar, Los Andes, Machu Picchu and a host of other hotels. Other popular hotels, such as Lenny's Lodgings, are located away from the square, which is where those travelers who spend a lot of time in Cuzco are more likely to stay. We decided to stay at the Plateros, right on the square, because it wasn't full and we wanted a room right away. Our Peruvian friend said goodbye and took off to stay at a relative's house. Mark, Bob, Steve, and I got a large room with four beds and a bath, and began to unpack.

The manager came up with coca tea, which is customary in Cuzco. It is made with coca leaves, from which cocaine is also derived. The leaves are legal in the Altiplano of Peru and Bolivia, though cocaine is not. Coca leaves for chewing, a popular habit with the Indians, are available at the markets everywhere.

We were soon out on the streets looking for dinner. There being quite a few restaurants around the square, we chose one on the north side where Inca music was being played by a live band. Taking a table, we ordered a round of Cusqueña beer, and began to listen. This pleasant music is played using traditional Inca instruments: la quena, flutes of varying length and pitch; la antara, the pan pipe; la charango, the guitar-like stringed instrument; and the bombo leguero, a massive willow and goat-skin drum. The music was light and strangely alien; as we ate our dinner and sipped our beer, we were swept back to the days of the Incas.

The next day we were off to see the fortress of Sacsay-huaman. The road leads up from the Plaza de Armas to a hill on the north side of Cuzco. At a leveling off of the hill, looking over the Cuzco Valley, is the colossal fortress, one of the most imposing edifices ever constructed. Walking around, we could hardly believe our eyes! Here was a stone structure that covered the entire hill; it appeared almost unworldly.

Gigantic blocks of stone, some weighing more than 200 tons (400 thousand pounds) are fitted together perfectly. The enormous stone blocks are cut, faced, and fitted so well that even today one cannot slip the blade of a knife, or even a piece of paper between them. No mortar is used, and no two blocks are alike. Yet they fit perfectly, and it has been said by some engineers that no modern builder with the aid of metals and tools of the finest steel, could produce results more accurate.

Each individual stone had to have been planned well in advance; a twenty-ton stone, let alone one weighing 80 to 200 tons, cannot just be dropped casually into position with any hope of attaining that kind of accuracy! The stones are locked and dove-tailed into position, making them earthquake-proof. Indeed, after many devasting earthquakes in the Andes over the last few hundred years, the blocks are still perfectly fitted, while the Spanish Cathedral in Cuzco has been leveled twice.

Even more incredibly, the blocks are not local stone, but by some reports come from quarries in Ecuador, almost fifteen-hundred miles away! Others have located quarries a good deal closer. Though this fantastic fortress was supposedly built just a few hundred years ago by the Incas, they leave no record of having built it, nor does it figure in any of their legends. How is it that the Incas, who reportedly had no knowlege of higher mathematics, no written language, no iron tools, and did not even use the wheel, are credited with having built this cyclopean complex of walls and buildings? Frankly, one must literally grope for an explanation, and it is not an easy one.[9,10,22,23,27]

When the Spaniards first arrived in Cuzco and saw these structures, they thought that they had been built by the devil himself, because of their enormity. Indeed, nowhere else can you see such large blocks placed together so perfectly. I have traveled all over the world searching for ancient mysteries and lost cities, but I had never in my life seen anything like this!

The builders of the stoneworks were not merely good stone masons— they were excellent! Similar stoneworks can be seen throughout the Cuzco Valley. These are usually made up of finely cut, rectangular blocks of stone weighing up to perhaps a ton. A group of strong people could lift a block and put it in place; this is undoubtably how some of the smaller structures were put together. But in Sacsayhuaman, Cuzco, and other ancient Inca cities, one can see gigantic blocks cut with 30 or more angles on each one.

At the time of the Spanish conquest, Cuzco was at its peak, with perhaps one-hundred-thousand Inca subjects living in the ancient city. The fortress of Sacsayhuaman could hold the entire population within its walls in case of war or natural catastrophe. Some historians have stated that the fortress was built a few years before the Spanish invasion, and that the Incas take credit for the structure. But, the Incas could not recall exactly how or when it was built!

Only one early account survives of the hauling of the stones, found in Garcilaso de la Vega's The Incas.[21,23] In his commentaries, Garcilaso tells of one monsterous stone brought to Sacsayhuaman from beyond Ollantaytambo, a distance of about 45 miles. "The Indians say that owing to the great labor of being brought on its way, the stone became weary and wept tears of blood because it could not attain to a place in the edifice. The historical reality is reported by the Amautas (philosophers and doctors) of the Incas who used to tell about it. They say that more than twenty-thousand Indians brought the stone to the site, dragging it with huge ropes. The route over which they brought the stone was very rough. There were many high hills to ascend and descend. About half the Indians pulled the stone, by means of ropes placed in front. The other half held the stone from the rear due to fears that the stone might break loose and roll down the mountains into a ravine from which it could not be removed.

"On one of these hills, due to lack of caution and co-ordination of effort, the massive weight of the stone overcame some who sustained it from below. The stone rolled right down the hillside, killing three- or four-thousand Indians who had been guiding it. Despite this misfortune, they succeeded in raising it up again. It was placed on the plain where it now rests."

Even though Garcilaso describes the hauling of one stone, many doubt the truth of this story. This stone was not part of the Sacsayhuaman fortress, and is smaller than most used there, according to some researchers, although it has never been identified. Even if the story is true, the Incas may have been trying to duplicate what they supposed was the construction technique used by the ancient builders. And certainly, while there is no denying that the Incas were master craftsmen, could they have managed and placed the 100-ton blocks so perfectly, a feat that we would be hard-pressed to duplicate today?

That the Incas actually found these megalithic ruins and then built on top of them, claiming them as their own, is not a particularly alarming theory. In fact, it is most probably the truth. It was a common practice in ancient Egypt for rulers to claim previously existing obelisks, pyramids, and other structures as their own, often literally erasing the cartouche of the real builder and subisituting theirs. Indeed, the Great Pyramid itself would seem a victim of such a ruse. The pharoah Kufu, or Cheops as he was known in Greek, had his cartouche chiseled into the Great Pyramid at its base. This is the only writing to be found anywhere on the pyramid, but every indication is that the pyramid was not built by Cheops. It may not have ever been meant to be a tomb, but that is another story.

If the Incas came along and found walls and basic foundations of cities already in existance, why not just move in? Even today, all one needs to do is a little repair work and add a roof on some of the structures to make them habitable. Indeed, there is considerable evidence that the Incas merely found the structures and added to them. There are numerous legends that exist in the Andes that Sacsayhuaman, Machu Picchu, Tiahuanaco, and other megalithic remains were built by a race of giants. Alain Gheerbrant comments in his footnotes to de la Vega's book, "Three kinds of stone were used to build the fortress of Sacsayhuaman. Two of them, including those which provided the gigantic blocks for the outer wall, were found practically on the spot. Only the third kind of stone (black andesite), for the inside buildings, was brought from relatively distant quarries; the nearest quarries of black andesite were at Huaccoto and Rumicolca, nine and twenty-two miles from Cuzco respectively.

"With regard to the giant blocks of the the outer wall, there is nothing to prove that they were not simply hewn from a mass of stone existing on the spot; this would solve the mystery." [21]

Gheerbrant is close in thinking that the Incas never moved those gigantic blocks in place, yet even if they did cut and dress the stones on the spot, fitting them together so perfectly would still require what modern engineers would call superhuman effort. Furthermore, the gigantic city of Tiahuanaco in Bolivia is similarly hewn from 100-ton blocks of stone, definitely of pre-

71

Inca origin. Proponents of the theory that the Incas found these cities in the mountains and inhabited them, would then say that the builders of Tiahuanaco, Sacsayhuaman, and other megalithic structures in the Cuzco area were the same people.

Again quoting Garcilaso de la Vega, who wrote about these structures just after the conquest, " ...how can we explain the fact that these Peruvian Indians were able to split, carve, lift, carry, hoist, and lower such enormous blocks of stone, which are more like pieces of a mountain than building stones, and that they accomplished this, as I said before, without the help of a single machine or instrument? An enigma such as this one cannot be easily solved without seeking the help of magic, particularly when one recalls the great familiarity of these people with devils."

The Spanish dismantled as much of Sacsayhuaman as they could. When Cuzco was first conquered, Sacsayhuaman had three round towers at the top of the fortress, behind three concentric megalithic walls. These were taken apart stone by stone, and the stones used to build new structures for the Spanish.

Sacsayhuaman was also equipped with a subterranean network of aqueducts. Water was brought down from the mountains into a valley, then had to ascend a hill before reaching Sacsayhuaman. This indicates that the engineers who built the intricate system knew that water rises to its own level. [23]

Garcilaso said this about the tunnels beneath Sacsayhuaman: "An underground network of passages, which was as vast as the towers themselves, connected them with one another. This was composed of a quantity of streets and alleyways which ran in every direction, and so many doors, all of them identical, that the most experienced men dared not venture into this labyrinth without a guide, consisting of a long thread tied to the first door, which unwound as they advanced. I often went up to the fortress with boys of my own age, when I was a child, and we did not dare to go farther that the sunlight itself, we were so afraid of getting lost, after all that the Indians had told us on the subject... the roofs of these underguound passages were composed of large flat stones resting on rafters jutting out from the walls." [21]

§§§

"Can you beleive this place?" marvelled Steve, walking up to me across the great field to the west of the fortress. This green area, in front of the old walls with the largest stones, reminded me of a football field. Down at one end, nuns still wearing their habits were playing volleyball. To the west some carpenters were building a platform for the Pope to use when he visited Cuzco the next month.

Bob walked over to join us and looked around. "Now, that's not something that you see every day," he said, "Atlantean stone construction and nuns playing volleyball!"

We all laughed at that one. "What makes you say this is Atlantean?" asked Steve.

"Well, construction like this can be found in Morocco, Malta, and beneath the ocean in the Caribbean. Take for instance the Bimini Road. Some authors call it 'of the Atlantean style'," Bob said, scanning the gigantic wall in front of us. Meanwhile, Mark had started to climb up on one of the biggest stones, a 200-ton, thirteen-sided boulder to our left, trying to pull himself up the wall like a rock climber.

"Maybe your Atlanteans that built those missing tunnels that are supposed to be around here," Steve conjectured.

"Possibly," Bob replied as we started to walk to the north. "I've heard that these cities were built by a group of people called 'The Atlantean League.' They were traders at the time of Atlantis, and supposedly later became the Phoenicians and Carthagenians. They may have built these cities, using Atlantean techniques, sometime after the sinking of Atlantis, which was supposed to have happened around 9,000 BC. Tiahuanaco is said to have been built at about the same time, but then, who knows? Maybe the Incas just dragged these stones into place a few hundred years ago. I suppose anything's possible."

"That doesn't seem likely," said Steve, as we reached Kenko, just beyond Sacsayhuaman. "I mean, these ruins look a whole lot older than anything you see in Europe or England that's that old."

"What about our friendly nieghbors from outer space?" quipped Mark, running to catch up with us. "Didn't aliens build all this for the Incas?"

"It doesn't really fit in with what we know about prehistory," Bob answered, perfectly seriously. "There are plenty of legends of great civilizations like Atlantis in the past. They weren't aliens, they were humans."

"Still, what about the legends about Gods coming in spaceships, teaching people all kinds of wonderful knowledge?" asked Steve.

"Well, those legends may be correct," Bob returned. "But just because someone lands in an airship and gives you some information, doesn't mean that the guy is an alien. During

73

World War Two, aircraft landed in the jungles of New Guinea and other remote places doing just that. The people thought of them as gods and created whole religions around them. In the past, people landing at Lake Titicaca or Nazca, may have been men like you or I. They just would have had an advanced technology, much as we have today compared to other con- temporary cultures.

"Stories of past cultures having airships are so numerous that there are hundreds of books on the subject. King Solomon supposedly had an airship, as did many figures in ancient India. The Bible has many references to such airships. Model planes have been found in Egypt, Columbia, Yugoslavia and other areas that are hundreds, even thousands of years old. The Incas even supposedly had gliders!"

"You're kidding!" said everyone in unison.

"Sure!" Bob smiled, pleased to be able to shock us, we who thought we had heard everything. "Monks with Pizarro reported that the Incas built gliders for rapid transit from high peaks to distant valleys. A lookout could complete a fifteen-day journey in fifteen minutes, in a glider like our own hang-gliders. The Aztecs had similar gliders, made out of stork feathers. These Aztec machines were called 'criers' by the monks. A Franciscan monk named Francisco Xavier Clausijaro stated in his history of Mexico that Aztecs could 'fly like birds' in these 'criers'."

Bob later showed me a story reprinted from the New York Times, July 23, 1934, which said that a Polish archaeologist named Professor Tanenbaum had found a stone in Mexico which depicted a glider. He said that an Aztec ruler named Netzahualcoyotl made regular flights from a high mountain to valleys far below.7 Also, in 1972, the Egyptian Museum in Cairo exhibited fourteen models of gliders found at various sites in Egypt. The most famous Egyptian glider was found at a tomb a Sakkara in 1898. It is now exhibit number 6347 at the Egyptian Museum.

§§§

One interesting theory about the building of the gigantic and perfectly fitted stones is that they were constructed by using a now-lost technique of softening and shaping the rock. Hiram Bingham, the discoverer of Machu Picchu, wrote in his book Across South America, of a plant he had heard of whose juices softened rock so that it could be worked into tightly fitted masonry.

In his book Exploration Fawcett, Colonel Fawcett told of how he had heard that the stones were fitted together by means of a liquid that softened stone to the consistency of clay. Brian Fawcett, who edited his father's book, tells the following story in the footnotes: A friend of his who worked at a mining camp at 14,000 feet at Cerro di Pasco in Central Peru, discovered a jar in an Incan or pre-Incan grave. He opened the jar, thinking it was chicha, an alcoholic drink, breaking the still intact ancient wax seal. Later, the jar was accidentally knocked over onto a rock.

Quotes Fawcett, "About ten minutes later I bent over the rock and casually examined the pool of spilled liquid. It was no longer liquid; the whole patch where it had been, and the rock under it, were as soft as wet cement! It was as though the stone had melted, like wax under the influence of heat." [33]

Fawcett seemed to think that the plant might be found on the Pyrene River in the Chuncho country of Peru, and described it as having dark reddish leaves and being about a foot high. In his bookThe Ancient Stones Speak, David Zink quotes a "psychic reading," giving the name of the plant as Caochyll, saying it has sparse leaves with reddish veins, and stands about three to four feet high. [40]

Another story is told in South America, of a biologist observing an unfamiliar bird in the Amazon. He watched it making a nest on a rock face by rubbing the rock with a twig. The sap of the twig dissolved the the rock, making a hollow in which the bird could make its nest.

All of this speculation may be put to rest by new findings, reported in Scientific American (February, 1986). In a fascinating article, a French researcher, Jean-Pierre Protzen, relates his experiments in duplicating the construction of Inca structures. Protzen spent many months around Cuzco experimenting with different methods of shaping and fitting the same kinds of stones used by the Incas. He found that quarrying and dressing the stones were easily accomplished using the stone hammers found in abundance in the area. He repeatedly dropped these hammers, made of a hard stone, against the larger blocks from eye-level. Each impact chipped away a small amount of rock, and he caught the hammer as it bounced back up to easily repeat the maneuver. Even the precision fitting of stones was a relatively simple matter, he says. He pounded out the concave depressions into which new stones were fitted by trial and error, until he achieved a snug fit. This meant continually lifting and placing the stones together, and chipping at them a little at a time. This process is very time consuming, but it's simple, and it works.

Protzen believes that Inca stone masonry was surprisingly unsophisticated, though efficient. He would like to debunk ideas of anti-gravity devices, stone-softening, or lasers used to cut and place the the stone. Yet even for Protzen, some mysteries remain. He was not able to figure out how the builders transportated and handled the large stones. The fitting process necessitated the repeated lowering and raising of the stone being fitted, with trial-and-error pounding in between. He does not know just how 100-ton stones were manipulated at this stage, while some stones are actually far heavier.

According to Protzen, to transport the stones from the quarries, the Incas built special access roads and ramps. Many of the stones were dragged over gravel-covered roads, which in his theory gave the stones their polished surfaces. The largest stone at Ollantaytambo weighs about 150 tons. It could have been pulled up a ramp with a force of about 260,000 pounds, he says. Such a feat would have required a mimimum of some 2,400 men. Getting the men seemed possible, but where did they all stand? Protzen says that the ramps were only eight meters wide at most. Further perplexing Protzen is that the stones of Sacsayhuaman were finely dressed, yet are not polished, showing no signs of dragging. He could not figure out how they were transported the 22 miles from the Rumiqolqa quarry.

Protzen's article reflects good research, and points out that modern science still cannot explain or duplicate the building feats found at both Sacsayhuaman and Ollantaytambo. Continually lifting and chipping away at a 100-ton stone block to make it fit perfectly is just too great of an engineering task to have been practical. Protzen's theory would work well on the smaller, precisely square, later construction, but fails with the older megalithic construction beneath. Perhaps the theories of levitation and softening stones can not be discarded yet! One last intriguing observation which Protzen makes is that the cutting marks found on some of the stones are very similar to those found on the pyramidion of an unfinished obelisk at Aswan in Egypt. Is this a coincidence, or was there an ancient civilization with links to both sites?

The four of us walked the half-mile or so to the incredible and mysterious ruins of Kenko. Most visitors miss these ruins, but for the traveler in search of lost cities and ancient mysteries, they are an absolute requirement!

At Kenko (or Qenqo), large rocks, cliffs, and hills are all carved with a most bizzare menagerie of steps, tunnels, seats, niches, windows and other shapes. One begins to imagine an architect doodling with modeling clay, but on an enormous scale. Staircases at odd angles lead nowhere. Other paths, tunnels and staircases are so weather-worn, they give the impression of being many thousands of years old. As we walked around, we even found what looked like an ancient set of parallel cogs cut into the stone, as if it was part of some set of gears or a levering device.

This is one of the strangest ruins I have ever seen. The area is unmistakably ancient, far older than the ruins of Sacsayhuaman and Cuzco behind us. You will not find Kenko in most archaeology books or tourist guides, simply because it cannot be explained! Kenko's appearance gives the impression of construction that was toppled and destroyed in a great South American earthquake of ages past. Everything appears to be tilted by about 30 degrees, which would have required an earthquake of tremendous magnitude to have done the damage. Portions remain visible, but the hard stone has been badly weathered over many thousands of years.

Farther up the hill is an Incan bathing area, nearby a shrine called Tambomachay, which has a beautiful spring coming out of its walls. The construction is a combination of megalithic and rectangular Incan stones, suggesting that it too may have been built first by the Atlantean League (or whoever), rather than the Incas. When comparing Kenko, Sacsayhuaman, Tambomachay and other ruins in and around Cuzco, one cannot help but notice the several different styles.

The most recent style is Spanish. Perhaps the most primitive of all, it is characterized by the masonry and tiled roofs so common throughout colonial South America. The Incan construction of 500 to 1000 years ago is evident on top of the larger, more perfect, more ancient works. This Incan technique is easily recognized by its square or rectangular blocks, typically weighing from 200- to 1000-pounds. Beneath it we find the megalithic construction of odd-angled blocks weighing from 20-to 200-tons, all perfectly fitted together. This construction may date from between 7,000 BC and 3,000 BC. Finally, there are the ruins at Kenko, old, worn, and baffling. Are they a joke, or they from some pre-cataclysmic culture that built on a very large scale? Stones at Kenko weigh as much as 500 tons. Incredible as it may seem, this physical reality is there for anyone to see. Unfortunately, as many academians have successfully discovered, it can also be ignored.

§§§

After dinner, I left the hotel in Cuzco alone, grabbing my tan stetson and raincoat, heading out into the night. My companions were tired, and the altitude was getting to them, so they went to bed early. As I stepped out onto the Plaza des Armas, it started to rain.

Turning my collar up against the wind, and zipping up my coat all the way, I walked the stone paved streets of Cuzco in the rain. I was too excited to sleep or rest, and needed to walk off some of my excess energy. I walked the streets in the pounding rain for awhile, stepping carefully on the slick stones and steep alleyways.

My mind reeled with the sights and possibilities of the last few days. The gigantic construction I had seen today was like nothing else I had ever seen! It was no wonder that the Spanish believed that these structures had been built by demons, or that later writers would claim that they were the works of visitors from outer space. They have to be seen to be believed! Engineers, mathematicians, historians, archaeologists and Egyptologists have made a big deal about the construction of the Great Pyramid of Egypt, built with stones averaging three tons. We were talking 200 tons here!

I couldn't help thinking about the tunnels and treasure. I've never thought of myself as a particularly materialistic person, but the thought of all that treasure, and the adventure that went along with it, created a pleasant thrill up my spine that warmed me briefly. Who had made this tunnel system, and did it really stretch for hundreds of miles through the Andes? It hardly seemed possible!

I walked south through the twisting alleyways of Cuzco, the rain pouring off the wide brim of my hat and onto the street. Turning a corner, I passed an Indian woman, her long black braids hanging on her colorful, wet poncho. I decided to find a café, before I got soaked to the bone.

Leaving an alley onto a main street, I abruptly found myself facing a sign to my right, "ABRAXAS." Abraxas? That rang a bell...It was the title of a Santana album of many years ago, as well as part of a Herman Hesse novel, Demian:

"We stood before it and began to freeze inside from the exertion. We questioned the painting, berated it, made love to it, prayed to it: We called it mother, called it whore and slut, called it our beloved, called it Abraxas ... "

I stood there for a moment in the pouring rain ,wondering whether to enter a place with such a name. Abraxas was once the name of a diety in the ancient Middle East, later becoming the name for a certain type of magical charm. But this mystical image didn't match the music coming from inside; pop music, not Incan at all. In fact, I thought I recognized a Santana tune.

Suddenly from behind me, someone urged, "Hey! Don't just stand there! I'm getting wet!" As I turned, a woman buried in a raincoat and hat pushed herself past me into the tavern. "Come in!" she cried.

I followed, dragged inside by her voice and the seductive warmth of the music and light. As I wiped my glasses, I took a good look around the room. It was full of young people, mostly foreigners, drinking and dancing. At a bar on the far side, several bartenders were busy serving hot drinks to help fight off the chill of the weather outside.

Soon, my companion and I were sitting at a small table, drinking hot pisco. She was tall and beautiful. Red hair flowed down one side of her red cheeks and onto her soft sweater. Her name was Shelly, and she was from Canada. I never was quite sure what she did for a living, but we talked for hours, and danced until the hour changed from late to early. Abruptly, between songs, she asked me to take her back to her hotel.

"It would be my pleasure," I replied, and we took our leave of Abraxas, the café, the ancient charm.

The doorman ushered us into the quiet warmth of her modern hotel. Shelly invited me into her room to warm up. Once inside, she closed the door.

"You'd better get out of those wet clothes. You could catch a cold." I felt like resisting, but could not. She helped me remove my jacket, then the rest of my wet clothes. Within moments, she had shed her clothes as well. She pressed her lips, full and red, against mine. Indeed, I thought as she pushed me back onto the bed, there was an ancient charm at work here...

INCA TAHUANTINSUYO

CARACAS

TAIRONA   CAQUETÍ

QUIMBAYÁ

BOGOTÁ
TIERRA DENTRO
SAN AGUSTÍN   CARIB   ARAWAK
CHIBCHA
QUITO   EQUATOR   0°
LUCANO   MAYAPÍ
SARRIANA
CAÑARIS   JÍVAROS   WITOTO   BORA   MANAO   MARAJÓ
TUMBES   CHIMÚ   PARÓMAS   SANTARÉM   BELÉM
                     MIRAÑ   ANDOKES
CHIMÚ

AMAZON BASIN

LIMA   MATO GROSSO   CAYAPÓ
        CUZCO
        LAKE TITICACA   SHAVANTE   BOTOCUDO
        LA PAZ   TUPINAMBA
                     GRAN CHACO

                                          CARIJÓ
TROPIC OF CAPRICORN
                     PAMPAS   CHARRÚA   RIO DE JANEIRO
                     QUERANDÍ
SANTIAGO
                     PUELCHE   BUENOS AIRES

SOUTH AMERICA

Showing the Ancient Inca Empire and Major Tribal Divisions
of South American Indians

PATAGONIA
TEHUELCHE

SCALE
0   250   500
MILES

10°
0°
10°
20°
30°
40°
50°

N

CHINCHAYSUYO   ANTISUYO   COLLASUYO   KOLLAS   CUNTISUYO

A megalithic wall at Sacsayhuaman. This is the most durable, earthquake-resistant construction found anywhere in the world. To this day, the builders of these walls remain unknown.

Another wall at Sacsayhuaman. The man stands in front of the largest block in the complex, weighing over 250 tons.

Detail of a megalithic wall at Sacsayhuaman. Each oddly-shaped block fits perfectly with the others, making the wall earthquake-resistant. The larger blocks in this photo all weigh well over ten tons.

PERUVIAN BIRD MAN

CUZCO

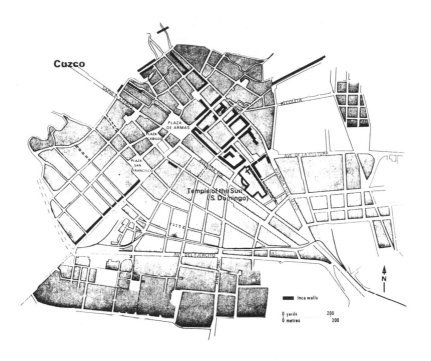

Cuzco

PLAZA DE ARMAS

PLAZA CABILDO

PLAZA SAN FRANCISCO

Temple of the Sun (S. Domingo)

RECOLETA

AVE. DE LA CULTURA

AVE. DEL EJERCITO

N

Inca walls

0 yards   200
0 metres   200

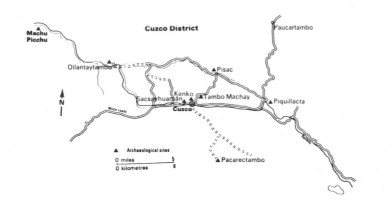

Cuzco District

Machu Picchu

Paucartambo

Ollantaytambo

Pisac

Sacsayhuamán
Kenko
Tambo Machay

Piquillacta

Cuzco

N

Motor roads

Pacarectambo

▲ Archaeological sites

0 miles   5
0 kilometres   8

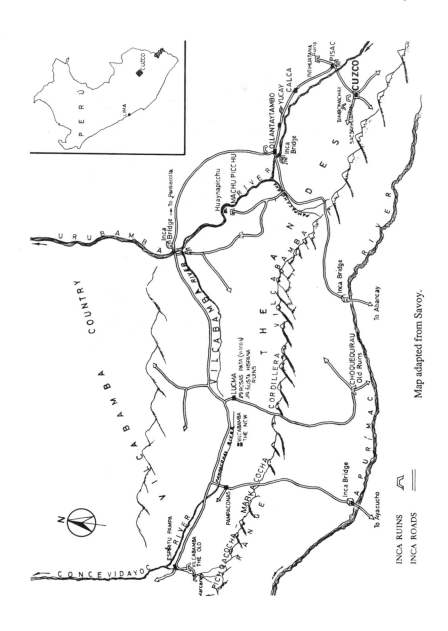

Map adapted from Savoy.

INCA RUINS

INCA ROADS

Machu Picchu, the incredible, self-sufficient, megalithic city, nestled high in the Andes.

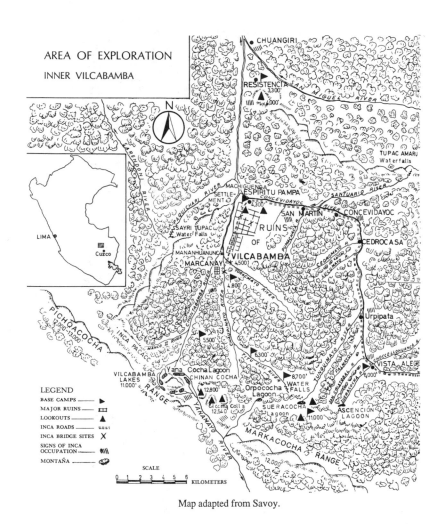

Map adapted from Savoy.

Peruvian archaeologist, Professor Edmundo Guillen, believes these ruins, found near Machu Picchu, to be the real Vilcabamba.

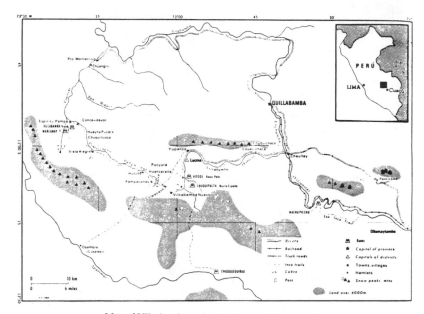

Map of Vilcabamba region by Gregory Deyermenjian.

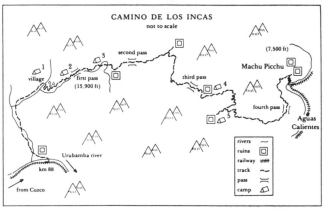

The Inca trail to Machu Picchu, adapted from The Weaver and the Abbey.

Circular tower and staircase at Machu Picchu.

Temple of
the Three Windows

Lower

Urban Area

Royal
Palace

Upper

Lower

Agricultural Area

Upper

Machu Picchu

0 yards   50
0 meters   50

Entrance

A rectangular-construction wall, split during a massive earthquake. Note that the irregularly-shaped megalithic walls would survive better. The largest block, behind explorer Richard Kieninger, weighs approx. 150 tons.

Machu Picchu PERU

Inca town
15th–16th centuries AD

Reconstruction of Machu Picchu with the thatched
roofs restored on buildings where these were known
to have existed

The northwest corner of Machu Picchu, looking up the hill to the "Hitching Post of the Sun," as seen from the "Room with Three Windows."

The "Hitching Post of the Sun."

Chapter Four

Machu Picchu and the Urubamba:
The Atlantean League
and the Irish Incas

...this is the land of our beginning,
where we went from the old red land before it sank,
because this land is as old as the dragon land of the fire god.
-*Sioux Indian Chief*

The Cuzco area is home to some of the world's most interesting and mysterious archaeological sites. Megalithic ruins
well worth visiting include Pisac, Puka Pukara and Ollantaytambo, north of Cuzco on the way to Machu Picchu. Pisac is
a beautiful Inca city on the Urubamba just east of Cuzco, consisting of temples, forts and modern reconstructions, complete
with the thatched roofs in the old Inca style. Its ancient
terraces, spread out over a wide area, are still in use by farmers
today. Amazing views, looking down the valley to either direction, are considered by many people to be as stunning a sight as
Machu Picchu. The stonework is excellent, apparently of Inca
origin, which makes it 500 to 1000 years old.
    Further down the valley is Ollantaytambo, 45 miles north of
Cuzco along the Urubamba, and reached by the same narrow-
gauge train that one takes to Machu Picchu. It guards the entrance to the narrow Urubamba Gorge.
    We four traveling companions were on the train heading
north, downhill toward Machu Picchu. Passing below Ollantaytambo, we gazed upwards at its magnificence. Its huge walls
towered above the river as we steamed past; I imagined the
rebel army of Manco Inca holding out against the Spaniards,
hurling stones down upon the armoured conquistadors. When

97

the Spanish attacked, one of them later reported, "When we reached Tambo we found it so well fortified that it was a horrifying sight... So many men suddenly appeared on every side that every visible stretch of wall was covered in Indians." [28] The Spanish were driven back, escaping at night back to Cuzco.

Most impressive at Ollantaytambo are the six large stones that face the river. The largest is about 13 feet (4 meters) high, 7 feet (2.1 meters) wide, and about 6 feet (1.8 meters) thick, and weighs approximately 50 tons (45,500 kg). Made from red porphyry, a very hard type of rock, much of their surfaces are very finely polished. On the fourth giant stone from the left is a stepped motif, identical to those found at Tiahuanaco in Bolivia, but not found elsewhere in the Cuzco area. Even more unusual is a stone in which a "keyway" has been carefully cut into the stone to hold a metal clamp, presumably to hold two colossal blocks together as earthquake protection. This unusual technique is found at Puma Punku in Tiahuanco and nowhere else. Tiahuanaco-style pottery is also found in the area.

The stones were apparently quarried across the river, 200 feet below the fortress, and about 3,000 feet up the opposite slope. A 250- ton stone from this quarry lies at the bottom of the river. While the Incas used Ollantaytambo as a fort to guard the entrance to Cuzco from up the Urubamba Valley (or down the Urubamba Valley, as was to be the case as the Incas retreated), it appears that Ollantaytambo, like Sacsayhuaman, was already in place before the arrival of the Incas.

After the conquistadors under Francisco Pizarro had executed the Inca Atahualpa, they marched on Cuzco and entered the city in late 1533. They installed a "puppet Inca" as ruler of Peru and the Inca Empire, the native prince Manco. Two years later, Manco Inca led the rebellion of 1536 against the Spaniards. He recaptured Cuzco, and even threatened to take the new Spanish city of Lima, meanwhile setting up his new headquarters at the heavily fortified Calca, in the Yucay Valley north of Cuzco. Later realizing that this was too close to Cuzco, he moved to Ollantaytambo.

Still later, after the successful defense at Ollantaytambo, Manco Inca made an attempt to relocate his army again, this time to the still-lost city of Urocoto. Urocoto is believed to lie far to the southeast, in the forests east of Lake Titicaca, where the secret monastery of the Andes is also rumored to be located. Manco Inca never made it to Urocoto, though, and instead retreated over an Inca road which ran from Ollantaytambo to the northwest, through the Panticolla Pass, and emerged at the Urubamba near the present-day town of Chaullay.

Manco's force crossed the bridge at Chaullay and followed the road westward along the Vitcos River, entering the Vilcabamba region. They then made their headquarters at Vitcos. Today the Vitcos River is called the Vilcabamba River.

Feeling secure from the pursuing Spaniards at Vitcos, the Incas failed to destroy the bridge at Chaullay. This allowed the conquistador Rodrigo Orgonez to pursue Manco right to Vitcos. But the Incan army escaped from Vitcos, retreating further into the interior of the Vilca- bamba region. Meanwhile, Manco's half-brother, Paullu, had been proclaimed the new puppet-Inca by the Spanish. Paullu Inca supported the Spanish in their pursuit of his renegade half-brother, and even led an army of native auxiliaries into battle against Manco's army.

The Spaniards pursued the Incas no further into the mountainous jungles of the Vilcabamba region that year. Manco set up a capital in an area known as the Espiritu Pampa, calling the city Vilcabamba. Here they built palaces, temples, stone dwellings, canals, bridges, fountains, and squares. Unfortunately, this capital did not remain a peaceful refuge for long. In April 1539, a force of conquistadors led by Gonzalo Pizarro reached Vitcos, then pressed on for Vilcabamba. Manco Inca's force attacked them 14 miles (22 kilometers) from the new capital, hurling boulders down on the invaders at a spot known as Chuquillusca. But Gonzalo's men climbed up higher, outflanked Manco, and defeated the Inca army. Manco himself escaped only by swimming across the Concevidayoc River and hiding in the deep forests. Manco's wife and many Inca nobles were captured and taken back to Cuzco by the Spanish invading force, after they had first gone on to briefly occupy Vilcabamba.

Manco returned to Vilcabamba to reorganize the Inca state after the Spaniards left. He conducted raids on Spanish-held towns, and even started to seek refuge in Quito, but turned back after he learned that the route was overrun with hostile tribes and armed Spaniards.

Meanwhile, in 1541 the Spanish fought among themselves for control over Peru, and Diego de Almagro lost his bid to gain control. He was executed, but later followers of Almagro assassinated Francisco Pizarro, thus ending the long and bitter feud. In 1542, seven members of the now defeated Diego de Almagro faction sought refuge at Vilcabamba. The Inca welcomed them to his capital, hoping they would instruct his army in the use of European weapons. However, hoping to gain pardon from the Spaniards, they stabbed Manco while he was playing the Inca game *quoits* , which is similar to horseshoes.

They were in turn killed by the Incas.

Manco's son Sayri-Tupac then became the ruling Inca. He was left alone until 1548, when the Spanish once again turned their attentions to Vilcabamba, determined to subdue every last bit of Inca power. Negotiations for Sayri-Tupac to leave Vilcabamba began, and in 1557 the Inca emerged to accept an estate in the sacred Yucay Valley just north of Cuzco.

But still, a royal fringe of Inca power remained at Vilcabamba with Sayri-Tupac's half-brother, Titu-Cusi. With Sayri-Tupac's death in 1560, Titu-Cusi became the reigning Inca. There followed an uneasy, negotiated peace for several years, and in 1569 both Titu-Cusi and his son allowed themselves to be baptized by two priests they had allowed into Vilcabamba province. For years, Titu-Cusi played a cagey game with the Spanish, being careful not to go too far, and giving them just enough to keep them happy.

Then, while visiting the site of his father's death in May 1571, Titu-Cusi fell ill following a night of heavy drinking and fencing. He died the next morning, and one of the priests was forced to say a mass over the dead Inca. When the Inca failed to come back to life, the Spanish priest was tortured and killed.

The new Inca was Tupac-Amaru, destined to be the last. Under his rule, Vilcabamba closed its borders and destroyed all vestiges of European contact, including some churches that had been built. In March 1572, a prominent Spaniard bearing a letter from the Viceroy at Cuzco was killed. On April 14, 1572, Viceroy Toledo of Lima declared war on Vilcabamba.

A force of 250 Spanish and 1500 native auxiliaries commanded by Martin Hurtado de Arbieto entered Inca territory and marched on Vilcabamba. After outflanking an ambush with help from a traitorous native, they arrived at Vilcabamba to find the city burned and abandoned, with the Inca Tupac Amaru gone.

Spanish parties ranged northward in pursuit, even taking to the Urubamba in rafts, relying on information from captured Indians. Deep in the jungle, they came upon and captured Tupac Amaru. He was led by a gold chain around his neck back to Cuzco, where he was beheaded on September 24, 1572.[29]

The hopes of a resurgent Vilcabamba state were now crushed, and the Spaniards began to exploit the region, using the inhabitants as slaves for the production of sugar, cocoa, and silver. By the mid-seventeenth century, the area had become unproductive and only two small villages remained. The province fell into a state of sleepy isolation and neglect for 200 years. The location of Vilcabamba was never recorded, and it became a legend; a lost city in the jungles.

And so it was that the legend of Vilcabamba came into being. Expeditions seeking Inca treasure searched for the city in 1820 and 1834, but the site could not be found. Until 1911, most experts believed that Choqquequirau was the site of Vilcabamba. But on July 24 of that year, archaeologist Hiram Bingham, who went on to become a professor at Yale and a United States Senator from Connecticut, discovered the fan-tastic city of Machu Picchu. He had been told about a city on the saddle of a mountain by a local Indian. Bingham believed his find to be Vilcabamba, and this belief held for almost 50 years. However, a significant bit of evidence was to emerge: Machu Picchu showed no evidence of ever having been looted by the Spanish, nor of having been torched by the escaping Inca army.

Even today, the location of the lost city of Vilcabamba remains in dispute, generally between two sites. One was discovered by the intrepid American explorer Gene Savoy in 1964, who identified the Espiritu Pampa Ruins as Vilcabamba. In 1966, Tony Morrison and Mark Howell visited this site, and found evidence of a fire. Further- more, this site shows signs of Spanish influence, Spanish-style tiles being used on the roofs of the burned-out buildings. Interestingly, it was Hiram Bingham who first visited the Espiritu Pampa ruins and Vitcos, just prior to his discovery of Machu Picchu.

The other site given for Vilcabamba was discovered by the Peruvian archaeologist Professor Edmundo Guillen, who poured over maps and accounts of the city for ten years. In 1976 he went to what he believes is the site of the lost city, in a valley in the Vilcabamba region twenty-five miles (forty kilometers) by rail beyond Machu Picchu, and thirteen miles (twenty kilometers) further by trail into the jungle. Accompanied by a television crew from the series, *In Search Of...* , Guillen discovered a city with an area of 2 square miles (five square kilometers). While exploring his find, the party discovered a nearby cave with a mummy inside. At first, this was thought to be the mummy of the Inca Titu Cusi, but when unwrapped, it turned out to be a simple tailor with samples of his work tied around his head.[30]

§§§

The train journey to Machu Picchu from Cuzco takes about four hours. We had left early in the morning, and it was eleven o'clock as we arrived at the station at Machu Picchu. There is really nothing at Machu Picchu except a railway station and the ruins. The closest town is a mile back down the tracks toward Cuzco, called *Agua Caliente* , or "Hot Water," because of its hot springs. It has several inexpensive hostels, among them the Hostal Caminantes, Hostal Municipal, and Hospedaje Machu Picchu. Others crop up and disappear from time to time, depending on the tourist flow.

Further down the railway line by two hours is Chaullay, where you would start if you wanted to head into the Vilca-bamba region. This would have to be done by foot or possibly with mules, bringing all your expeditionary equipment with you from Cuzco. The rail line follows the Urubamba River to its end another few hours down the line at Quillabamba. From Quillabamba, there is a road further down the river to Puerto Monterrico. One can also reach the Espiritu Pampa this way, and make a circuit back around to Chaullay.

Our group was feeling extravagant by this time, so we opted to spend the night at the expensive and luxurious Machu Picchu Hotel, which is located right at the ruins. We had met a Peru-vian on the train, a tall, handsome fellow named Adelqui, who worked as a tourist guide. He was coming to pick up a group, and told us he would show us around.

We all ran off the train to the buses, Adelqui in the lead, and caught the second one going up the mountain. The buses whined and howled up the steep road, switching back and forth as the road climbed up and up. As we turned each corner, people on either side of the bus would look straight down and gasp, seeing the river over a thousand feet below over the sheer cliff.

Sitting near the front, I glanced at the bus driver. His face was grim, and he gripped the steering wheel and followed the road with an intensity only an Andean bus driver could have. As we turned each corner, he would step on the gas, and we would surge up to the next switchback. I glanced at Aldequi, but his brown, strong face was calm. He had evidently survived this trip many times.

He smiled at me, sensing my nervousness. "Don't worry, these buses rarely go over the edge on the way up. It's the way down that's dangerous." Hiram Bingham never had to do this, I thought.

At the summit, we ate a quick lunch, then entered the ruins with Adelqui. Words can hardly describe the beauty of Machu Picchu and its surroundings; this is undoubtedly one of the most spectacular views in the world. One could hardly ask for a better location for a lost city.

After passing through the entrance gate, set up on the path next to a cliff, we ducked through a tunnel and into the lower terraces of the ancient citadel.

We strolled up the stairs, past terraces and buildings of awesome construction. Looking down, we could see the Urubamba River far below us, a rushing blue and white river winding through the dense green mountain forests. To the north, the peak Huaynu Picchu towered steeply above the city. Machu Picchu was green and grand. It had stairways for streets, and for water it had rushing streams that cascaded down beside the stairs. But for inspiration, it had some of the most beautiful mountain scenery in the world. No wonder Hiram Bingham said of Machu Picchu, soon after he discovered it, "Like the Great Pyramid and the Grand Canyon, rolled into one."

When we reached the top of the saddle, we stood on a wide green field, like a large athletic field, probably used for assemblies and games. Around us were great walls, and public buildings with large porches and balustrades carved out of gigantic blocks of granite. Further up the mountain is the Hitching Post of the Sun, and the Court of Three Windows. Here particularly, one could see the combination of Inca architecture with earlier megalithic construction, lesser, square Inca blocks atop gigantic blocks of stone weighing up to 80 tons. At one spot, the megalithic stones are cracked open, almost ready to tumble, where a powerful earthquake has managed to force them apart.

The purpose of Machu Picchu has always been a mystery. It is invisible from below, and is perfectly self-contained. The city itself is well protected by its isolation, and it would be very difficult to attack, if ever it was discovered. It seems to have been designed as a secret city, totally self-sufficient. Its water is pure and originates from springs on the mountain. The terraces around the city are sufficient to grow whatever food the inhabitants might need. In fact, the peak of Huaynu Picchu is terraced all the way up its steep slopes to its summit. There is a trail to the summit which passes through a short tunnel before entering a smaller group of ruins.

Interestingly, skeletal remains found here indicate a ratio among the inhabitants of ten females to one male. This has led some to regard Machu Picchu as a sanctuary for the *Nustas* , "Virgins of the Sun." These ritual virgins may have been sent to this secret city to keep them safe from the marauding Spaniards. A royal Inca trail leads from the city to Cuzco, over the mountains. Some researchers feel that the site may even have been used by the Incas before Cuzco.

If we assume that the theory that the Incas discovered and moved into the megalithic construction is correct, what conclusions might we draw from these magnificent ruins? Could survivors of an advanced civilization, marooned in South America, have built Machu Picchu? In this case, it is possible that savage Indian tribes, probably the Quechua Indians themselves, forced the survivors to retreat further and further into the mountains. Eventually, they may have built this impregnable city in the mountains, abandoning their cities around Cuzco to the wandering tribes of savages living along the river valleys.

Incredible as this supposition may seem, it is the story told by some American Indians. L. Taylor Hansen, daughter of one of the authors of the Continental Drift Theory, tells the following story in her book, *The Ancient Atlantic* :

Shooting Star, an America Sioux chief, told Hansen of a conversation he had had with a guide at Machu Picchu. The guide told a legend about giants coming to the city and throwing rocks at each other, thus creating the strange ruins. People laughed, but Shooting Star went to the Indian guide separately and asked, "Is this the city of the thunderbirds?"

The guide answered, "It is the city of the bird of lightnings. Every street is feather, but one does not see that is so unless from an airplane."

Hansen continues, quoting the Sioux chief. " 'Where are the caves where people lose themselves?'

" 'They are under the city. Some of the entrances are secret. Others are closed.'

"'Have you ever been down in them?' I asked.

"He shook his head. 'It is forbidden.' That answer I expected, and he knew that I did. We smiled our recognition.

" 'Where is your tribe?' he asked.

" 'Thousands of miles to the north, through the United States and almost to Canada.'

" 'It is well,' he said, and we clasped arms in the ancient manner (grasping forearms above the wrist).

"A few days later, after the ceremonial length of time, he brought an old man. I had expected him. Altogether there were eight of us. We spoke of legends and words. 'I tell you, my friends, this is the land of our beginning, where we went from the old red land even before it sank, because this land is as old as the dragon land of the fire god.' " [27]

The Red Land was Atlantis, according to Hansen and quite a few other researchers. The ancient Mexicans commonly referred to their homeland as a sunken land to the east called

"Atlan." The story of their ancestors building these megalithic structures thousands of years ago is still told in North American Indian campfire tales. The story continues that eventually they were forced out by hostile tribes. Machu Picchu may have been their last hold-out. The people then migrated north into Mexico, abandoning their gigantic cities in Peru.

These wandering people eventually moved north to the American Southwest, where they were assimilated by the native Apache Indians; the men killed and the women taken as prisoners to become part of the tribe. The Apache Indians supposedly have retained the legends which speak of the build-ing of the terraces and the great stone walls. Later, a tribe of Apaches moved southward again into Mexico, and became the Aztecs. When Cortez and his conquistadors invaded Mexico, Montezuma may have sent most of his treasure back to their ancestral homeland in the four-corners area of New Mexico, Arizona, Utah, and Colorado. But that's another story!

§§§

We spent the afternoon exploring Machu Picchu, looking inside the remains of buildings, jumping up on walls, and walking the ancient trails. Adelqui smiled condescendingly at Bob's explanations for the origin of the city. As a guide, he had been trained to give the official explanation of Machu Picchu, which was that it had been built by the Incas a few hundred years ago, and that it was their last refuge, the city of Vilcabamba. This, of course, has been proved wrong, but the official story dies hard.

We decided to take a walk along the old the Inca trail leading up from Machu Picchu to the southwest. The trail went through the forest, past flowers and trees, with quite a drop beneath us into the Urumbamba River. "Watch your step!" I called back to the others, as I scrambled on ahead.

It was really exciting to explore this lost city. Words like *fantastic, remarkable, incredible* and *astounding* kept coming up over and over again in our conversations. The history of the Incas was fascinating in its own right, even if they hadn't built Machu Picchu, Sacsayhuaman or the other megalithic structures. But who were the Incas, anyway? They were a mysterious bunch, to say the least, and there is a great deal of confusion about them.

The Incas were a race of people descended from the first Inca, Manco Capac, according to their own legend. He was a red haired, bearded chap, who appeared with his wife at Lake

105

Titicaca probably between the fourth and eighth century AD. With him were his three brothers and their wives. Manco Capac declared to the people that he had been sent by God to his teach His children, and that this was the beginning of the new Inca dynasty. While I had read and discarded the ridiculous theories that Manco Capac was a space traveler, I was not ready for Bob's next suggestion—that he and his crew were actually Irish missionaries!

"Irish missionaries?" I almost shouted at Bob. "You have a lot of convincing to do for that one!" I looked around the Inca trail which we had hiking, then out at a collapsed bridge to a sheer cliff hundreds of feet high. It seemed an appropriate place to pause to hear Bob's theory of the Irish Incas. We all looked his way expectantly.

"No, I'm not crazy," Bob defended himself to Steve, Mark, me, and a scowling Adelqui. "Irish monks were apparently sailing up and down the west coast of the Americas since about the second century AD. They sailed in leather boats, and often made long voyages in the Atlantic. The most famous of these Irish monk-sailors was Saint Brendon, who is believed to have sailed to the Americas in the sixth century. *National Geographic* did an article on him a few years ago."

"That's not so surprising," I sighed with resignation, "if we accept that the Phoenicians, Egyptians, Greeks, Romans, Celtics and everyone else you've been telling us about were sailing over here." I felt like I was back in grade school, reciting my geography lesson. But this time, the sequence of history was a bit different!

"Sure," Bob went on, without skipping a beat, "and the Irish were Celtic as well. Christianity came to Ireland early, well before the rest of Europe. It was not the Christianity of Rome, but came from Anatolia in Turkey, where the Apostle Paul had preached. Somehow, mission- aries from Anatolia reached Ireland by sea, without stopping in Gaul. The Irish monks were still affiliated with Rome, though they were sort of renegade Catholics.

"Irish monasteries were quite unusual. Ireland was separated from the rest of Europe, and didn't suffer through the turmoil and invasions that the rest of Europe went through at that time. Irish monks were about the best-educated people in Europe in the first millenium AD. Irish monasteries also had a great deal of wealth, but they were continually raided by Vikings and local Irish kings who stole their gold. The monks wanted the gold for the glory of God, not for trade, and zealously sought for more in their boats.

"One land in Irish legend was Hy-Brazil, thought to be a wealthy kingdom full of gold across the Atlantic. This land would seem to be South America. Irish monks probably reached Peru from Columbia, having heard of the fabulous gold artifacts and endless gold mines in the Andes."

"Manco Capac sounds alot like 'Monko Catholic'," said Mark.

"Exactly," Bob agreed. "Manco Capac told the people that he had been sent by God to take care of them and save them, which is just the sort of the thing that a Christian missionary would tell primitive people. Manco Capac may genuinely have wanted to help these high- land people, poor and undernourished, as well as to pick up some gold.

"He taught them to live as monks did in Ireland, which is a unique system. All property was held in common, belonging to a small city state which the monks founded, probably at ancient Cuzco. Work, not gold or other metals, was the medium of exchange, just as in an Irish monastery. For a certain number of hours' work, a person received food for his family and a place to live. Gold and silver were used for ornaments and decorations."

I could see that Mark, the youngest and most impressionable of our group, was beginning to like Bob's version of South American history. Adelqui, on the other hand, was doing everything possible to ignore Bob, as the latter continued with his story. "The Irish were good organizers and worked hard to improve the life of the natives. The natives were grateful, and added their own skills to the newly formed Inca state: road building, metal craftsmanship, and other skills that the Irish lacked. There weren't all that many roads in Ireland at that time. As the Inca state prospered in a communal utopia, other tribes wanted to be part of their success. Later, when the Inca Empire became more powerful, they forced others to join.

"It seems that succeeding generations of Irish-Inca rulers lost sight of their religion and purpose. They became rather cruel and authoritarian God-kings, and called themselves the 'Sons of the Sun,' taking on what was probably a mixture of an earlier sun-worshipping religion, perhaps left a thousand years earlier by the Egyptians."

"There's not much difference in the religions of Aton and the Incas, anyway," said Mark. "Both are the worship of one God, symbolized by the sun. Even Christianity has vestiges of Atonism."

Steve handed out sections of an orange he was quietly peeling. Adelqui tossed a stone over the edge of the trail, watching it fall a thousand feet into the dense jungle below. "Are you going to give us any evidence for this tale of yours?" he asked.

"There is other evidence," Bob replied, popping the juicy orange slice into his mouth. "For instance, Francisco Pizarro wrote about the Inca Atahualpa and his family, 'They were even whiter than the people of Spain.'' A group of Indians speaking what appeared to be pure Gaelic or Erse were discovered earlier in this century in the southern Andean cordilleras, somewhere west of Miraflores and San Rosario, in northwestern Argentina. Wilkins wrote that these Patanian Indians weren't emigrants, as their ancestors had inhabited that region ages before the arrival of Spanish conquistadors. Wilkins had a colleague whose Irish uncle had met these Indians, while on the Argentinian pampas in 1910. The uncle spoke Erse well, and for some time lived and worked with them on the Pampas Enthral, near Miraflores. Some members of this tribe of Patanian Indians have the blue eyes and reddish hair of the Irish Celt."

"Yeah," I remembered suddenly, "there were those red-haired mummies at Nazca!"

"White people with light hair and beards abound in South American legend and literature," Bob agreed, nodding. "But not all of them were necessarily Irish. Many were probably Vikings or even Iberian Celts. Brazil was supposedly named by the Portuguese because dye-wood, or brazil-wood was found there. However, this may not be the case, as the name Hy-Brazil was used by the ancient Irish. As a matter of fact, an Irish priest told Pope Zacharias in 780 AD that the old Irish habitually communicated with a transatlantic world! The Pope had him ex-communicated for saying this.

"When Saint Brendon sailed for Hy-Brazil with 50 monks over 1,500 years ago from the Abbey of Clonfert, he was gone for seven years. When he returned, he wrote about '...the fairest country a man might see; clear and bright, neither hot by day, nor cold by night, the trees laden with fruit, the herbage glorious with blooms and gay flowers...' It's not likely that Saint Brendon was speaking of Labrador or even New England; he was probably speaking of Central and South America. It would seem that the land of Hy-Brazil was the New World, where the ancient Irish began the great Inca civilization modeled after Irish monasteries. Indeed, only the Inca empire and Irish monasteries had such a unique communal system."

"Well, you've convinced me!" said Mark with a smile.

"That's not all, you guys," Bob went on. He was on a roll! "In 1516 Sir Thomas More published a classic book on economics and politics, called *Utopia* . Part of the book was a satire on England, describing a land where the poor work but own nothing, while the rich do no work and own everything.

"The book then describes a far-away land where everyone works and has plenty. Utopia has good roads and the granaries are full of food. There are reed boats on an inland lake just like on Lake Titicaca. People are given food and housing according to their needs. Gold is mined in abundance and used for lots of things, but not for money. No money is needed or used, and all land is held in common.

"Sir Thomas More was describing perfectly the contrasts between England and the Inca Empire. He goes to great length to state that his book is fact and that he got the information from a sailor named Hythloday in the Netherlands. More had many friends in Ireland where he probably got his information on the Incas. The book was published sixteen years before Pizarro landed in Peru, effectively putting an end to the Inca Utopia."

"Maybe it's just a coincidence," said Adelqui.

"There is no such thing as a coincidence," said Steve, obviously now a believer like Mark. I had thought that quiet, stable Steve would have held out longer.

"Anything is possible," Bob repeated the line that had become his trademark. "It's also interesting that many his-torians feel that the Mexican messiah, Quetzal Coatl, may have been an Irish monk, possibly Saint Brendon himself. There may have even been several Quetzal Coatls, Saint Brendon being the second, or even third.

"The Mexicans called the land of Quetzal Coatl *Hapallan* , or 'Holy Island,' and said it was over the ocean to the east. Indeed, Ireland would fit nicely into the idea of Hapallan, especially since it was also known in the early centuries of the Christian Era as the Holy Island. Quetzal Coatl was a white, bearded man who wore a robe adorned with crosses, just like an Irish monk.

Adelqui was never going to buy all of this Irish Inca talk, that much was obvious from the ever-deepening scowl he wore. But Mark and Steve were now firm believers as Bob finished up. "Furthermore, Quetzal Coatl was supposed to have built a boat out of serpent skins and sailed back to his 'Holy Island.' This sounds like legendary nonsense, except when interpreted in light of the Irish currahs, or ox hide boats. The monks built these to sail up and down the Irish coast, and over to Europe and Iceland. Lacking oxen or other large animals in America, Quetzal Coatl could have made his boat from the skins of alligators." As Bob wound up his unusual tale, instead of Irish monks sailing the Atlantic, all I could picture was how my junior-high school history teachers would have rolled over in their graves.

§§§

We all walked back down the trail to the ancient city. It was getting late, which meant the gates would soon be closed. Back at the cafeteria, we had dinner, then sat on the veranda and slowly drank a beer. All the tourists from Cuzco had all gone back on the afternoon train, so the hotel was strangely silent. Out on the square, a white, wooly alpaca named Pancho was munching on the grass. Watching him eat, admiring his fine coat, we followed the clouds drifting between the mountains in the background. I soon retired to my luxurious room, for which I had paid $50 a night, a king's ransom in Peru.

I suddenly had the inspiration to go back up to the ruins to take some sunset photographs. I grabbed my camera and went up to the gate; it was locked. Scaling around the locked gate, and briefly hanging in mid-air over a small cliff with a drop of thirty feet, I swung my foot around onto the other side. With a heave, I pulled myself onto the trail. Glancing furtively back to see if any guards had seen me, I strode quickly along the path to the lower stairs of the city.

The feel of the ruins was quite different now, walking alone among the magnificent stairs and walkways of Machu Picchu. Clouds were just coming through the valley as I ran up the ancient stairs. The clouds had hung up near the peaks of the mountains earlier, but now they were rolling down into the valleys, leaving the high ridge tops exposed.

I ran quickly upward toward the southern terraces on the trail to the Gate of the Sun. Arriving out of breath, I turned to look back on the city, all green and empty in the last few minutes of daylight. Clouds rolled up Huaynu Picchu as I snapped a few photos. It was magnificent.

A large, white-fading-to-gray cloud passed through, for a time totally obscuring the city, so I turned to watch the sunset and the clouds in the valleys of the Andes to the west. It was if the entire, beautiful vision was being played out especially for me, in an open-air theater that wrapped around all my senses.

I photographed Machu Picchu while the clouds drifted through the city. My vantage point above the city to the south was perfect, so I sat on a rock overlooking the city with a view of the sunset to the west. I marveled at the city's construction and antiquity; it was so perfect, so superb! These people had been great realtors as well as great builders, obviously understanding the realtors' adage, "Location is everything."

I thought about the legends of the Atlantean League and the American Indians of the Southwest. Were they true? I wondered about Bob's theories of the Irish Incas as well. Many historians would call them ridiculous. But if the Incas were not Irish or other European voyagers, then who were they? They were certainly not Quechua or Aymara Indians–that much is known.

I looked down at the round, windowless tower in the city. I had once seen a similar tower, in Zimbabwe, southern Africa. I also recalled the round towers of, guess where? Ireland! Round towers are found all over Ireland, and they are unusual in that the access door is built quite some distance above ground level, which would seem rather inconvenient. One Irish tower on Devenish Island in county Fermanagh is 82 feet (25 meters) high, with the access door about one quarter of the way up. But the towers at Machu Picchu and Zimbabwe have no doors whatsoever. Another similar tower which is found in New England, now half submerged, was the subject of a Longfellow poem, *A Skeleton in Armour* . Longfellow believed that the tower was built by Vikings. Was there a common thread, tying them all together?

I glanced to my left at the orange sun, which was setting the western mountains on fire with its last rays of light. Some higher clouds had turned a burnt red, with the mountain peaks silhouetted on the horizon. A few still-white clouds nestled in the valley far below. A shiver suddenly ran up my spine; I felt that I was on the edge of time, spanning the magnificent past with the approaching future. A mystical crack between these worlds had opened up to let me in, and I knew that I was lucky to be there.

But I also knew I had return to the hotel before it got too dark. I started down the stone steps for the city, now enshrouded in clouds drifting through the streets and stairways, like the ghosts of the lost architects. I marveled at their work, and could almost feel their presence as I moved through the streets, down the steps, and back to the gate. As I maneuvered back across the small cliff and around the locked gateway, I glanced back at the city, giving a nod of respect to the spirits of Machu Picchu.

"Thanks for all the good times," I whispered.

Hiram Bingham, discoverer of Machu Picchu.

Chapter Five

Lake Titicaca:
The Search for the Hidden City
of Gran Paititi

If thou seekest El Dorado thou must ride,
boldly ride over the Mountains of the Moon
through the valley of the shadow...
-Edgar Allen Poe

The next morning, we rose early, checked out, and headed
to the city for another look around. We took a walk up to the
Gate of the Sun on the Royal Inca Highway (Camino Real del
Inca), which continues to Cuzco. It is about a two-hour walk
there and back to the saddle on the ridge where the gate stands.
About an hour further on, down the next valley, are the Inca
ruins of Wiñay Wayna. If you want to backpack the Inca trail,
try starting at Qoriwayrachina, then spend the night here. You
can also enter Machu Picchu in the evening from this trail if
you have backpacked in. The Inca trail hike is a good one,
taking about five days, with plenty of Inca ruins to stay in on
the way. Contact the tourist office in Cuzco before embarking
on this trip, as they can give you up-to-date information and
advice. Gear can be rented in Cuzco as well.

When we got back from the Gate of the Sun, Bob and I decided to climb to the top of Huaynu Picchu, the sharp peak to
the north of the city. Signing a register as we started up the
trail, we immediately found ourselves climbing ancient stone
steps up the steep face. At a number of places the trail got so
steep that a rope had been fixed to the trail to help climbers. It
reminded me a bit of climbing in the Himalayas, though this
was steep, slick forest, not walls of ice.

Sweating profusely, we made it to the top in about thirty-five minutes. Near the top, the trail passes by terraces built precipitously just below the summit. One false step by a gardener up here would send him tumbling a thousand or more feet to his death below.

"Who would want to grow crops up here?" I asked Bob.

"Well, if this was a secret, self-sufficient city," he answered, "they probably wanted to utilize all the farming space available."

"They sure did! This would make a good lookout, too."

We dropped through a low tunnel and emerged at the summit, a rock outcrop where we had an excellent view of Machu Picchu and the whole Urubamba Valley far down below us. After a short rest, we went back down through the tunnel, and down the several thousand steep, stone steps. Bidding Machu Picchu a fond farewell, we boarded a bus to take us back down the long, steep road to the train station.

About a third of the way down, just as our old bus cornered a sharp turn, we were all frozen to our seats by a gut-wrenching scream, trailing off like a skydiver's last cries before hitting the ground without a parachute. Seeing the driver smile calmly, we searched for the source, our hearts still pounding. At the next turn, we heard the same scream, but this time were able to locate its maker. As the bus wound down the steep road, a boy ran along a trail that intersected the road in between each switchback. Passing the bus each time, he would let out his scream. After the initial shock, we found his antics quite amusing, laughing each time he went by. And sure enough, he was waiting for us at the bottom, with his hand out. Most of the tourists paid him for his efforts, and later I found out that he performed for all the buses this way. This kid would be a millionaire by the time he was twelve.

The four-hour train back to Cuzco was relaxing. Women met the train at many of the stops to sell sweaters, mittens, scarves, Inca Cola, or hot corn on the cob. As we arrived in Cuzco, a great rainbow hung over the valley, and the sun glinted off the city's many tiled roofs.

We stayed for a few more days in Cuzco, drinking beer in the cafés, eating at restaurants where Quechua bands played Inca music, and wandering the back streets. Just past the Cathedral is the Alley of Hatunrumiyoc, where a famous twelve-sided stone is located. This stone is also featured on the labels of Cusqueña Beer.

Walking down this alley, I marveled at the construction. I could clearly see the different levels again here, as elsewhere. Lowermost, the older "Atlantean" construction, large stones cut

114

at odd interlocking angles. Higher, the rectangular Inca blocks, then the Spanish stonework on top of that. Other areas of Cuzco with ancient Incan and older construction include Choquechaca, Tullumayu, Santa Clara, Loreta, Maruri, and San Agustin. Actually, as you wander the streets of Cuzco, just look around, and more often than not you will see an ancient wall.

Eventually, we felt we had seen the best of Cuzco, and boarded the train for Lake Titicaca, a full day's journey away. We were retracing our journey from Juliaca, this time on to Puno on the shores of the lake. We sat back in our seats, facing each other with a table between us. Mark brought out a deck of cards, and we played a few games of Hearts as we traveled upward into the Andes Cordillera.

Peru is utterly full of lost cities. I could go on forever relating the stories I have heard of cities and incredible wealth locked in the vastness of the mountains. But perhaps the one lost city that is most talked about is the true final refuge of the Incas, El Gran Paititi.

When the Spanish finally entered Vilcabamba in 1572, they found the city deserted, burned, and devoid of treasure. They were able to capture only the reigning Inca, Tupac Amaru, and take him back to Cuzco where they executed him publicly.

What happened to the rest of the Inca royalty, and to the treasure associated with Vilcabamba? Some believe that the Incas retreated once more, this time to El Gran Paititi. Also known as the "White House" and "House of the Tiger King," it was generally believed to have been a major Inca jungle outpost. One early source of information on Paititi is a book written in 1537 by a Silesian priest, Juan Carlos Polentini, entitled *Las Rutas Por Paititi* ("The Routes to Paititi"). This old text relates that after the defeat of the Incas by the Spaniards at Ollantaytambo, a splinter group of Incas migrated eastward into the jungle of Madre de Dios, bearing the Inca treasure to Paititi. Paititi has, up to now, never been found.

El Gran Paititi, or just Paititi (sometimes spelled Paytiti), has been synonymous with "El Dorado" in Peru for 400 years. Indeed, it may actually have been Paititi that was the origin of the El Dorado legend. It was this legend of gold treasure and adventure, one of a lost city of incredible magnificence, that was to spur on explorers, adventurers, and treasure-hunters for hundreds of years, to drive much of the early exploration of the Amazon.

It is well known that the Incan Empire at its height stretched from north of Quito in Ecuador, south along the Andes and west to the coast, all the way down into central Chile. What is not generally known is just how far east the Incas had set up their roads, trade routes and cities. The Incas did have a trade network that stretched eastwards deep into the jungles on the east side of the Andes. Salt was frequently carried across the mountains in exchange for gold and feathers. According to Jorge Arellano, director of the Institute of Archaeology in La Paz, Bolivia, Inca ruins have been found in the Bolivian State of Beni, which is several hundred miles east of the Andes and in dense jungle. He says that a series of small fortresses in the jungle form a line in an easterly direction. He believes that the Incas used these fortresses as stopovers on their migration from the Madre de Dios area of Peru, believed by some to be the site of Gran Paititi.[31]

Furthermore, in August 1984, a Brazilian archaeologist, Aurelio Abreu. discovered the ruins of a city he believes to have been constructed by Incas in the Brazilian state of Bahia. He believes these ruins at Ingrejil were built by "refugees from Incan or pre-Incan Peru who found there the mountainous terrain and cool climate that suited them." These ruins are located more than two thousand miles from Cuzco as the crow flies, through some of the most dangerous and dense jungle in the world, most of it unexplored. This serves to illustrate just how far east some historians believe the Incan empire may have stretched—virtually to the Atlantic beaches of Brazil!

Though there is little doubt that Paititi did exist, there is a great deal of myth surrounding this lost city. Harold Wilkins writes about Paititi in his books, *Secret Cities of South America* and *Mysteries of Ancient South America.* Wilkins believes that the Incas escaped from the Spanish after the battle of Ollantaytambo by fleeing through a branch of the tunnel system discussed earlier, heading east toward Paititi. This may well be true, though it was hardly necessary for the Incas to have fled through a tunnel. They could have left by canoe, then crossed the mountains using the excellent Inca roads.[22,43]

Assuming a tunnel from Vilcabamba did exist, Wilkins thinks it went due east from Cuzco, through the jungles, to the empire of Paititi. He indicates that Paititi was a separate kingdom, ruled by mysterious white men whose king was known as the "Tiger King." (Wilkins seems to forget that the Incas were White men themselves). According to Wilkins, Paititi means "jaguar." The Tiger King, or Jaguar King, lived in a white house by a great lake.

Many people seem to confuse Gran Paititi and El Dorado, though the legends locate them thousands of miles apart. El Dorado is often believed to be in the vicinity of the Orinoco

River near the borders of Columbia, Venezuela and Brazil. In early 1559, the Viceroy of Peru wanted to rid his country of unemployed soldiers and troublesome Spanish adventurers, so he sent a party of 370 Spaniards and thousands of Andean Indians on an expedition down the Amazon in search of El Gran Paititi. This expedition was an utter failure, during which the men mutinied, and a psychopathic soldier, Lope de Aguirre, killed the leader Pedro de Ursua. Taking over the expedition, he abandoned the search for El Dorado, vowing to return and conquer Peru itself. This wild and incredible adventure, during which the women warriors known as Amazons were first reported, and the Amazon River was first navigated, was made into a German movie a few years ago called, *Aguirre: The Wrath of God* .[32,23]

This disastrous expedition was the beginning of the confusion between El Dorado and Paititi. It searched in an area far removed from where Paititi appears to be located, and this is why most adventurers after El Dorado searched in the vicinity of Columbia and Venezuela.

One adventurer who searched for Paititi was Pedro Bohorques, a penniless soldier who pretended to be a nobleman. In 1659, after serving in Chile, Bohorques became a wanderer. Calling himself Don Pedro el Inca, he swore that royal Inca blood flowed through his veins. Bohorques set himself up as emperor of an Indian kingdom at the headwaters of the Huallaga River south of Cuzco. He converted almost ten-thousand Pelados Indians into his service, and declared all Spaniards fair game. He also sent some of his followers on a search for Paititi, hoping to find the treasure.

When these men did not come back with gold, Bohorques left his empire and went to Lima. Unfortunately, the Spaniards had heard of his decree against them, threw him in prison, and sentenced him to death. He pleaded for his life, promising to reveal the location of the Kingdom of Gran Paititi if he was re-leased. The judges refused his offer, but many gold hunters visited him in prison, begging him to share his secret with them. He refused, and went to the gallows in 1667, much to the chagrin of the treasure-hunters of Lima.[23]

Actually, it is not likely that Bohorques knew the location of Paititi, though he was in the correct area, and may have learned the general location. Also, Paititi was probably still a living city at this time, so it would have been difficult for Bohorques or anyone else to enter.

Sometime later, the son of a prominent landowner in

Paraguay, Don Alonso Soleto Pernia, wrote, *Memorial of What My Ancestors and I Have Done in the Quest for El Paititi.* The original copy of this now-faded manuscript is kept in the archives of the Council of the Indies in Spain. Pernia and his family settled in San Lorenzo in what is now the state of Beni in Bolivia. In fact, they founded the town of San Lorenzo, and had to subdue a band of marauding Chiriguana Indians to do so.[43, 23]

Captured Indians told Pernia stories about Gran Paititi, claiming that their forefathers had ventured into the land, but had been forced back by white men with gleaming silver armour and weapons. They also met an Indian lady spinning the wool of a sheep, and saw an animal with a long neck, that was unlike a horse or mule. This animal was probably a llama or alpaca.

Pernia took a group of his men in search of Paititi. They discovered unusual forts built from uprooted trees, bearing strange signs. Later, they attacked another fort, taking fifteen Indians captive. Pernia writes, "Presently we came to a pueblo with a road that was so broad, and swept so clean, that we were astonished. We entered this place and found it was abandoned. We presumed that the inhabitants had run away when we came up the road. In this village, we found a building in the plaza with thirteen sculptured images. All of the figures were standing up and we presumed them to be monks of some type. They were dressed in robes like our friars and their faces were sculptured with the look of priests. These images had hair shirts hanging from their girdles. They all looked at each other. The building was like a church.

"... we passed along the road and came to another village. We found a statue there of a naked man crucified on a sort of cross. It had the appearance of our Jesus. The Christ-like image had arms, legs and feet like ours. Nearby was an altar stone (or pulpit). We inspected this pueblo for some time and debated about pressing forward into the great beyond. But Alonso de Solis, our captain, insisted that our food and supplies made it imperative that we return home. Thus we left that mysterious pueblo with the crucified figure that no artist could ever improve upon ... "

After returning home, Pernia was encouraged by his father to make another trip to find Paititi. They were told by an Indian who agreed to take them to Gran Paititi that their were white men in the city, and that they had firearms!

Pernia writes, "... and six of us went to the top of the mountain the Indian had guided us to at that time. Looking north, I saw a highland running along before us. The highland was in a valley that was surrounded by great towering mountains. On the side was a lake and around the lake was a great pueblo. We watched the place for some time and wished we were six hundred instead of six so we could march into that place. With sinking heart, we left Gran Paititi without knowing more about that city."

Let us pretend for a moment that this report is true. First of all, the lost city they seem to have found would be in the right general area to be Gran Paititi: in the mountainous forests east of Cuzco and Lake Titicaca. Indeed, the Province of Bolivia has many lakes, and Gran Paititi is said to be next to a lake in most legends. We also know that there are Inca ruins in the Beni Province, and that the Incas used the Madre de Dios River for access from the Cuzco area into the eastern mountain jungles and the Beni area. From Vilcabamba, the Incas could have gotten fairly easily to the Madre de Dios by canoe and mountain trail.

It is interesting to look at Pernia's description of the robed people, crucified deities, and church-like buildings in the light of Christianity. Thirteen "friar" statues were noted, reminding us of the Last Supper of Jesus and his apostles. The builders of Pernia's lost city would appear to be Christian monks of some sort; dare I venture to say Irish ones, at that? Certainly, this bizarre story could make more sense if we believed that the Incas were founded by Irish monks who set up their "Empire of the Sun." But, to be fair to the skeptics, it is also possible that Pernia's group had merely stumbled onto a Spanish settlement without realizing it!

The idea of light-skinned men living in numbers in the jungles of South America is not such a big deal. South America is literally teeming with tales of white, blond-haired Indians, and they are not just the kids of lost and captured explorers. It has been the habit of remote Indians tribes to capture explorers and keep them captive, the chief often forcing them to marry one of his daughters. Blond explorers are preferred, and I personally know one explorer whose life was saved because he had these features. During the 1930's, while exploring a remote area of eastern Peru, his Indian guides showed him shrunken heads of two White explorers who had preceded him. "We don't kill you like them, you have gold hair," they told him.

I looked out the window, and fingered my own blond hair. Would it save me if the going got tough? No! I have green eyes! If I were captured by headhunters, maybe I could fake it, or maybe they would be colorblind. Marrying the chief's daughter didn't seem like such a bad fate; better than ending up as a shrunken head!

We had come to a small station, and I got out to rustle up a snack. Indian women crowded the platform, selling corn and potatoes while kids sold candy. A policeman wearing green fatigues and an automatic pistol was leaning up against the station house. Like a Peruvian cross between Clint Eastwood and Charles Bronson, he had a thick black mustache, and seemed relaxed and cool as he surveyed the station, his territory. Under his stern gaze, I bought a boiled potato and slowly reboarded the train.

As we pulled out of the station, I carefully ate my hot snack, still thinking of all I had read and been told about the search for Gran Paititi. I remembered a letter that Colonel Percy Fawcett had written to his son Brian back in the 1920's. Colonel Fawcett was one of the great South American explorers of the early part of this century. He disappeared in the jungles of Brazil in 1925, while searching for what he thought was an Atlantean city. He wrote, "...I have heard from Indians about 'collections of stone houses' and clothed Indians who worship the sun and guard the approaches of their cities with savage determination. Records in the archives of missions and governments also talk of clothed white Indians occasionally sighted but never contacted, of lost cities in the Brazilian forests on a scale grander still than those of the Incan empire. My own investigations lead me to believe that two of the ancient city sites I propose to investigate are inhabited by the remnants of the same race that built them, now degenerated into a state of savagery due to their complete isolation, but still having traces of their original culture.

"I expect the ruins to be monolithic in character, more ancient than the oldest of Egyptian discoveries. Judging by the inscriptions found in many parts of Brazil the inhabitants used an alphabetical writing allied to many ancient European and Asian scripts. There are also rumors of a strange source of light in the buildings, a phenomenon that filled the Indians with terror who claim to have seen it." [33] Colonel Fawcett disappeared while on this search, and the resulting search for Fawcett or his diaries has lasted until today!

In 1681, a Jesuit missionary named Fray Lucero wrote of information given to him by Indians in the Río Huallagu area of north-eastern Peru. They told him that the lost city of Gran Paititi lay behind the forests and mountains eastwards of Cuzco.

The Jesuit wrote, "This empire of Gran Paytite has bearded, white Indians. The nation called Curveros, these Indians told me, dwell in a place called Yurachuasi or the 'white house.' For king, they have a descendant of the Inca Tupac Amaru, who with 40,000 Peruvians, fled far away into the forests, before the face of the conquistadors of Francisco Pizarro's day in AD 1533. He took with him a rich treasure, and the Castilians who pursued him fought each other in the forests, leaving the savage Chuncho Indios, who watched their internecine struggles, to kill off the wounded and shoot the survivors with arrows. I myself have been shown plates of gold and half-moons and ear-rings of gold that have come from this mysterious nation." [43] This story is independently documented in the book *Amazonas y El Maranon* by Fray Manuel Rodriguez, published in 1684.

Of course, the search for Gran Paititi still continues, and many explorers feel that they are getting close. Today, many feel that Paititi is somewhere in the Paucartambo area of Peru, east of Cuzco toward the Madre de Dios River. This is the same area in which Fray Lucero indicated that Gran Paititi could be found. Some expeditions, however, because they either found the city or disturbed the Indians too much in their search, end up dead.

In 1971 an American-French expedition was led by Bob Nichols, an American with years of experience in the jungle, who wrote travel articles for the *Peruvian Times* the 1960's. This group of three explorers attempted to reach Paititi by going up Río Pantiacolla from the south. But they disappeared after several months, and a search party financed by their families shortly afterward turned up nothing.

Then, in 1972 Japanese explorer Y. Sekino was able to contact the Machiguenga Indians in the area and confirm that the three explorers had been killed. Although rolls of film and a few notebooks were recovered, the bodies were never found. Gregory Deyermenjian, an American anthropologist, believes that the Nichols party had gone up the Río Pantiacolla to reach Gran Paititi, which they believed to be located in the mountains between the Río Pantiacolla and the Río Pinipini.

However, the valley of the Río Pantiacolla is very steep and narrow. Nichols and his group were trapped in the valley, not able to climb higher into the mountains. They continued forward through the valley for weeks, but their Indian guides left Nichols after their 30-day agreement expired. The three explorers continued to push up the valley alone, and presumably ran out of food, because there is very little wild game in the area. Deyermenjian theorizes that they then entered the house of a Machiguenga Indian, and not finding anyone home, took some food.

"The Machiguenga Indians are very friendly, and if you ask them for anything, they will give it to you. But if you take it without asking, they will kill you," says Deyermenjian. This is apparently what happened to Nichols and his two companions.

An amateur archeologist from Arequipa, Peru named Carlos Landa Neuenschwander led an expedition into this area, followed later by a French expedition. Neither expedition met with success. The French were fortunate to make it out alive, having had a poor rapport with the local Indians. All of these expeditions followed a single clue that indicates that Paititi is in this area around Paucartambo, in the mountains to the northeast of the central Cordillera Paucartambo, an area known as Mameria.

Gregory Deyermenjian and British photographer Michael Mirecki mounted their own expedition into the same area in 1984. Starting first by truck from Cuzco, they drove one day to Paucartambo, where they formed a mounted party of six on ten horses. They then headed out up the Río Paucartambo and over the Cordillera Paucartambo.

In personal correspondence to me, he wrote, "It took us five days to cross the mountains at altitudes reaching four thousand meters, offering some of the most spectacular scenery in the world. We located a *tambo* , which in Quechua means 'Resting Place.' This was the gateway to a rocky Inca trail which ascended a steep mountain known as Huascar. On the rockfaces, we saw drawings of llamas, condors, and human faces, which (the priest, who authored the book *Las Rutas Por Paititi*) Polentini claims are signs indicating the direction northwards to Paititi. We left the horses on a high plateau, to begin a steep descent into the jungle. Three days later we arrived at a settlement of of the Machiguenga Indian tribe where we met the chief, Goyo. The following day, we accompanied him deeper into the jungle, crossing fast-flowing rivers and hacking our way through the dense vegetation with machetes.

"Suddenly we came across some stone terraces known as *andenes* which the Incas used for cultivating coca plants. Coca leaves were of great importance in the daily life of the Inca; when chewed they provided energy. They are still chewed today by most of the campesinos of the Altiplano in Peru and Bolivia. Now we were high up above the River Mameria and we found ruins of walls, about two meters high and ten meters long. They were evidently the remains of Inca dwellings, their thatched roofs long disappeared. The simple stone-work was practically identical to that of the ruins at Vilcabamba

(Deyermenjian refers to the ruins at Espiritu Pampa, which he visited in 1981), examples of later construction.

"There were also various round tombs known as *chullpas* where we found various silver objects, including Inca bells and a large *tupi* , or cloak fastener. Higher up the slope stood an Inca furnace which was once used for firing the abundant ceramic pieces that lay scattered everywhere. These included plates with geometric motifs and vase handles portraying carvings of ducks, frogs, foxes, and llamas. The whole area is now covered in tropical vegetation and we had to clear the ruins with machetes in order to see their true form and to take photographs.

"We had discovered the ruins of Mameria, where the Incas had fled from Spanish persecution. Goyo, the Machiguenga chief, informed us that the city of Paititi lay high up on a nearby mountain. The various books and documents that we had consulted confirmed this statement. Unfortunately, the rainy season had come early to Peru and we were short of time and food, and lacked appropriate climbing equipment. Apparently, this mountain had not been climbed since Inca times, because the ascent is very difficult. Giant slippery roots make progress almost impossible. Goyo said that in Inca times, a path ascended the mountain to Paititi, and offered to spend the ensuing months searching for its existence." [31]

According to many sources, the mountain on which Paititi is located is called *Apukatinti* , though exactly which mountain is really Apukatinti is open for debate. The word means "Lord of the Sun" in Quechua, and any mountain with this name (there are several) is a good candidate for having Paititi on it. However, according to Peruvian anthropologist and explorer Fernanado Aparicio Bueno, author of the book *En Busca del Misterio de Paititi* (*In Search of the Mystery of Paititi* , 1985, Editorial Andina, Cuzco), Paititi is located on another Apucatinti farther north of the Mameria region.

Interestingly, literally translated, *Paititi* comes from the Quechua word "*Paikikin* " which means "the same as Cuzco". What could it mean, "The same as Cuzco?" Deyermenjian thinks that this indicates Paititi is another stone city, similar in its construction to that found at Cuzco and Sacsayhuaman; a megalithic city like Machu Picchu. On the other hand, it may mean that Paititi is like Cuzco in the sense that it is the abode of the Inca kings, as Cuzco once was. If Paititi was built from scratch by the retreating Inca royal fringe, then the ruins are more likely to be similar to those found at Espiritu Pampa: small and unimpressive.

Historically, Gran Paititi was not reported as being located on top of a mountain, but rather by a lake. If these older reports are correct, Paititi may be further into the jungles to the east or south. Some researchers even believe that it may still be a living city, where the Inca tradition is still carried on. Many areas, particularly to the east, could have remained under Inca control for quite some time after the Spanish conquest.

Then again, Apucatinti may well be the site of a long-dead Paititi. Demoralized and cut-off from their former empire, the surviving Incas could have existed on top of this remote mountain in a self-sufficient city much like Machu Picchu, until they died out. Deyermenjian backs this theory, and thinks that the city effectively died about the year 1600, a mere 30 or 40 years after the Incas escaped to their refuge there.

In June of 1986, I accompanied Greg Deyermenjian and a party of Peruvians to scale the Apucatinti in Mameria. It took one week by horseback to the edge of the jungle, and a further two weeks of living with Machiguenga Indians in effort to scale the peak. We discovered Inca buildings, ovens, tombs and coca plantations, as well as the first ever structures in the Madre de Dios department of Peru, but the ascent to the top of the mountain was extremely difficult. The mountain has no fresh water, and is covered in thick, almost impenetrable jungle. We ascended the mountain for five days from the base, with Machiguenga Indians leading the way. However, after running out of food and water, we had to return to the Indian village.

In August of 1986, Deyermenjian returned to Mameria by himself, and made it to the summit of Apucatinti with his Indian guides. To their disappointment, neither Paititi nor any other structures were at the summit of the mountain.

Deyermenjian's Apucatinti was a dead end, but Paititi still exists somewhere in the remote high jungles of eastern Peru or Bolivia. An English explorer named Sebastian Snow claimed to have discovered Paititi in 1954. The abandoned fortress that he thinks was Paititi is situated some fifty-five miles west-north-west of Pangoa on the Urubamba, near the headwaters of the Rio Montaro. He writes about his discoveries in the 1956 book *Half a Dozen of the Other* (Hodder and Stoughton, London). While his discoveries are of interest, it seems doubtful that the ruins Snow found are actually of Paititi, but rather of one of the many Inca outposts to be found in Antisuyo region of Peru.

Perhaps more interesting is an article called *Gold Raiders of the Amazon* that appeared in the June, 1982 issue of Swank magazine. The story is about a gold panning expedition led by an adventurer from Ohio named Phil Miller in the Madre de

Dios department of Peru, just east of Cuzco. After hearing of two massive stone towers similar to those at Sillustani near Lake Titicaca, they are determined to investigate the local rumours of a lost city nearby. Just as they sighted the tops of the towers, they were confronted by "one of the largest humans Phil had ever seen. Brown-skinned, with a peculiarly angled nose and high forehead, dressed in brightly colored animal skins and carrying a bronze-tipped spear," the giant figure signaled to the party not to continue further. Wisely they retreated. Was Miller about to enter the sacred territory of Paititi? At least he is alive to tell the story!

§§§

The setting sun's reflection sank slowly into Lake Titicaca as our train moved along its shore. The sun's last rays glinted off the water as we rolled into Puno, the last major town in Peru heading along the Altiplano into Bolivia. As I stared at the golden glow on the lake, fantastic images of lost Inca gold and the city of Gran Paititi lingered with me.

At the station in Puno, we made our now-standard mad dash off the train into a waiting taxi to find a hotel. We were higher in the mountains than at any other time in our trip, so the cloudless night was soon as cold as any Siberian outpost.

But try as we might to find one, there just didn't seem to be a warm hotel in that town. Our eventual choice, the Sillustani, is supposedly the second-best hotel in Puno, but we couldn't even get hot water in our rooms. The woman at the desk, with the fervent emotion of innkeepers the world over, insisted that her hotel had hot water in all its rooms. Unfortunately for our now-freezing feet, none of our attempts to prove her correct succeeded. She told us to let the water run; we did so for about half an hour, then got tired of waiting and left to find hot food instead.

A number of other hotels in Puno are all less expensive than the Sillustani, and probably offer much better value. Around the main plaza, you can find the Hostal Torrino, Hotel Colon, Hotel Tacna, Hotel Venezia, Hotel Colonial, Hotel Tursitas, Hotel Extra, Hotel Roma and others. If your are travelling on a tight budget, several people can share a room for a couple of American dollars. Puno is not a very big town, and most people just stop here on their way to and from Cuzco, Bolivia, or Arequipa.

We soon found the International Restaurant and stopped for dinner. It is a lively place, full of cheery Peruvians and the odd traveler, so the four of us spread out to meet and talk to others like us. As I waited for my Chinese meal of fried rice, I struck up a conversation with an American at the next table, who introduced himself as Dan. He was tall and thin, and had come to Peru to find the secret monastery which was supposed to still hide the most intriguing Inca artifacts.

This monastery is the subject of a book, *Secret of the Incas,* by George Hunt Williamson, written under the pen name Brother Philip.[25] While at times the fact and the fancy in its pages seems to merge, the book still makes good reading. According to Williamson, a "Lord Muru" arrived at Lake Titicaca at some time in the remote past, when the Andes Mountains were first uplifted in a cataclysmic event that also sank the Pacific continent of Mu. Lord Muru set up the "Monastery of the Brotherhood of the Seven Rays," which was to keep the secrets and treasures of his race in its archives.

Among these treasures was the Golden Sun Disc of Mu. Williamson maintains that this Sun Disc was later given to the Incas, when they had advanced enough spiritually to appreciate it. But when the Spaniards conquered Peru, the Sun Disc was removed from the Sun Temple at Cuzco, and placed back in safe keeping at the monastery.

Unfortunately, Williamson's tale cannot be verified. Most researchers feel that the Sun Disc of Mu was hidden in a tunnel. That such a Sun Disc did exist is certain; it was seen by the very first Spanish to enter Cuzco. There is even some evidence that a now-lost continent or civilization in the Pacific may have existed. But there is no indication, apart from Williamson's book, that the Sun Disc came from "Mu," though no one knows where it did come from or when it was made. Indications are that it was a valuable golden artifact, but in Williamson's book, it takes on a mystical quality. Some independent evidence does exist for a secret monastery somewhere in the Andes, just north of Lake Titicaca in Peru. Williamson may have been there, or heard about it on one of his trips to Peru in the 1950's. According to him, this monastery is also known as the Valley of the Blue Moon.

While Williamson's book could be classified as fiction, the first part is quite interesting reading, appealing to people with a sort of idealistic, romantic, or mystical outlook on life. (None of them hereabouts, right?) And a surprising number of them, after reading the book, have come to Peru from Europe, North America, and Australia, bent on finding the secret monastery. I have met several people who have set out on this quest, though nobody seems to have succeeded —except one!

In the late 1970's, a New Zealander named Michael Brown, was given a copy of *Secret of the Andes* by his karate teacher. In his book, *The Weaver and the Abbey,* Brown tells the story of his own subsequent quest. It is a tale of human courage and inspiration, more of a man in search of himself than in search of Inca treasure. Yet, at the very end of the book, Brown claims to have found the hidden valley and monastery.[34]

Brown gives few details, though he maintains others had found the valley before him. "...the abbey dominates the landscape. It's normally sombre grey walls have taken on some of the colourful evening light... Like the others before us, Julie and I have undertaken not to reveal the location of the abbey, nor to describe its interior, nor to describe the teaching methods employed. The purpose of this restriction is to encourage the seeking for first-hand experience of the nature of the abbey." [34]

While Brown will not reveal the exact location of this mountain paradise, he gives some clues. Everyone who searches for the "Shangri-la of the Andes" leaves from Juliaca, just north of Puno. From Juliaca, one heads due east on the road and from there into the mountains.

At dinner that night in Puno, Dan introduced me to Williamson's book, then told me about his own unsuccessful quest. "I went searching for the monastery," he began. "You need to go to a small town east of Juliaca called San Juan del Oro, which is Saint John of the Gold. I took an old Ford taxi there from Juliaca. I was running out of money, so I traded the driver an old camera and some film for the ride. I had to register at each little town. They didn't see many tourists around there, I'll tell you that!

"In San Juan del Oro, there were these Swiss medical missionaries who said that a few people had been there before me. They told me that the others thought San Juan was the lost monastery. One of the Swiss women told me about some old ruins back down the road, so I went there and spent the night. It was just a bunch of old Inca walls, but it was something.

"I was tired, but I kept driving myself on. The next day I walked around until I met a lady who gave me some potato soup. I pitched my tent there, and hung out for a day. The next day, my intuition told me to leave and go back to Juliaca, so I wandered out onto the road, and immediately got a lift in a truck. That night a terrible storm hit. I was lucky to get out of there when I did!"

"Do you think those ruins were the monastery?" I asked him, sipping an Arequipeña beer.

"Oh, no," replied Dan. "Not at all. Those were just some

old walls. The real monastery is somewhere near there, but farther on. I think that you would have to backpack for several days from San Juan del Oro. But I don't think that it's too far." Interestingly enough, this is pretty much what Michael Brown indicates in *The Weaver and the Abbey* .

George Hunt Williamson died in Los Angeles a few years ago, but not without revealing one of the secrets of the Monastery. At a seminar in the early 1980's in Spain, Williamson said that he would reveal the location to the participants, who paid handsomely to spend a weekend with "Brother Philip". Williamson revealed the location of the Monastery as being, not in Peru, but at a location in Bolivia, to the north-east of La Paz! There is, however, no monastery or any other structure at this sight.

It may be that Williamson, "Brother Philip", just couldn't really reveal the location, however, informed sources have told me that Williamson himself had tried to stop the republication of the book when he realized how his "hoax" was being taken all too seriously. Another clue as to the truthfulness of the book is "Brother Philip's" reference to an expedition to Paititi undertaken from the monastery. If the monastery was truly populated by "Masters" and other members of the "Brotherhoods" they would know where Paititi was, and would not have to go "looking for it". Williamson's secret monastery is more likely an analogy for Paititi itself, often said to be occupied by living "Inca Masters", rather than a separate place. It is also doubtful that Williamson was ever there. As to Brown and his book, "The Weaver and the Abbey", it is also doubtful that he reached the monastery, as the monastery just doesn't exist.

The real secret of Andes, which is more than the monastery and the Sun Disc, may not be decoded for a long time. The mountains, valleys and jungles hold many secrets. But sometimes, when talking to other travelers like Dan, I would begin to wonder why we did it, what it was we were looking so hard for. Lost cities and treasures may abound, though no treasure is so great as the treasure of true love. Maybe this is the true secret of the of the Andes, the one that every person needs to discover for themselves.

Chapter Six

Tiahuanaco and La Paz:
Antidiluvian Remnants in Bolivia

When you have eliminated the impossible,
whatever remains, however improbable,
must be the truth.
-Sherlock Holmes

We woke up early the next morning and decided to leave
Puno for Bolivia. Eager to continue our exploration of South
America, we hurried to catch the fast hydrofoil ferry across
Lake Titicaca, which leaves from Juli.

On our way to Juli, we passed the interesting ruins of
Sillustani. These consist chiefly of a series of towers and battle-
ments, called *chulpas* , along the lake. A group of stone circles
stand nearby which are sacred to the Indians who live in the
area, called "Sun Circles," Most interesting are strange round
towers, constructed with great skill out a large blocks of
andesite stone. Like their twins at Machu Picchu and elsewhere, their origin and purpose remains a mystery. They are
constructed using the same pre-Incan techniques found at
Cuzco, Sacsayhuaman, and Machu Picchu.

The Sillustani towers are wide at the top and taper to a nar-
rower diameter at the bottom, like a funnel. They have only
two small openings, one at the bottom and one toward the top.
These openings are too small to have been used as doors, as
only a child could squeeze in through them.

In the 1905 edition of *American Anthropologist*, Adolph F.
Sandelier discusses many of the theories behind the towers and
Sun Circles. He suggests that the towers were probably used as
grain storage silos, the small doors ideally suited for protecting
the crop. He also states that it was the opinion of most of his

contemporaries that the towers were burial chambers. Yet, it would have been difficult to put an adult body inside with any dignity, and one can hardly imagine the doors were for visitors! In reality, few remains of any type have been found inside any of the towers. Also interesting is that construction of a few towers seems to have been abandoned while in progress.

Sandelier also mentions that the Sun Circles would appear to be intended for some astronomical purpose, even though they are not on level ground. Archaeologist William Corliss comments, "A fascinating possibility in connection with the sun circles on inclined ground is that they were built on level land originally, but were tilted by a later cataclysm (which perhaps also interrupted tower construction). The region around Lake Titicaca was apparently tilted in recent times."[38]

Victor von Hagen visited the towers in the early 1950's and reported them in his book, *Highway of the Sun.* Calling them the Towers of the Dead, he writes, "...fourteen feet high, some circular, others square, the Towers of the Dead were wonderfully fashioned of stone in the megalithic style with huge polygonal rocks fitted together so exactly that even moss could not find lodgement. The corbeled vaults inside, almost as high as the towers, were of meticulous stonework. There were a few bone fragments lying about, and some bits of pottery—not much more, for these tombs had been sacked first by the Incas and later by the Spaniards, and so thouroughly that just who built the houses of the Dead has never been discovered."[63]

Von Hagen also quotes a curious passage from the historian Cieza de Leon, who indicated that they were tombs. "...the tombs were built in the form of small towers...according to the rank and wealth of those who built them. They carry the corpse to the place where the tomb is prepared...there they burn ten or more llamas...kill the women, boys and servants who are to accompany him on his last voyage. All these are buried in the same tomb with the body. The mourners then walk along uttering sad and mournful songs...while an Indian goes before them beating a drum. The great tombs are so numerous that they occupy more space than is given to the living."[63] This ceremony sounds incredibly similar to that used by the ancient Egyptians! Certainly Cieza did not witness either the building of the towers or the burial ceremony, though what he reported was the tradition. One wonders if Cieza had been reading too much about ancient Egypt and China when he visited the stone towers. Were they originally built for some other purpose, but then later used as tombs by the Incas?

At Juli, several older women were changing Peurvian and

American currency into Bolivian. We found out later that they were not giving us a very good deal. Slightly poorer for our transactions, we boarded the hydrofoil and were soon skimming east across the lake toward Copacabana. The hydrofoil is run by a Bolivian company, Crillon Tours, and seats about forty people. This modern ferry stands in stark contrast to the reed boats which still ply the lake's waters, passing mightily by them in transit between Juli on the Peruvian shore and Copacabana on the Bolivian side. Soon after we left the port, which was little more than a dock, the ship lowered its ski-like foils to cruise smoothly across the lake at four times the speed of the old steamers it replaced.

Lake Titicaca is the highest navigable lake in the world, at an altitiude of 12,500 feet (3,810 m). It has a maximum depth of 1,214 feet (370 m), also making it one of the deepest lakes in the world. The lake has an area of about 3,200 square miles (8,190 square km), about half the size of Lake Ontario

Copacabana is famous for its Independence Day celebrations, which take place in early August. The festivities are well worth participating in if your schedule permits. Copacabana is also the home of the church of the "Holy Indian Virgin" statue, where a miracle took place a hundred years or so ago. Many South American Catholics now make a pilgrimage to the church, offering gifts to the carved wooden stature made by a local Indian boy in the 1800's.

Copacabana is a pleasant-enough town; we walked the streets for a bit, and shopped along the street market. I was amused to see one store which sold nothing but batteries! Every brand and size you could ever want for any style radio, flashlight, or gizmo. Next time I was deep in the jungle and needed a battery...

After Bolivian immigration had checked our passports and stamped us in, we were off in the hydrofoil again to the Inca ruins at the Island of the Sun. Some legends state the first Incas appeared on the island, while others have them appearing at a cave on the lake's shore. Another legend says that a group of White men like the Incas lived on an island in the lake until the time of the Spanish conquest.

As we walked up the old Inca steps to terraces on the hills at the Island of the Sun, it appeared to us that the ruins were of Incan origin, rather than being pre-Incan construction. The stairs did remind me a little of Machu Picchu, with a small stream flowing down next to them. A little Quechua girl followed us up these stairs, proffering what was, compared to her small size, an immensly oversized basket of flowers. She was about five, wearing a black dress, with long black hair in braids, and rosy red cheeks. Bending over, I smelled her assorted wares, then gave her a few cents and a pat on the head for a small bunch. The hydrofoil's sharp whistle ended our quick interlude, calling us back down to the shore.

Back on board, heading for the Bolivian port of Huatajata, I pondered the mystery of Lake Titicaca. Explorer and oceanographer Jacques Cousteau had come here in the late 1970's, to search the bottom of the lake in a mini-submarine. He found giant frogs, but not much else, admittedly only covering a small part of the entire lake bottom. What was the famous French oceanographer looking for? Would you believe sunken cities?

Local Indians have reported observing buildings and roofs in the lake, and that after long droughts when the water level was low, they could even touch the tops of the buildings with their poles! This was written off as superstitious talk until the early 1970's, when an American dive team discovered what was literally a sunken city on the eastern shore of Lake Titicaca! Near Bolivia's Porto Acosta, in about 65 feet (20 m) of water can be found the ruins of an ancient city. There are reports of other sunken cities in Lake Titicaca, and it was these rumours that may have piqued Jacques Cousteau's interest.

A Bolivian archaeologist has an explaination for the existance of a sunken city in the lake. He theorizes that the water was very low at one time after a severe drought, and people living on the lake foolishly built their city too close to the water. Later, when the drought ended and the water level rose, the city became submerged, a lost city to be discovered many years later by puzzled archaeologists.

This is not a bad explantion, trying to explain in simplest terms how a sunken city got in Lake Titicaca. Such an explanation does not work when one tries to explain other sunken cities, located in the English Channel, in the Caribbean, and in the Pacific. But there are other possibile explainations.

Presently, there are two schools of geology competing for respectability in scientific circles, Uniformitarian Geology and Cataclysmic Geology. Uniformitarian Geology holds that the earth's external and internal geological processes have been operating unchanged, and within the same range of rates, throughout the earth's history—and that these rates are typified by currently observed processes that are clearly gradual in nature.

Cataclysmic geological theory states that these changes are not always uniform. According to this school of thought, sudden changes occur during which mountain ranges can be raised in a matter of days, and a continent or island can sink overnight. There is evidence to support both sides, though most scientists prefer to support the uniformitarian view. Not because there is necesarily more evidence, but because it is startling to think that sudden devastation may come upon the earth.

Ancient books, legends, and myths, on the other hand, tend to support the cataclysmic point of view. After all, water rising one inch per century is hardly the stuff legends are made of! Whether considering the Old Testament flood, the Sumerian Epic of Gilgamesh, or similar stories in Hopi books, Mayan texts and other ancient records, many tales from "long, long ago" tell of an upheaval of tremendous size which devastated civilization.

Some researchers postulate that the earth's surface 24,000 years ago was radically different than it is today. A continent may have existed in the Pacific Ocean, named variously Lemuria or Mu. The South American tectonic plate was depressed, making it a cresent shaped continent, and most of what is now the Amazon Basin was the Amazonian Sea. During a possible pole shift, created by a huge build-up ice at both poles, the Pacific tectonic plate sank, and South America assumed the form we see today.

Hugh Auchincloss Brown, in his book *Cataclysms of the Earth* speculated that these pole shifts happen every seven to nine thousand years, depending on the build-up of ice at the poles. In fact, some navigation maps used as recently as the 1500's show Antarctica *ice free* ! Today, 90% of all the fresh water on the earth is estimated to be incased in the Antarctic ice mass, growing at a rate of 52 billion tons annually.

This does not take into account the loss of some ice to melting, creation of icebergs, etc. Even so, Brown cites a 1960 study that showed that the Antarctic ice mass increases its accumulation by 293 cubic miles annually. This is considerable, even in relationship to the total mass of the earth. Brown also shows that the South Pole's center of mass is approximately 350 miles off-center from the geographic South Pole, along the 80-degree East Meridian. According to one of the cataclysmic theories, the earth will flip like a top once it has been destabilized enough by the ice cap. The idea that the Antarctic ice will melt and flood coastal cities is far less likely. Just the opposite is actually happening, with more and more ice accumulating every day.[35,36,37]

Could the sunken city near Porto Acosta actually be a city from the pre-cataclysmic times, when this area contained a canal that crossed the continent? Precious little archaeological work has been done at this sunken city, as underwater archaeology generally centers around salvaging shipwrecks.[39,40] I decided that if the earth was about experience another cataclysm, I'd better continue my trip quickly!

§§§

When we arrived at the other side of the lake, we had lunch of fresh trout at the Crillon Tours cafeteria. Near the port, an Indian was fishing from his reed boat. Built from the local fresh-water reeds, these boats are quite strong and sea-worthy. In his book *The Ra Expeditions* , Thor Heyerdahl narrates his attempt to cross the Atlantic to the New World in a papyrus boat built by Mediterranean craftsmen. When this boat disintigrated mid-voyage, he brought two Bolivian reed boat builders back to his North African starting point. The boat they subsequently built completed the Atlantic voyage successfully, proving the possibility that primitive technology would have allowed trans-oceanic exploration.

Leaving the port, we took a three-hour bus trip across the dry, cold and desolate Altiplano to La Paz, the largest city of Bolivia and the highest capital city in the world. The city is located in a deep canyon, and as we came over a crest in the Altiplano, we got a spectacular view of its beauty. The old city, with its cobblestone streets and colonial houses, clung tightly to the canyon's sloping walls. At the valley floor were the skyscrapers of new La Paz, glass and steel towering over narrow, twisting streets. In the distance, the snowy peaks of the Andes shot up from the high plateau of the Altiplano, tall rock brothers of the skyscrapers in the valley.

Darting frantically to and fro, our bus shot down the steep road and into the canyon like a hungry baracuda among a school of fish. Soon we were in downtown La Paz, where we disembarked at the Hotel Andes. Most of the inexpensive hotels in La Paz can be found in the old city down the hill from the railway station. The Hotel Italia, Alojamiento Central, Hotel Capitol, and many "Residencials" around the train station are all just a few dollars a night. Try to get ahead of the crowd from your bus to find one with a vacancy, or get another traveler to recommend one for you.

When we arrived in La Paz, the inflation rate was almost 1000% per year, and sometimes as much as 20% per day. If you have ever wondered what super-inflation is like, take a trip to Bolivia. You will feel the power that your stable currency holds, as if you were carrying some magic talisman. But watch out for those who would relieve you of your magic!

We checked in, then immediately walked down to the central district, where we were approached by black-marketers offering to buy our American dollars. The police were keeping a close eye on everyone, as all black-market currency changers were illegal, so the atmosphere of the entire area was a tense one, filled with danger and caution.

But I had been entrusted with not only my small group's funds, but also those of several other hotel guests. They had placed on me the onerous responsibility of converting this sum to Bolivian currency at a good rate, and to try staying alive through the process. Separating from the group on a back street, I struck a deal with a young man who took me through several dark streets, down an alley, then up some stairs. Inside an unobtrusive door, we entered a small room where several armed men and a woman huddled around a desk, counting huge stacks of money.

The mound of money, carelessly thrown all over the desktop, reminded me of the megalithic building blocks at Cuzco. If it had been any currency other than Bolivian, it would have been worth a fortune. I received millions of Bolivian dollars for several hundred American dollars at an exchange rate of over 90,000-to-one. Just three years before, the rate had been eight-to-one!

With my millions, almost more than I could stuff into my large day pack, I escaped to the street with the young Bolivian who had brought me. All the way back to the hotel, he hurried me along, looking back over his shoulder as if we were being followed. When we arrived, he told me that the police had spotted us together earlier, and had tried to find us at the building with the money hoard. I got a sudden chill as I pictured myself rotting away in prison, surrounded by rats eating my worthless Bolivian millions.

Back in the room, I dumped the money onto the coffee table, stacks and stacks of hundred-dollar bills. It looked like we had robbed a bank! We divided up the loot like gangsters, each of us ending up with a stack of bills that looked like an accordion. As I handed Steve his stack, I told him, "Don't forget I gave you a million dollars once!" Steve winked, and we all laughed.

The next morning we're off to Tiahuanaco, probably the most controversial archaeological ruins on the planet. Even to conventional archaeologists who laugh at theories of upheaval, Tiahuanaco is a source of controversy and debate. All agree that these megalithic ruins predate the Incas. Yet just how old are they, and who built them? The depth of the mystery is indicated by the fact that texts state only that Tiahuanaco was built by the "Tiahuanaco Culture," a rather clever deduction!

I found it hard to deduce anything better, though, as my brain was bounced along in a bus back toward Lake Titicaca, on a different road than we had used the day before. Stopping at the village of Tiahuanco on the way, we found a colorful Indian market open. We wandered among the different stalls for a while, taking photos and making an occasional purchase. Mounds of fresh vegetables, piles of tantalizing coca leaves, and garments of brightly colored yarn all beckoned, an Aymara Indian woman wearing several black wool skirts sitting behind each selection of merchandise, collecting stacks of Bolivian dollars. Resisting temptation to buy too much, we took a quick look around the town. Its church is unique, built from stones taken from Tiahuanaco, and even including a few statues from the ancient city.

Half an hour later we arrived at the ruins themselves. Situated in a remote, desolate area of the Altiplano, these ruins overlook barren hills, in stark contrast to the stunning setting of Machu Picchu. The cataclysmic theorists point out that it is unlikely that such a fantastic city would be built at such a desolate location and altitude. This unlikely reasoning is used to further the theory that Tiahuanaco was built at a lower elevation, and later uplifted.

We walked into the ruins from the south side, stopping to inspect what is supposed to be a small model of the site, carved in stone by the ancient builders. We continued to walk, to the top of the city's pyramid. This pyramid was partially destroyed by treasure hunters, seeking gold in the middle of its earthen structure many years ago.

From the summit of the pyramid, we got a good look at the entire city of Tiahuanaco. Feeling like kids in a toy store, we didn't know what to explore first in this incredible, ancient place. Finally deciding, we hurried first to the restored temple of Kalasayaya. Megalithic blocks make up the steps, walls, and arches around the temple. At the turn of the century, Bolivian engineers broke up the stones and carried away all the smaller blocks to be used as ballast on a railway. What remains today of Tiahuanco is what could not be carted away for use in other structures, only the biggest blocks of stone. And the city is still impressive! In 1864, E. George Squire visited Tiahuanaco and was quite impressed by the ruins; he called them the Baalbek of the New World. (He was referring to the ruins of Baalbek in Lebanon, which contain some of the most astounding megaliths to be found anywhere in the world.)

In the center of Tiahuanaco is a stone arch, cut from a solid chunk of andesite weighing about twelve tons, now cracked by what must have been a pretty good earthquake. On the upper portion of this arch is a series of carvings, believed to be a calendar. In the center a figure, holding a staff on each side, appears to be weeping. He is known as "the Weeping God."

When the Spaniards first arrived, they were told by the Indians that this city had been found in ruins by the Incas. Cieza de Leon, one of the first chroniclers of South America, visited the site in 1540, when much of the stone still remained. He reported two colossal, stone figures, with long robes reaching to the ground and ornamental caps on their heads.

Cieza de Leon wrote "...the natives told me...that all these marvels sprang from the ground in a single night...There are not stones in any of the hills beyond." The Spaniards generally believed that these monuments "...were more the work of demons than of men."[22,39,40] A similar legend told at the time was that, "Tiahuanco was built in single night, after the flood, by unknown giants. But they disregarded a prophecy of the coming of the sun and were annihilated by its rays, and their palaces were reduced to ashes..."[39]

In the 16th century, missionary Diego de Alcobaso wrote, "I saw a vast hall carved on its roof to represent thatch. There were the waters of a lake which washed the walls of a splendid court in this city of the dead, and, standing in its fine court, in the shallows of the water, on the platform of a superb colonnade were many fine statues of men and women. So real they were that they seemed to be alive. Some had goblets and upraised drinking cups. Others sat, or reclined, as in life. Some walked in the stream flowing by the ancient walls. Women, carved in stone, dangled babies in their laps or bore them on their backs. In a thousand natural postures, people stood or reclined." One of the statues wore a beard, and as we know, South American Indians are beardless.[22]

Today, most of these statues have been destroyed. All that remains are the monolithic figures of bizarre, bug-eyed men who stare vacantly over the desolate ruins of Tiahuanco. They look more like men from outer space than beautiful people at a party in the hills. The Spaniards destroyed everything they could at Tiahuanaco, thinking it idolatrous. These larger figures were spared because they were so massive, but they have been badly damaged.

In the 1800's, a controversial French anthropologist named Augustus le Plongeon visited Tiahuanaco and observed a strata of seashells, which hinted that the site had once been at sea level. (I found a fossilized trilobite myself while we explored the ruins.) British Colonel James Churchward used the argument that Tiahuanaco is a former port city as a major piece of his evidence for the lost continent of Lemuria.[41,42]

The great South American explorer, Colonel Fawcett said at the turn of this century, "These megalithic ruins of Tiahuanaco were never built on the Andes at all. They are part of a great city submerged ages ago in the Pacific Ocean. When the crust of the earth upheaved and created the great Andean Cordilleras, these ruins were elevated from the bed of the ocean to where you now see them." [33,22]

Yet, I'm afraid that all of these upheaval theorists are at least partially mistaken. The gigantic city of Tiahuanaco was not built at sea level and uplifted with the Andean mountains, but was most likely built where it stands, thirteen thousand feet above sea level. The city and statues stand largely intact, which would be quite unlikely if they had been thrust 13,000 feet upward in a mountain-making cataclysm.

If one is looking for ruins which could have suffered through such an upheaval, one needs look no further than those of Puma Punku. Infrequently visited, Puma Punku is only a mile or so to the north of Tiahuanaco, toward Lake Titicaca. Its most fascinating feature is what appears to be an ancient canal. Huge sandstone and andesite blocks up to twenty-seven feet long and weighing as much as 300 tons are scattered about like a child's building blocks. The normally- conservative *Reader's Digest* reported, "A jumbled heap of stones looking as if they were hurled to the ground by some great natural catastrophe, is all that remains of Puma Punku..."[39]

Here was once a great canal, according to some archaeologists, destroyed in an earthquake of massive proportions. The construction at Puma Punku is different from that at Tiahuanaco, in that the stones were fitted together with clamps, like the one stone at Ollantaytambo. Puma Punku has none of the statues found at Tiahuanaco, but instead has geometric designs precisely cut into the andesite, such as concentric Swiss-style crosses and triangles.

While Bolivian archaeologists insist that ancestors of the local Aymara Indians built both Tiahuanaco and Puma Punku, it would seem that their culture has certainly taken a slide back, as they now can barely make a subsistence living on the high, barren plateau. Neither they, nor the Spanish government of impoverished Bolivia are capable of duplicating the engineering feats of Tiahuanco or Puma Punku.

Traditional archaeologists explain the former canals at Tiahuanaco by saying that it was once near Lake Titicaca, twenty miles away. The lake theoretically covered a greater area at that time, extending to the port of Puma Punku. It is interesting to contrast this explanation with that for the sunken city near Porto Acosta, which the same experts claim was built when the waters of the lake were very low. This adds up to quite a variation in the depth of the lake!

Yet, if a massive earthquake tossed down the 300 ton stones of Puma Punku, scattering them about the plain like a bunch of toys, then why were not the buildings of Tiahuanaco likewise destroyed? Is it because they were built at a later time, after the cataclysm?

An alternate theory to explain this mystery involves a possible cataclysm which sank the lost continent of Lemuria. This theoretical continent received its name in the late 1800's as a proposed land bridge between Africa and India, in a effort to explain the existence of Lemurs in both areas. As used today, the term Lemuria refers to a continent which encompassed much of the Pacific tectonic plate, including California west of the San Andreas fault. It does not include the Indian Ocean, as it did originally. If this continent sank at the same time that the Amazon Basin rose, then the canal at Puma Pulku could have been built before the upheaval to serve the same purpose which the Panama canal serves today.

Tiahuanaco could then have been built after the raising of the Andes. Some say that Tiahuanaco was built about 15,000 years ago. Archaeologist Arthur Posnanski, who studied Tiahuanaco for thirty years at the turn of the century, decided that the city was from 10,000 to 12,000 years old. Traditional archaeologists scoff at this ancient date, citing radio carbon dating of artifacts indicating that the city was occupied at 1,700 BC. Even this figure is astounding, considering that some vanished culture was constructing buildings that we can hardly duplicate, four thousand years later.

And who would have built Tiahuanaco? Perhaps none other than those mysterious seafarers who mapped Antarctica before it was covered with ice, sailed the world spreading a megalithic culture, and wore red turbans over their blond hair—the Atlantean League! But why would anyone want to come to one of the most desolate, inhospitable places on earth and construct a megalithic city? This has always been the most puzzling question of Tiahuanaco, no matter who you decide actually built it.

There are two possible reasons for choosing this location. First, it is significant that the older ruins of Puma Punku are nearby. Could it be that the builders of Tiahuanaco put the city here because it was near the ruins of the even more ancient city? This would seem to be the case. They may have wanted to draw attention to the ruins of Puma Punku, perhaps just stumbling upon them while searching for a place to build Tiahuanaco.

Peruvian historian Montesinos wrote in his *Memorias Antiguas, Historales, Politicas del Peru* : "Cuzco and the city of ruins Tiahuanaco are connected by a gigantic subterranean road. The Incas do not know who built it. They also know nothing about the inhabitants of Tiahuanaco. In their opinion it was built by a very ancient people which later on retreated into the jungle of Amazonia."[54] So, even here at desolate Tiahuanaco, we have the mysterious tunnel system popping up again! If it doesn't exist, why does every one talk about it?

The second possible reason for locating Tiahuanaco in the mountains is that the builders were refugees, building their city in a place where they would not be disturbed. This same attitude exists today among survivalists, who create their own retreat from the insanity of our world. Had the builders of this city tried to create their own retreat?

As we left Tiahuanaco, I tossed around all of these possibilities in my head while gazing out the back of the bus at the ruins quickly disappearing into the distance. Had mankind always been savage, battling and warring against one another? Did human nature lack the spiritual refinement and emotional capability needed to really love one another? I reflected that nearly every religious figure, including Buddha, Confucius, Lao Tzu, Jesus, and even Viracocha and Quetzal Coatl, had admonished mankind to do just that.

With the sun setting over the snow covered Andes to the west, I considered one of the most radical theories of Pacific civilization, which maintains that Lemuria (Mu) supported a culture where many different races lived in harmony. Then Lemuria was destroyed by a natural cataclysm. Could it be that mankind would again progress to where we would all live together peacefully, in a new golden age of civilization? Maybe there was hope that mankind might once again live in peace, with the sun bathing down upon a loving culture like that of the Incas, "Sons of the Sun." This thought brightened me just as the last golden rays of the sun died behind a great icy mountain peak in the distance. The wind came up suddenly, whistling icily through the bus windows. This new age could not come too soon, I thought, zipping my coat up against the chilling wind blowing down hard from the mountains. It would probably get darker before the dawn...

The Incas were fantastic road builders, but they did not use the wheel for transportation, as it would have been impractical in the mountainous terrain.

In one El Dorado-Gran Paititi legend, the king was covered with gold dust before bathing.

In this early print, Manoa, "City of Gold," was depicted as similar to a Middle-Eastern city.

Gregory Deyermenjian points to Apucatinti.

The Machiguenga Indians of the Apucatinti area.

Photos courtesy Gregory Deyermenjian.

Square and round chulpas near Lake Titicaca. Not the megalithic construction, similar to that at Sacsayhuaman.

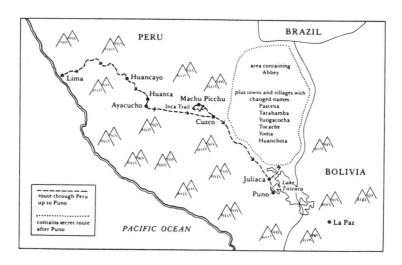

Map to the secret monastery in the Andes, adapted from <u>The Weaver and the Abbey</u>.

The spectacular highway from La Paz drops down into the valleys from the snow covered slopes of the Andes.

The central figure on the Gateway to the Sun in Tiahuanaco. He is depicted with tears in his eyes, and is said to be crying for "the sunken Red Land"--Atlantis?

An Aymara fisherman in a totora reed boat on Lake Titicaca.

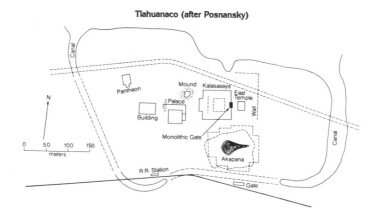

Tiahuanaco (after Posnansky)

Main temple area of Tiahuanaco. Puma Punku is approx. one mile to the left.

A statue found by Colonel Fawcett at Tiahuanaco.

View from the sunken temple looking into the Kalasaya area of Tiahuanaco.

Conduits and partially-reconstructed wall at Tiahuanaco. Who really built this city?

The massive Gate of the Sun at Tiahuanaco, hewn from a solid piece of andesite.

Keystone cuts in the blocks at Puma Punku.

A keystone cut in the blocks at Puma Punku. An unusual and sophisticated method for fastening megalithic blocks together, a similar cut can be found at Ollantaytambo.

Portions of the canal at Puma Punku.

Another view of the ruins at Puma Punku, showing blocks weighing up to 200 tons, tossed about by an earthquake of enormous proportions.

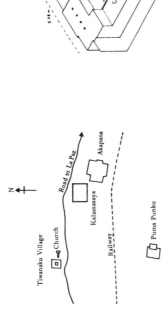

An architect's drawing of blocks of stone found at the "canal" of Puma Punku.

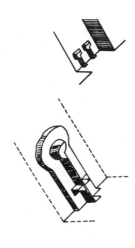

These keystone cuts in the andesite were used to hold the gigantic blocks together. Silver or copper clamps were placed in the key cuts.

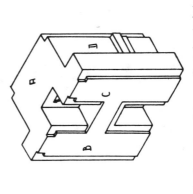

An architect's drawing of the complicated articulation of blocks of andesite lava found at Puma Punku.

Tiwanaku Village

Church

N

Road to La Paz

Kalassasya

Akapana

Railway

Puma Punku

Two proposed "Pole-Shift" mechanisms, possibly caused by build-up of ice at the poles. Such a shift could generate the tremendous destructive forces required to cause the damage evident to the ancient ruins in South America.

For over 1,000 years the world's largest man has stood etched into the side of a lone desert mountain in Chile's remote, starkly beautiful Atacama Desert.

Rediscovered in 1967 by Chilean Air Force General Eduardo Jensen, the great ground drawing has become popularly known as the "Atacama Giant."

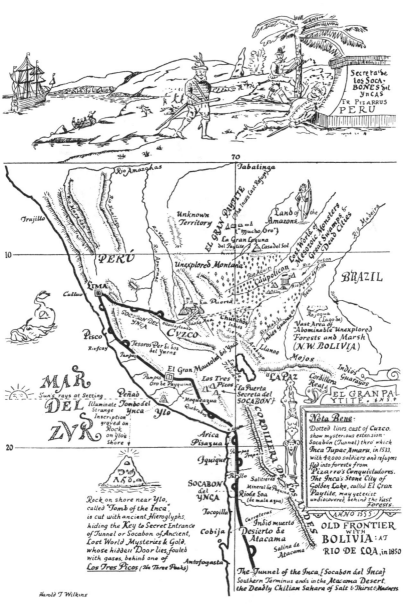

The following text labels appear on the map:

Secreta de los Socabones del Yncas
Fr. Pizarrus
PERU

70
Rio Amazonas
Tabatinga
Trujillo
Unknown Territory
EL GRAN PAYTITE (The Inca Last Refuge)
"mucho Oro"
La Gran Laguna del Paytite
Casa del Sol
Land of the Amazons
Lost World of Mesozoic Monsters & Great Swamps & Dead Cities
Rio Madeira
10
PERÚ
Unexplored Montaña
Caupolican
BRAZIL
Callao
LIMA
La Puerta
SOCABON DEL YNCA
Ollantaytambo
CUZCO
Chunchos
Indios
Rio Grande de Jujuy
Jagua (Lago Se)
Vast Area of "Abominable Unexplored" Forests and Marsh (N.W. BOLIVIA)
Pisco
Rio Ycay
Tesoros Per Si los del Ynca
Llanos
Indios Guarayos
Mojos
El Gran Mausoleo del Ynca
Los Tres Picos
"LA PAZ"
Cordillera Real
Indios Guarayos
MAR
Sun's rays at Setting illuminate Strange Inscription graved on Rock on Ylo Shore
Pampas Oro se Payquina
La Puerta Secreta del SOCABON
EL GRAN PAYTITE
DEL
Peñao
Tombo del Ynca
Ylo
Moquegua
Quebrada
Nota Bene:
Dotted lines, cast of Cuzco, show mysterious extension Socabón (Tunnel) thro' which Inca Tupac Amaru, in 1533, with 40,000 soldiers and refugees fled into forests from Pizarro's Conquistadores. The Inca's Stone City of Golden Lake, called El Gran Paytite, may yet exist undiscovered behind the Vast Forests.
ZVR
Arica
Pisagua
CORDILLERA DE
(ANNO 1555)
Iquique
Pampa Tamarugal
SOCABON del YNCA
Rollo
Salitreras
Mineral de Paquina
OLD FRONTIER WITH BOLIVIA: AT RIO DE LOA, in 1850
Rock on shore near Ylo, called "Tomb of the Inca" is cut with ancient Hieroglyphs, hiding the Key to Secret Entrance of Tunnel or Socabon of Ancient, Lost World Mysteries & Gold, whose hidden Door lies, fouled with gases, behind one of Los Tres Picos (the Three Peaks)
Rio de Loa (de mala agua)
Tocopilla
Cobija
Indio muerto
Desierto de Atacama
Carreteras
Salina de Atacama
Antofogasta
The Tunnel of the Inca, [Socabon del Inca] Southern Terminus ends in the Atacama Desert, the Deadly Chilian Sahara of Salt & Thirst & Madness

Harold T Wilkins

Harold Wilkins' map of the Andean tunnel system.

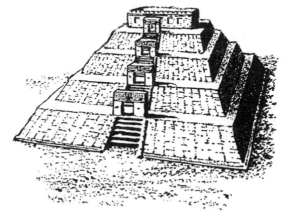

A reconstructed version of the Akabana Pyramid at Tiahuanaco.

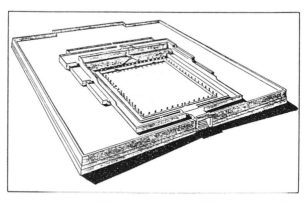

A reconstructed version of the sunken temple, Kalasasaya, at Tiahuanaco.

Chapter Seven

Across the Andes into the Atacama: Mysteries of the World's Driest Desert

It is strange, but true;
for truth is always strange;
stranger than fiction.
-*Lord Byron*, Don Juan

Back in La Paz, we spent a few more days wandering the city and visiting such sites as the Valley of the Moon, the archaeological museum, the outdoor Tiahuanaco Park, and the shopping area around the Basilica of San Francisco. This last is a good place to buy sweaters and other souvineers, and to change money on the black market. With inflation so high, the exchange rate per American dollar sometimes rose by *ten thousand* dollars daily! The situation was getting so extreme that some people were starting to panic, believing that the economy was about to collapse.

It was on this crazy note that my companions, Bob, Mark and Steve, planned to fly back to Lima and Miami. For our last night of South American adventure together, we headed to the top of the Sheraton Hotel, which sports the most expensive restaurant in town. The view of the city from the top is excellent, well worth a nighttime visit even if your aren't hungry. But our group was quite hungry, stuffing ourselves on a feast complete with Bolivian wine (Bolivia is not really known for it's wine). After dinner came the proverbial bad news, amounting to well over a million dollars! Quite up to the task, we all pulled out wads of money, huge stacks which ultimately amounted to only a few American dollars. Imagine the scene:

"That will be one million, two hundred and sixty thousand Bolivian dollars, sir," says our waiter, a friendly young man in a tuxedo. We hand him a stack of bills three feet high. He diligently counts the hoard, taking almost twenty minutes to do so. With a deep sigh, he announces we are fifty-thousand dollars short. I dig into my pocket, pull out another wad, and hand him sixty-thousand with a flourish, ten-thousand as an added tip. Waiters have to be trained as accountants in Bolivia.

That night I took my three companions to the airport. They were booked on a late AeroPeru flight to Lima, and we arrived only about an hour before departure. The airport was a mad house! It was full of all kinds of people: Bolivians, foreign businessmen, and tourists, all trying to escape the economic madness which had taken over.

We discovered that all the flights were double booked, and that my friends had been bumped. "Are you crazy?" raged Bob, "We just reconfirmed yesterday!"

"I'm sorry, sir," replied the receptionist curtly, from behind the protection of her counter, "but you are fifteen minutes late checking in. Others have taken your place."

I moved quickly past Bob, who was going into shock. "May I speak to the manager, miss?" I asked politely.

"I'm sorry, he's busy," she said. Just then, a tall, dark man in a uniform came out of an office behind her.

"Excuse me, sir, but are you the manager?" I asked him, as the receptionist grimaced and cast me a dirty look. I guessed that she had probably taken a bribe to bump my friends off their plane, probably to let an escaping businessman and his family out of the country.

"Yes, I am. What can I do for you?" he asked me.

Bob came up close, along with the others. "My friends here just reconfirmed their reservations yesterday, and now you tell us that they have no seats! They really must get back to the United States. Surely, there has been some mistake?" I said with my most sincere face, looking him straight in the eyes. I was the calmest of the group, since I wasn't planning to leave yet.

"Let me see your tickets," he said. Examining them, then checking a list behind the counter, he concluded, "Yes, there seems to have been some mistake. There are seats for you."

"Thank God!" crid Bob, as he received his boarding pass from the now rather sullen receptionist.

"Thank you, miss!" we all sang in unison, and headed for the boarding gate. This would be the last time that we would all be together, so we all shook hands vigorously and embraced, then I waved to them as they disappeared around a corner. Their flight was already boarding.

I was left standing by myself at the airport, suddenly feeling very alone. I took a taxi back into the city and my hotel. Once again, on my own, a vagabond drifting from country to country, in search of romance, adventure, and lost cities on the physical and mental plane.

Corny as it may sound, I'd always found it pretty exciting. But at that moment, alone in the Bolivian taxicab, I wasn't too thrilled. Instead, I felt a little depressed, and more than a little lonely. The hotel was even worse, so I decided to go out on the town, and ended up walking the main street along Avenida de 16 Julio, looking for a night spot. I had a Pilsner Centenario beer in one of the beer cellars along the street, then found myself in a rather run-down discoteque called "The Pink Panther." Another beer there didn't make me feel any better, so I hit the streets again, walking back up the steep road through the center of La Paz.

By this time, the streets were nearly empty. The skyscrapers were tall and cold, and the old stone buildings crowded next to them did not seem any warmer. Why should I feel depressed? Sure, I had parted ways with my friends, and I was now alone in a foriegn country where I knew no one. Nobody, not one person in all of South America! Suddenly, this thought cheered me. That I didn't know where I was going, who I would meet, and what adventures I was going to have along the way was exciting and exhilarating!

Now alone, I could hitchhike again, just as I had done years before on my journeys in Africa and Asia. Never immune to cliché, I would throw my destiny to the wind, and take each moment as it came, living life like I had in my crazy youth, and enjoying every single minute! A sudden chill ran up my spine with the thought of adventures to come. The entire continent of South America now lay before me, and I had only scratched the surface!

Hitchhiking follows no fixed itinerary; it is vagabonding with whatever form of transportation presents itself. It is both an art and a science, a meditation and a form of expression. Hitchhiking is not being in a hurry, taking time to reflect on your life and to court your own destiny. There is nothing like standing at a crossroads in the desert, a range of majestic mountains in the distance and your bag at your feet, watching a lonely truck approach, streaming a cloud of dust behind it. Your heartbeat quickens, your mind races, and you ask yourself, "Who are they? Where are they going? Will they stop?"

163

But hitchhiking is also walking the fine line between fate and free will. As another hithchiker said to me while we were waiting for a ride in the wilds of Sudan many years ago, "By using mental attraction, we create our own rides. We should think of the kind of ride we want, and attract it into our environment."

Pumped up by this sudden motivation, I headed back to my hotel. On the way I gazed up, this time looking beyond the cold skyscrapers and silent stone buildings, at the stars that twinkled high above. They shone with extraordinary brilliance and clarity. I smiled broadly, thanking them for lighting my path, both spiritually and physically. It was good to be alive. Sometimes I just needed to remind myself of that.

§§§

Like an omen blessing this next phase of my South American adventure, the sun shone brightly through my windows as I woke. I packed up and checked out of the hotel, not exactly sure where I was going, but eager to hit the road. I went to the train station, and with a sudden inspiration to head south through Bolivia towards Chile, bought a train ticket to Oruro, about a hundred and fifty miles south of La Paz. This was the only train which headed the direction I had chosen. From Oruro, I could get other trains toward Chile, but the ticket agent warned me it would not be easy. I didn't care, I was in no big hurry, I was free!

I got a visa for Brazil, the only country in South America for which one is required. In the back of my mind, I was hoping to get to Rio de Janeiro in time for the famous Carnival, a month or so away. Armed with my visa, I got back to the train station just as the train was boarding, jumping on with an eager smile of anticipation.

Hauling my pack down the aisle of one of the carriages, I moved slowly down the crowded isles. Around me were hundreds of Aymara Indians, contrasting nicely in their colorful wool clothes and plain vinyl luggage. The women all wore a traditional English-style wool bowler hat, with their long black braids hanging down on either side. They circulated throughout the train, chattering among themselves, but still keping keeping their eyes on the many young children that ran up and down the aisles.

I took my seat by the window, next to a handsome young Aymara woman. She had long black hair, tied in a pony tail and flung over one shoulder, but minus the ever-present bowler hat. She was in her early twenties, I supposed, and very pretty, with fine straight features, reddish-brown skin, and a pronounced, straight nose. She wrapped herself in a rainbow colored pancho, and wore a black wool skirt beneath it. In her arms was a small girl, about three, wearing a new, blue cotton dress, probably just purchased in La Paz.

The woman smiled at me as we pulled out of the station, and we talked in Spanish for some time. She laughed easily, and was very outgoing, asking me many questions about my trip. I gathered that she was married, but separated from her husband. She was traveling to Oruro with her parents, who were sitting in front of us. Hearing his name, her father turned around and smiled at us. He was a very large man, with a dark complexion, and I got the immediate impression that he had worked many hard years outdoors. His greased-back hair was turning grey, giving him an old appearance, though age can be deceptive in the Andes. His eyes bore the bloodshot marks of a lifetime of chewing coca leaves and drinking the the local spirits.

The woman and I talked off and on throughout the trip, though I never learned her name. In the west was a terrific sunset, which we watched together for some time; it was a deep orange line against the mountains in the distance, on the edge of the plain. Dark clouds hung above the fiery peaks, creating a scene that seemed painted and unreal.

I suddenly turned to the woman and looked her in the eyes. She smiled at me, and drew close. "You are very beautiful," I said in Spanish. It was true, but I don't know what suddenly inspired me to say it. Perhaps it was the sunset.

"Thank you," she whispered, fingering the blonde hair around my ears. I wanted to kiss her, but that is not something that one does in public in South America. Especially with strangers.

The train arrived in Oruro after nine, and it seemed my short affair with the beautiful Aymara woman was over before it began. As we all stepped out onto the platform, I asked the family where the hotels were, half hoping that they would invite me to stay with them. The invitation did not come; instead, they politely pointed the way to the main street.

Oruro is a small city, a tin mining center in a rather bleak spot just north of Lake Poopo. All of the hotels are located around the train station, including the Hotel Prefectural Alojamiento Provenir, the Residencial's Pagador, the Ayacucho and the Scala. But I had a difficult time finding a hotel, as each one I checked was full. I started to become suspicious after the fifth hotel—did they not want foriegn tourists? This has happened before.

Then I met a young Bolivian couple from La Paz who had been on the same train, and who were having the same problem. We went around to a few hotels together, and finally found a spare room in a hotel. Where else? Just opposite the station! The husband and I each got a bed in the men's dormitory, while his wife took the room.

Now half starving, I went out to walk around the street market. The small food stalls sold hot dogs, hamburgers, and other fried food. Looking at the unsanitary condition of the these little carts, and imagining what mysteries might be discovered in the meat these old ladies were serving up, I decided not to explore their sandwiches. Buying a candy bar instead, I dropped into a café for a beer before turning in.

This little café was just a small room, though it did have a pool table in the back, which was surprising. They had no beer, only the distilled wine known as Singani from which the national Bolivian cocktail *chufly* is made. I ordered one, sat at one of the four tables, and looked around. There were about a dozen Indians in the bar, all of them dead drunk, a few even slumped over on their tables, unconcious. I had read that it was a miserable existance in the tin and silver mines of Bolivia, and that the miners work hard all day in the suffocating air of the deep mines, then burn their guts out with fire water at night.

The next morning, I tried to get a train over the pass to Antofagasto in Chile. I found that there was only one passenger train each week, and that this was not due for five days. Well, I didn't want to wait for five days in Oruro, so I tried to get a ticket to Uyuni, a small town that is the railway junction to northern Argentina and the Atacama desert.

The conductor I talked to told me the train to Uyuni was not going to leave until nine that night. I wanted to buy a ticket then, but he said I would have to buy it later. So I wandered out into the street, to kill the day. This town had certainly not been spoiled by tourists; I rather doubted that many travelers spent more than a night here.

I planned to by-pass Potosi, once the richest city in the Americas because of its vast silver mines. The town was founded by the Spanish in 1545, and still retains much of its colonial charm. Today largely a ghost town, the Indians who still work in the mines are desperately poor. The town is even higher than La Paz and bitterly cold at night, the winds of the high altiplano sweeping in from the mountains. The only interesting activity in Potosi is a tour of the Pailaviri Mines, which have produced billions of dollars worth of silver over the years. The tin from the mine is still the basis for Bolivia's legitamate econony, though the real economy is probably tied up in cocaine.

These mines predate the Spanish, originating as either Inca or pre-Inca works. Since the Spanish takeover, over eight-million people have died working the mines, many of them imported Indian slaves.

The tale of Potosi is one of human bondage and greed, in which the wealthy Spanish royalty made fantastic fortunes at the expense of the local population. Today, the lot of the miner has not improved a great deal, though miners earn a good wage by Bolivian standards. The life expectancy of a typical Bolivian miner is about 37 years, largely due to the miner's disease silicosis, or tuberculosis.

I asked a young man on the street for directions to the bus station, as I still had thoughts of trying to leave town sooner. The man, a youthful college student of twenty-four named Erasmus, said he would take me there, rather than just pointing the way.

As Erasmus and walked down the street, he told me that he was from Potosi, going to school here, studying to be an engineer. He was a nice kid, clean cut and friendly, though he did not speak any English. It just so happened that he was leaving this evening for Potosi by bus, and also had much of the day to kill. At the bus station, we checked to see if there were any buses to Uyuni or the Chilean border, but that was another disappointment. The train was the only way out of this town.

Erasmus bought me some coca tea and bread at a small cafeteria at the station, then we both walked downtown. I bought him an ice cream cone as we walked around the main square, and he said he would like to show me his house.

His was a small room in a rather run-down courtyard villa. I picked my way upstairs to his room, past the chickens and a sleeping dog, onto a landing built into the adobe walls of this two story house. Rather tired, I rested on his bed while he made us each a cup of tea downstairs in the villa kitchen.

Looking up from the bed in the cool room, I noticed that he had some posters on the mud walls, pictures of Spanish singer Julio Iglesias, a tiger, a parade of heavily-armed military vehicles, and Michael Jackson. Commenting on this interesting selection when Erasmus came back, he said that these four posters represented life in South America: glitter, the military, and the wild. He was a devout Catholic, and handed me his well-worn Bible to look at. I flipped through it momentarily, then asked him what his thoughts were on two of the mysteries I had run into, the tunnels and the ancient ruins. Suprisingly, he regaled me with his personal versions, seemingly oblivious of the contradictions inherent between Church doctrine and many-thousand year old civilizations.

Thanking Erasmus for his hospitality, I took a taxi out to the Oruro Archaeological Museum, which had a small collection of wild Carnival masks (far-out!), mummies (dead and shriveled), and trepanned skulls (bizarre!). Trepanning is the process used to make peoples skulls appear long and thin, like those of the mummies in turbans at the Nazca Museum. In this process, pressure is applied to the back of a child's head from birth, in order to shape the bones of the skull while they are still soft. The pressure was usually applied by laying the child in a cradle with a long, flat extension at the top, to which his head was bound tightly with cloth wrappings. Skulls that have been trepanned look quite strange, with the back of the head elongated, looking almost alien. In South America, this custom probably originated to deliniate the royalty from common folk, kings and their family having the long, misshapen skulls. Trepanning was aparently quite popular among certain cultures, though not the Incas. The custom seems to have a pre-Incan origin.

Interestingly, I went to high school near Flathead Lake in Montana. The area named for the Flathead Indians, who also had a tradition of putting babies on a flat board so that their heads would be elongated. This is similar to the trepanning process, though without the bindings. Flathead Indians ranged from Montana up into Canada, still living today around Flathead Lake. It is interesting that this rather singular custom should appear in two widely-separate areas.

My final stop was the zoo, which had in its collection a number of interesting animals, including condors, monkeys, and coati-mundis. The zoo itself was rather tacky and run-down, reminding me of a zoo in Khartoum, in the Sudan. That zoo had the same run-down look, and went so far in its tackiness as to have a dog on display!

Having exhausted the limited possibilities of this town, I headed back to the train station. This time, the ticket seller told me to come back at 4:30 for a train to Uyuni departing at 6:30. But the first conductor had told me that the train was at nine!

Deciding to stay close to the station, I had lunch at a café nearby, then saw a movie at the local cinema, a terrible Italian fantasy called *Sinbad and the Caliph*. Fortunately, I am a Sinbad fan, so my tolerance was high. It rained heavily during the movie, so that the whole dusty town seemed a bit cleaner and fresher when I came out. Feeling lucky, I tried the station again.

This time I was informed that the train would be departing shortly, but that there were no more seats. With a smile, the ticket agent invited me to enjoy the town's hospitality until the next train came–in three days!

I may have thrown my destiny to the wind, but the wind in this town was not for me. I bought a second-class ticket without a reservation. When the train arrived, I took a seat, but was soon kicked out by the passengers with reservations.

I wanted to go to Uyuni, and didn't really care where I rode, so I asked a conductor where I could sit. Looking at my ticket, he told me matter-of-factly, "The baggage car."

The idea of riding in a baggage car rather was rather thrilling. I climbed into one that was empty; it was a little wet from the rain, but I relished the thought of standing there by the open door, watching the sunset, rumbling over the altiplano and past Lake Poopo.

But the thrill faded as more people piled into my damp sanctuary, and wanted to close the door against the cold. I got off, and started to look for a place with a window. As I walked down the platform, some sort of skuffle broke out in the second-class car. Using this as a distraction, I quickly entered the carriage and took an empty seat, only to be removed by the real occupant and his reserved ticket.

I was back on the platform again, the train was getting ready to leave, and it was getting dark. I thought momentarily about going back to the baggage car, and riding there in the dark. Instead, tried the dinning car, hoping to hang out there without a seat, but a waiter quickly kicked me out. Desperately, I walked up to first-class, on the chance that there would be an empty seat I could take and pay the conductor extra.

The Sun God must have been watching over me that day, because a Bolivian suddenly came up, trying to sell two first-class tickets to the Argentine border! I nearly cried out in joy, and offered to buy one from him, even though I was only going half way. Losing the subsequent bargaining session for lack of time, I settled into my two seats with both tickets as the train began to move. I had a great view, with reflections off the lake and small marshy pools of water. As the sunset faded off into the distance behind the Andes, I drifted off as well.

I dozed in my seat until we arrived at Uyuni. In a sleepy fog, I got off the train. It was now nearly two in the morning, and according to the station master there would be a train at four to the Chilean frontier. Shivering, I looked around for a place to sleep, but the first- and second-class waiting rooms were already packed with sleeping Indians with stacks of blankets and baskets of food. I finally found a bit of floor to stretch out on, pulling my sleeping bag over me, and dozing fitfully for several hours.

There was no train at four, but the station master said that it would leave at 8:30. At 8:30 he said it would leave at 10:30, and this later became 11:30. I was starting to get the idea that trains in Bolivia left and arrived at no particular fixed time. Worse, getting a straight answer from station agents seemed next to impossible.

Sometime during this perpetual wait, I met a young man from the

169

Canary Islands, a Spaniard named Francisco. Francisco was a tall, handsome man, just turned 30. He had light brown, curly hair, and his face was dusty, his lips chapped as if he had just walked here across the desert and mountains.

In fact, he was riding a motorcycle around South America, a small Yamaha 150 which he had bought duty-free in Venezuela. He had ridden it across Venezuela, and through Colombia, Ecuador, Peru and Bolivia to get here. He was on his way to Santiago, where he planned to sell the bike, then head back to the Canary Islands.

When the train finally did arrive, Francisco got his bike loaded, then climbed into the passenger car with me. This was a freight train, going to the top of the pass that is the frontier between Bolivia and Chile. It was nearly empty, with only a few other passengers besides Francisco and myself in the single passenger car. The rest of the train seemed to be empty box cars going to the top of the pass.

I asked Francisco why he didn't ride his bike to the top of the pass, as my map indicated that there was a road over the summit into Chile. "That road is very bad," he said. "In Uyuni, they told me not to try to ride it. Everyone said to take the train." I wanted to mention that he could get old waiting for the trains here, but I stayed silent. Instead, I welcomed his company and conversation as we wound our way along the salt flats of the Salar de Uyuni. This is a huge salt pan that covers an area of one hundred square miles. It occured to me that it might have been created by evaporating sea water, trapped in a basin at the altiplano by the rising continent.

I dozed for some time, and then woke up at Chiguna where we waited for a new engine to take us the twenty miles to the border. This was one of the most desolate places I had ever been, high and windy in a weird alpine salt desert. Snow capped volcanoes, some smoking like a recently-fired gun, dotted the bleak brown landscape. Adding to the bleak effect were a collection desparate, grey buildings, abandoned railway cars, and a few strange beehive-like buildings that were painted in camoflage. No one else but the military would live here!

Relations between Bolivia and Chile have been poor ever since the War of the Pacific fought between Peru, Chile and Bolivia from 1879 to 1883. Bolivia supposedly started the affair by threatening an embargo on the guano factories worked by Chileans in Bolivian Antofagasta. The Chilean navy responded by siezing Antofagasta in Febuary 1879. Peru sided with Bolivia, and the fighting lasted for four angry years before the Chileans finally won. They annexed the Bolivian coastal provinces of Antofagasta and Tarapaca, as well as the Peruvian provinces of Tacna and Arica. Tacna was returned to Peru in

1929, but Bolivia had lost its only costal access, becoming a land-locked country. Sporadic negotiations with both Peru and Chile for a sea outlet have failed, keeping Bolivia bitter and poor. All this over guano: bird dung!

It was nine in the evening when our ghostly freight train finally limped into the cold and dark border station at the top of the pass. We certainly weren't going anywhere that night, so Francisco and I started to settle down for the night. I had just finished making a bed out of two seats, and fluffed up my down sleeping bag, when Francisco came in from outside, saying that the station master wanted us to sleep in the station.

We obliged, sleeping on the hard mud floor of a dark adobe brick building beside the tracks, Francisco's motorcycle by the door. The next morning, I shouldered my pack and started walking for Ollague, the small station on the Chilean side of the pass. On my right and left were volcanoes, tall cones of dirt and snow towering up to twenty-thousand feet.

The quiet of this high-altitude desolation was abruptly shattered by a loud roar from back along the tracks. Francisco rode up on his motorcycle, and I climbed on for the short ride to the border. At Chilean customs, I filled out a form, and was cheerily greeted by the customs officer, who I gathered did not have a great number of tourists come through his lonely post. Francisco had some problems with the gentleman, however, not having the proper stamp on his motorcycle documentation. Here we were, the first tourists this guy has seen in years, and he's worried about a stamp. Not wanting to interfere in what was developing into an international incident of major proportions, I walked over to the Interpol office across the tracks, where a policeman acting as Immigration officially stamped me into Chile.

Waiting for Francisco, I inquired about any trains to Calama, the next major town down the mountains and into the Atacama desert. According to the officer, there weren't any trains or buses for about five days! How was I going to get out of here, I asked?

He looked up and down the dry, windswept pass, and shrugged his shoulders. "I don't know," he said in Spanish, "try walking."

Well, it was about one-hundred and fifty miles to Calama, through the driest desert in the world. Maybe I could pay Francisco to take me to Calama on the back of his motorcycle? He was still negotiating a multilateral motorcycle importation treaty, but took a moment out to apologize that it was out of the question to get a lift with him to Calama. The road was bad, and his bike could never take the extra weight over such a long ride.

171

Wondering what I was going to do, I walked back to the Interpol office. As I began to steel myself to the thought of hitchhiking, I wondered what my friend back in the Sudan would have had to say about creating a ride in this place!

Suddenly, the policeman came running out of the station, pointing and yelling in Spanish, "There, there, that train is going to Calama!" A hundred yards down the tracks in the direction he was pointing was another freight train, just pulling out of the station! Running up alongside it, determined to jump on as the train built up speed, I searched for a handgrip or foothold. My pack was growing heavy on my back, and the train was picking up speed. I had to jump this train, and it had to be then!

I caught up to a boxcar which had its door jammed partly open. Taking a deep breath, I slung one arm out of my pack, unhooked the belt strap and tossed it in. The train continued to accelerate as I took a mighty leap and flung myself headfirst into the car. But I only made it halfway in, my legs dangling down under the car near the wheels.

"I've got to make it!" I cried out loud, and struggled to get a knee up inside the car without pushing the other leg furhter under the car. Finally succeeding, I pulled myself in, and lay panting on the floor.

Gazing out at the desert rolling quickly past, I sighed with a combination of relief and pleasure. Relief that I didn't have to stay in Ollague after all; pleasure in successfully hopping this train across the Andes and down into the Atacama desert. This sure beat five days on the pass!

The area I was passing through was reputed to contain one of the entrances to the vast tunnel system through the Andes. Much has been written about these tunnels, some of which is believable, some of which is not. Since much of the exploration of the tunnel fragments which have been found was done as much as four-hundred years ago, it is often difficult to tell the fact from the fancy.

Between 1848 and 1850, a Russian-American woman traveled in Peru, named Madame Helena Petrovna Blavatskaya, founder of the modern "Theosophical Society." She had heard the rumours of the mysterious tunnel network, and reportedly met the Italian hypnotist who had extracted the secrets from the priest (see the story in a previous chapter).

The Italian said he had since visited what he believed to be one of the tunnel system's entrances. Madame Blavatskaya joined him on a journey south from Lima toward Arica. She wrote, "We reached Arica near sunset, and at a certain point on the lonely coast we were struck by the appearance of an enormous rock, nearly perpendicular, which stood in mournful solitude on that shore, and apart from the cordillera of the Andes. As the last rays of the setting sun strike the face of the rock, one can make out, with an ordinary opera-glass, curious hieroglyphics inscribed on the volcanic surface."

According to Madame Blavatskaya, there were also certain mystic signs at the Sun Temple in Cuzco. It was only by interpreting these signs, invisible except when the sun's rays struck them at a certain angle at a certain hour of the day, that one might learn the secret of the tunnels and how and where they might be entered. This is the stuff movies are made of!

According to Blavatskaya, one tunnel segment is intersected at a certain point by a royal tomb. This tomb is supposedly equiped with a number of booby traps, making entry difficult even for Indiana Jones. The ancient engineers of these tunnels and tomb had cunningly arranged doors consisting of two enormous slabs of carved stone, pivoted to turn and close so tightly that one can see not the faintest sign of crack or joint. Supposedly, reading secret signs is also required to discover the key to entering the tomb.

According to Harold Wilkins, a branch of the tunnel leads then to Lima, and the other branch leads further south to the Atacama. The southward tunnel passes beneath the towns of Tarapaca and Cobijo. The story gets hazy here, as Wilkins seems to be quoting from Madame Blavatskaya on this point. Tarapaca does indeed exist in the Atacama desert, while Cobijo is known today as Gatico, located south of Tocopilla. This bit of information is rather confusing, as Gatico is on the coast, while most tunnel reports indicate that they stayed inland. Perhaps a tunnel opening is located near Gatico. I should say that most information coming from Madame Blavatskaya, a strange person to say the least, is suspect, and should be taken with a rather large grain of salt.

The southern extreme of this tunnel ends, according to Wilkins and Blavatskaya, in the "mysterious salt desert of Atacama, a thirst-striken waste of llanos and alkaline deserts, out of which flow only scanty runlets of brackish water." Looking around from my perch on the train, I could see why Wilkins described it that way. The Atacama is the driest desert in the world, according to the Guiness Book of Records, with less than half an inch of rainfall a year on the average. Calama, my destination for the night, has had absolutely no rainfall in recorded history!

The secret to the entrance of the tunnels appears to lie in the decipherment of the hieroglyphs cut into the enormous rock on the shore near Arica, called the "Tomb of the Incas." The actual entrance, according to Blavatskaya, is near one of three peaks, a landmark triangle close to the Rio de Loa.

Blavatskaya and her companions traveled northward to Ylo (Ilo) in the vicinity of the three peaks. At this point, information from both Wilkins and Blavatskaya gets shaky. Blavatskaya names the river Payquina as the boundary between Peru and Bolivia at the time, yet there is no record of there ever having been such a river. According to Wilkins, a hill named Payquina is located just inland from Ylo. There is also a question of just where this enormous rock with the carved hieroglyphs is located. Wilkins and Blavatskaya both locate it near Arica, yet on his map of the tunnels, Wilkins puts it at Ylo. Certainly, there are three peaks inland from Ylo.

Wilkins seemed to think a great deal of Madame Blavatskaya, and was probably himself a Theosophist. It would appear that he has gone to quite a bit of trouble to try and cover for Blavatskaya's inconsistancies. These conflicts in the story could have any number of explainations: perhaps she could not remember the details; was deliberately trying to confuse further explorers; or was just making the whole thing up. Yet, the story of the tunnel system originated hundreds of years before she was born.

According to Blavatskaya, an old Quechua Indian told her that the only practical entrance to the tunnels is cut into one of the three peaks. Located on the borders of the Peruvian provinces of Tacna and Moquegua, each measures about nineteen-thousand feet. They cover a lot of area, and a secret door into a tunnel system would certainly be difficult to find.

The Quechua supposedly told her, "A thousand soldiers, were they in that tunnel, would be forevermore one with the dead, did they attempt to force their way into the treasure-tomb of the dead Inca. There is no other access to the Arica chamber, but through that hidden door in the mountains near the Rio Payquina, Arica. Along the entire length of the immense corridor, from Bolivia to Lima and royal Cuzco, are smaller hiding places filled with treasures of gold and gems and jewels, that are the accumulations of many generations of Incas. The aggregate value of the treasures is beyond the power of man to estimate."

Said Madame Blavatskaya herself, "We had in our possession an accurate plan of the tunnel, the sepulchre, the great treasure chamber and the hidden, pivoted rock-doors. It was given to us by the old Peruvian; but if we had ever thought of profiting by the secret it would have required the co-operation of the Peruvian and Bolivian Governments on an extensive scale. To say nothing of physical obstacles, no one individual or small party could undertake such an exploration without encountering the army of brigands and smugglers with which the coast is infested, and which in fact, includes nearly the entire population. The mere task of purifying the mephitic air of the tunnel not entered for centuries would also be a serious one. There the treasure lies, and tradition says it will lie till the last vestige of Spanish rule disappears from the whole of North and South America."[22]

This map which Madame Blavatskaya spoke of is said to be now in the Theosophical archives in Adyar, India, though no one that I know of has ever seen it. Wilkins drew his map from other independant and "secret" sources.

§§§

The train stopped in the middle of the mountainous desert, so I jumped out of my private boxcar. A conductor spotted me and strutted over.

"What are you doing on this train?" he asked me officiously in Spanish. A small man in a dark blue conductor's uniform, he was acting very important, but I got the impression it was just that: an act.

"I'm on my way to Calama," I answered him politely, also in Spanish. "I hope this train is going there."

"Who said you could ride on this train?" he fired back sternly.

"The policman at Ollague told me to jump on this train," I replied.

"He has no authority," said the conductor, taking off his cap and wiping his forehead. "Do you know what kind of trouble we would be in if our superiors found out you were riding our train?" He then proceeded to give me a lecture in Spanish about insurance, risks, responsibility, permission and red tape. I knew I wasn't in Bolivia anymore; they would never have worried about such things. Of course, they never knew if and when their trains were actually running, either. I listened politely, nodding my head as the conductor made each point.

In the end, I made my excuse, a good, all-purpose excuse for the traveler in a foreign country who has done something wrong. "Sorry, I didn't know. What should I do now?"

Softening in the face of my admission, he said, "Grab your pack, you can ride in the caboose with me." How could I refuse?

After some time of slowly winding down out of the Andes into the desert, we stopped. This time, the same conductor invited me to ride up front with him in the engine.

Having gone through the responsibility and red tape lecture, we could now get to know each other. He was a friendly man, with a small black mustache and eager smile, named Daniel. His mechanic was Luciano, a part-Indian with long, straight black hair and a sharp nose. They were very pleased to have me riding with them in their engine, and showed me every little nuance of the workings of a diesel-electric locomotive. This one was made by General Electric in Chicago.

I soon gathered that they didn't get too many hitchhikers hopping their trains through the desert. None in fact. They must have saved all of their important issues to discuss with me, the American hitchhiker-explorer; because we were soon deep into a serious one: Yogi Bear! Daniel did a great imitation of Yogi; "Hey, Booboo!" We all laughed, passing the time until sunset. As we passed the world's largest open pit copper mine, Chuquicamata, its poles and long strings of lights set against the stars gave it the stark appearance of a lunar outpost from a science-fiction movie.

Yogi Bear?

Since my new friends were not supposed to have allowed me on the train, they had to let me off just outside the Calama station. They slowed down to a fast walking pace, enabling me to leap down to the rocky railbed. Fighting to keep my balance, I was soon standing and waving to my hosts in the glare of the first station lights.

Gathering myself together after the jump and dusting off my hat, I shouldered my pack, looked around, then took a deep breath and started into town. Almost immediately, I started wondering what had happened to Francisco. If I read in the papers that another guano war had started on the desolate border of Chile and Bolivia, with Francisco's native Canary Islanders chipping in what little bit they could, I would rest in the assurance that I knew the inside story.

Chapter Eight

Hitchhiking in Chile:
Frozen Mummies and Earthquakes

There are tracks of strange beasts,
huge and unrecognised
in the beaches of these lakes behind unknown forests...
-*Colonel Fawcett lecturing before the
Royal Geographic Society, 1911*

No sooner I had I reached a main street, than a young man approached, asking me in English if I was looking for a hotel. Standing there with my blond hair, dusty jeans and backpack, it was not a particularly difficult assumption to make.

"Sure," I said, looking him over. A young kid with curly black hair, about seventeen, he looked quite friendly. "Which is the best bet?"

"Most foriegners stay at the Calama Hostel, over on that street," he replied. We headed for the hostel, and on the way introduced ourselves. His name was José.

At the Calama Hostel, a surprisingly new building, José waited while I went inside. Two young auburn-haired women, possibly French, were sitting by the door. I tipped the edge of of my fedora and greeted them, "Buenos Noches."

The women said nothing, but drew away slightly, giving me a strange look. I realized then that I must have been a pretty odd sight, just in from the desert, covered with dust, unshaven, and carrying a large pack. Their eyes grew wide, and neither dared to speak. It was time to move on.

The hostel was better than most, but it cost a bit more than the new vagabond within me wanted to spend. Back outside, I told José that I wanted to find a less expensive place.

"The cheap residentials are down here," he grinned, emphasizing the word, "cheap." I checked into the Residential Splendid, one of a half-dozen to be found around the center of town. After washing the dust off my face, José and I went out on the town.

I had developed a powerful thirst on that train ride over the Andes, so we stopped at the first sign for *chop*, the Chilean version of draught beer. Over a schooner of beer and a pizza, we talked in Spanish. José's favorite topic turned out to be trains—he had been hanging out at the station that night, just before we met. We spent a good half-hour discussing the relative merits of General Electric diesels—he was quite impressed with my apparent depth of knowledge. I couldn't bear to tell him that I had just learned it all that day! Which reminded me of something important:

"José, are you by any chance a Yogi Bear fan? You know, 'Hey, Booboo!' " I could tell from the look on his face that this was not something all Chilean train men had in common. Soon it got late and José left, thanking me for the food, but still giving me a funny look.

The next day, I took an early morning bus to San Pedro de Atacama, a small oasis sixty miles southwest of Calama in the dry Andean foothills. A Belgian Jesuit priest had worked with and studied for the Atacameno Indians here for many years, eventually founding a small archaeological museum, which is now internationally famous. This area of Chile is rather dry and deslolate, with its only water source being streams of Andes snow melt. But this desolation is in marked contrast to its richness in archaeological sites and lost cities.

At Pintados, near Iquique, are found large drawings on the mountains of condors, llamas and huacanos (an animal similar to a llama), much like those found on the Nazca plain. Indeed, all along the dry coast of Chile and Peru, vestiges of great drawings and lines can be seen on the hills. What great culture lived here in pre-history, marking up the desert like a sand box?

One clue might be the many "Tiahuancao type" artifacts found at the Jesuit priest's museum. Whoever those Tiahuanaco people were, they seemed to have at least influenced, if not controlled this area. Were these people part of Bob's Atlantean League? How wide spread was travel and communication in the Ancient Americas, and across the oceans to Asia, Europe and Africa?

The Molle Indians of the Atacama desert used a ceramic "plug-beard," an artificial, ritual beard, as a symbol of authority. The ancient Egyptians used exactly the same sort of fake beard to denote authority. The pharoah and his court are often depicted with the stylistic beards in artwork. The Molle Indians went so far as to insert the ceramic beard through a hole cut into their jawbone!

There is evidence that the Huentelaguen Indians of the Northern Coast of Chile also lived in Southern California, as judged by the similar, distinctive tools found in both places. How could two cultures exist in such widely separate area? The Humbolt current goes right up the South American coast to North America, but this would imply the Huentelaguen Indians had seafaring skills that they were not supposed to have. Maybe nobody told them they didn't know how to sail!

How old are these ancient cultures of the Atacama? The answer is surprising, and it may give us an idea as to the age of Tiahuanaco. In November 1983, a treasure trove of extremely well-preserved, mummified human remains were discovered in Arica by a water company, while exavating a forty meter sandstone mound near the city. A total of ninety-six mummies were eventually uncovered by a team of archaeologists, who said they were so well preserved because of the dry climate.

The team, headed by American pathologist Dr. Marvin Allison, carbon dated the mummies, finding them to be approximately 8,000 years old! The occupant of Tomb 761 was dated as 7,810 years old, about 2,600 years older than the oldest Egyptian mummy! Allison believes these mummies to be the world's oldest.

Prior to this discovery, it was believed that the Chinchoro culture came into existance at about the time of the 16th-century Spanish conquest, which yields a difference between the two estimates of more than seven thousand years! This discrepancy has cast some doubt on the opinioins of the established experts on civilization in the Americas.

"I think we have found this society was a lot more complicated than originally believed," said Allison, in a newspaper interview at the University of Tarapaca in Arica, where he is on staff. "Their system of burial obivously required a well-developed social structure." Allison also contends that the accepted theory that Asian people migrated down the coast of North America across the then-existant land bridge cannot account for this culture, as they could not have moved fast enough to reach Chinchorro by the date of the earliest proven settlement here. "We don't know where they came from," he said.

Sivia Quevedo, an anthropologist at Chile's Museum of Natural Science, claims that these mysterious peoples' knowledge of anatomy "...was much superior to that exhibited by the mummies of Egypt." The ancient Egyptians disembowelled the bodies of their royalty, salt-dried them for up to 70 days, then wrapped them in linen bandages and buried them with their gold and jewelry. The early Chinchorros aparently possessed no such wealth, or they didn't bury it with their dead. They skinned their dead, removed major organs and muscles, fire-dried the corpse, and reinforced the bones with straw matting and carved wooden struts.

However, in the procedures which gained them Quevedo's respect, the ancient Chinchorro doctors pulled the skin back onto the skeleton like a glove, then covered the head with a clay mask and a wig made from the dead person's hair. Finally, they painted the corpse and erected it as a statue! Later mummies from the same cemetary found at Arica were not skinned, but were covered with a thin layer of cement, apparently to make a better statue.

The Chinchorros left no writings as clues to their origins, only their uniquely-preserved bodies. Because of a lack of research funds, more than 100 bodies were left inside the now-covered cemetary at the Arica mound, and other known burial sites remain untouched. "The desert is a better preserver of these mummies than any museum, so they will stay buried until future generations can take care of them," said Rene Lara Quiroz, a University of Tarapaca spokesman.

If, as some researchers have done, we infer that the age of Tiahuanaco is similar, it would make the gigantic city older than any city in Egypt, Sumeria or Babylon. This would also date it just after the sinking of Atlantis by Plato's report, and support the theory that the city was built by survivors. Atlantis or not, no matter where I went in South America, I couldn't shake the mystery of the ancient builders of these cities!

§§§

Also near San Pedro de Atacama is Toconao, where a branch of the legendary Camino del Inca, the Inca road system, can be found. The geysers at Tatio are also worth a visit. I wanted to hitchhike out that direction, but was told that there was virtually no traffic out there, and furthermore, that it was a dead end. I decided to hitch back toward Calama, then catch a ride to Antofagasta and the coast.

After buying a plastic bottle of mineral water at the local store, I started walking out of town, hoping to get a lift the sixty miles back to Calama. It was several hours, half my bottle of water, and nearly ten miles later when a truck finally stopped. And what a truck! A huge

180

semi-tractor dragging an even bigger trailer loaded with a steamroller.

I flung my pack up onto the trailer, then climbed into the seat of the steam roller. The truck started up again and we were off, roaring mightily through the desert. My hands gripped the steering wheel as the barren hills rolled past, the hot wind in my face, my hair streaming behind. It was great! I felt exhilarated, and as the heat started to get to me, I imagined myself as Captain Childress, Lost Airman of the Atlantean League, piloting my steamroller-airship down to an emergency landing at Nazca. Too much of Bob's alternate history!

At the crossroads at Calama, the truck let me off, a bit sunburned on the forehead and a little dizzy from a crash landing at Nazca. After taking a good drink from my water bottle, I started walking toward the coast. Only half an hour later I got a ride with two young guys in a mini-van half way to Calama, letting me off in a small town called Salinas. I ate a quick sandwich washed down with a beer in a small café, and then hit the road again. Mid-afternoon had arrived, meaning I would have to get a ride soon if I was to get to Antofagasta before dark.

I had not walked far down the road when three more young guys in a club-cab pickup stopped. With their hair greased back, they looked like a cross between sixty's greasers and eighty's New Wavers. But they took me right into Antofagasta and dropped me at the center of this major Northern Chile port.

I got a room for about a dollar fifty a night at the Residential Familair. There are other inexpensive Residentials in Antofagasta, all around the center of town, especially on Calle Baquedano. These include the Residencials Colon, Plaza, Splendid-Gran, Paola, O'Higgins, Riojanita, and the Hotel Chile-Espana.

Quite tired by this time, I was probably suffering from heat exhaustion from walking the desert all day and flying my steamroller-airship from the back of that trailer. Despite all this, I did manage to get out for a walk in the plaza in the center of town. Antofagasta was a small, sun-bleached town, reminding me a great deal of similar costal towns in Sicily, Spain or Greece. The main street here was closed off to traffic, which created a pedestrian mall with shops and sidewalk cafés. After a light dinner, washed down with plenty of water, I slept well.

The next morning, after changing some money at a bank, I took a bus out of town to the Pan American Highway to start hitching. The bus deposited me just past a police roadblock, which was stopping the cars leaving town. Several cars approached, stopping first at the roadblock. I would wave my arm widely at them first, gesturing down the road and then at my feet. Simply holding out your thumb out and waiting by the road doesn't really cut it in South America. I had developed the method of using my whole body many years before in Africa and Asia, and I found that it worked in South America as well.

I got a lift almost right away, with a man in a dump truck who was going sixty miles down the road to a gravel pit. He let me off at a junction, and I found myself walking down a two lane highway in the desert, without a car, house or person in sight. I stopped and took a drink from my full canteen; I had prudently left Antofagasta with food and water. Sitting on my pack, I looked around at the brown hills in the distance to the east, and at the dry, barren earth all around me. Who could live out here, I had to wonder?

I was just getting up to start walking down the road again, when a white Ford appeared in the distance, slowly coming closer. I took off my hat and wiped my brow against the blasting heat, then began waving my arm and hat wildly, motioning for the car to stop. To my great relief, it slowed, allowing me to jump into the back seat as it passed. Surprisingly, I found myself riding through the desert with three Franciscan priests. One was a Belgian, in his forties and obviously the superior of the other two younger priests, both Chilean.

We rode together for some time, conversing in both Spanish and English. I asked them if they had ever heard of the tunnel system, as it was rumoured that the end of one branch was located somewhere here in the Atacama. The Belgian priest found the idea ridiculous, replying, "Of course not, these things do not exist."

More quietly then, one of the younger Chilean priests said tersely, "I have heard of the Socoban del Inca. There is an entrance here in the desert. Perhaps near San Pedro de Atacama."

The Belgian priest was shocked. But I questioned the Chilean brother further: where had he heard of these tunnels, had he seen them himself? He would not say more, or even tell me where he had gotten his information. This may have been because of his Belgian superior, who so obviously took a dim view of our subject. Perhaps he thought it superstitious and "un-Catholic."

The three priests finally let me off at dusk at the port town of Caldera, after covering about half the distance between Antofagasta and Santiago. At a nearby fruit inspection checkpoint, a bus driver said he would give me a special price to Santiago. Looking forward to a comfortable ride in the half-empty Mercedes coach, I accepted.

Shortly thereafter, we had a long stop at a restaurant for dinner. Inside was a Chilean cowboy with a Texas accent. Discovering that I spoke English, he invited me to sit with him and drink Chilean wine .

He had recently retired from an American firm that had been exploring for oil in the Chilean desert. Lamenting that he didn't attract the young women anymore (he was 65), he finished off another glass of wine and looked longingly at the young, well-proportioned waitress. "She don't like me," he mourned. "I got money, but she don't care! She like the young men, like you!" We were speaking English, but the waitress shot me a glance anyway. I smiled nervously.

"I got money, but I'm old," he repeated. He must have finished off quite a few glasses of that wine to work himself into this mood. "The girls, they don't like me!" I felt sorry for this old, retired roustabout with nothing to do. I didn't know what to tell him, so I kept him company for awhile, drinking his wine.

Soon, the bus was getting ready to go. I got up to leave, and thanked him for the wine and stimulating conversation. "Please, don't go," he pleaded. "Stay and we drink wine! Don't go, I'm an old man!" He was pitiful. Fortunately, the honking bus gave me a great excuse to leave.

"Sorry," I said, "but I have to go with the bus. Good luck!" And I was off into the night, back on the bus, heading down the dark, lonely road south.

On arrival the next morning in Santiago, I met another passenger on the bus, Alex, an Argentine on his way from Peru back to Buenos Aires. He was fun, friendly, and pudgy. WIth his long black hair, held back by a band of beads, he looked like a small, chubby Argentine hippy from the sixties, somehow held in suspended animation until the eighties.

Alex took me to the Youth Hostel in Santiago, a well-located place, with a few large rooms upstairs where hostelers slept in their sleeping bags on mattresses on the floor. Plenty of inexpensive hotels can be found around the railway station, with names like the Continental, Florida, Mundial, Caribe, and Valparaiso. Most single travelers seem to stay at the Youth Hostel.

With over four million people, Santiago is the fourth largest city in South America. Still, it is a very attractive city which I liked more than any of the other major cities I had visited on this continent. It has a subway system, a good shopping area downtown, and many fine restaurants. Unique mountain-parks in the center of the city provide excellent views, and one has a funicular railway to the top. The Las Condes suburb to the east of the city is quite posh, with the finer restaurants and cafés. Santiago has a distinctly European feel, and just as in Buenos Aires, the visitor sometimes thinks that he is in Southern Europe.

What do Santiago's people do for fun? Many go to the ocean resort of Valparaiso, which is the second largest city in Chile, as well as a modern industrial port and tourist center. The water here is very cold, but the night life is famous, with a reputation for "swinging singles."

For several days I wandered Santiago, either together with Alex or on my own. We visited the Chilean National Museum, which has some excellent exhibits, including plenty of fascinating archaeological material. This is a good place to see artifacts from Easter Island, a Chilean possession, as well as the mummy of an Inca boy found frozen on a mountain top within sight of Santiago in 1954.

Discovered with one pouch of coca leaves and another of teeth and nail clippings, this mummy is believed to be about five hundred years old. He may have been a sacrifice to the sun, though no one really knows why this child was buried in the small shelter where he was found. Unfortunately, this mummy is no longer displayed, as it had begun to rot.

Our third day in Santiago turned out to be Alex's birthday, so we took the funicular railway to the top of Cerro San Cristobal and watched the sun set over the city. I had brought a bottle of Chilean wine (thirty cents a bottle), and we celebrated Alex's twenty-first birthday while watching the lights of the city turn on in the west, and the growing dusk cover the Andes to the east. Just behind us was Mount Aconcagua, which at 22,835 feet (6,960 meters) is the highest mountain in the Western Hemisphere.

I left Santiago the day after Alex's birthday, catching a bus to the southern suburb of Buin. My plan was to hitch all the way south to Tierra del Fuego if possible. It would take several days of hitchhiking down the long, narrow coastal valley that is Chile, until I reached the end of the road, Puerto Mont and the beautiful fiords and glaciers of the south. To get to Tierra del Fuego, you can either take a ship from Puerto Mont down to Punta Arenas, or drive through Patagonia on the Argentine side. I planned the latter.

Shortly after I left Santiago, an earthquake measuring more than eight on the Richter scale hit, devasted a great deal of the city. At least 150,000 people were left homeless, though, miraculously, only a few hundred were killed. I felt that I was fortunate to have left the city when I did, and to have seen Santiago before the quake had hit. Quakes such as this are common in the Andes, an area where two tectonic plates meet.

As I waited for the bus to Buin, a young, blond-haired Chilean woman introduced herself as Nancy. She asked me in English, "Are you American?"

"Yes, I am," I replied. "Are you?"

"No, no. I am from Chile, but I lived in America for several years."

She spoke perfect English, with an American accent. She was taking her daughter to visit her uncle's wine estate near Buin. We boarded the bus, and I sat with her and her charming child, a quiet, blonde haired girl of about four. Nancy and her Chilean husband had moved to New York City some seven or eight years before, but had broken up about the time that the child was born. Nancy and her daughter moved to California, but she never divorced her husband, who still lives in New York. She was now living with her parents in Santiago.

In Buin, she invited me to have lunch at her uncle's estate. We took a taxi past the vineyards, down a dirt road and up to an old villa. Chile is quite famous for its wines, which are of very high quality. Many people believe them to be the best in the world.

Her uncle's family greeted me warmly; a large family of mom, dad, grandmother, five frisky kids, and a few other relatives. Lunch was ready just as we arrived, and soon we were sitting down to a delicious, traditional Chilean meal: corn-mush tamales, bean soup, onion and tomato salad, and lots of wine. The whole meal took hours, with lively conversation in Spanish, plus a bit of English with Nancy's uncle.

Interestingly, the topic at one point turned to UFOs. Nancy's uncle insisted that they were real, relating his own experience of seeing some flying saucers near his vineyard back in the 1960's. I told him that UFOs undeniably existed, since any flying object that has not been identified is an "unidentified flying object." Just what UFOs really were, either weather balloons, clouds, military craft, or men from Atlantis, was the question we talked about all that afternoon.

UFOs are a popular discussion topic in South America, and many, many people believe in them. Nancy's uncle expressed his belief that some of the flying saucers are actually American military ships, and told me that the Chile's Marxist government had accused the U.S. of "zapping" one of Chile's communications installations from the air with some kind of laser or particle beam.

After our long lunch, we retired to the garden with a glass of liqueur, to relax among the peach and plum trees. We watched as the children played in the yard, and cats stalked birds in among the flowers. Eventually, Nancy jumped up and said that it was getting late. She grabbed her daughter, and giving our thanks, we left.

By this time, it was late afternoon, which made it hard for us to find a taxi on the lonely road. When we had walked to the end, Nancy asked me where I was going to stay that night. I replied that I might camp out, or if I caught a lift, I might get to a town with a hotel.

"I'm going to stay in my father's cottage a few miles from here.

You're welcome to stay there for the night."

"That would be great. I have a sleeping bag I can unroll on the floor." I know a good deal when I see it.

"Good. You can get a fresh start in the morning, and tonight you will have roof over your head." We finally got a country taxi to her father's cottage, a cozy three-room house among the vinyards. We were still stuffed from the afternoon's huge meal, but Nancy found a bottle of her uncle's wine. I lit a fire in the small fireplace.

With her daughter asleep in the next room, we lay by the fire, sipping red wine. She was beautiful, I thought, though I was too shy to tell her so. When on the road, a vagabond becomes self-sufficient, but still misses certain comforts. Dusty, thirsty and tired, I have often walked in from the desert, mountain or jungle with just two things on my mind: a cold beer and the arms of an affectionate woman. The former can be easy, but the latter is rare. After all, it is difficult to cultivate romance when one is constantly on the move.

As if she were reading my mind at that moment, Nancy turned to look at me. "Do you ever get lonely when you're traveling?"

"Yes, I do sometimes," I answered, still shy.

"What do you miss most of all?"

I had nothing to lose. "I think I miss most being close to another person. I miss romantic evenings in the arms of a beautiful woman."

She moved close to me, her long blonde hair falling back on on her shoulders. "Will you put your arms around me, weary traveler?"

"With pleasure," I whispered as we drew closer together, kissing deeply, in front of the warm fire. The life of a rogue archaeologist could be hard and lonely, but sometimes it wasn't so bad...

§§§

After sharing breakfast and saying a wistful goodby, I caught a ride south on the Pan American highway almost imediately after stepping out onto the road. My first ride was with an Arab-Chilean, who took me many miles down the road to where he had just planted some orchards. During the ride, he told me that he was bisexual.

"What do you think of making love with a man? Did you ever do this?" he asked, glancing hopefully in my direction.

I told him matter-of-factly that I really wasn't interested, but thanks for the ride anyway. He dropped me off soon after, and I got a ride with a young Chilean guy into Talca. Another friendly young guy who worked with the Chilean dairy industry picked me up there, then I caught a lift on the back of a truck to the crossroads near Concepcion.

I decided to skip Concepcion, and keep heading south. As I stood there at those lonely crossroads waiting for a ride, a truck approached. As it passed, I was bombarded by watermelon rinds thrown by passengers in the back, one of them hitting me hard in the mouth. I lost my balance and fell back, holding my face, as the truck sped away down the road. Hitchhiking is not always as romantic as I make it out to be.

But shortly thereafter, I caught a ride with a Chilean who had lived in Australia for some years, and a Canadian. I jumped into the back of his pickup with their kids and leaned back on my pack to watch the Chilean forests pass by.

An ancient city was recently found in Southern Chile. According to an article in *Scientific American*, a settled community 13,000 years old was discovered at Monte Verde, near Puerto Mont at the end of the Pan American Highway. The settlement showed foundations for at least twelve buildings, made up of small logs and roughly cut hardwood planks, held in place by stakes driven in the ground. The arrangements of these foundations shows that the structures were rectangular and that the huts were joined by their walls to form two parallel rows.[44]

Wrote Tom Dillehay, author of the article, "The remarkable wealth of artifacts these people left forms a rich and eloquent record of the social system, the economic strategies, and the technologies through which they adapted to their postglacial forest habitat...The relatively high level of social development represented by the community at Monte Verde indicates that New World culture in the late Pleistocene was much more complex than has been thought."

Radiocarbon analyses of wood, bone and charcoal from the site have yielded a series of dates between 13,000 and 12,500 years ago. The foundations of this settlement, said to be agricultural, are the oldest known architecture in the Americas. Two significant observations can be made here. First, this discovery continues the recent trend of continually pushing back the dates assigned for the beginning of civilization. Second, the oldest known architecture in the Western Hemisphere is found near the very southern tip of South America. Yet, according orthodox history, man migrated slowly from Alaska down to Tierro del Fuego, so this should have been the last place reached!

There is a tradition in Chile of another lost city in the south, called *Ciudad do los Cesares*, or City of the Caesars. Colonel Fawcett relates the fanciful story: "...the city, inhabited by cultured people of high order, is said to lie in a hidden valley of the high Cordilleras...The city is paved with silver and the buildings roofed with gold. The inhabitants lead an existence of blissful isolation under the benignat rule of an elightened king; and there is some magic property about the place that makes it visable only to a few chosen seekers from the outside, invisible to all undesirable adventurers. Many people, even in modern times, are said to have set out in seach of the Cuidad de los Cesares never to be heard of again."[33]

Harold Wilkins said the city is also known as the Enchanted City (La Ciudad Encantada) and was located in the headwaters of the Rio Baker in southern Chile. Strange boomings are heard in this area by cattlemen who sometimes roam this remote area. Said one Chilean cowboy to Wilkins, "Our fathers have told us that, behind the unknown region from which this river issues, there dwelt...a white, blue-eyed, bearded race of men who live in a green valley where are shining white towers gilded temples, splendid palaces of lords and kings, stone causeways and bridges and much gold."[43] Here we have a tale of a lost city resembling a South American version of Shangri-la.

Even stranger are the persistent legends and stories which abound in South America of giant winged creatures. These stories have been told since before the Conquistadors arrived, and some seem to be based on far more recent sightings. Some radical thoerists have gone so far as to say that these sightings can be attributed to still-living flying dinosaurs, the pteradactyls or more precisely, pterodons.

There are literally hundreds of reports of giant birds and pteradactyls showing up around the world. The skeleton of a pteranodon was discovered in Big Bend National Park, Texas, in 1975. It had a wingspan of 51 feet and is the largest such fossil of a flying reptile so far discovered. Other pteradactyls had wingspans from 8 to 20 feet. Such creatures are believed to have become extinct about 65 million years ago, though that is not necessarily the case. Many creatures which lived at that time are still alive, such as crocodiles, turtles, and the famous coelocanth.

The following article appeared in a magazine called *The Zoologist* in July, 1868. "Copiapo, Chile, April 1868. Yesterday, at about five o'clock in the afternoon when the daily labours in this mine were over, and all the workmen were together awaiting their supper, we saw coming through the air, from the side of the ternera a gigantic bird, which at first sight we took for one clouds then partially darkening the atmosphere, supposing it to have been separated from the rest by the wind. Its course was from north-west to south-east; its flight was rapid and in a straight line. As it was passing a short distance above our heads we could mark the strange formation of its body. Its immense wings were clothed with something resembling the thick and stout bristles of a boar, while on its body, elongated like that of serpent, we could only see brilliant scales which clashed together with metallic sound as the strange animal turned its body in its flight." [45]

Almost every Indian tribe from Alaska to Tierro del Fuego has legends of a gigantic flying monster so large that, "...it darkened the sun." The clapping of these giants' wings created thunder, so they were known as "Thunderbirds." The Navaho Indians still perform their Thunderbird dance, and tell the legends of the "cliff monster" which lived in high craggy roost, descending to carry people off to feed to its young. Some South American Indians believed that the bird was constantly at war with the powers living beneath the sea, particularly a horned serpent, and that it tore open large trees in search of a giant grub which was its favorite food.

Carvings of what appear to be pterodons can be found in Mayan ruins at Tajin, northeastern Vera Cruz state in Mexico and on a bluff facing the Mississippi River near Alton, Illinois.[20,45] One amazing story that appeared in the Tombstone, Arizona Epitaph on April 26, 1890 related:

"A winged monster, resembling a huge alligator with an extremely elongated tail and an immense pair of wings, was found on the desert between Whetstone and Huachuca mountains last Sunday by two ranchers who were returning home from the Huachucas. The creature was evidently greatly exhausted by a long flight and when discovered was able to fly but a short distance at a time. After the first shock of amazement had passed, the two men, who were on horseback and armed with Winchester rifles, regained sufficient courage to pursue the monster and after an exciting chase of several miles, succeeded in getting near enough to open fire with their rifles and wound it. The creature then turned on the men but owing to is exhausted condition they were able to keep out of its way and after a few well directed shots the monster partly rolled over and remained motionless. The men cautiously appproached with their horses snorting in terror and found that the creature was dead. They then proceeded to make an examination and found that it measured about 92 feet in length and the greatest diameter was about 50 inches. The monster had only two feet, these being situated a short distance in front of where the wings were joined to the body. The head, as near as they could judge, was about 8 feet long, the jaws being thickly set with strong sharp teeth. Its eyes were as large as dinner plate and protruding about half way from the head. They had some difficulty in measuring the wings as they were partly folded under the body, but finally got one straightened out sufficently to get a measurement of 78 feet, making the total length from tip to tip about 160 feet. The wings were composed of a thick and nearly transparent membrane and were devoid of feathers and hair, as was the entire body. The skin of the body was comparatively smooth and easily penetrated by a bullet. The men cut off a portion of the tip of one wing and took it home with them. Late last night one of them arrived in this city for supplies and to make the necessary preparations to skin the creature, when the hide will be sent east for examination by the eminent scientists of the day. The finder returned early this morning accompanied by several prominent men who will endeavour to bring the strange creature to this city before it is mutilated."

Since no mention of this creature is made in any following issues of the Epitaph, it would seem to be a hoax, possibly created to boost the circulation of the paper or enliven a boring week in Tombstone. Especially considering the incredible size of this creature, it would seem that there was at least some exageration involved. Still, one wonders if these two cowboys encountered one of the last of the Thunderbirds.[46]

Even as late as 1976, two sisters spotted a huge and strange "bird" by a pond near Brownsville, Texas. They identified it out of a book of prehistoric animals as a pteranodon. Investigators discovered that there were many reports of giant "winged lizards" in the Rio Grande Valley around Brownsville. The San Antonio Light newspaper reported on Februrary 26, 1976, that three local school teachers were driving to work when they they saw an enormous bird sweeping low over cars on the road. It had a wingspan of 15-20 feet and leathery wings. It did not so much as fly, as glide. They later scanned encyclopedias at their school, then identified the creature as a pteranodon.[48]

Getting back to South America, a Mr. J. Harrison of Liverpool said that when he was navigating an estuary of the Amazon in 1947 called Manuos, he and others observed from the boat's deck a flight of five huge birds passing overhead and down the river in a V-formation. But they were no ordinary birds, said Mr. Harrisson in a letter, "The wingspan must have been at least twelve feet from tip to tip. They were brown in colour like brown leather, with no visible signs of feathers. The head was flat on top, with a long beak and a long neck. The wings were ribbed." He said that the creatures "were just like those large prehistoric birds."[48]

§§§

The folks in the pickup eventually stopped for lunch, inviting me to join them. The two men were both agricultural inspectors, who had been working together for a long time.

Over our soft drinks and sandwiches, the Canadian suddenly said to me, "Do you believe in UFOs?"

He was the second person to ask me this in the last few days. I said that I had read about them and found the subject quite interesting.

"We saw a UFO here just a few years ago. Both of us, together!"

"Really?" I asked. "What did it look like?"

"It was lit up, and shaped sort of like a doughnut. As it flew, it expanded!" said the Chilean. I smiled and finished my drink. What else could I do?

They dropped me off in Temuco at sunset, where I spent the night in the Youth Hostel. This place was full of young Chilean students who were heading south for the holidays, which unfortunately meant that the next morning they were all on the road hitchhiking. I walked several miles down the road, past dozens of students with backpacks.

It seemed that I would never get a ride, what with all the hitchhikers on the road in front of me. Just when I had resolved to flag down the next bus that came by, a nun in a mini-van stopped. Inside were a half-dozen other hitchhikers, all picked up by this kind sister.

By fate, she drove through Villarica to Pucon, via Villarica, along a back road to one of the beautiful lakes in Lake District. From Pucon there was a dirt road over the Andes into Argentina. After a light lunch I hit the road out of town into the mountains.

Several short lifts took me quiclky into the mountains. The country was green and wooded, with the soaring, snow covered peaks of volcanoes looming above the forest. Streams with filled trout and willows on their banks cut through the rugged terrain, reminding me of similar mountain territory in Colorado and Montana. Looking back now, I can say that the time I spent walking along that country road between lifts, admiring the beauty of the wooded farm country, was perhaps the most peaceful and refreshing part of my whole trip, in striking contrast to the mountain desert where I had spent the last few days.

I was scanning the mountains hopefully for a glimpse of an ancient pteradactyl soaring among the volcanoes, when I heard the sound of a pickup truck coming down the road. My heart quickened as I prepared myself to hitch this lift. As I sighted the truck, I made large waving motions with my right arm, then motioning down the road in the direction I was going. As I the truck got closer, I waved cheerily.

The truck sped by me without slowing down, engulfing me in a cloud of dust. Then it skidded to a sudden stop a hundred yards down the road, swirling dust obscuring it from view. I grabbed my pack and ran, panting by the time I jumped in.

The occupants turned out to be a family from Argentina, their teenage daughter driving. I envisioned the discussion they might have had as they first approached, not resolving to pick me up until they had passed by. Settling in the back of their truck, I grinned foolishly at the sky as we ripped along the road east. They were going a long way, and I would be over the mountains and into Argentina that night.

We passed through a small Chilean check post and then into Argentina. Everyone had to get out and push the truck to get it started after customs, then we were off to San Martin. We also passed the beautiful Lanin Volcano, a white smoking cone, spectacularly rising into the sky on the border.

Crossing the mountains, we had made it to Patagonia, and the scenery was great. Gauchos rode their horses through huge herds of cattle which seemed to stretch to the horizon. We passed endless forests, streams and mountain pastures. The sunset was superb as we barreled past the green hills on this lonely dirt road. Standing up, I grinned with joy at the sunset and the awesome beauty of that rugged land.

After dark, they let me off in San Martin, a small tourist town on the edge of a lake. Grabbing my pack, I thanked them for the ride as I jumped out and began down the main street, which was only about four blocks long. Walking through the chilly, dark night, I could see people in the few open shops stared out at me, a stranger whistling merrily. I had been told once before, many years ago in Africa, that I should live each day as if it were my last. I bought it then, and I buy it now.

Chapter Nine

Across Patagonia:
Giants in the Earth

There were giants in the earth in those days;
and also after that when the sons of God came
in unto the daughters of men, and they bare
children to them, the same became mighty men
which were of old, men of reknown.
-Genesis 6:4

If I had only arrived in town a few months later, I would have been able to do some skiing. But since the Southern Hemisphere's winter begins in June, I was still too early. I got a single room for four dollars at the Hotel Lacar, a ski lodge. The next morning I got up to find it pouring rain. All I could think of is what good snow it would all make!!

I needed to change some money into Argentine pesos, so I headed out through the rain to the only bank in town, then decided to head out for Bariloche, Argentina's most popular mountain resort. The rain was still coming down as I hit the road, but I was bent on hitchhiking to Bariloche. My enthusiasm was literally and liberally dampened by the time I got to the edge of town, however, so I stopped at the bus station to check the schedule. There was no bus due to leave San Martin headed anywhere until late in the afternoon. Just then it stopped raining, at least momentarily, so I decided to try my luck on the road again.

I was quite fortunate to get a ride quickly in a Volkswagen van with a young couple from Buenos Aires. Dad was an architect, and they had a pretty, blonde haired daughter in the back who was about five years old and rather bored by the trip. The couple had driven a similar van up to Colombia once, sold it, and then traveled around the United States for a year.

We took a leisurely trip through the hills, lakes and forests, stopping frequently to take photos of the superb alpine scenery. They dropped me off later in the afternoon at a small village called San Angostura, on the shores of Lago Nahuel Huapi. On the opposite shore of this mountain lake was my destination, San Carlos de Bariloche.

Flagging what few cars came by this small country road, hoping that it wouldn't start raining again, I got a few rides down the road toward summer cabins on the lake, then finally caught a great ride just as the sun came out, in the back of a big truck loaded with hay. They let me off at a crossroads, and I caught one last ride into Bariloche, arriving in town just as the sun was setting. I was dropped off right in front of the Hotel Mirador, which was more like a guest house than a hotel. I was able to get a bed in a room with five beds for only three dollars; quite inexpensive in Argentina's number one ski resort.

Bariloche is on the northeast corner of Patagonia. It has a large shopping area, and is reminiscent of a Swiss alpine resort, complete with chocolate factories. I happily wandered Bariloche for a few days, enjoying its people and good nightlife. There are plenty of residentials available for a few dollars a night, including the Villa Elfrida, Los Brothers, El Retalito, Gran Luz, Candeago and Los Andes.

One night in a bar I met a *Peronista*, the title he bore so proudly indicating his right wing Argentine political party affiliation. Friendly and talkative, he tried quite hard to sell me a lottery ticket. About forty, he was dark and fairly good looking, but seemed to be having a tough time of late. The way he talked, quite eloquently in both English and Spanish, I gathered that he considered himself quite a hit with the ladies.

"Come on!" he said, finishing his glass of red wine. "I'll show you bars in Bariloche tourists never see!" His enthusiastic invitation, something you don't get very often on the road, convinced me to go.

Our first destination was his friend's house, on the wrong side of Bariloche. Sharing some wine in the rather bare and dirty living room, we were serenaded by the most annoying sound known to man—the hiss of a television blaring away, tuned to an empty channel.

"Why don't you turn it off?" I asked them.

"What for?" said my Peronista friend, "Something might come on!"

Finishing that bottle of wine, we left for an Indian bar. The Peronista explained mysteriously that because he was part Indian, he could get us in. Located on the corner of two dirt raods in the same run-down neighborhood, from the outside I couldn't tell it apart from any of the other old buildings.

But as we stepped inside, fifty grizzled, brown faces turned to look us over. These men were tough, with nasty scars worn as the insignia of rank in their obviously-violent lives. It was as if we had just walked into the set of a Hollywood western movie, just before the umpteenth take of a fight scene: you could feel that everyone was ready to pull their knives and start slashing. Obviously getting some gratification out of the attention the toughs were giving us, my Peronista friend casually tossed out something in Spanish like, "It's okay, he's with me."

A toothless old man, who looked like he had spent most of life fighting and drinking, poured me a glass of red wine. Thanking him, I tried to pay for both of us, but he magnanimously (and forcefully) refused. Great, now I had a debt to one of these guys.

Meanwhile, it seemed like everyone else in the bar was still staring at me grimly. I was beginning to think that maybe the Peronista had set me up. I felt my front shirt pocket for the small tear-gas clip which I sometimes carry, the size of a marking pen. I had left in the hotel.

Failing that, I eyed the half empty bottle of red wine standing on the rotting wood of the bar. I tried to picture myself seizing the bottle by the neck, smashing it on the bar, and wielding it like a knife while I escaped out the back door into the night...

I nearly jumped through the roof as the attention of the room abruptly shifted, this time to the opening door. As it pushed open wider, two women walked in, looking nearly as dangerous as the men staring at them. Obviously favorites of many of the bar's patrons, their well-timed entrance left me a forgotten gringo, sitting in the corner. I downed my wine in one relieved gulp, and quickly poured another.

We hung out in this nameless bar for a while, drinking more wine. "Come on," said my host, somewhat less lucidly than when we had arrived, "now we go and find some women!" With that we took off into the chilly night, stalking down the dirt roads of Bariloche.

I was starting to understand my host. He had lost his job, and was hustling lottery tickets to make money. I was now his blonde-haired American buddy, who he wanted to show off to his friends, and who he would now use to try impressing some women.

Our destination was disco-cabaret, where ladies of the evening did their business. Young and bored, they were mainly poor Indians from the country who had come out of the pampas to the big city, and were now turning tricks. The whole thing seemed so above-board that I wondered if prostitution was legal in Argentina?

We had no sooner sat down and ordered a glass of wine, when

several girls began quarreling over who would get to dance with the gringo first. The winner was a tall woman with dark black hair and dark eyes, wearing a long, slinky dress. She rubbed herself against me as we danced, and then continued the rubbing back at our table.

"Buy me a drink, honey," she coaxed me in Spanish.

"Buy her a drink," said the Peronista, who was buisy rubbing himself against another woman, with bleached hair.

"How much is a drink?" I asked.

"It's only a thousand pesos," said the Peronista.

That was about four American dollars at the time, far too much. "Sorry," I told her. In a huff, she left, but two more immediatelytook her place, continuing the rubbing routine. I told them all that I wasn't going to buy them drinks.

Well, if I wasn't going to buy them drinks, what was I doing there, they wanted to know? I didn't know, so I left the Peronista with a woman still on his lap. Rubbing doesn't come free in Bariloche!

§§§

Argentina is the second largest country in South America after Brazil, measuring a full one-third the size of the United States. Geographically, the country is formed plain rising from the Atlantic west to the Chilean border in the towering peaks of the Andes. The northern area is the swampy and partly wooded Gran Chaco, while the southern area is the cool, arid plateau of Patagonia. The population density over the 450,000 square miles of Patagonia is one person per square mile, kept company by 40 sheep. Quite a few Welsh arrived in Patagonia in the 1800's to tend these sheep, founding a number of Welsh towns found there today. Patagonia itself means, "the land of the people with long feet," a title which refers to the stories of the Patagonian Giants.

Giants have long caught the fascination of mankind, with a revival of "giant conciousness" in Europe taking place in the middle ages. Some scientists and historians at that time argued that there must still be a race of giants somewhere in the world, the legends were so numerous.

When Ferdinand Magellan discovered Patagonia in 1520, on his way around the world, he anchored at Port San Julian, just north of Tierra del Fuego, "The Land of Fire." While Magellan's fleet laid at anchor in the natural bay, a native of extremely large proportions appeared on the beach. "This man," wrote Pigafetta, a companion of

Magellan, "was so tall that our heads scarcely came up to his waist, and his voice was like that of a bull." Other natives emerged, and according to a historian in Spain, the smallest of them was taller and bulkier than any Spaniard. So was born the story of the Patagonian Giants, appearing to vindicate those historians who had insisted that such a race must exist.[49]

Sir Francis Drake anchored in the same harbor in 1578, also reporting men of great stature, who he described as being well over seven feet tall. Anthony Knyvet, who took part in an expedition to the Straits of Magellan in 1592, wrote of having seen Patagonians from ten to twelve feet in height, and of having measured several bodies of the same size at Port Desire. Several skeletons ten or eleven feet long were discovered in 1615 by two crewman from the Dutch schooner Wilhelm Schouten.[49]

By this time, the existance of a race of giants seemed well established, though other natives of Patagonia were of normal size. However, for nearly one hundred fifty years after this last sighting, no other reports were made of these Patagonian Giants. Other natives did insist, however, that giants lived in the interior of the land.

When Commodore Byron visited the Magellan Strait in 1764, he reported sighting some natives on horseback who waved at his party. Byron later wrote in his log that the chief of these natives, "was of a gigantic stature and seemed to realize the tales of monsters in a human shape: he had the skin of some wild beast thrown over his shoulder."[49]

Upon meeting with five hundred more of these giants, each taller than the tallest of the British, one of Byron's officers wrote, "...some of them are certainly nine feet, if they do not exceed it. The commodore, who is very near six feet, could but just reach the top of one of their heads, which he attempted, on tip-toe; and there were several taller than him on whom the experiment was tried."[49]

It is worth noting here that most people over-estimate the height of a person who is taller than they are, and that a man of Byron's height could probably only reach up to about eight feet. Yet these sightings were the last of the Patagonian Giants. To this day, no one has identified who these giants were, while some doubt that they even existed. Some who still believed the stories felt that they lived somewhere in the interior of Patagonia, rarely coming to the coast.

It is also interesting to note that in 1895 a discovery was made of the reportedly fresh skin of a giant ground sloth (Mylodon) in a cave at Consuelo cove at Last Hope Inlet, on the western coast of Patagonia. These creatures stood about fifteen feet tall, and were thought to have been extinct for thirty-thousand years. But this skin was rolled up and carefully buried in a cave which also contained human remains, including a mummy![53]

Evidence suggested that ground sloths were actually penned in in the cave, fed and later slaughtered. Did ancient, or not-so-ancient man actually domesticate giant ground sloths in Patagonia? What sort of man would do this—perhaps one of great stature?

Another fascinating mystery involves the Cave of Fell north of the Magellan Strait. According to a report sent to me by the Museum of Natural History in Santiago, human remains found in this cave date from at least ten-thousand years ago. Mastadon, Mylodon (giant ground sloth) and horse bones were found, the sharp cuts on the bones indicating that they had been killed and eaten by men. Of the several layers in the cave, the last is "sealed with another layer of large stones which were produced due to a cataclysm."

A fascinating thought comes to mind considering this last statement. Could South American survivors of a cataclysm or pole-shift have suddenly found themselves at lower latitudes, with whatever buildings they had constructed destroyed in the resulting earthquakes and tidal waves? Even quite advanced and civilized people would be forced to live in caves, literally reverting back to a "cave man" existance. This raises the question: have stone ages occured between eras of more advanced science and technology? A global cataclysm occuring as recently as the nineteenth-century would have left very little in the way of permanent remains for archaeologists ten-thousand years hence, except for our few cities made of stone!

Most of the tribes living in North America at the time of European settlement literally lived in the stone age—they had no knowlege of making tools, weapons or implements of metal. Yet, ancient copper mines have been found around the Great Lakes which were worked in some ancient age. And, someone had to have built all the ruins I had been visiting.

One interesting tribe that lived in Tierra del Fuego at the time of the European discovery was the Onas. They were quite an unusual bunch, wearing no clothes, but covering themselves with mud to keep warm. Somewhat taller than average Indians at nearly six feet, they often wore a piece of wood on the top of their head, giving them extra height. This custom may have started in imitation of the Patagoinian Giants, but their tradition claims they dressed like this to frighten their own women, to keep them in line.

According to an ancient legend among the Onas, in an earlier time, the tribe's women managed the society and educated the children. There was a conspiracy among the women to keep the men afraid of them and their power, until one man discovered the women's trick, and the tables were turned. Now it is the men who keep the women in fear...

Back to the giants themselves, did they really exist? In 1925 a group of amateur "investigators" destroyed one of the most important finds of its kind. Digging into an Indian mound at Walkerton, Indiana, they had unearthed the skeletons of eight prehistoric humans, ranging from eight to almost nine feet tall, all wearing substantial copper armor. Unfortunately, the evidence was scattered and lost.[51]

Author Ivan T. Sanderson relates a letter he recieved regarding an engineer who was stationed on the Aleutian island of Shemya during World War Two. While building an airstrip, his crew bulldozed a group of hills, discovering under several sedimentary layers what appeared to be a graveyard of seemingly human remains, consisting of crania and long leg bones. The crania measured from 22 to 24 inches from base to crown. Since an adult skull normally measures about eight inches from back to front, such a large crania would imply an immense size for a normally proportioned human. Furthermore, every skull was said to have been neatly trepanned![50]

Sanderson tried to gather further proof, eventually receiving a letter from another member of the unit who confirmed the report. The letters both indicated that the Smithsonian Institution had collected the remains, yet nothing else was heard. Sanderson seems to be convinced that it was not a hoax, but wondered why the Smithsonian would not release the data. To quote him, "...is it that these people cannot face rewriting all the text books?"

In 1833, soldiers digging a pit for a powder magazine at Lompock Rancho, California, hacked their way through a layer of cemented gravel and came up with the skeleton of a man about twelve feet tall. The skeleton was surrounded by carved shells, huge stone axes, and blocks of porphyry covered with unintelligible symbols. The giant was also noteworthy in still another respect: he had a double row of teeth, both upper and lower.[52] When local Indians began to attach a religious significance to the skeleton and artifacts, the authorities ordered it secretly buried, to be lost to science.

It's amazing, the trivia you can come up with, reading up for a trip to South America.

§§§

At Bariloche, I had boarded a train across Patagonia, heading east through the state of Rio Negro toward the Atlantic. But once I took my seat in second-class, the man next to me explained that he was with his wife and son, but for some reason, his son had a first-class ticket. He wanted me to sit in first-class and let his son have my seat, so that they could all sit together. This sounded fine with me, so we traded places.

Up front in first-class, I gazed out at the endless pampas and rolling plains with the odd gaucho. Patagonia reminded me a bit of Wyoming or eastern Montana. Further south are the icy peaks of the Patagonian Andes, sharp and glaciated, providing some of the most difficult ice climbing in the world.

Suddenly, in the middle of nowhere, the train stopped. Getting out, I saw a policeman running back down the tracks. It turned out that the conductor had asked a teenager for his ticket, and not having one, he had lept off the train travelling about forty miles per hour. A while later, the policeman came back, dragging the frightened youth by his collar. He was apparently unhurt by his daring leap, but I imagined he would spend the rest of the trip under arrest.

I slept comfortably in the first-class seat until the crack of dawn, when the conductor came by and wanted to see my ticket. Well, this was a bit of a problem, as I still had my original second-class ticket. When the conductor saw this, he turned a little red, and I imagined myself joining the train jumper in the jail car, the policeman snuffing out his cigarettes on my arms.

I tried to explain, asking him to come with me back to second-class. Here, the father explained the story, but I had to pay a little extra for my first-class seat, because his son had been on a child fare. It all worked out well in the end, the conductor taking my extra pesos with a smile.

We pulled into Buenos Aires, the capital of Argentina, rather late that night. I didn't know where to go, but decided to try the Youth Hostel listed in my travel guide. Taking a subway to a distant suburb, I then walked the midnight streets in search of the hostel, which was sure to be closed.

When I finally found it, the door was locked, but I noticed that a second floor window was open with a light shining through. Walking closer, I could hear voices. People speaking English! I climbed the wrought-iron fence, pulled myself up to the second story, and called in, "Hey, will you guys help me with my pack?"

Several people lept up. "Sure, man," said one with an Australian accent. I jumped down and lifted my pack to him, then climbed up again and crawled into the room. Inside, four other travelers all drank red Argentine wine. They poured me a glass, and I settled down on the floor next to them. Patagonia was behind me, the giants and prehistoric animals left out there in the icy wastes of the south.

A Pteradactyl with an Archaeopteryx–are flying lizards extinct ?

Do prehistoric animals still survive in remote regions of the world?

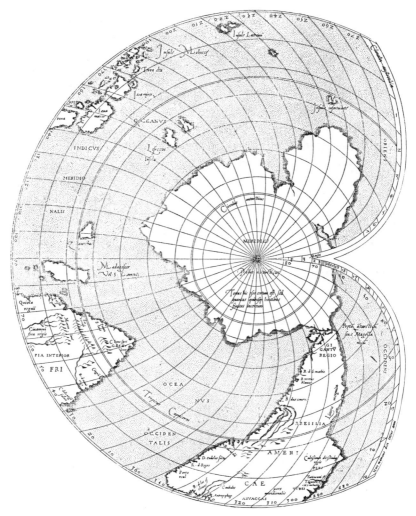

G. Mercator's 1538 copperprint map of the Southern
Hemisphere. Note the caption in what is now Patagonia:
"GIGANTU REGIO."

COMMODORE BYRON AND THE GIANTS

From Hawkesworth's "Voyages of Byron, Wallis, Carteret, and Cook"

Sloth

Armadillo

Megatherium

Glyptodon

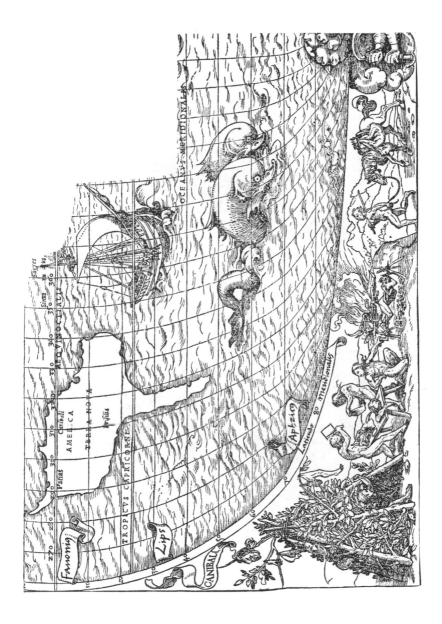

Rare photo of colossal structures on the bottom of Lake Titicaca just off the Bolivian port city of Puerto Acosta. They are most certainly pre-Inca.

Another rare photo of the massive, cut and dressed stones found underwater on the east side of Lake Titicaca. Do more ruins lie beneath this mysterious lake? Photos from the book *Enigmas, Misterios y Secretos De America* (Enigmas, Mysteries and Secrets of America) by Federico Kirbus published in Argentina in 1978.

Map showing the location of underwater structures alone Puerto Acosta. From *Enigmas, Misterios y Secretos De America.*

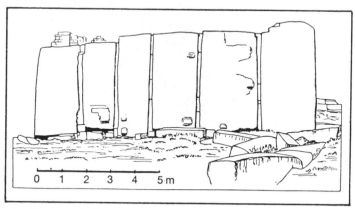

Massive blocks at the former "Temple of the Sun" at Ollantaytambo. The largest of the blocks weighs aproximately 300 tons! Other massive blocks are scattered about as if a massive earthquake had hit it. The construction technique is the same as that used to build at Puma Punku, similarly scattered gigantic ruins near Tiahuanco.

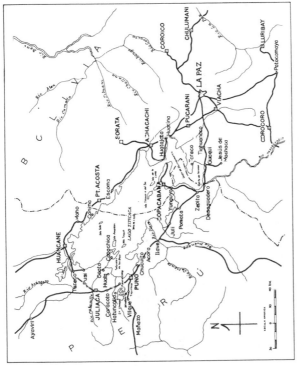

Map of Lake Titicaca, highest navigable lake in the world. Underwater structures have been found near Puerto Acosta and Isla des Sol.

One of the ancient Bug-eyed statues at Tiahuanaco.

Old print of the Gate of the Sun. Note the huge split from an earthquake, and woman sitting on the ground selling souvineers.

Chapter Ten

Northern Argentina and Paraguay: Mystery of the Megaliths

Facts do not cease to exist because they are ignored.
-Aldous Huxley

Sunshine streamed in through the windows of the hostel shortly after dawn the next day. Judging only by what I had seen last night and the sounds now drifting in from the street, I got the distinct impression that Buenos Aires was quite different from other capitals that I had visited so far; according to my guide book, it was the most sophisticated city on the continent.

First founded in 1536, the city was later abandoned after Indian attacks, but settled again in 1580. Buenos Aires became the capital of and independent and newly-unified Argentina in 1862, growing into an urban colossus by the late 1800's. At that time, railroads built and owned by the British penetrated the the agriculturally abundant pampas to the west, beginning to supplement the great inland river transport system that linked the city with Uruguay, Paraguay and Brazil. Immigrants from Europe swelled the city's population, adding to its cosmopolitan flavor, and helping to make Buenos Aires today the second largest city in South America, after Sao Paulo.

The vast, fertile land of Argentina's interior, breadbasket of South America, encouraged a huge influx of imigrants. French, Germans, Swiss, British, Austrians, Poles, Scandinavians, and Slavs all came to this promising land, but still, the majority of immigrants were Spanish and Italian. Today, Indians are outnumbered by the people of European descent, prompting one observer to describe Argentina's peolpe as,

"…a bunch of Italians who speak Spanish, but think they are French."

Buenos Aires has hundreds, probably thousands of hotels and residentials in which to stay, and most can deliver you a bed for three to five dollars American a night. The Youth Hostel is a good deal, but is located in the Avenida La Plata area, at Calle Marmol 1555, which is a fair distance from the center of town.

The center of Buenos Aires could easily be said to be the junction of Avenida Florida and Avenida de Mayo. Avenida Florida is the main shopping street, a plaza many blocks long with hundreds of shops, all closed to motor traffic. Inexpensive hotels can be found in this area, between Avenida Florida and Avenida 25 de Mayo. Examples are the Torino, Viena, Intrnacional, Victoria, Varela, Cambridge, Ocean, Fenix, and many others. The area sports a good number of sidewalk cafés, and the plazas Colon and de Mayo are near by.

I spent several days in Buenos Aires, and had a great time. That first morning, I officially checked into the hostel, then left to explore the city with friends I had met after crawling into the window the previous night. My new companions were a young, dark haired Australian named Bruce, a blond-haired German in his thirties, known around the hostel as "Klaus the Kraut," and a rather charming anthropology student from Alaska named Joni. Joni was quite tall, wearing her long blond hair down straight, which she told us had attracted a significant amount of attention from members of both sexes as she traveled around the continent. I gathered that she was driving both Bruce and the Kraut crazy with desire—she certainly had that potential.

Our first destination was Avenida Florida, but being Sunday, many shops were closed. At the International Telephone Exchange, I tried to call a woman I had met many years before in Afghanistan, an attorney named Melida. She was the only person I had known in South America before my trip. I wondered if she would even remember me, as we had had only met for a few minutes, in which time she had given me her address and told me to look here up when I got to Argentina.

"Hello?" asked a voice on the other side of the phone.

"Hello, is this Melida?" I asked cautiously.

"Yes," she answered in English. "Who is this?"

"You probably don't remember me, but we met one day on the border of Afghanistan and Iran, as we left Herat, and you gave me your address and said I should give you a call if I was ever in Argentina…"

"Afghanistan? Herat? Oh, I remember you! Where are you? How long have you been in Buenos Aires?"

"I just got in last night from Patagonia. Are you sure you

214

remember me? I don't want to bother you or anything, but I thought we could have lunch or something."

"But of course I remember you! Where are you now? What are you doing today?"

"I'm down at the International Telephone Exchange. I don't have any plans for the day, really..."

"Stay there, I'll come down and get you. Stay right there!"

And so it was that I made a date with my only friend in South America. Bruce, the Kraut, Joni and I waited for Melida for nearly half an hour at a sidewalk café. I didn't recognize her when she showed up; in fact, I couldn't even remember what she had looked like when we first met. Her's was just an address of a fellow traveler on a page in my tattered journal.

Melida was Italian, about forty, with short auburn hair. She had brought her car with her, and insisted on showing all of us around the town. We piled into her Peugeot, then took off on a whirl-wind tour of the city. We stopped first in La Boca, "The Mouth," an Italian area by the docks famous for its working class cafés and nightclubs. We dropped by one of the fashionable clubs along the Rio de la Plata which separates Argentina from Uruguay. Here people were windsurfing and sailing in the wide, brown river. Beautiful women in the latest swimsuits from Paris tanned in deck chairs, while other people played tennis. Buenos Aires is said to have more tennis courts per person than any other city. It was certainly as sophisticated and cosmopolitan as any other city in the world. I was a world away from the windswept Altiplano of Peru and Bolivia, with the Quechua and Aymara women in their long skirts, braided hair and bowler hats.

Melida then drove us through the upperclass suburb El Sidro, where we shopped at a Sunday market by the El Sidro Cathedral. Later, she and I shared a steak at one of the famous steak bars along the Rio de la Plata. Argentina is famous for its beef, and unless you are a vegetarian, don't miss having a steak while you're there.

Joni remarked that this was really a treat, to be chauffeured around Buenos Aires. "I've been here a week, but you've shown us more today than I've seen the rest of the time put together!"

Melida was fantastic and generous. "I've been a traveler myself," she said. "I know what it's like to be on the road. This is really my pleasure." She was obviously enjoying herself, too. "There's a certain comraderie between travelers on the road, and I miss it. My heart still goes out with you, who are traveling the world."

After seeing what seemed like the whole city, Melida eventually dropped us off back at a café La Boca. Sharing a carafe of wine, the

215

others all ordered spagetti bolonaise, but I was still full from the steak Melida and I had shared. This café was popular with dock workers; old men in dark clothes and greased-back hair. Nearly everyone was an Italian immigrant to Argentina; most of them were speaking Italian now. Hearing the language and catching snips of conversation, I felt I could easily be somewhere in Italy; Naples, perhaps.

Outside, Carnival was beginning, a spectacle and celebration which goes on for several weeks. A parade came down the street toward the café, and people were spraying each other with cans of shaving cream. As we left the café to get a bus back to the Hostel, we were all caught by the foamy spray. There was no escape! We ran, leaving a mad spraying party continuing in front of the café. If this was a taste of Carnival in Argentina, the rest was going to be pretty wild!

When I woke up the next morning in the hostel, the sharp realization hit me that I was almost broke. I was deep into the Southern Hemisphere, had not brought a credit card because of the risk of theft and misuse, and had just over one-hundred dollars left to my name.

One can always teach English in many foreign countries, though I knew it was a time-consuming way to make money, having taught several times before in the Far East. Working as an English writer or journalist could also be fun, but I couldn't see myself trying to save money in a country with over one-thousand per cent inflation per year.

What I did have was the Nikon camera I had bought just before leaving the U.S., and I was determined to sell it. Cameras and electronic goods are fairly expensive in Argentina, so selling mine could probably keep me on the road quite a while longer.

Taking the subway down to Avenida Florida where there were many camera shops, I shopped around, comparing prices. When I told the owners of one store that I wanted to sell mine, one man took me next-door to a jean shop, where a young Jewish-Argentine kid was found to translate the negotiations.

All three of us then walked around the corner to a used-camera store. Here the proprietor, a rather rotund, bald-headed man of German descent, examined my camera, telephoto lens, and other accessories. After looking it all up in a price book, he offered me $300 American in cash for everything, which was more than I had paid for it in the States.

I accepted happily. Feeling suddenly rich, I immediately went to the bathroom to stuff the twenty-dollar bills into my money belt. Though $300 doesn't seem like much, it would allow me to travel in South America for several more months, if I kept expenses way down. I had lived on less than five dollars a day in Asia and Africa, so I was

216

confident of success. Plus, I still had a plane ticket back to Miami, which I could use any time from Peru, Ecuador or Columbia.

Now loaded, I tripped around town for a couple of days with my friends. Bruce, due to leave soon for Uruguay with Joni, was quite excited about the prospect of traveling with her. But late on the night they were supposed to have left on the steamer to Montevideo, he returned to the hostel, disappointed in his amorous intentions because he had neglected to get an Uruguayan visa. Joni, an American, didn't need one, but Bruce was from Australia.

"I'll never find a woman in South America," he lamented to Bruce, the Kraut, and me, sitting around a small table in the hostel's dormitory room. Just the three of us were staying there, drinking wine until the wee hours of the night. Occasionally the manager would knock on our door and tell us to be quiet.

"She was just a tease anyway," the Kraut consoled. "She would never have wanted to sleep with you."

"Why do you call her a tease?" I asked.

"You don't know her like me," he replied mournfully. "I was staying with her for a week here before you two came. I know!"

Conversations like this can go on all night, especially if you have a large bottle of wine. We did. Beautiful women on the road usually elicit a strong response from other travelers. I had also found Joni attractive, since she was so self-confident and outgoing. But while Bruce and Klaus argued about what Bruce's romantic prospects with her would have been, my mind wandered back to thoughts of lost cities.

There are actually several lost cities in Argentina that are worth investigating. James Churchward, a British Colonel who wrote a number of popular travel and historical speculation books back in the thirties, claimed to have seen a map of ancient South America in a secret monastery on his last trip to western Tibet. This monastery had in its possession a number of clay tablets engraved with maps of various parts of the world. According to Churchward, the maps were dated by the positions of stars shown in certain constellations. Astronomers had supposedly told him that these positions indicated the maps were made twenty-five thousand years ago.[42]

Before relating more of Churchward's theories, I should mention that much of what he writes is unsupportable elsewhere. While his stories are quite attractive to those who believe that ancient history holds more mystery than school textbooks show, his books are often found on fiction shelves.

According to Churchward, the South American map showed how colonists moved from a now-sunken Pacific continent into the Atlantic,

217

and thence to Atlantis, Africa and Europe, by crossing the center of South America in boats. They theoretically crossed through the gigantic canal at Tiahuanaco and into the Amazonian Sea.

Wrote Churchward, "What is now the Amazon Valley, which is intended to include the Amazon Swamp and the Amazonian watershed, was then an equally large land-locked Sea like the Mediterranean Sea today. The Amazonian Sea at its eastern end was connected with the Atlantic Ocean and at its western end with the Pacific Ocean by canals. These canals were intact up to the time the mountains were raised...The shore lines of this Amazonian Sea are very distinctly marked today: the northern shores were along the foothills of the Venezuelan highlands; along this shore line are some wonderful white quartz beaches.

"...Various cities are shown, some with names, some without. One to note especially is situated quite close to the canals. It has no name showing but it stands exactly where the ruins of Tiahuanaco are today. The second city is situated along the southwest shore of the Sea. It bears a name which reads: "The Jewel city" or "City of Jewels." The third city was situated abot half way along the southern shore but a little inland and was called "The City of Gold," without doubt the legendary Manoa. Another one lay far south on the sea coast about, I think, where the River Platte is today. No name is given to it. Still another lay to the north of the sea. From its position I should think somewhere in Venezuela. There is no name given to this one either.

"...On the top of the Andes Mountains 13,500 feet above the level of the Pacific Ocean on the shores of Lake Titcaca, are the ruins of a prehistoric city called Tiahuanaco. This is at the exact spot shown on the Tibetan map. Among the ruins of his city there is a wonderful monolith called by archaeologists 'one of the archaeological wonders of the world.'

"Near the ruins of this city are remains of ancient stone-lined canals, thus again corroborating the Tibetan map. These canals have been the wonder of all who have seen them and much speculation has been indulged in as to who built them and for what purpose. They are now very much out of alignment and broken up. They are up and down like the swells of the ocean.

"At many spots west of the ruins of the city and canals one comes across many sea shells, showing that much of the land west of the city was emerged when the mountains went up. It also proves that once both city and canal were at sea level.

"The remains of the ancient city of Manoa are known but have never been explored as far as I know.

"...Colonel Fawcett discovered in the center of Brazil, 1500 miles inland, between the headwaters of the Rivers Huigu and Tapajos, an ancient city. This part of Brazil is an immensely large unexplored region. The Rivers Huigu and Tapajos are the two principal southern branches of the Amazon. A few years ago Colonel Fawcett brought out a small statue across the breast of which was written an inscription. I saw it only for a few seconds. The inscription however, was easy to translate as it was Cara Maya and not over 2000 years old. I think Fawcett must have run across the ruins of Manoa. Two of my friends who have been exploring this very region returned a short time ago. They found many remains, also the remains of the ancient bridge called Tia Chanca. They tell me that about 500 to 600 feet remain intact. The roadway is 300 feet above the ground."[42]

Lastly, Churchward makes this cryptic remark: "Some prehistoric ruins are to be found on the banks of the River Platte, Argentina. Some time since, a tablet was found in these ruins with an inscription which was discovered to be an exact duplication of one found in Mongolia, Asia."[42]

I have a few comments on the above text, written by Colonel Churchward in the late 1920's after a lifetime of "research." First of all, it must pointed out that Churchward's work is very poorly documented. He constantly refers to documents, maps, clay texts and artifacts that no one else has ever seen. Nor does he give sources for the many fascinating "facts" he casually tosses out. For instance, where is this Mongolian tablet now? Did Churchward see it? As far as I can tell, no one else had ever seen or heard of this tablet, before or since.

On Churchward's map of South America, drawn supposedly from the Tibetan clay tablet, he shows several ancient cities. Churchward comments that his canal city is located exactly in the place where Tiahuanaco is found. However, there is a gross mistake in his map, as the canal remains are to the north of Tiahuanaco, not to the south. Assuming that the canal is in the right place, then the city that he has marked is not Tiahuanaco, but is located aproximately where Lake Titicaca is today. Can the sunken city off the east shore of Lake Titicaca be the city Churchward is talking about? We also have the problem, discussed before, of how Tiahuanaco can still be standing, while the canal has been tossed about as if by a cataclysm. Almost certainly, the Tiahuanaco seen today was not around when the canal was being used.

It is interesting to note Churchward's location of the city of Manoa. This seems to be in the Matto Grosso, aproximately where Colonel Fawcett's lost city is located. The stone statue that Churchward speaks of is authentic, and was given to Colonel Fawcett by either author H.

Rider Haggard, or O' Sullivan Beare, the British Consul to Brazil. The artifact had come from one of the lost cities which Fawcett sought. Churchward saw the statue for only a few moments, but says that the inscription "was Cara Maya and not over 2000 years old." Churchward, I think, can be likened to the infamous Erich Von Daniken. Whereas Von Daniken sees every prehistoric carving as proving the existence of prehistoric visitors from outer space, Churchward sees all scratches and unintelligeble symbols and writings as a derivative of some text from a sunken continent in the Pacific. The writing on the idol has in fact since been interpreted as Mediterranean in origin by far more reliable university sources, a topic which will be covered in more detail in Chapter 14.

Churchward's description of Manoa sounds surprisingly like that of Gran Paititi, the still-lost city to which the Incas finally withdrew to after the Spanish conquest. Legends of Manoa and Gran Paititi spurred the search for El Dorado by the conquistadors and their successors, though it was usually thought to be located north of the Amazon, rather than south, as Churchward depicts it on his map. If an accurate map ever showed up for a "City of Gold," it wouldn't be golden for long!

The River Platte which Churchward mentions is none other than the Rio de la Plata which flows past Buenos Aires. As a major transportation artery into the interior, it is not suprising that an ancient civilization would build a city on its banks. Unfortunately, I can find little other information on these ruins either.

Most interesting is a small dot placed on Churchward's map, indicating an unnamed city, located in what is now northwestern Argentina. But in this area are found several mysterious remains, about which very little is ever heard. For example, in the Province of Tucuman, near the small town of Rioha, in the wide valley of Tafi, are some 2000 monoliths, some as much as ten feet tall, placed in rows of three and five. According to an article in *Science* in 1897:

"Tafi is the name of a broad valley in the Province of Tucaman, Argentine Republic. The well-known scientist, Professor Ambrosetti, in a recent visit there had his attention called to an extraordinary collection of monolithic pillars and stone enclosures, erected in remote ages by the native inhabitants. He describes them in *Globus*, Bd. LXXI., No. 11. The monoliths are from six to ten feet in height above the soil, some plain, others decorated with conventional designs, others rudely chipped into the likeness of faces, etc. They extend over a considerable area and their purpose is problematical.

"Ambrosetti is inclined to attribute them to the predecessors of the Calchaqui Indians, who occupied this territory at the Conquest. He suggests that they are the work of the same people who erected the buildings of Tiahuanaco; a suggestion which I think is extremely probable for some of the decoration shown in his cuts is strikingly like that on the stone pillars of Hatuncolla two leagues form Lake Titicaca, portrayed in Squier's *Peru*, pp. 385-6."[17]

From my understanding of the site, which is vast and ancient, it looks like a cross between Stonehenge in Britain, and Carnac in Brittany, Northern France. This area is an unfortunately remote desert, quite difficult to get to, or it would be a major tourist attraction for Argentina. My plan once I left Buenos Aires was to see the Tucaman megaliths as a detour on my way up to Rio de Janeiro for Carnival.

Just south of Tucuman in San Juan Province is the Valle de la Luna at Ichihualasto, close to the Chilean border. Besides the rows of monoliths which are found here, similar to those at Tucuman, on cliffs in this remote valley can be found petroglyphs of bears, "airplanes," and people wearing what appears to be circular helmets or "halos." But this is also a difficult area to get to. One experienced traveler recomended that I hire a jeep and the local guide, an Indian named Dorivio at San Juan, and take plenty of food and water to venture into the wasteland of the Valley of the Moon. It sounded like quite an adventure, what with glyptodons, pteradactyls, and mysterious megaliths!

§§§

On my last day in Buenos Aires, I invited Melida out to dinner. Instead, she invited me to a home cooked meal in her apartment. With a time set, I walked down to the Lacroze Station to find a train to Tucuman, to check out the megaliths. Armed with a ticket, I wandered about the Florida shopping area for the afternoon, popping in to see my friends at the jean shop who had helped me sell the camera.

We had only been talking for a few minutes when Alfredo from the camera shop next-door joined us. He soon began regaling us with stories of his heroics in the Falklands War (he had been wounded early in the fighting and evacuated). These remote, windswept islands were once a whaling station, occupied by various whalers from different countries. With lots of sheep and a few lonely English shepards ("The Falkland Islands, where men are men, and the sheep are nervous," is the way one Argentine put it), the ownership of the Falklands has been disputed between Argentina and Britain for many years. Obviously a big topic in Argentina, some cirtics have made rather startling charges about the war's necessity and motivation.

In December, 1981, Argentina's deteriorating economy lead Lt. Gen. Leopoldo Galtieri to lead a junta and take over as President. As the peso continued to be devalued and inflation soared, Galteiri saw an opportunity to rally his countrymen and bind them together; he landed thousands of Argentine troops in the Falklands on April 2, 1982, reclaiming them as the Malvinas, their Spanish name.

The Thatcher Goverment of Britain responded with a 40-ship task force, which sailed from Portsmouth on April 5. Soon after May 21, when 5,000 British troops landed on the islands, Argentine cheers died, 11,000 Argentine troops eventually surrendering to Britain. General Galtieri resigned three days after the surrender of the island garrison on June 14.

This war seemed to be just a silly dispute over some small islands in the south Atlantic, both countries fighting to save face. Yet, according to the critics, the whole story hasn't been told. Supposedly, ten days before the war, Britain announced plans to cut it's naval force by 10,000 men and to rely more on submarines than surface ships in the future. But after the war rallied public opinion, the Thatcher goverment not only cancelled the cutback, but decided to replace four old ships with new ones, and to spend $37 million monthly keeping a naval presence in the south Atlantic.

Argentina may have also benefited from the war, diverting attention from its internal troubles, and getting a chance to use and replace some outdated military hardware. This, and the fact that Britain and Argentina are actually allies, lends some credence to the theory among disgruntled Argentinians that the leadership of the two countries cooked the whole thing up together.

Alfredo told us that during his evacuation back to the mainland, he heard interesting talk of something secret happening with regards to South Georgia Island, farther to the east and south of the Falklands. Supposedly uninhabited except for a British weather research station, the island is one huge rock, at 1,450 sq. mi. (3,700 sq. km.) nearly the size of Puerto Rico. And it is reputed to be more than just a weather station, according to Alfredo. "I heard in the army that there was a base under the island. The rock is hollowed out, and a whole underground city is built inside. Submarines and ships can sail straight in."

I had heard something like this before, so I wasn't too surprised. Similar bases do exist; one is the NORAD Command Center inside Cheyenne Mountain in Colorado Springs. Another American city underground is supposedly located at Pine Gap, near Alice Springs in Central Australia, plus another somewhere in Virginia for Pentagon brass. The Israelis discovered an underground submarine base, in a coastal cave on the southern coast of Lebanon, built the Russians.

Later, at Melida's apartment over dinner, the two of us enjoyed a bottle of wine and traditional Argentine meat pies. Her apartment was lovely, decorated with art and artifacts she had collected on her many travels. She had been educated in France, and still enjoyed spending as much time as she could in Europe.

Soon the conversation turned to the Falklands war, lost continents, and cataclysms (you expected maybe Yogi Bear?). As we finished the last of the wine, she asked me leadingly, "Do you suppose that these tunnels in the Andes are like the base in Colorado Springs? Could the Incas, or their predecessors, have built them for protection?"

At that instant, I knew I had uncovered a conspiracy at work. She had obviously been in contact with Bob. "I guess that's possible."

"Have you read any of the ancient Indian texts, like the Ramayana or the Mahabarata?"

"Yes!" I exclaimed. "They're all about terrible wars. Bob claims they were fought with ray guns and airships!" I could sense a story coming, so I put some more food on my plate.

"What do you remember about ancient cities excavated in India?"

"There was a strange one," I told her, fishing the last of a pie from a plate and popping it into my mouth. "When they first dug up..."

"Don't talk with your mouth full!" she admonished.

After swallowing and then laughing with her, I said, "When they first dug up Mohenjo Daro, an ancient Indian city in Pakistan..."

"I've been there, too" she reminded me.

"...they found remains of people just lying in the streets, some of them holding hands! It was like some doom just took over the city."

"When did this war take place?" Melida asked.

"Well, the last one in the Mahabarata, the Battle of Kurukshetra, took place around 4,000 BC."

"That would correspond with some of the dates around Tiahuanco, wouldn't it?" Melida asked.

"Yes, I suppose so." Now Melida was trying to relate ancient texts of India to the South American ruins! She was worse than Bob! I quoted his favorite phrase, "Anything's possible."

"Indeed, it is!" she said, and then jumped up. "Let's take a drive!"

Back in the Peugeot, she gave me a tour of Buenos Aires at night. We walked around the Cultural Center, then drove to the old part of the city and sat in a café, listening to some old Italians playing tangos on the piano and accordian. Considering the decor, this café hadn't changed for sixty years. A tall, thin man, with his hair slicked back, looking something like Rudolf Valentino, came to our table and sang us a tango love-ballad. It was great!

We then went to a student bar decorated with posters of movie and music stars. They served draft beer and had a huge bathtub of unshelled peanuts from which we just helped ourselves—we could have been in the student quarter of any city in Europe or the U.S. The night rolled by quickly, as we talked until two about life in India and Kathmandu. When Melida finally dropped me off at the Hostel, I thanked her for all the good times and attention she had given me and my friends in Buenos Aires, then crawled back inside through the window.

I was off the next morning by train to Tucuman, sitting in a second-class window seat. Between staring out the window at the vineyards outside the train on the way to Tucuman, I read the English newspaper from Buenos Aires. Inside was an interesting story that caught my eye. It was an interview with a man who claimed that near Tucuman a Glyptodon was being kept. These creatures grew up seven feet high, twelve feet long, and were heavily armoured, resembling in many ways a giant armadillo. Thought to be extinct thousands of years ago, their remains can be seen at the La Plata museum in Buenos Aires. However, it is a fact that Indians today still use the shells from these creatures, using them right-side-up for housing, and up-side-down for bathing! Calling them *Tatu-Carreta*, the natives insist that these creatures are still living, but are rarely seen because they live underground. The glyptodon allegedly kept in near Tucuman was supposed to be about five feet high, though the source in the article somheow failed to provide the name of the owner or a photograph of this strange creature. But living glyptodons could also account for stories of "dinosaurs" being seen in the jungles of South America, as they were large, scaly and rather frightening to bump into on a dark night.

When I arrived in Tucuman, rain had begun to come down hard. I stepped off the train and out into the streets, the rain pouring off my hat and pack, down onto the dark and muddy streets. I spotted a café at the end of the street and headed for it.

Inside the café, I plopped down my pack, and after shedding my parka, took a seat near the door. A small place, only about six people sat at the sixteen or so tables drinking *matte*, a type of tea popular in the pampas of Argentina and Paraguay. This tea, which is quite a stimulant, is sipped from a bottle-like container with a straw. Hot water is continuously added to the container, the matte brewed and re-brewed over and over again.

Tucuman is a major town, with a population of nearly 400,000. Founded in 1565, it was moved to its present site in 1685. Nestled just east of the Andes, the area around it is heavily irrigated and forestry is a major industry. But I was here to try to get to the megaliths.

I ordered a meat pie and matte tea. Everyone in the café watched me carefully, as I suspected that they didn't get too many travelers here. As I began to sip my tea, a tall man, about fifty walked up, and without introducing himself said, "Where are you from, señor?"

His face was weathered, but kind. He wore a wool jacket and dark wool pants, typical of Argentine men in the country. His face was cleanshaven, his eyes were dark. I suspected that he might be part Indian. After pausing for just a moment to study him, I told him I was from the western United States. He spoke quite good English, so I asked him how I might get to the Valley of Tafi, to the megaliths.

"You must hire a jeep to get to Tafi. But you should be careful, it is very dangerous. There are smugglers and bandits in those mountains. Plus, there is treasure!" His voice emphasized these last words, but his whole tone was serious. He was definitely not going to offer to take me out there. "A gringo snooping around Tafi is not good. I advise you not to go by yourself." He looked genuinely concerned.

"I'm not after any treasure," I assured him. My meat pie arrived, and I took a bite.

"That might be true, but not everyone will believe you. People are poor here, and they think gringos are rich. Many people here are watching at night for *la luz de dinero* . Do you know what that is?"

Replying that I didn't, he continued. "It is the money light! Along the trails of the old ones, the Incas and those who came before, one can sometimes see a light, a strange dim green and white light hovering above the ground. Where you see the light, there is treasure! The man searching for *tapada*, for treasure, pounds a stake into the ground where he sees the light, and then drinks wine until the morning. It is dangerous to stay out late at night, for the *tapada* hunter believes in *demonios*. He will return in the morning, and dig up the treasure!"

"Have you ever found such treasure?" I asked the man, as I filled my matte bottle with more hot water.

"No, never. It does not matter to me. I am a happy man. I have everything I need. What about you, señor, what treasure do you seek, so far from home? Where are you going from here?"

"I am planning to go to Paraguay and Brazil from here," I told him. "I hope to be in Rio de Janeiro for Carnival."

"Ah, but that is only a few days from now. It will take you some time to get to Rio de Janeiro from here. I do not think you have time to go to the Valley of Tafi. There is a train tonight for Resistencia. Perhaps you want to be on that train?"

I glanced outside at the pouring rain. The thought of going to Tafi did not appeal to me much at the moment, I had to admit. Going into the Andes in this region was sort of like going into parts of Mexico a hundred years ago; men were armed, desperate and had a dislike for foriegners. Besides, I had been planning to be in Rio for Carnival for quite some time. "Perhaps you are right, señor," I said, "when does that train leave?"

"At midnight. It is not a passenger train, but I have a friend at the station, who can help you. We will go there after you are fininshed."

I finished my meal, eating a salad after the pie, then one more refill of the matte. The stranger and I left for the station, pounding across the road in the pouring rain. When we got there, we had to wait for a few minutes for someone in the station office to finish an animated telephone call. While we waited, my new friend expressed his concern for my welfare.

"Most people do not take responsibilty for their lives," he said. "They are victims of the forces and wills that surround them. They are like the leaf blowing in the wind. They have no control over their life, and blame their misfortunes on others. Do not be like them."

"I take responsibility for my life," I said, in my own defense.

"Good. Your thoughts and actions are like ripples in a pond. They spread out in front of you to make all things happen. Life is a great cycle, like a wheel turning around and around. Learn your lessons well, so you will not have to repeat them. Such is life." he stated with finality.

"That sounds like good advice. I thank you." I was getting treated to philosophy as well as hospitality!

After talking quickly with the man in the station office, he came out and said, "Follow me." He led me down a long line of boxcars, to one near the end. "I think it is this one," he said, and opened the car door, sliding it back. It was empty, so I tossed my pack up, and climbed in.

"The train leaves in one hour! In the morning you will be in Resistencia! Good luck, and remember: things happen to you for a reason! It is your challenge to understand the reason!"

"Thank you!" I called to the stranger, then he disappeared into the rain. I wondered privately what had prompted the man's apparent concern for my well-being, as I settled into a corner, and unrolled my sleeping bag. Shortly I heard the train whistle, and I closed the boxcar door. Over the clackety-clack of the rails, I could here the pounding of the rain on the roof of the car. With the stranger's words in mind, I drifted off to sleep. Little did I know how pertinent these words would become, at Carnival.

§§§

In the morning, the train arrived in Resistencia, just as the stranger had promised. I imediately got a bus up to Formosa and then on to the capital of Paraguay; Asuncion. With only 600,000 people, still by far the largest town in Paraguay, Asuncion is still small and easy to navigate.

Good hotels can be found in the town center. I ended up at the Pension Asuncion, conveniently located between the Plaza de los Heroes and the Plaza Uruguay. Other hotels include the Hotel Savoy, Pension Santa Rosa, Residencia Royal, and the Hotel de Mayo. There are not many tourists in Paraguay, so getting a room is usually not much of a problem.

About the size of California, Paraguay is a land-locked country with the majority of its population in the eastern, upland grassy region. The western Chaco area consists primarily of marshes, lagoons, dense forests and jungle. Also located in western Paraguay is a Mennonite colony, Filadelphia, which is largely independent, a sort of country within a country. And, while the largest hydroelectric dam in the world is located in Paraguay at the Itaipu, the major industry is said to be smuggling.

Paraguay became a duty-free country some years back, so now a large quantity of luxury goods are smuggled out to other countries, especially Bolivia. This can make travel rather dangerous in the west. As there are no buses or public transport, you will have to hitch on a truck, and that truck is probably smuggling.

I met two Peace Corps volunteers who were traveling through this area, coming from Paraguay into Santa Cruz province of Bolivia. They said that some truck drivers who had given them a ride were discussing openly how they were going to, "kill these two gringos." The volunteers managed to convince the smugglers that it would not be advantageous to do so.

Paraguay became independant from Spain in 1811, the only South American country that did not have to fight for independance. In the 1600s, Jesuit Missionaries had a great deal of power in the country. They set up a rather unique series of traditional communes called *reduciones* for Indians, using music to lure them out of the forests, rather like the Pied Piper of Hamlin. These communities were primarily agricultural, with traditional crafts greatly encouraged. Money was not used, and all trading had to be done a good distance from the community.

The demise of these communities, and the terror of early Paraguay, were the large slave raiding parties parties which came from Brazil. Whole communities were sold into slavery, to work on plantations in the Amazon Basin. Slavery is still rumoured to exist in some areas of Brazil.

Currently, the President of Paraguay is Dictator General Alfredo Stroessner, who came into power in 1954. Labeled a neo-Nazi, he has been accused of brutally suppressing all political opposition and of harboring former Nazi War Criminals. Indeed, by asking too many questions in the wrong place about the wrong person, one could find oneself in a lot of trouble. Most Nazi war criminals are getting pretty old these days, but there are plenty of strange goings-on and behind-the-scenes power struggles in Paraguay, Argentina, and Brazil. I was told once that there is an entire city in central Argentina full of ex-Nazis and their families. No journalists, investigators or strangers are allowed into the city, and just who is living there is largely a secret. One Japanese journalist barely escaped with his life a few years ago after trying to do a story on this "lost city of the Third Reich."

I quite enjoyed my short stay in Asuncion. The people were friendly, making it fun to wander along the river and through the plazas. Paraguay is also known for its unique folk music. On Benjamin Constant street behind the Post Office are a collection of cafés and bars where Paraguay's folk music is played with gusto and character.

But soon I had boarded a bus for Iguasu Falls, a six hour ride in an *autobus rapido*. Leaving early from a station in Asuncion, it was a fast ride through the countryside of forest and farms. The Iguasu Falls are in the corner where Paraguay, Argentina, and Brazil meet, but the best view of these spectacular falls are on the Brazilian side.

As we crossed the bridge into Brazil, one step closer to Rio, I could'nt stop thinking aboutthe words of the stranger back in Tucuman who had put me on the train. "Life is like a great cycle: learn your lessons well and you will not have to repeat them."

Chapter Eleven

Rio de Janeiro:
The Carnival and the Sphinx

You never know what enough is,
until you know what more than enough is.
-William Blake

After getting stamped into Brazil, I jumped into the back of a waiting dump truck full of kids which then sped toward Foz de Iguasu. We arrived in the late afternoon, and I wearily checked into the Hotel Brasil, one of the inexpensive hotels near the bus station. There are a number of these, including the Hotel Colibri, Cisne Hotel, Hotel Excelsior, and the Dormitorio Estrela. Foz de Iguasu is quite a small town; its downtown is only about two blocks long. Two travel agencies on the main street will exchange money.

I slept well. After the adventures and exhausting travel of the last few days, the saggy mattress felt like a fresh bed made for a prince. Rising during mid-morning, I ate a breakfast of scrambled eggs at a café near the bus station. You will see a lot of bus stations if you travel around Brazil, as they constitute one of the centers of life in the country. Generally clean and modern, they support a bus system which is fast, cheap and reliable. You will often have to pay to use the bathrooms in the stations, which helps keep them clean and sanitary—a welcome contrast!

The Iguazu Falls are one of the most incredible natural sights in the world, and one of the great tourist spots in South America. Having seen Victoria Falls in Africa and New York's Niagara Falls, I can easily say that Iguazu tops them both in its spectacular beauty, not to mention the amazing wildlife found in the jungle nearby.

I caught a bus down to the falls, which were only ten minutes away, and spent the afternoon exploring the area. The experience was fantastic! One unusual aspect is that there is not just one, but a whole series of cataracts, each pouring down terrific quantities of water. Walking along the dense forest trail along the falls, you are treated at every turn to another misty section. At each corner, I was awed by more astounding beauty.

An observation post stands at the end of the trail, near the farthest cataract. I moved through the spray onto a walk that goes over to the edge of one of the falls. Looking down, I saw the water pour out below the walk and over another cataract. Feeling suddenly dizzy, I gripped the rail for support. The drop seemed like miles! By this time, the spray was starting to soak through my clothes, so I headed back up along the trail.

A bit hungry, I bought an ice cream cone at a stand near the observation post. But as soon as I began to eat it, a sudden tropical rain began. Beginning to realize that being dry just wasn't in the cards for me today, I joined the crowd running for shelter. The rain picked up into a genuine tropical torrent, but typically, by the time we made it to one, the rain stopped. I felt like a car wash sponge after a long summer weekend.

After a quick beer, I wrung out my wet clothes and caught a bus from the falls back into Foz de Iguazu. Realizing that Carnival started the next night in Rio, I caught an overnight bus to Curitiba, about 400 miles away near the coast. I slept most of the way, waking up early the next morning as we pulled into the Curitiba bus station.

After a shave and wash in the rest room (ten cents admission!) I grabbed a bus to São Paulo, the largest city in South America. It was only a few hours away, and again I dozed, resting up for Carnival.

São Paulo is a vast, sprawling city, which threatens to engulf all the surrounding territory in its expansion. At almost ten million people, it is three times the size of Paris, and may soon be a contender for the largest city in the world. When it was a sleepy little Jesuit town in 1554, no one ever dreamed it would become the dynamic, industrial focus of South America. "São Paulo can never stop," say the natives affectionately.

Today a city of tall concrete and steel skyscrapers, its outskirts are haphazard shantytowns, the homes of the country people who flocked to the city for work. Brazil is a country of contradictions, with large upper- and lower-classes, the separation of these classes broadening yearly. If this rich-get-richer, poor-get-poorer cycle continues, a social and economic disaster of gigantic proportions could be the inevitable result.

There are literally thousands of hotels around São Paulo, including several Youth Hostels. Some are always located around the train and bus stations. Try the Hostel Ellis Regine at Av. Diego de Corvalho 86 Capi Vari, Campos eo Jordao, or the Hotel Chaves near the Sorocabana railway teminal and central bus station.

My bus arrived at about noon from Curitaba. I was not particularly interested in staying in São Paulo, because Carnival began that night in Rio, and I did not want to miss this once-in-a-lifetime experience. However, when I tried to get a bus to Rio, the agent said the buses were fully booked for the next three days, and that it was absolutely impossible to get a seat. This news left me severly disappointed.

"How can I get to Rio today?" I pleaded in Portuguese.

"I don't know," he replied courteously. "It is impossible."

"But what will I do?" I asked, dreams of Carnival in Rio shattered.

"Spend Carnival in São Paulo!" said the man cheerfully.

I thought I would cry.

At this point, a gentleman standing beside me asked in broken English if he could help. He seemed as eager to help a stranded foreigner as to practice his English, which was fortunate, because my Portuguese is horrible.

"Yes," I told him, "can you help me get on a bus toward Rio?" I was determined to get there, and I realized that there was still one way to do so. I had hitchhiked the length and breadth of both Africa and Asia, so I could certainly hitchhike from São Paulo to Rio de Janeiro, only about 200 miles along a modern, four-lane highway.

My plan was to catch a city bus on the main highway toward Rio, then get off at the last stop, which I hoped was on the outskirts of the megalopolis. From there, I would hitchhike into my Promised Land. The man took me outside to a bus stop, and helped me find a bus going the right direction. But he gently tried to disuade me, saying that it was fruitless. "There is no hitchhiking in this part of Brazil. No one will give you a ride. No one will stop."

Well, he was right, and he was wrong. There really was no hitch-hiking in that part of Brazil, and it was possible that most drivers would not give me a ride. However, it was not true that no one would stop!

I can explain: I tried hitching from the outskirts of São Paulo for an hour, but no one would give me a lift, as they were all moving too fast on the super-highway. But eventually, a bus approached and I flagged it down, as one can do on highways in Brazil. To my good fortune, the bus stopped, I paid the driver, and he took me as far as he could, about

231

twenty or so miles down the road. I repeated this trick several times during the day, leap-frogging toward Rio until, by late afternoon, I was about half way there.

As six o'clock approached, I stood on the highway, trying to flag down cars and trucks, when another bus appeared. I waved my arms wildly, motioning for the bus to stop. This was my last chance to get to Rio before dark!

The sleek, new, red Mercedes bus sped up at first, but the driver must have then changed his mind, because he slowed down and came to a stop a hundred yards down the road. I grabbed my pack and ran. Out of breath as I boarded, I wheezed out one word, "Rio." He nodded and replied, "2000 cruzeiros."

What luck! I couldn't believe it; I would make it to Rio for Carnival! Holding my pack over my head, I moved to the back of the bus, glancing left and right for a seat. I found one in the back, put my pack down next to the toilet, and collapsed into the seat.

Sitting next to me was a Brazilero about five-and-a-half feet tall, with dark hair, a mustache, and an extremely muscular build. He seemed to be in his mid-twenties, but judging from the scars on his face and hands, those years had been rough ones on the street. We talked for a while in Portuguese, but my vocabulary was limited, so the going was slow.

He was eventually able to communicate to me that his name was Victor, and that he lived in São Paulo. He was on his way to Rio for Carnival, as was everyone else on the bus. At a rest stop ja few miles outside Rio, we met another traveler, a red-haired German traveler also from our bus, named Conrad. His English was excellent, and his Portuguese was very good, so he became our natural translator.

The three of us, Conrad, Victor, and myself, struck up a friendship, and decided to "paint the town red" together for the next few days. The first thing we did when we arrived in Rio that evening was to take a bus out to Copacabana, to the apartment of a Swiss friend of Conrad's. We couldn't stay there, but we could leave our packs and valuables with him, while we tripped the light fantastic. Carnival is a notorious time for crime: pick-pockets, muggers and worse all did a thriving business, so it was best not to carry any more than we were willing to lose. Victor, however, seemed oblivious to the danger; he carried all his worldly possessions in a small bag which never left his shoulder.

With our packs safely stored, we took a bus to Centro, the downtown area. There we were fortunate enough to get two rooms in a dive, the Hotel Dez de Novembro, for about four dollars each. It was located in a sleazy neighborhood, but then again, one might say that all

232

of downtown Rio is a sleazy neighborhood. I had a room on top of the old brick building. To reach it, I had to go outside onto a rooftop terrace, then climb up a fire escape. I had a large double bed, my own bath, and a window with a splendid view of the rooftops. For four dollars, this was a great deal, expecially considering this was the busiest week of the year.

The least expensive places to stay in Rio are the youth hostels. There are three, though only the Casa do Estudiante on Praca Anna Amelia 9, 10, &11, ZC 39 Castelo Street is open year-round. Some of the less expensive hotels are: The Hotel Monte Blanco and the Hotel Rio Claro on Rua do Catete; Hotel Braganca and Hotel Mudo Nova on Avenida Mem de Sa 85; Hotel Cruzeiro Tefe on Rua Sacadura; and the Hotel Rio Grande on Rua Senador Pompeu. Many others exist; in fact, there is a hotel on almost every block. You would be hard pressed, however, to find reasonably priced accomodations near Copacabana, the world-famous beach resort just to the south of the city.

Finally, we hit the city and began dancing in the streets at samba parties, which were breaking out all over the city. Although Carnival officially begins on the Sunday night leading up to Ash Wednesday, in Rio the action starts at 11 PM on Friday, when the first Balls begin and the samba parties start.

Throughout the year, the samba schools prepare for Carnival. Because they live in poverty the rest of the year, many lower-class natives want to "act rich" during Carnival. They practice on weekends, making their costumes, and working out routines for their special, chosen samba. As many as three-thousand people may belong to a particular samba school, each with his or her own job to do in the pageant. Each school also has its own band, which can number up to three-hundred musicians.

Rio literally goes insane for Carnival. Down from the hills stream the poor, gaudily bedecked in satins and tinsel, their faces smeared with paint, powder and make-up. Out of the swank apartments come the rich in their expensive costumes, embracing and kissing everyone they meet. Entire streets downtown are blocked to traffic, as parades, samba schools, and their bands turn neighborhoods into one big dance party. As Martha and the Vandells proclaimed in the their early sixties song, there is literally "Dancing In the Street."

Wild parties continue twenty-four hours for four days and five nights, theoretically ending on Wednesday morning. Inhibitions are generally tossed out the window, and Carnival is about as Dionysian a party as you can find anywhere. Fancy, expensive balls for the upperclass (tickets cost from $50 to a $1000) often end in what seems, to the prudish, an orgy. Hawkers on the street sell photomagazines showing some of the last year's balls, as risqué as any issue of Playboy or Penthouse. Of course, most people in the photos are wearing (or removing!) outlandish costumes, their faces hidden by elaborate make-up so no one will ever recognize them.

Victor, Conrad and I partied on the street with everyone, drinking Antartica brand beer, and dancing with the half-naked women who continually approached in sequins and ostrich plumes. This was only the first night of Carnival, so we took it easy, going to bed at a fairly early hour: before two. There were four more nights of the Carnival, and we thought that it was best to warm up slowly.

The next morning, I was awakened by Victor's furious pounding. Opening the door, he appeared as a character from a nightmare I hadn't had: baggy orange overalls, a matching floppy cap, and a wide push broom. "Come on, we're going to the beach!" he yelled in Portuguese.

On the way to Copacabana, Conrad explained that Victor was a street sweeper. This was a working holiday for him; he had to sweep the streets of Rio every morning after the parties. He had slept on the floor of Conrad's room last night for a few hours, then was up before dawn to begin sweeping.

When we arrived, we found Copacabana, we found it packed along its entire length, from the water to the road. Thousands of tanned and white bodies lay frying in the sun. Rio cuties, many of them topless, wandered up and down the beach and among the sidewalk cafés. Perhaps they hoped to spot a movie star, and certainly this was as good a place as any to do so. Transvestites even flirted with the tourists (after all, anything goes during Carnival!)

As I lay on the beach after a good swim, I managed to forget the moving scenery and thought instead about the lost cities that might be located around Rio. It appears that Rio de Janeiro, a superb and beautiful natural harbour, may have been a major port in the pre-Colombian past.

South of the city is found the "Sphinx of Rio." This enormous rock outcropping overlooking the Atlantic has what looks like the huge head of a Sphinx carved into it. What more natural feature for ancient sailors to take advantage of as a landmark or signal to their fellow sailors; a kind of giant billboard sign saying, "Here we are!"

While some people claim that the rock is nothing more than a natural formation that coincidentally looks like a Sphinx, others claim that it is indeed an ancient carvied landmark. And who else do they claim would carve a Sphinx into a rock except...the Egyptians! They say that the Rio de Janeiro Sphinx is a sort of Egypto-Brazilian Mount

Rushmore, carved more than 3,000 years ago.

Well, there is no proof that this Sphinx was carved by Egyptians, or by anyone for that matter. But is there proof that ancient seafarers did sail to America?

In 1872, a Portuguese land owner discovered some stones near the Paraiba River (not far from Rio de Janeiro) with strange writing carved into their surface. He sent them to the president of the Instituto Historico in Rio de Janeiro, where a well-traveled naturalist, Dr. Ladislau Netto (1838-94), identified the script as Phoenician. Dr. Netto then forwarded a few excerpts of the inscription to Professor Ernest Renan (1823-92) of Paris, who replied that, while no one can really pass judgment on artifacts he has not personally examined, he was nonetheless confident they were a forgery!

Dr. Cyrus Gordon, a professor at New York University, aquired a copy of the inscriptions in 1967, later identifying the script as Sidonian, close to the letter-forms of the Eshmunazar inscription of the early fifth century BC. However, two letters were more archaic, suggesting a sixth century BC date.

Certain linguistic oddities in the text, thought a century ago to discredit its authenticity, now actually lend to its credibility, according to Dr. Gordon. He writes, "No forger who knew enough Semitics to compose such a document would have committed so many apparent errors. Now that nearly a century has passed, it is obvious that the text is genuine, because subsequently discovered Phoenician, Ugaritic, and other Northwest Semitic inscriptions confront us with the same 'errors.' "[6]

Dr. Gordon translated the inscription as follows: "We are Sons of Canaan from Sidon, from the city where a merchant (prince) has been made king. He dispatched us to this distant island, a land of mountains. We sacrificed a youth to the celestial gods and goddesses in the nineteenth year of Hiram, our King. Abra! We sailed from Ezion-geber into the Red Sea and voyaged with ten ships. We were at sea together for two years around Africa. Then we got separated by the hand of Baal and we were no longer with our companions. So we have come here twelve men and three women, into one island, unpopulated because ten died. Abra! May the celestial gods and goddesses favor us!"[6]

Gordon quotes Zelia Nutttall from the book, *The Fundamental Principles of Old and New World Civilizations*, published by the Peabody Museum in 1901; "...the role of the Phoenicians, as intermediaries of ancient civilization, was greater than has been supposed and...America must have been intermittently colonized by the intermediation of Mediterranean seafarers."

In the mid-sixties, Roman wine *amphorae* were recovered in Guanabara Bay, just 15 kilometers from Rio de Janeiro. American archaeologist Robert Marx created quite a stir in Brazil in the seventies, bringing up other Roman artifacts, as well as more amphorae, and even locating the sunken vessel itself. Reaction to these claims were so strong in Brazil that Marx was proclaimed an Italian agent, and banned from re-entering Brazil! It seems that there is still a certain sensitivity about the issue of which European power, Spain or Portugal, discovered Brazil "first!"

Professor Elizabeth Will of the University of Massachusetts at Amherst declared the amphorae to be from the second century BC, and that they were Roman. They were probably manufactured at Knouss on the coast of Western Morocco, an ideal spring-board for voyages to Brazil.[4] Other amphorae, of Carthaginian origin, were found off the coast of Honduras in 1972.

This all would seem to prove that Mediterranean sailors from several different civilizations were sailing to the New world from as early as 1000 BC right up to several centuries after the birth of Christ. The Vikings and other European sailors continued to make the journey until just before Columbus. However, the Egyptians seem to have been the first of the Mediteranean cultures sailing to the Americas, beginning as long ago as four or five thousand BC.

In the appendix of his remarkable book, *The Chronicle of Akakor*, late German researcher Karl Brugger wrote: "The Egyptian Books of the Dead in the second millennium BC speak about the kingdom of Osiris in a distant country in the west. Rock inscriptions in the region of Rio Mollar in Argentina are clearly linear in the Egyptian tradition. Symbols and ceramic objects were found in Cuzco that are identical with Egyptian artifacts. According to the American researcher Verrill, they provide evidence for the visit of King Sargon of Akkad and his sons in Peru in the years 2500-2000 BC. Consecration sites and temples in Guatemala seem to have been fashioned after the Egyptian pyramids. Their architecture, which follows strict astronomic laws, points to the same origin or the same builder. But the most distinct indications are in Amazonia and the Brazilian federal state of Mato Grosso. Meter-high inscriptions on barely accessible rock faces unquestionably show the characteristics of Egyptian hieroglyphics. They were collected and interpreted by the Brazilian scholar Alfredo Brandåo in his two-volume work *A Escripta Prehistorica do Brasil*. He writes in the preface: 'Egyptian seafarers left traces everywhere, from the mouth of the Amazon to the bay of Guanabara. They are about

4,000-5,000 years old, and so we can surmise that communications by sea between the two continents were broken off at a later date.' "[54]

§§§

Victor threw a towel on my face, disturbing my playful mental superimposition of an Egyptian headdress on a passing Brazilian beauty. "Come on," he said in Portuguese, "let's grab a beer!" Gazing at the collection of near-naked, bronzed bodies sizzling on the packed beach, I was amused by the thought of Romans and Egyptians suntanning on this same beach. Rio had certainly changed quite a bit since since the heyday of its Sphinx.

Carnival was still in full swing, so there was plenty of madness in the air. For the rest of the afternoon, we wandered Copacabana and Centro, stretching and preparing for the wild night ahead. Conrad and Victor had turned out to be the ideal companions. Conrad was fun and crazy. He got along well with Victor, so they spent a great deal of time together, talking excitedly in Portugese.

Victor, mad Victor! He was a janitor at that time, but before that he had been a criminal. Conrad called him a gangster. Victor pulled his shirt up over his brown, muscular chest and showed us two very nasty scars, souveniers of a shootout with the police. I was curious, but didn't ask for the full story!

Victor didn't seem to have much money left from his criminal career, so Conrad and I treated him to meals and an occasional beer. But as the streetwise gangster, he was constantly warning us of danger. He would often look around corners at night to make sure we weren't being followed, or to keep us from stepping into a "trap." He was our bodyguard, faithfully keeping an eye out for his two gringo friends during the wild and dangerous Carnival. For the price of a rice dinner and beer, Victor kept us safe.

Conrad told me once that Victor was a good guy, but that we could only trust him "so far." When we passed a pretty girl on the street, he would say something to her with a glint in his eye. I never heard what he said to the women, but from their reactions I guessed it was obscene. Conrad later told me Victor's line was, "I love you, I want you, let's screw!" This approach did not seem to work very well. On other occasions, we would be walking along the street, Mad Victor the bodyguard chattering away, when he would suddenly fall to his knees to scoop up a box of matches or some other bit of choice garbage, for which he had a keen eye. In time, I became quite fond of him, even though he was rude to women and I could rarely understand anything he said.

That night at Carnival downtown, while we danced to the samba and drank beer on the street, I chanced to meet a young lady in front of the National Library. I was taking a breather from the wild street scene, and had climbed up the steps. She was a charming woman from the Matto Grosso who worked at the library, and was living in Rio with her brother. Her name was Vilma, and she was twenty-three. Petite, with short black hair and sparkling brown eyes, she had a wonderful smile and shy demeanor. She was completely unlike the tall, buxom blacks in sequined bikinis and feathers dancing in the parades down below.

Perhaps the Carnival atmosphere and beer got to me, but I suddenly kissed Vilma on the side of her neck. She turned to me, and I put my arm around her waist. "I'm not like these girls that you can buy with your American dollars," she said. "You can't pay me!"

We laughed and hugged. She was so sweet, I was afraid of falling in love with her. "Let me walk you to your bus," I suggested. As she boarded her bus, I asked what she was going to do the next day. She suggested that I meet her at the Hotel Gloria at Florida Beach the next morning at eleven. Turning back toward the crowd, I found Mad Victor and Conrad standing there, Conrad with a patronizing smile of his face, and Victor saying something in Portuguese, undoubtably obscene. Red with embarrassment, I pushed the two jokers back toward the party

But I was not destined to meet my dream woman again. I woke up much too late the next morning, and when we finally made it to the Hotel Gloria, it was past one in the afternoon. We went down to Florida Beach to look around anyway, but it was useless: the crowd was too large. Swimming and playing volleyball for a while, we prepared for yet anothernight of craziness.

That night, after Mad Victor showed up, we all had dinner together before hitting the streets of Centro. As usual, I walked ahead, while Conrad and Mad Victor chattered away in Portuguese behind me. As we turned down a fairly dark street, I had made it a fair distance ahead of them both.

Suddenly, two shadows separated themselves from the gloom of the alley. Startled, I spun around to see two men rushing me. One hit me hard on the back of the head, just behind my right ear. I staggered forward, pain searing through my head and body.

My attacker intended me to fall, but I didn't. I managed to keep on my feet, even though he and his partner shoved me up against a wall and began groping at my clothes for valuables. I hardly knew what was happening as I clutched my head and tried desperately to keep on my feet.

But as I tried to turn to face the assailants, Mad Victor and Conrad came to my rescue. Victor punched one of the attackers in the face, while Conrad grappled awkwardly with the other. Quickly dispatching his victim, Victor grabbed the man who had meanwhile pinned Conrad to a wall, pulled him away, and tossed him head-first into a door.

It was over in a matter of moments. Faced with the wrath of Mad Victor, the two men fled. I had fallen against some trash cans, where both Conrad and Victor came to pick me up. Was I okay, they asked? Yes, I was okay, though already I had a splitting headache.

Not wanting to let this spoil Carnival, we tripped on down to main street, where we proceeded to drink more wine. This had a fortunate anaesthetic effect on my now-pounding headache. The evening progressed, and I drank more wine, dancing the samba with the crowds. At some point during that evening, I met a young woman, and we danced and drank wine together. The night wore on, and the samba and wine continued. As the lights became a blur, so did my memory.

I woke up late the next morning in my hotel room bed, mid-day sun pouring into the room. Lying next to me naked, a ravishing woman with shoulder-length brown hair and tanned white skin slept soundly. My head throbbed as if the samba dancers were still pounding their rhythm inside it. I felt like a detective waking up in some cheap Mickey Spillane novel. Who was this woman? She looked French. Why did my head hurt so much? Was it the woman? Was it the wine? Then the details started slowly coming back into focus: the mugging, Mad Victor in action, and the ensuing party.

I awoke again some hours later to find my companion awake. Rather than being French, she hailed from São Paulo. She asked me who I was, and in my daze I told her I was a rogue archaeologist who explored lost cities. "How interesting," she cooed, and bit my ear. It was my bad ear, but after all, I wasn't in that much pain...We spent the early afternoon together, getting to know each other in the privacy of my room, until she said that her husband was waiting for her on their yacht in the harbor.

"Really?" I squeaked, only now aware she was married. "Your husband is waiting?"

"Yes, of course," she said, rising and turning on the shower. "He will be expecting me back soon. What time is it?"

"Does he know where you are?" I asked. Remembering Mad Victor, I scanned the rooftops for trouble. I'd had enough for one day.

239

"No, of course not! I don't even know where I am!" Wrapping herself in a towel she came in and kissed me. "Really, I have to go! It's been fun!"

"Where's your yacht?" I asked.

"In Copacabana," she replied.

"I'll come with you." We took a taxi to Copacabana, where I put her on a launch toward the yacht. As I walked down the main avenue along the beach, I wondered what more was going to happen. There were still two nights of Carnival left, but I didn't know if I could take anymore.

At that very moment, a man in his twenties rode up on a motorcycle. "You want to change some money, gringo?" he asked. Mentally counting my Brazillian currency, I told him yes, so he took me on a ride along the waterfront on his bike. When we stopped at Ipanema Beach, he told me that his name was Antonio, and that he was actually from a suburb of Buenos Aires called Olivos. He seemed Italian, had a thick five-o'clock shadow, and dark black, greased-over hair. But he was quite friendly, and drove me around Rio for half an hour, with total disregard for all traffic laws.

When we fianlly stopped, he said, "I like you. We go to a ball tonight. I get you tickets. You still want to change money?"

I said that I needed to. "Give me the money, and wait here. I change the money for you. I be back in ten minutes."

Feeling wary, I said I should go with him. That was impossible, he said. If I just waited here, he would be back soon with the money, then we would go to a ball. He even showed me the tickets. My head still hurt, and I wasn't thinking clearly. I'm sure that had the street-wise Mad Victor been there, he would have stopped me.

"Well, OK, here's fifty dollars," I said, handing him the precious money to change into cruzeiros at the black market rate.

Taking my money, Antonio was off on his motorcycle. "I be back in ten minutes," he called over his shoulder. Did he seem to ride off even faster than before?

Well, I waited for about half an hour, and, of course, he never came back. Why should he? He had my money, he was a scam artist, what more did he need? Disgusted and disappointed, I headed for Conrad's Swiss friend's apartment. On the way, I had to squeeze through a crowd to board a bus, and during the crush, lost my wallet to a pickpocket. The little money Antonio had left me with was now gone; I didn't even have bus fare! I graphically explained my predicament to the ticket taker, showing her my empty pockets. She let me ride free.

Back at the Copacabana, I went up to the Swiss man's apartment, where fortunately I had kept the rest of my cash. When I told him what had happened, he shook his head. "I thought you knew about those guys," he said, "or I would have said something. Everyone knows about them in Copacabana. They're always ripping off the tourists, either changing money or selling cocaine. They just take your money and disappear."

Finally making it back to the hotel late that afternoon, I told Conrad and Mad Victor that I had decided to leave Rio. They both laughed at my confession that one more night like the last few would probably kill me. I gave Victor a hug and thanked him for saving my life. Two hours later I was on a bus heading north for Salvador, the cultural capital of Brazil.

Yet another spectacular sunset bathed over the landscape as I leaned back in the bus speeding out of Rio. I thought about Carnival—it was not over yet! There were still two nights left of the crazy once-a-year party. Tonight I could spend recovering on the bus, but the last night I would be in Salvador. Perhaps by then my wounds would heal. Touching the tender skin behind my ear and closing my eyes, I remembered the stranger who had put me on the train in Argentina, and his unsolicited theory that we attracted to ourselves everything which happens in our lives. Idly, I wondered how I had managed to attract quite so much into my life in Rio!

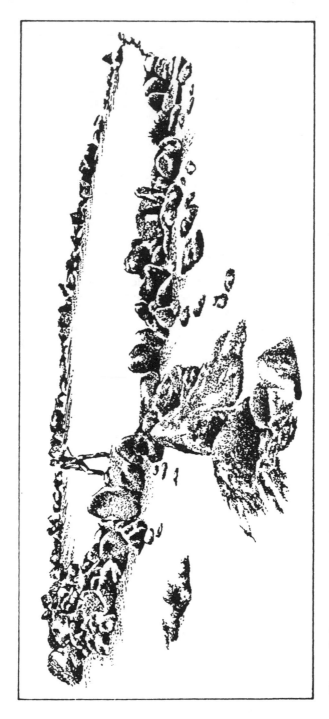

One of the stone circles, possibly an astronomical observatory, found at Tucuman.

Chapter Twelve

The Amazon Jungle:
The Secret City of Akakor

The ancient Masters were subtle, mysterious, profound, responsive.
The depth of their knowledge is unfathomable.
Because it is unfathomable,
All we can do is describe their appearance.
Watchful, like men crossing a winter stream.
Alert, like men aware of danger.
-Lao Tzu, Tao Te Ching

Great was the knowledge of the Former Masters; great their wisdom.
Their vision reached to the hills, the plains,
the forests, the seas, and the valley.
They were miraculous creatures.
They knew the future.
Truth had been revealed to them.
Farsighted they were and of high resolve.
-The Chronicle of Akakor

This chapter is a reprieve from the story of my South American odyssey. Here, you will find perhaps the strangest of all the ancient stories and legends to emerge from this mysterious continent. As you read this tale, try to be less critical than I was when I first encountered it; rather than looking for the points which might prove it false, search instead for the threads which may indeed come through from a truly ancient time.

The Amazon jungle is one of the last true frontiers left on earth. To the Amazon basin are nearly the same size as the continental United States. Most people's image of South America is that it is somewhat smaller than North America, but they forget that not only do most maps exagerate the northern latitudes of the latter, but also that Canada itself is larger than the U.S.! Imagine that everything west of Washington D.C. was a huge, virtually impenetrable jungle filled with anacondas, fierce cats, huge crocodiles, savage Indians, and, in case you thought I forgot, lost cities. That will give you an accurate mental image of the Amazon basin.

The Amazon jungle is situated primarily within the borders of Brazil, but significant parts are located in Bolivia, Peru, Ecuador, Columbia, Venezuela, and the Guianas. It is generally these border areas that are the least known or explored. Within this dark world, rarely penetrated by civilized men, the incredible story of Akakor takes place.

The primary trading center of the Amazon basin is the old rubber capital Manaus, a city surrounded by jungle with a population of over 600,000. Of late it has become a major river port, accommodating ocean-going vessels. Founded in 1669, it grew rapidly during the rubber boom of the late 19th century and then fell silent when rubber prices crashed from competition with the British rubber estates in Malaysia. With the recent increase in interest in developing the Amazon basin, Manaus has sprung back in importance, and is a boom town once again.

In Manaus, on March 3, 1972, a German journalist named Karl Brugger met Tatunca Nara, prince of Akakor in a backstreets tavern, *Gracas a Deus*. The meeting had been arranged by some friends, who believed that Brugger should hear the incredible tale that Tatunca Nara had to tell. Brugger interviewed this Indian chieftan several times, tape recording the tale, then accompanied him on his subsequent attempt to return to the secret city of Akakor. Brugger tells the entire story in his book, *The Chronicle of Akakor*.[54]

Brugger describes Tatunca Nara as tall, with long dark hair and a finely molded face. He had brown eyes, narrowed and full of suspicion. He was a half-breed, a Mestizo. When he met Brugger, he was wearing a faded tropical suit, the gift of some Brazilian military officers, girded with a broad leather belt with a striking silver buckle. In broken German (the language anomaly is described later) the chief told Brugger the amazing tale of his tribe, the Ugha Mongulala, a people who were "chosen by the Gods" 15,000 years ago. He maintained throughout his narrative that what he said was all recorded in a tribal book, the *Chronicle of Akakor*, written in their own script.

This itself is incredible, as no written language is supposed to exist among South American tribes, including the Incas. He goes on to say that the language they spoke was Quechua, which has a written language of 1,400 symbols, each yielding different meanings depending on their sequence. Not even the Incas, who also spoke Quechua, knew "the script of the Gods."

The *Chronicle of Akakor* starts at the year zero, which corresponds to the year 10,481 BC on the Gregorian calendar, according to Tatunca Nara. During this year, "...the great Masters left the Ugha Mongulala. Before the year zero, men lived like animals, without laws, without tilling the soil, without clothing themselves." The great Masters brought "the light" (shades of the Prometheus story, bringing light, or knowledge, from the heavens to mankind).

Before year zero, said Tatunca Nara, the continent was "...still flat and soft like a lamb's back, ...the Great River still flowed on either side." At a time before the year zero, no one knows when, but Tatunca guessed 3,000 years before, "...glimmering golden ships appeared in the sky. Enormous blasts of fire illuminated the plain. The earth shook, and thunder echoed over the hills."

The strangers who came in the golden airships said that the name of their home was Schwerta, and talked of cataclysmic upheavals that happened every 6,000 years. These strangers looked very much like men, with fine features, white skin, bluish black hair, and thick beards. The only difference was they supposedly had six fingers on each hand and six toes on each foot! Tatunca Nara at one point spoke about the knowledge of the Former Masters. "We have no tools as they did which, as if by magic, suspend the heaviest stones, fling lightning or melt rocks." The strangers civilized the tribe, and built three great cities of stone: *Akanis, Akakor , and Akahim* . The names indicated the order of their construction: Aka means "fortress," and Kor, "two." The third fortress, Akanis, was built "...on a narrow isthmus in the country that is called Mexico," according to Tatuca Nara, "...at a place where the two oceans touch" (Panama?). Akahim, the third fortress, is not mentioned in the Chronicle before the year 7315, but its history is closely linked to that of Akakor.

The city of Akakor lay far up the Purus River, in a high valley in the mountains of the frontier between Brazil and Peru. Both the Madre de Dios province of Peru and the Acre Province of Brazil are likely locations, as both these areas are still largely unexplored. "The whole city is surrounded by a high stone wall with thirteen gates. They are so narrow that they give access only to one person at a time. The plain in the east is additionally guarded by stone watchtowers where chosen warriors are always on the lookout for enemies.

"Akakor is laid out in rectangles. Two intersecting main streets divide the city into four parts corresponding to the four universal points of our Gods. The great Temple of the Sun and a stone gate cut from a single block sit on wide square in the center. The temple faces due east, toward the rising sun, and is decorated with symbolic images of our Former Masters...A strange script that can only be interpreted by our priests tells of the foundation of the city."

According to Tatunca Nara, "The most impressive building in Akakor is the Great Temple of the Sun. Its outer walls are unadorned and are made from artfully hewn stones. The roof of the temple is open so that the rays of the rising sun can reach a golden mirror, which dates from the times of the Former Masters, and is mounted at the front. Life-size stone figures flank both sides of the entrance to the temple. The interior walls are covered with reliefs. In a large stone chest sunk into the front wall of the temple are the first written laws of our Former Masters.

"Next to the Great Temple of the Sun are the buildings for the priests and their servants, the palace of the prince, and the lodgings of the warriors. These buildings are rectangular in shape and are made from hewn stone blocks. They are roofed with a thick layer of grass supported by bamboo poles."

Tatunca Nara spoke of secret documents that were kept in the Temple of the Sun, including pictures, maps and drawings telling of the history of the earth. "One of the maps shows that our moon is not the first and not the only one in the history of the earth. The moon that we know began to approach the earth and to circle around it thousands of years ago. At that time, the world still bore another face. In the west, where the charts of the White Barbarians only show water, was a large island. And a gigantic mass of land was in the northern part of the ocean as well. According to our priests, these two were buried under an enormous tidal wave during the first Great Catastrophe, the war between the two divine races. And they add that this war did not only lay waste to the earth but also to the worlds of Mars and Venus, as they are called by the White Barbarians."

Tatunca Nara then went on to explain that there were another twenty-six stone cities around Akakor, the largest being Humbaya and Paititi in Bolivia (probably in Pando province or possibly in Beni province), Emin on the lower reaches of the Great River, and Cadira in the mountains of Venezuela. "But all these were completely destroyed in the first Great Catastrophe thirteen years after the departure of the Gods."

"Apart from these mighty cities, the Ancient Fathers also erected three sacred temple complexes: Salazere on the upper reaches of the great river, Tiahuanaco on the Great Lake, and Manoa on the high plain in the south." These temple complexes were supposedly the residences of the Former Masters, and were off limits to the tribe. A giant pyramid was erected in the center of these sacred temple complexes, and a broad stairway led to the the platform where ceremonies were conducted (note that Tiahuanaco, the only place named that is actually known today, does indeed have a pyramid located in its center.)

Said Tatunca Nara, "Of the sacred temple precincts, I have seen only Salazere with my own eyes. It lies at a distance of an eight days journey from the city that the White Barbarians call Manaus, at a tributary of the Great River. Its palaces and temples have become completely overgrown by the Liana jungle. Only the top of the great pyramid still rises above the forest, overgrown by a dense thicket of bush and trees."

Besides the fortress on the surface, there existed a series of underground dwellings. "We have thirteen cities, deeply hidden inside the mountains that are called the Andes." Inside the Temple of the Sun, said Tatunca Nara, there are twelve entrances to the tunnels that link "lower Akakor" with other underground cities. The tunnels are large enough for five men walking upright, and are so extensive that many days are needed to reach one of the other cities.

Of the thirteen underground cities, twelve were lit artificially. These were: Akakor (the underground city), Budo, Kish, Boda, Gudi, Tanum, Sanga, Rino, Kos, Aman, Tata, and Sikon. The thirteenth city, Mu, which is also the smallest, is lit by high vertical shafts that reach to the surface, while an enormous silver mirror disperses sunlight over the whole city. All the subterranean cities are crossed by canals carrying water from the mountains.

These tunnels and subterranean cities were built by the Former Masters. According to the written *Chronicle of Akakor*, quoted from memory by Tatunca Nara:

"And the Gods ruled from Akakor. They ruled over men and the earth. They had ships faster than birds' flight, ships that reached their goal without sails or oars and by night as well as by day. They had magic stones to look into the distance so that they could see cities, rivers, hills, and lakes. Whatever happened on earth or in the sky was reflected in the stones. But the underground dwellings were the most wonderful of all. And the Gods gave them to their Chosen Servants as their last gift. For the Former Masters are of the same blood and have the same father."

After the Former Masters left in the year zero, according to the chief, some sort of global catastrophe occured. Just before the catastrophe, there was some sort of "War between the Gods," something horrible and devastating. After this war and catastrophe, the Ugha Mongulala and the surrounding tribes lapsed into 6,000 years of barbarism.

During this first cataclysm in the year 13 (10,468 BC) the course of the rivers was altered, and the height of the mountains and the strength of the sun changed (volcanic dust in the air?) "Continents were flooded. The waters of the Great Lake flowed back into the oceans. The Great River was rent by a new mountain range and now it flowed swiftly toward the East. Enormous forests grew on its banks. A humid heat spread over the easterly regions of the empire. In the West, where giant mountains had surged up, people froze in the bitter cold of the high altitudes. The Great Catastrophe caused terrible devastation as had been predicted by our Former Masters."

"After the first Great Catastrophe, the empire was in a desperate situation. The underground dwellings of the Former Masters did withstand the tremendous landslides and none of the thirteen cities was destroyed, but many of the passages that linked the borders of the empire were blocked up. Their mysterious light had been extinguished like a candle blown out by the wind. The twenty-six cities were destroyed by a tremendous flood. The sacred temple precincts of Salazere, Tiahuanaco, and Manoa lay in ruins, destroyed by the terrible fury of Gods."

Then in 3,166 BC was a second catastrophe, ending the "Years of Blood," the six thousand years of barbarism that South America had fallen into after the first. Apparently, just after this catastrophe, the Gods returned to Akakor and resumed power. "But only a few ships reached our capital, and the gods stayed with the Ugha Mongulala for barely three months." Only two brothers stayed on, Lhasa and Samon, theformer remaining at Akakor, Samon flying to the east, to establish his own empire.

Lhasa, now king of the Ugha Mongulala, fortified the kingdom, and supposedly had Macchu Picchu built as an outpost of the empire. "Lhasa was the decisive innovator of the Ugha Mongulala empire. During the 300 years of his rule, he laid down the basis for a powerful empire. Then he returned to the Gods. He convened the elders of the people and the highest priests and passed his laws on to them. He ordered the people to live according to the Gods' bequest forever and to obey his commands. Then Lhasa turned to the East and bowed low before the rising sun. Before its rays touched the holy city, he ascended the Mountain of the Moon, which looms over Macchu Picchu, in his flying disk and forever withdrew from the humans." Somewhat contradictorily, the chief also said that Lhasa's flying disc, which is the color of gold, is still kept in the Temple of the Sun. How Lhasa left without his flying disc is not explained.

§§§

Lhasa was often absent with his flying disk.
He visited his brother Samon.
He flew to the mighty empire in the East.
And he took a strange vessel with him
that could pass over water and mountains.
-*The Chronicle of Akakor*

Supposedly, Samon's empire was a mirror image of that of Akakor, built by a mighty river. Lhasa often visited his brother with his flying disc, and to form a strong link between the two nations he commanded the construction of a great city at the mouth of the Amazon in 7425 (3056 BC), named *Ofir*. "For almost a thousand years, ships from Samon's empire docked here with their valuable cargos. In exchange for gold and silver they brought scrolls with writing in the language of our Ancient Fathers, and they brought rare woods, finest fabrics, and green stones that were unfamiliar to my people. Soon Ofir had become one of the wealthiest cities of the empire and a target for the savage tribes in the East. They stormed against the city in repeated attacks, raided the ships at anchor, and disrupted the communications with the interior. When the empire disintegrated a thousand years after Lhasa's departure, they succeeded in conquering Ofir in a mighty campaign. They ransacked the city and burned it down. The Ogha Mongulala yielded the coastal provinces at the eastern ocean and withdrew into the interior of the country. And the connection to Samon's empire was severed."

Tatunca Nara then talked about Akahim, a city which is mysterious even to his tribe. Supposedly located on the borders of Brazil and Venezuela, the entrance to the gigantic stone city, shaped "like an outstretched finger," lies behind a great waterfall. Akahim has lain in ruins for 400 years, though it was in close alliance with Akakor for thousands of years. The former occupants of Akahim also decided to

249

go underground, when the White Barbarians began to advance into their territory. He also goes on to say that Akakor and Akahim are linked together by a subterranean passage and an enormous mirror device. "The tunnel starts in the Great Temple of the Sun in Akakor, continues below the bed of the Great River, and ends in the heart of Akahim. The mirror device extends from the Akai over the range of the Andes to the Roraima Mountains, as the White Barbarians call them. It consists of silver mirrors of the height of a man mounted on large bronze scaffolds. Every month, the priests relay the most important events across the device in a secret sign language. In this way, the sister nation Akahim learned for the first time of the arrival of the White Barbarians in the country called Peru."

Tatunca Nara then goes on to say that the Inca foulder of legend, Viracocha, was an Ugha Mongulala who had been banished from the tribe as a law breaker. Viracocha then founded the Inca dynasty, and built Cuzco. This was in 7951 (2470 BC) according to Tatunca Nara, further stating that the Inca Empire later became a sister nation of the Ugha Mongulala.

In the year 11,051 (570 AD) a curious thing happened to the Ugha Mongulala and Akakor. Up the Amazon came white, bearded strangers sailing in long ships with a fierce dragon-head at the prow. They called themselves "Goths" and allied themselves with the people of Akakor. "The iron armor, the black sails, and the colored dragon heads from the ships of the Goths have been preserved to this day, and we have kept them in the Great Temple of the Sun. According to the drawings of our priests, their ships could carry up to sixty men and were propelled by a sail of fine cloth that was rigged to a high mast. More than 1,000 warriors reached Akakor on forty ships."

That Goths arrived in Akakor, according to Tatunca Nara, in 570 AD is quite interesting. The Germanic tribe of Ostrogoths, a race of warriors that conquered Italy within a period of sixty years, were defeated by the East Roman General Narses at the battle of Mount Vesuvius in 552 AD. The last survivors of this formally powerful tribe disappeared without a trace. Linguists claim to have found traces of their language in the southern regions of France and Spain, though definite proof of where they migrated has never been offered.

According to *Chronicle of Akakor*, the Ostrogoths united with some bold sailors of the north, and ended up in South America. The subsequent union of the Goths and the Ugha Mongulala again strengthened Akakor. They built new walls and defenses, and the Goths showed the Ugha Mongulala how to make iron and armor. This story curiously corresponds to one of the Gran Paititi legends, in which

250

"white Indians" were said to wear armor and have constructed wooden fortifications and roads.

Later, of course, "The White Barbarians" invaded South America, and conquered the Incas. Five years after the Spanish arrived, the Ugha Mongulala decided to withdraw into the inner recesses of Akakor. They left Macchu Picchu, according to Tatunca Nara, and ordered their frontier cities abandoned and destroyed. Only the subterranean passages were left unsealed, for they could not be used without understanding the signs within.

The struggle of the Ugha Mongulala to maintain their empire failed as the Spanish continued to conquer more and more of South America. With Spanish and Portuguese landing at the mouth of the Amazon, Akakor's sister city Akahim came under attack by hostile tribes and was abandoned. The men wanted to retreat, but curiously, the women insisted on fighting the White Barbarians. And so, according to Tatunca Nara, the legend of the Amazons was born.

According to Brugger, Tatunca Nara said that in 1920 the Spanish captured fifteen Inca nobles, holding them prisoner in Lima. Tatunca Nara's father, Prince Sinkaia decided to attempt to free them, sending eighty warriors through the tunnels, a branch of which led to Lima. That Inca nobles were still around in 1920 is incredible in itself. Where did they come from, Gran Paititi?

The tunnel walls are light colored, said Tatunca Nara. "Black stones which we call 'hour stones' are sunk into the walls at regular intervals to mark the distance. The ways in and out are protected by signs of our Gods, traps, and poisoned arrows. Not even the Incas know the course of the tunnel. After the arrival of the White Barbarians, they had constructed their own subterranean passage. It went from Cuzco via Catamarca into the interior yard of the Lima Cathedral. A stone slab bars the passage from the outside world. It is so cleverly sunk into the foundation that it cannot be distinguished from the other slabs. Only those who know the secret can open it.

"The eighty selected warriors went through Lhasa's passage. For three moons they moved like shadows through the country of their enemies. Then they reached the capital of the White Barbarians. At dawn they broke out of the underground passage and tried to free the captive Incas. In the ensuing battle, 120 White Barbarians were killed. But the enemy's advantage was too great. None of Sinkaia's warriors returned to Akakor. They gave their lives as faithful servants of the Gods for the Chosen People."

Later, in the year 12,143 (1932), the Ugha Mongulala attacked a White settlement on the upper reaches of the Santa Maria River, killing all the men, and taking four women captive. Three drowned in an attempt to escape on the return to Akakor, but one survived, a German missionary named Reinha. Entering Akakor, she took a liking to the ancient city and its people, eventually marrying Prince Sinkaia. Together they gave birth to, you guessed it, Tatunca Nara. This whole story, a bizarre one to start with, at this point gets even stranger!

Four years later, after Tatunca Nara was born, Reinha left Akakor to returned to Germany as an ambassador to Hitler's Third Reich. She was gone for one year, then returned to Akakor with three German leaders. After long negotiations, the leaders of Akakor and the Germans reached an agreement; the Germans and the Ugha Mongulala would be allies. In the year 12,425 (1945), the Germans would land on the coast and occupy the larger cities. The Ugha Mongulala were to support the campaign by making raids on the white settlements in the interior. After the expected victory, Brazil would be divided into two territories: the Germans would rule the provinces on the coast; the Ugha Mongulala would reclaim the region on the Great River that had been given to them by the Gods 12,000 years before.

According to Tatunca Nara, the first German soldiers reached Akakor in the dry season of 12,422 (1941). New groups of soldiers arrived secretly at Akakor throughout World War Two. They left Marseilles on U-boats, told before they left that they were going to England. Once on board, they were told that they were really going to Akakor.

The Germans armed and trained the Ugha Mongulala. The last of the soldiers arrived in 1945, but the planned invasion never took place. Still, the Germans and the Ugha Mongulala planned for war.

However, for some years, things were calm in the empire of Akakor, and the German soldiers lived the life of the Ugha Mongulala. But in 12,444 (1963), fighting broke out between them and Peru, the Germans and Ugha Mongulala killing a number of white settlers in the Madre de Dios region. The Peruvian government counter attacked, forcing the Ugha Mongulala to withdraw back to Akakor.

In the year 12,449 (1968), a plane crashed in the vicinity of Akakor. Prince Sinkaia ordered his son, Tatunca Nara, to go to the site to slay the survivors, who were being held captive by another tribe. But Tatunca Nara disobeyed this order, and conducted the survivors to Manaus. This was the first time Tatunca Nara entered a White Barbarian city.

The twleve survivors were officers of the Brazilian Government, all obviously thankful to Tatunca Nara. He said it was they who gave him his second name, "Tatunca, my first name, means 'great water

252

serpent.' I bear this name since I defeated the most dangerous creature on the Great River. In the language of my people, Nara means 'I do not know.' That was my reply when the white officers asked me for the name of my family."

During his subsequent ceremony to become the new tribal leader, he entered the Akakor temple complex, and passed through successive secret rooms. In an inner chamber he found four bodies, he said, three men and one woman. Mummified, these bodies were extremely well preserved, and noremal in every respect—except they had six fingers and six toes!

As new leader of the tribe, Tatunca Nara felt it was useless to fight the White Barbarians any longer, especially since another cataclysm was predicted (in 1981, according to the *Chronicle of Akakor*. This date has come and gone without the cataclysm, in case you haven't noticed). With the help of the aging Germans, they destroyed the above-ground parts of Akakor, so the White Barbarians could not see them from the air, and retreated into the underground cities.

Tatunca Nara decided to go back to the nearby town of Rio Branco, to see if he could make some sort of treaty with the White Barbarians. A Catholic Bishop was even admitted to Akakor and given a portion of the written Chronicle. He returned to the outside world, but was soon killed in a plane crash. The written text was supposedly sent to the Vatican, where it allegedly remains. Tatunca Nara was even imprisoned once by the whites when he tried to negotiate with them, but he escaped. While in Manaus, still trying to negotiate with the White Barbarians in 1972, he met Karl Brugger, and our tale comes full circle.

§§§

To simply call this story strange would be an understatement. We have here all the elements of the wildest science-fiction and occult fantasy: Gods from outer space, lost continents, vast tunnel systems, flying saucers, bold Vikings, forgotten cities in the jungles, even Hitler and the Nazis! Stand back, Steven Spielberg, here comes the *Chronicle of Akakor*!

But can there be any truth to this story? Perhaps, for your own sanity, you would like me to tell you why it cannot possibly be true. Maybe I just made up the whole thing, to liven up my otherwise-dull book!

No discussion of lost cities and ancient mysteries of South America can be made without touching on the subject of Akakor. As objectively as possible, I would like to examine this material. Karl Brugger claims to have checked out as much of Tatunca Nara's story as possible, saying he didn't believe the man until certain facts were verified. But a friend of Brugger's in the Brazilian Secret Service said he had known Tatunca Nara for four years, and confirmed at least the end of his adventurous story. The chieftain had definitely saved the lives of twelve Brazilian officers, whose plane had crashed in the province of Acre. Both the Yaminaua and Kaxinawa Indians revered Tatunca Nara as a chieftain, even though he was not of their tribe. These facts were documented in the archives of the Brazilian Secret Service, according to Brugger.

Brugger researched Tatunca Nara's story in the archives of Rio de Janeiro, Brasilia, Manaus, and Rio Branco, coming up with astonishing results. Independent newspaper documentation of the tale is available starting in 1968, according to Brugger, with mention of a white Indian chieftain who saved the lives of twelve Brazilian officers by obtaining their release from the Haisha Indians and leading them to Manaus. With their help, Tatunca Nara was granted a Brazilian labor permit and an identity card. Witnesses said that he spoke broken German, a number of Indian languages from the upper Amazon, and a little Portuguese.

Fighting did indeed break out in 1969 in the Peruvian province of Madre de Dios, and the leader of the Indians was a man named Tatunca. When this man fled to Brazil, the Peruvians applied for extradition, but the Brazilians refused to cooperate, as a result of which Peru closed their common border.

In 1972, Tatunca Nara appeared in Rio Branco, establishing a connection with the Catholic Bishop Grotti. Together, according to Brugger, they solicited food for the Indians on Rio Yaku in the churches of Acre's capital. Since Acre province had been considered "free of Indians," no help was given. Three months later, Bishop Grotti died in a mysterious plane crash.

But according to Brugger, Tatunca Nara did not give up. Again with the help of the officers whose lives he had saved, he got in touch with the Brazilian Secret Service and appealed to the Indian Protection Service, FUNAI. He also told the West German Embassy about the 2,000 German soldiers who were reportedly still living in Akakor. The consul did not believe his story, denying him further access to the embassy.

The Indian Protection Service agreed to make contact with the tribe, but while making preparations in Rio Branco, Tatunca Nara was arrested by local authorities in Acre Province to be sent to Peru to stand trial for the uprising he had led. Shortly before his extradition, his officer friends got him out of prison and had him brought back to Manaus. There, Brugger met Tatunca for a second time, having meanwhile checked out the story. Wrote Brugger, "Some points could be explained, but I still thought much was quite incredible, such as the subterranean settlement and the landing of the 2,000 German soldiers."

Tatunca Nara, after telling Brugger the whole story again, suggested that the journalist accompany him to Akakor. Brugger accepted, and on September 25, 1972, the pair left Manaus by river, accompanied by a Brazilian photographer. Their plan was to motor up the Rio Purus, then continue by canoe up the Rio Yaku on the border of Peru and Brazil. They would then continue on foot through the foothills of the Andes to the secret city. The chief estimated that the entire trip would take six weeks.

With a Winchester rifle, two revolvers, machetes, food, hammocks, jungle clothes, medicine and other equipment, they ascended the Rio Purus to the Rio Yacu. On October 5, Brugger reports that they abandoned their boat for the canoe at Cachoeira Inglesa and began the final journey to Akakor; it had been ten days since they left Manaus. Two days later, rounding a bend in the river, they came across some gold prospectors who had constructed a primitive factory on the river bend, running the coarse-grained sand through sieves. The small party stayed the night with these prospectors, listening to their strange tales of red-haired Indians painted blue and red, who used poisoned arrows and may have practiced cannibalism.

As they drew ever nearer their destination, Tatunca Nara prepared himself for the return to his people. Before them, they could see the snow capped peaks of the Andes. They must have been in Peru, far up the Rio Yaku. Behind them stretched the green sea of the Amazonian lowlands. Tatunca Nara painted red stripes on his face and yellow stripes on his chest and legs. He tied back his long black hair with a yellow band decorated with the strange symbols of the Ugha Mongulala.

Brugger wrote that he and the photographer began to grow uneasy with the expedition at this point. Though he was still fascinated with the concept of Akakor, the trip was rapidly becoming a nightmare. To their combined relief and dismay, on October 13, their canoe was caught in an eddy and capsized, after passing over dangerous rapids. Half of their food and medical stores were lost, plus the camera equipment was partially ruined. This became their excuse to give up the expedition, only ten days from Akakor, and return to Manaus.

Tatunca Nara, however, would not be deterred so easily. The last the two White men saw of him, he took a bow, a small quiver of arrows, and a hunting knife, and disappeared into the wild land.

§§§

Wrote Brugger, "Does Akakor exist after all? Perhaps not exactly as Tatunca Nara had described it, but the city is undoubtedly real." There is always the possibility that he made up the whole story, winding it cleverly around existing legends, and interwtiwning it with 20th-century history. This may be the case, though it seems somehow unlikely. I believe that he is telling the truth, as far as he knows it. Brugger has written the book as an investigator, so it would be rather easy to verify a few of his facts.

An odd epilogue to the story is that Karl Brugger was murdered outside his Manaus apartment a few years ago, shot by an unknown assailant. Whether his death was connected somehow to his book and his knowledge of Akakor is not clear.

Let us assume then, that Brugger reported everything as he heard it and experienced it. Does this mean that the *Chronicle of Akakor* is true? Hardly. Separating the fact from fiction in this story would be almost impossible. But there are several interesting aspects to the story.

In view of the many earlier legends and stories from South America, one cannot help but draw certain parallels between the *Chronicle of Akakor* and the Peruvian legends of Gran Paititi. Was it to Akakor, known as Paititi to the Incas, that the last of the Incas fled, knowing they would find safe refuge?

Throughout Brugger's book, there is a distinct implication in Tatunca Nara's words that the "Former Masters" were of extraterrestrial origin. While this possibility appeals to Erich von Daniken's fans, the evidence does not support such a hypothesis. It is worth noting that the ubiquitous von Daniken wrote the forward to the book, which discredits the whole work for some people right away.

Naturally, von Daniken finds that Brugger's book supports his own writings. Though, except for a few phrases, the Former Masters could easily be accounted for as Atlantean, or even other, more mundane humans. Let us not forget that legends become twisted and exaggerated over time, the inevitable fate of an oral tradition. The stories of the Ugha Mongulala are thirteen thousand years old, by their own

256

reckoning! Surely they have "evolved" somewhat, if they had any validity in the first place.

Perhaps Brugger, having enjoyed a few of von Daniken's books, interpreted Tatunca Nara's statements to indicate extraterrestrials. I doubt quite seriously that Nara actually gave him a credible reason to do so. After all, Tatunca Nara spoke only broken German, and even less Portuguese. I gathered that Brugger didn't speak Quechua. I would also venture to guess that the dating of the Chronicle is a bit off. I wonder what the Ugha Mongulala thought when 1981 came along, and the third cataclysm did not come.

It is interesting to note that at Tiahuanaco, the few remaining statues do indeed have six fingers and six toes! But were the models extraterrestrials? Not necessarily. It is quite possible that some people, perhaps an entire race, had an extra digit at some time in history. There is, in fact, a tribe of bushmen who live in Namibia who have six fingers and toes. They live rather primitively, and do not fly around in airships or anything of the kind, though they did make onto South African television once. I saw them!

Necessarily false is Tatunca Nara's statement that Tiahuanaco was one of the sacred temple complexes built before the first cataclysm, then destroyed with the rising of the mountains. Nearby, the ruins of the canal have been heaved about as if by an earthquake, yet at Tiahuanaco, only a short distance away, many of the giant stones still stand straight and tall. It is simply inconceivable that a cataclysm would wipe out Puma Punku, the canal area, and still leave the statues and structures of Tiahuanaco standing as they are today.

The idea of the ancient gold mining city of Ofir, or Ophir, located at the entrance to the Amazon is interesting and hardly unique. A map for "...facilitating the explanation of Holy Scriptures," prepared in 1571 by Benedictus Arias Montanus in Antwerp, indicated that Ophir was located in the Rocky Mountains of the United States and in Peru (he gave it two locations). Near the mouth of the Amazon, he located another Biblical city called Iobab. Further in the interior of Brazil he situated a city called Sephermos. Salazere, one of the cities mentioned by Tatunca Nara, is located around the area indicated as Sephermos.

The monk Montanus may have been reflecting an esoteric tradition of ancient gold mining cities in the Americas. Ophir was the source of the fabulous gold which King Solomon mined jointly with King Hiram of Tyre, his Phoenician father-in-law from Lebanon. Ophir was a three year voyage from Solomon's court, traditionaly one year in transit, one year at the city, and one year for the voyage back. It would appear to have been found quite a long distance away, almost certainly not along the Red Sea as many modern historians insist.

Samon, Lhasa's brother in the *Chronicle of Akakor*, is certainly a close word association for Solomon. Curiously, Solomon was said to possess "...a ship which flew through the air," just as did Samon and Lhasa, according to an Ethiopian text, the Kebra Nagast.[55] The Empire of Ethiopia (Abyssinia) was supposed to have been founded by the son of King Solomon, borne by the Queen of Sheba.

The tunnel system almost certainly exists. Though, I find it highly unlikely that the Incas could have built their own system of tunnels after the Spanish conquest of Peru, as Tatunca Nara said. They did not seem to have the technology in the first place, nor the time or resources after the Spanish arrival.

There are indications that some sort of global cataclysm may have occured at roughly 10,000 BC, the time specified for the first cataclysm in the *Chronicle of Akakor*. Mammoths which have been found flash-frozen in Siberia with semi-tropical plants in their mouths are usually dated at around 10,000 BC. They are thought to have been happily grazing at a temperate zone, when they suddenly found themselves in the Arctic, where they froze to death, en masse. A pole-shift phenomonon?

The clues that I think give insight to Tatunca Nara's incredible story and its possible inaccuracies can be found in the Ugha Mongulala's alleged association with the Third Reich. Tatunca Nara did indeed speak broken German and insisted, even to the West German consul, that 2,000 German soldiers were still living at Akakor.

Karl Brugger investigated the possibilities of the Nazis sending soldiers to Akakor and their alleged plans to invade Brazil. In the appendix to his book, he relates what he found. The Germans believed that strict neutrality on the part of Brazil was essential for German U-boat mastery of the south Atlantic, and that the future invasion of South America was a natural extension for the expanding Third Reich. However, the Americans managed to convince the Brazilian government that they should side with the Allies, and Brazil allowed the U.S. to install supply bases on its northern coast. Later, it broke off relations with Germany.

In the spring of 1942, when Field Marshall Rommel seemed to be about to conquer all of North Africa, Brazil was the topic of a General Staff meeting in Berlin. After a great deal of discussion, Hitler decided on a retaliatory attack, in order to "...punish Brazil for her leaning toward the U.S., and to warn the country off from further hostile actions."

The secret operation started in early July, 1942 from Bordeaux. A

U-boat flotilla left for the South Atlantic to sink as many Brazilian ships as possible in "free maneuvers." On August 15, U-507 torpedoed the Brazilian freighter Baendepi near Salvador, twenty-four hours later also sinking the freighter Araquara. One week later, on August 22, Brazil declared war on Nazi Germany.

This area became known as the Brazilian Front. Brazilian leaders became convinced that Germany was planning an invasion of their country. The Brazilian Foreign Minister Oswaldo Aranha expressed the opinion to U.S. Ambassador Jefferson Caffery in 1941: "We are convinced that the German Wehrmacht will try to occupy Latin America. Strategic reasons alone require the invasion to begin in Brazil." Furthermore, intercepted German cables discussed action to be taken against Brazil. On the Brazilian Front, as many as 38 Brazilian ships were sunk by U-boats during the war.

The landing of 2,000 German soldiers in Amazonia, and their making their way to Akakor, was an integral part of Nazi's plan for the conquest of Brazil, according to Tatunca Nara. Was such a feat even possible?

Eyewitnesses claim to have observed the landing of German U-boats on the coast of Rio de Janeiro. As early as 1938, a U-boat reconnoitred the lower Amazon. The Amazon river, at points so wide that both sides can rarely be seen at once, is navigable by submarine to Manaus and beyond. The Nazi U-boat established contact with the German colony at Manaus, performed a geographical survey, and made the first historical film of Amazonia, which is still preserved in East Berlin archives.

Another operation, documented in the archives of the Brazilian Air Force, was the voyage of the S.S. Carlino in June 1943 from Maceio to Belem, at the mouth of the Amazon. The orders of the German freighter can only be assumed; the Brazilian Air Force believed that it carried a shipment of arms for underground German agents, so it attacked the freighter, without success. There was neither a German colony in the Maceio area nor were there Brazilian military installation.

If we now assume then that the Nazis could have an alliance with the Ugha Mongulala, sending troops to Akakor, what does this mean in terms of the *Chronicle of Akakor*, the Ugha Mongulala book, and the 13,000 years of history related by Tatunca Nara?

For one thing, Hitler and most high ranking officers were literally "occult nuts." In 1920, Adolf Hitler encountered Dietrich Eckehardt, a poet and occultist, who shared with Hitler his bizarre theories of the origins of the Germanic tribes on the northern island Thule, of supernatural beings from a vanished civilization, and the imminent rise of a superior civilization in Germany. Later, a powerful secret organization known as the Thule Group was formed, and other secret societies built around it, including the Vril Society, the Ahnenerbe (Ancestors' Heritage), and the Waffen-SS.

The *Chronicle of Akakor* contains material virtually identical to this occult Nazi doctrine. Perhaps the tell-tale clue to the shared influence of Nazi theology and the *Chronicle of Akakor* is Tatunca Nara's statement, "One of the maps shows that our moon is not the first and not the only one in the history of the earth. The moon that we know began to approach the earth and to circle around it thousands of years ago."

The idea of more than one moon in the sky is not new. Tatunca Nara's statement implies that a previous moon crashed into the earth, creating the cataclysm. This "theory" was actually proposed at the turn of the century by an Austrian occultist, Hans Horbiger, in his glacial cosmogony and "Welteislehre" studies. He proposed that the earth had several moons, and that they descended slowly toward until they crashed into the planet. The gigantic city of Tiahuanaco is a key part of this theory, having been built, according to Horbiger, no less than 230,000 years ago! That was before the first cataclysm. The second cataclysm occurred about 13,500 years ago, when the next moon crashed into the earth, leaving the moon now visible in our sky.[22]

As incredible as this "theory" may seem, the Nazi's adopted it into their cosmology. Horbiger died just prior to World War Two, and was considered a prophet by the Nazis. The fact that this same bizarre tale appears in the *Chronicle of Akakor* is quite suspect, although it may be coincidence. Which influenced which?

§§§

The *Chronicle of Akakor* is like a mixture of Nazi cosmology, South American mythology, von Daniken's "Gods from Outer Space" phraseology, and a small smattering of known facts. The possibility exists that Karl Brugger made the whole book up, or that Tatunca Nara was the fiction writer.

Since the publication of *The Chronicle of Akakor*, at least one person has disappeared searching for the city. Gregory Deyermenjian, the American explorer who has spent a great deal of time in Peru searching for Gran Paititi, told me that he knew the son of a wealthy

American family who came to Cuzco in 1977, obsessed with the idea of reaching Akakor. He hired a hotel owner in Cuzco to get him as close to the headwaters of the Rio Yaco as possible, where he planned to meet an Indian who would take him to to the ancient city.

The hotel owner escorted him as far as Cosnipate. Unfortunately, the headwaters of the Rio Yaco are as remote a location as you are likely to find in the world, almost impossible to reach by his route from Peru. But the young American aristocrat was determined to try. Not surprisingly, he was never heard from again.

But is it possible that one or more stone cities still lie undiscovered in the jungle on the Brazilian-Peruvian frontier? On December 30, 1975, satellite *Landsat II* took a series of photos at 13 degrees south latitude, 71 degrees 30 minutes west longitude, over the jungles of southeastern Peru. These photos, when analyzed, showed eight pyramids, each only slightly smaller in height than the Great Pyramid of Giza in Egypt![61]

Close investigations of these pyramids has shown that there are actually twelve, all covered by trees. Several attempts have been made to reach these pyramids by land, yet, to this date no expedition has been able to reach this incredible archaeological find. The difficult jungle conditions have resulted in the death and disappearance of some of the explorers. Are these pyramids part of the Akakor complex?

We are left with the quite plausible theory that the Ugha Mongulala are real people with real cities and real traditions. Germans had some influence on these traditions, especially if Tatunca Nara actually had a German mother. Surely, Nazi doctrine could have influenced the mythology of the Ugha Mongulala, which seems to the case.

We can't end this crazy chapter without one more speculation. Germany surrendered in May, 1945, yet according to Tatunca Nara, Germany was still sending soldiers to Akakor at that time. Why? The Germans would certainly have long since abandoned their plans to invade Brazil.

On the day before the German surrender, two U-boats left northern Germany and headed into the South Atlantic. The passengers and mission of these U-boats, U-530 and U-977, remains a mystery; all that is known is that they surrendered in Argentina almost three months after the end of the war, at different times. There was immediate suspicion that the passengers on the U-boats were Hitler, Bormann, and other high ranking Nazi officials missing since the end of the war.[56] Both Eisenhower and Stalin expressed their belief that Hitler had escaped from Berlin.

This may seem too much to believe, but neither Hitler's, nor

Bormann's death were ever satisfactorily proven. Bormann was supposedly killed in a tank crashing through Russian lines, trying to escape Berlin. His body was never identified, and the witnesses were all Nazi officers. Hitler's "body" (at least a dozen "doubles" were found shot in bunkers in Berlin) could not be identified, though the Russians claim to have identified his body through dental records. Yet Hitler supposedly shot himself in the mouth!

The captains of the U-boats were turned over to the Americans, who interrogated them thoroughly. Had Hitler been on board? Where had the U-boats been for the last two and a half months? Why hadn't they surrendered at the end of the war, and what to what ports had they been?

Naturally, the captains answered that their were no important Nazis on board, and they had gone to Argentina because they did want to surrender to the British; it had just taken them a long time to get there. Tatunca Nara did not say if any Germans arrived after May, 1945. Is it possible that U-530 and U-977, plus other U-boats that never surrendered, took these last German soldiers to Akakor? Could it be that Hitler and Bormann were among them?

Tatunca Nara knew nothing of the war in Europe, except what the Germans told him. He would not know that important Nazis had come to Akakor. And what better place to hide from avenging Allies, than a gigantic "City of the Former Masters" deep in the Amazon jungles, where civilization would not penetrate for many years!

Let's see, did Tatunca say anything about the Kennedy conspiracy?

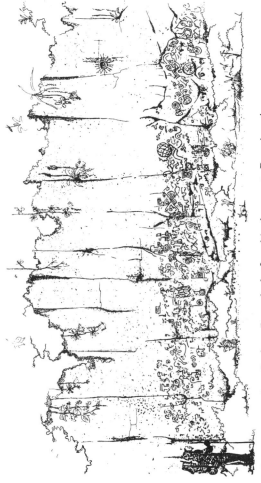

The strange pre-Inca Pusharo Petroglyphs found in the remote Peruvian Amazon. Do they point the way to some mysterious lost city?

Robin Palomino Rivet '85

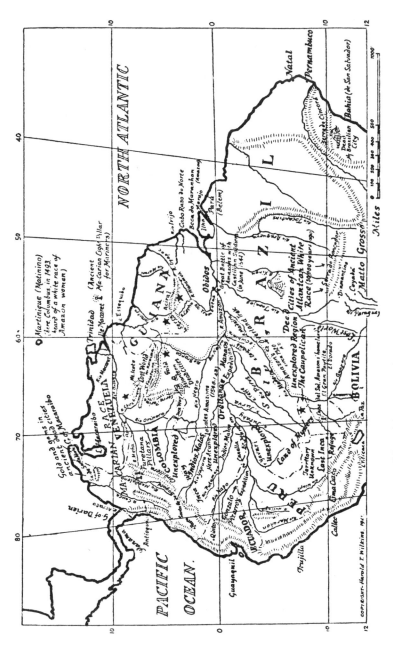

Harold Wilkins' map of the Amazon Jungle.

𐤟𐤟𐤟 (Paraiba inscription — Phoenician script, 8 lines)

FACSIMILE OF THE PARAIBA INSCRIPTION
A tracing of Netto's facsimile made from the master copy of the inscription. This facsimile was mailed from Rio de Janeiro to New York on January 31, 1874.

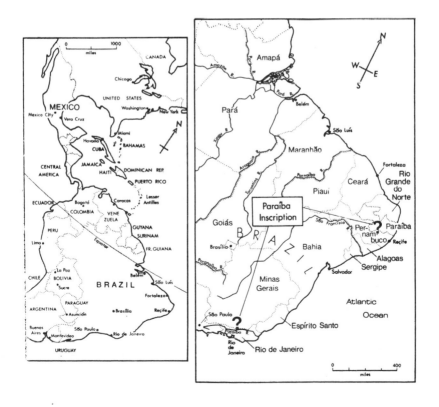

THE PARAIBA INSCRIPTION

MODERN HEBREW LETTER	PARAIBA (ca. 530 B.C.)	BAT CREEK (ca. A.D. 100)
א	𐤀	𐤕
ב		
ג		
ד		
ה		
ו		
ז		
ח		
ט		
י		
כ		
ל		
מ		
נ		
ס		
ע		
פ		
צ		
ק		
ר		
ש		
ת		

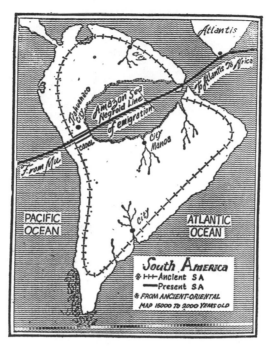

*South America showing the ancient Amazon Sea and canals
connecting it with the Pacific Ocean from a tablet 25,000 years
old in one of the western monasteries of Tibet.*

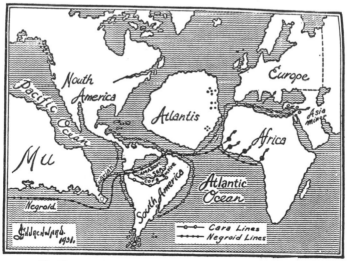

*The Lines of Colonization from Mu through the Amazon Sea
to Africa, Atlantis, the Mediterranean and Asia Minor.*

Churchward's maps of ancient South America.

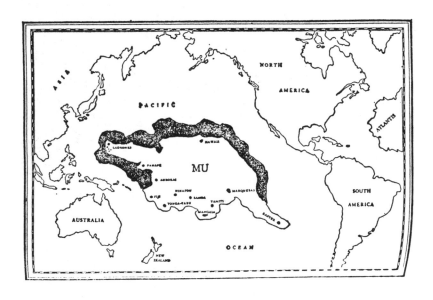

Churchward's map of Mu.

Karl Brugger.

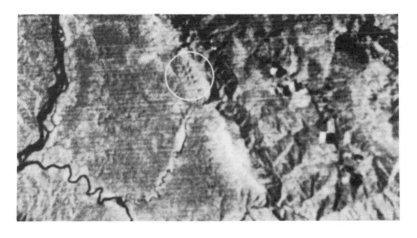

Landsat II satellite photo showing eight, pyramid-like structures in the Madre de Dios region of the Amazon.

Tatunca Nara with the expedition boat in Manaus

The flag of Akakor

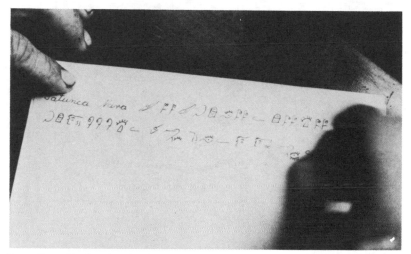

Tatunca Nara writing down the script of the Ancient Fathers

Sample of the simplified script of the Ancient Fathers following
the arrival of the German soldiers

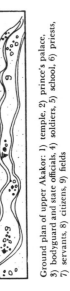

Ground plan of upper Akakor: 1) temple, 2) prince's palace,
3) bodyguard and state officials, 4) soldiers, 5) school, 6) priests,
7) servants, 8) citizens, 9) fields

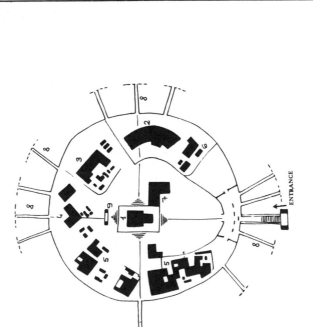

Ground plan of lower Akakor: 1) temple, 2) palace, 3) priests,
4) armory, 5) people, 6) palace of guards, 7) throne chamber,
8) connecting passages, 9) Gate of the Gods

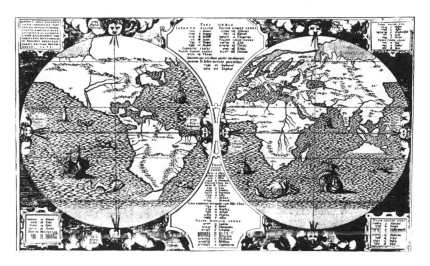

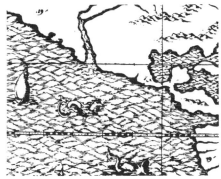

THE MAP OF BIBLICAL GEOGRAPHY

This map "for facilitating the explanation of Holy Scriptures" was prepared by Benedictus Arias Montanus (1527–1598) and published in Antwerp in 1571. The map is a copper engraving, 32 x 53 cm. It indicates the gold-bearing land of biblical Ophir by the number "19" on the west coast of both North and South America. By 1571 Arias Montanus would have heard of the gold pillaged by Pizarro from the Incan Empire, but hardly of the North American sources of gold now famous since the Gold Rush of 1849. If Arias Montanus is indeed reflecting an esoteric tradition about the ancient exploitation of gold in the Rocky Mountains, archaeologists should eventually find the old gold-mining installations there.

A tapir, a large mammal of the South American forests.

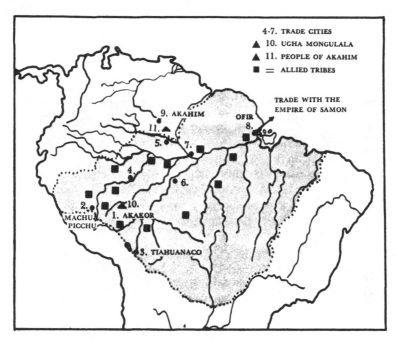

The empire of Lhasa, the Exalted Son of the Gods

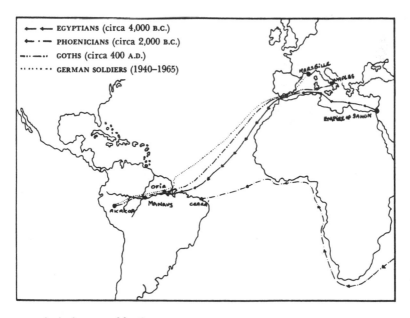

Arrival routes of foreigners

Tatunca Nara in war paint (before setting off to join his tribe)

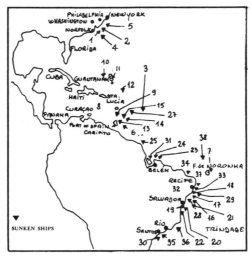

Brazilian ships sunk by German U-boats

The author and companions, catching dinner on a typical South American evening.

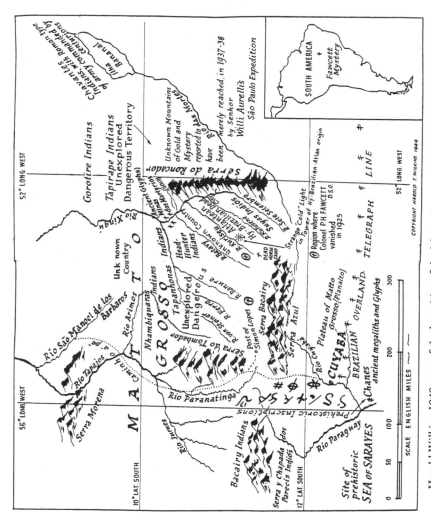

Harold Wilkins 1949 map of the lost cities of the Matto Grosso area Brazil.

Chapter Thirteen

Bahia and Northern Brazil:
The Lost Mines of Muribeca

Healthy, free, the world before me...
strong and content,
I travel the open road.
                -Walt Whitman

Memories of Carnival in Rio lingered in my aching head as the bus sped north through the hilly bush country towards Salvador. A deep orange sunset adorned the western sky. As it slowly faded into twilight, I faded into sleep, exhausted. When I awoke the next morning, the bus was still droning on towards Salvador.

All the rest of that day, as we wound along the narrow, paved road that is the main highway north of Rio, I slipped between daydreams and short naps. But the subject of both types of dreams was the same: the seemingly unfathomable ancient mysteries and still lost cities of this strange and vast continent. During the trip, my emotions flipped back and forth. At times, I was calmed by a smug confidence that I had cleverly deciphered the entire riddle; at other times, I lapsed back into confusion at the seeming contradictions and fictions which permeate each of the riddle's pieces. Truth is elastic, and the past fades away like so many soap bubbles in the wind.

Occasionally, I would follow my confusion with doubts which were fundamental to my entire South American trip, and even my life. What's the point of searching for lost cities? I guess that when you question your drive and passion seriously, you either quit, or renew your commitment. Having reached this point, helped along the way no doubt by remembering the origin of the still-tender area behind my ear, I made new my commitment to track these mysteries as far as I was able.

Through my research into history, lost cultures, ancient ruins, and legends, I understand how Arthur C. Clark must have felt when he wrote in the July 1986 issue of *Omni* magazine, "...I'm sorry to say that, owing to their misreading of the Bible, thousands of people still believe...the world was created around 4000 BC." I feel that my high school and college professors were similarly mistaken. They were repeating the errors which they had learned from their teachers, without thinking. Their paradigm, their reality structure, was simply being passed on from generation to generation of historians without analysis. These people, passing on what were often mistaken, biased, antiquated theories, had become experts at theories no longer valid.

But like so many other smart-alec kids, I read different books, had different experiences, believed about life and death differently than they did. I am not prone to hallucinations, and have never seen a "flying saucer." Yet, it occurs to me that UFOs might exist. What could possibly cause me to assume otherwise? This is my paradigm, which is admittedly different from that of others. I am open to the consideration of new alternatives.

The Chronicle of Akakor had shaken the foundations of my previous reality structure, even allowing for the possibility that significant parts of the story could be false. Most people would simply declare the whole thin fiction, rather than face the discomfort of rethinking, or at least critically questioning, their paradigm. But the ancient Chinese philosopher Chuang Tzu commented on the necessity of adjusting "upward" as you learn more about yourself, the world, and life. If you cannot adjust your thinking and grow both emotionally and mentally, he declared, "...you will be destroyed on the lathe of heaven."

The bus finally arrived in Salvador at dusk. It stopped at the Salvador bus station, located in a modern terminal on the outskirts of the city. I was searching for the right bus to take into the city center when a tall, blond Israeli with an artificial leg asked me, "Are you looking for the bus into the city?"

"Yes, as a matter of fact, I am," I told him.

"Then follow me, I'm heading there myself," he smiled. I followed gladly, and we boarded a bus into the downtown area, a ten-minute ride from the main terminal. "Are you also looking for a hotel?" he asked, as we got off the crowded bus.

You might think from his "on target" questions that this man was

280

either another South American scam artist or a psychic, but the real explanation is much simpler. When you see a wild-haired young guy with a backpack over his shoulder get off a bus, it doesn't take much horse sense to conclude that he's going into town, and will be looking for a hotel. "Sure," I said, then, remembering how Antonio had relieved me of my funds, asked, "Do you know any good, inexpensive ones?"

"The hotel where I'm staying isn't bad," he said, "Come with me." He headed for an elevator. The old city of Salvador is built at the edge of a cliff over a natural bay. To get from the modern part of Salvador central to the old city, where all the charm, action, hotels and restaurants are located, you take a gigantic elevator up to the top of the cliff. It costs about five cents.

As we waited in line for the ascent, I studied the Israeli. He was tall and young, with curly blonde hair and a Nikon camera slung around his neck. He had an artificial leg attached above the knee, and wore shorts and a T-shirt. I suspected that he had lost his leg while serving in the army, perhaps to a terrorist bomb, but I didn't feel that it was polite to ask him directly. I did, however, ask him from what part of Israel he came.

"How did you know that I was from Israel?" he asked.

"I lived on a Kibbutz in Israel some years ago," I told him, "and I could tell from your accent, as well as your sandals. Only Israelis wear sandals like those." They were, in fact, army-issue.

At the top, the tall Israeli led me down an alley to his hotel, The Hotel Vigo. The Vigo was full, but since the same people owned the adjacent hotel, the Center Hotel, I soon had a room there. I paid about three dollars a night for my own room with a bath.

Moments after dumping my luggage, I was out on the street. It was the last night of Carnival, and I was ready to party! I had been told that Carnival in Salvador would be a different experience from Carnival in Rio. The Salvador Carnival, I understood, was more authentic, more for the people—the blacks of northern Brazil were the heart of the festivities. In Rio, Carnival was more for the rich and the tourists, more for show than for fun.

On the streets of Salvador, I was swept up in a party. Soon I found myself dancing in the street with a beer can in one hand and a shapely brown lady in the other. Samba bands were playing on top of double-decker trucks: the top platform was an open air stage from which the bands cranked out their pulsing music. There were scores of these trucks and bands. They drove slowly through the streets, and as one drove slowly past, another glittery double-decker truck came along, playing a new tune. At least, I assumed it was a new tune, but I honestly couldn't tell the difference.

The street was one big, noisy parade, with the bands playing as if there were no tomorrow. I joined in the dancing and drank a few beers. After the bus trip, I was in the mood for a fling, and this was, after all, the last night of Carnival. As it was my first night in Salvador, and I didn't have Mad Victor as a guide, I quickly got lost.

Soon, it was getting quite late. Still, the bands continued playing as if the street party had developed a life of its own. I asked one Brazilian woman, a beautiful lady with bronze skin and long black hair, if she knew the direction back to the Hotel Central or Hotel Vigo. "Sure," she said, and taking my hand, led me through the streets. She was a school teacher and spoke good English, but had never met an American before since she taught far out in the country. She was excited to meet me.

I told her that I was pleased to meet her, and that I thought that Salvador was an interesting city. "Things get pretty crazy here during Carnival," she replied with an engaging smile.

Wanting to talk to her some more, I asked, "Can we stop at this café for a minute?" as we passed a small restaurant.

"Of course!" she exclaimed, smiling as I held open the door. We each ordered a cup of coffee as we began to get acquainted.

Sipping from the mug she held cupped in her hands, she talked about her brothers and sisters in a small town in the interior of Bahia, and about the children at her school. She was so charming that I could hardly take my eyes off her. She was fairly tall, with long black hair, dark, dark eyes, and thick black eyebrows. She couldn't help but notice my stare, and shyly looked down.

Seizing the moment, I said, "Sorry for staring, but you are very attractive."

"Thank you, young gringo," she replied softly. "So what brings you to Salvador besides Carnival?"

I didn't want to tell her about about being mugged in Rio, so said, "I'm here to look for the Lost Mines of Muribeca."

"The lost mines of Muribeca!" she exclaimed. "You must be quite an adventurer! They have been lost for more than 300 years!" With that, we both laughed.

Working our way through the crowd, we danced a bit, then had a beer in another café. Eventually, we got back to the hotel. "May I come in and see your room?" she asked. Inside, she slipped into nothing more comfortable, then kissed me hard on the lips. "Anything can happen during Carnival," she said. "Things get a little crazy." I didn't mind: I'm a little crazy myself at times.

§§§

Salvador is Brazil's most interesting city, according to many travelers. It was the first city built by the Portuguese, back in 1549. Until 1815 the country's busiest port, Salvador passed sugar, gold, diamonds and other goods across the Atlantic to Europe. The city's many old churches, colonial buildings and narrow, winding streets are a pleasant complement to its beaches, which make it a popular holiday spot.

In addition to the Hotel Vigo and Central Hotel, there are quite a few other inexpensive hotels located on the square. Just as you step out of the elevator at top of the cliffs, you will see the Hotel Lima, Hotel do Comercio, Hotel Queluz, Hotel Chaves, Hotel Monaco, Hotel Planeta, and many more. Accomodations can be harder to find around Carnival time, but generally you can get a room somewhere if you try.

Ask questions about lost cities around Bahia, and you will get some surprising answers. Back in the 1940's, a professor of geography at a Brazilian university informed Harold Wilkins, "There are no ancient ruins in the grasslands and forests of Brazil, señor. No vestiges of ancient culture, no ruins such as you have in Mayan Yucatan, or the jungles of Honduras and Guatemala. All that was here when dom Pedro Cabral sighted what is now Rio de Janeiro, in the year AD 1500, all that we have here now—primitive Indians at the fishing and hunting stage. They live in huts and clearings in the jungle...In our sertao are scrub, heath and wilderness, but no monuments like those of Peru."[22]

This is a sweeping statement by an "expert" in a country which is today largely unexplored. Naturally, Wilkins insisted that the professor was wrong, though probably not to his face—the Brazilian authorities can be rather sensitive about foreign "experts." But Wilkins was proved right in the end, although it took nearly fifty years.

In 1984, the lost city of Ingrejil was discovered in the northern Ingrejil mountains of Bahia state. The vice-president of the Sao Paulo Archaeology Institute, Dr. Aurelio Abreu, discovered the ruins of this legendary stone city, "dating from Incan times and sought by explorers for centuries in the country's remote interior." According to a Dallas newspaper, apparently the only American newspaper which considered the story important enough to run, Dr. Abreu and two researchers found, "ruins of a structure of stone giving the impression of a fortress and dating from remote times" in the mountains of Bahia.

For decades, these ruins have been known to local residents, who simply called them Ingrejil. They are constructed with "precision-cut stones fitted without mortar in the style of the Inca architecture of Peru," according to Abreu. Legends of stone cities in the interior have circulated for centuries, but this find was the first public mention of the ruins outside the towns in this remote region.

"We believe there must be other structures like Ingrejil in Brazil's interior—much of which is still feared and unexplored," said Abreu, who had first inspected the site on request from Brazilian authorities in late August, 1984.

Abreu is quoted as saying the ruins, "are nothing like structures built by Indians known to inhabit Brazil in pre-Columbian times. Ingrejil may have been built by refugees from Incan or pre-Incan Peru, who found there (in the highlands of Bahia) the mountainous terrain and cool climate which suited them."

Abreu described Ingrejil as "...a two-mile by one-half-mile plateau accessible only by mountain paths. There are piles of well-hewn stones and dolmens, crude stone arches, visible." To my dismay, I was not able to visit this city. The Brazilian government is not letting any foreigners into the site at this time, which in itself is rather mysterious. But there are several pieces of this brief newspaper report which are quite interesting and deserve some comment.

It is almost unbelievable to think that the Incan Empire extended, at one time, all the way to Ingrejil. Yet, its construction is very similar to so-called Incan architecture. One plausible explanation is that some refugees from the devastating wars in the highlands of western South America during the millenia before Christ came to the mountains of Bahia and built the city.

Buildings almost identical to "Incan construction" have been found on Easter Island. Here, we should speak about the earlier, megalithic construction, which as we have established, appears to predate the Incas. Also, this type has been found in Central India at Vihayanagara, known today as Hampi. A revealing article on this fascinating city, including other oddities such as the underwater ruins at Bimini, appears in the March,1986 issue of *Archaelogy Magazine*. Most probably, Ingrejil does indeed predate the Incas, as Abreu suggests.

Who, then, might have built it? Could this be one of the cities mentioned by Tatunca Nara when relating the *Chronicle of Akakor*? One thing is certain, as Abreu corroborates, where there is one lost city, there are usually others. Brazil may be full of megalithic cities, as many explorers, including Colonel Fawcett and Harold Wilkins, have believed for years.

284

It is also possible that Ingrejil was built by Egyptians, Phoenicians, or other Mediterranean seafarers. Was Ingrejil the legendary Ophir mentioned on maps of the middle ages which oddly placed that city in Brazil? Tatunca Nara placed Ofir in this area himself. If the architecture is similar to that of Macchu Picchu and Sacsayhuaman, the city may have been constructed by those mysterious, megalithic, world-travelling builders, the Atlantean League. At this point, it is all a matter of conjecture and speculation. But Ingrejil is a significant find, which has shaken accepted Brazilian archaeology to its foundations. Suddenly, Brazil has an ancient history that goes beyond Indians living a stone-age existence in the forest.

Rene Chabbert, an engineer from Pennsylvania, has recently discovered what he thinks is Colonel Fawcett's lost city, originally located by those Portugese soldiers in 1752. By pouring over satellite maps, he concludes that Ingrejil, like Colonel Fawcett's lost city, was part of an Egyptian colony. At first, this might seem to be a pretty outrageous statement, but let's take a further look at the evidence.

Do you remember the Sphinx near Rio, Tatunca Nara's city of Ofir, and the writing from Colonel Fawcett's lost city? The one thing that propelled the Egyptians all over the world—possibly as far as Sumatra, Australia, and North and South America—was their search for gold. The fabulous gold mines, worked by Solomon at Ophir, were probably first worked by the Egyptians, according to the Bible.

Would the Egyptians have come to South America looking for gold? Would they have found it, if they did come? Are any ancient mines located around Ingrejil or other areas of Brazil?

In the sixteenth, seventeenth and eighteenth centuries, many adventurers in Brazil were obsessed with locating gold and silver mines. Actually, they sought one mine in particular: the Lost Mine of Muribeca. It had been owned by a Mestizo named Roberio Dias. One of the wealthiest men in Bahia, Dias owned a fabulously rich silver mine, somewhere in the interior of Brazil. Worked by Indians, it was rumored to be thousands of years old.

Dias' father was a half-Indian named Muribeca. Muribeca had inherited the mines from his father, a Portuguese, the only survivor of a shipwreck who lived with a friendly Indian tribe and later married an Indian woman. These fabulous, ancient, mines, possibly Egyptian, were shown to Muribeca's father by his mother's tribe. Setting the Indians to work in them, Muribeca's family eventually became wealthy.

Dias had everything material: he was fabulously rich, yet he was still a commoner, and worse yet, he was part Indian, a mestizo. The one thing he wanted but couldn't have was a title, a certificate of nobility. He even travelled to Madrid, where he proposed an ingenious deal to the King, Dom Pedro II. Said Dias, "I offer your Majesty all the riches of my splendid, but secret, mines. There is more silver in those mines, I assure you, than all the iron in the mines of Bilbao in your Spanish province of Biscaya. All I want from your Majesty in return is the title of Marquis of the Mines."

Dom Pedro II, then king of both Spain and Portugal, would not give Dias the requested title in Spain. Instead, he had the orders sealed, stipulating that the commission of Marquis be given to Dias only after the location of the mines had been disclosed. Dias did not trust the king, however, and persuaded the ship's captain to open the orders before they reached Bahia on the return voyage. As Dias suspected, the King had no intention of making him Marquis of Mines, but had only dispensed a military commission as a captain! Naturally, Dias refused to turn over his mines, much to the dismay of the governor of Bahia.

Dias was then thrown into prison in Salvador, where he rotted away in a dungeon for two years. Still, he refused to talk. Eventually, he was allowed to buy his freedom for 9,000 crowns. He died in 1622, the secret of the mines never disclosed, the Indians not speaking, even under torture.

So, the secret of the Lost Mines of Muribeca went to the grave with Dias; but that did not stop the search. For the next 150 years, many hardy Portuguese explorers, known as *bandeiristas*, searched the dense and inhospitable forests for the fabulously valuable mines. Lured by the possibility of wealth, civilians banded together with armed Negro slaves and Indian guides. These exploration parties would take off into the dangerous forests, often never to return. There is a record of one party, 1,400 strong, from which only one man returned!

This expedition set out in 1743, when Francisco Raposo, a native of Minas Gerais province, led a group into the forests in search of the lost mines of Muribeca. They were a hardy lot, travelling on foot, living off the land, and combing the vast jungles in search of clues to the lost mines.

According to his own document, now kept in the archives of Rio de Janeiro under the name "Document 512," Raposo's party wandered in search of the mines for ten years. Much of document 512, reproduced here in full (see appendix), had been partially eaten by insects when it was rediscovered and translated into English by Mrs. Richard Burton in 1865. Yet the document is authentic, and it tells an incredible tale of a lost city and the discovery of what appears to be the Lost Mines of Muribeca.

Evidently, after wandering for years, the party approached a range of mountains which seemed to be lit by flames. Actually the fiery look was caused by the setting sun glistening off wet, quartz crystals covering the hillsides immediately after a rain. To the eager explorers, however, the mountains seemed to be covered with gems, and when a rainbow appeared over the crest of a ridge, they felt they had been given a hint of the treasure waiting inside those mountains.

After heading toward the mountains for several days, they found the bed of a road leading up into the peaks. Following this old path, the mammoth entourage came to the top of a ledge from which they could view the surrounding plain. To their amazement, about four miles away was a huge city!

Immediately, they flung themselves to the ground to avoid being seen. Keeping a low profile, they peered out at the city in search of inhabitants. No life could be seen: no people walked the streets, no smoke curled up into the air. Utter silence cloaked the entire area.

Carefully, they descended to the valley floor, where they spent the night. Scouts were dispatched the next morning, to see if the city was inhabited. They came back two days later, reporting it deserted. Cautiously, the party of over one thousand Portuguese, Negro slaves and Indian guides entered the city.

Raposo describes the city as "cyclopean." Ruins were everywhere, but many buildings were roofed with great stone slabs still in position. The men proceeded down the street and came to a vast square. Here, in the center, was a huge column of black stone; upon it was the effigy of a man with one hand on his hip and the other pointing toward the north.

One side of the square held a huge building, thought to be a palace. Partially ruined obelisks, carved of the same black stone, stood at each corner of the square. The walls and roof had collapsed in many places, but the great columns still stood in place. Frescos and carvings decorated the walls, and thousands of bats inhabited the dark recesses.

The figure of a half-naked youth with laurel around his head was carved above the door of the palace. Inscriptions were located below the figure. Opposite the palace was a temple-like building; beyond it the rest of the city lay in ruins. A great, bottomless chasm meandered aimlessly through the old metropolis.

An earthquake had apparently laid this fabulous place to waste. Tumbled columns and huge blocks of stone lay scattered throughout. A river sliced through the city, which the adventurous party explored further, eventually coming to another structure. A vast building with fifteen chambers, this structure had at its entrance a square monolith with deeply engraved characters. Inside, Joao Antonio, the only member of the expedition to be mentioned by name in the document,

287

found a small gold coin in the rubble. The coin reportedly had "...the image or figure of a youth on his knees" on one side, and "...a bow, a crown and an arrow" on the other. Rene Chabbert, who has studied Colonel Fawcett's city for years, says that the only gold coin fitting this description is the gold Daric, showing King Darius of Persia (521-486 BC) as an archer kneeling with bow, quiver and spear. Set into an adjoining cliff face, they saw what appeared to be ancient mine workings. They had no means with which to explore the deep mine shafts, but a great quantity of rich silver ore was littered about the entrances. Here and there were caves hewn out of the cliff, one sealed off by a great stone slab engraved with strange glyphs. The caves might have been the tombs of the city's monarchs and high priests. These seem reminiscent of the tombs at the Valley of Kings in ancient Thebes, or Luxor.

A smaller party continued down the river, where they encountered a canoe paddled by two White men with long black hair, dressed in some sort of *European* clothing! They fired a shot to attract attention, but the canoe apparently vanished. After several months of hard travel back to the east, they arrived at the San Francisco River, a small outpost. From there, they apparently made their way back to Salvador, or at least one of them did, carrying the document of their adventure.

The rare document hints at the discovery of a great treasure, but no details are given. It is unlikely that the men brought any of it out with them; gold is heavy, and they had a great distance to travel to re-embrace civilization. Their plan was to return to the city and claim their treasure. This document was sent to the Viceroy, Don Luiz Peregrino de Carvalho Menezes de Athayde, who incredibly did nothing with it.

We do not know what happened to Raposo or the other men. Did they return to the city? None of them, supposedly, were ever heard of again. For nearly a century, the document lay gathering dust in the archives at Rio de Janeiro. Finally it was rediscovered by the state government, and a young priest was sent out to investigate. He turned up nothing.

Rene Chabbert communicated to me a very interesting epilogue to this story. He hired a researcher who specialized in esoteric research of ancient documents to check into the whole story of Raposo and document 512. The researcher told Chabbert that a document about Raposo and the bandeiristas of 1753 could be found in the Vatican Library. The researcher said that, according to this Vatican document, Raposo and his men had encountered, possibly near the place where the men had discovered the mines, a tunnel and a strange man who guarded the entrance. Of the nine Portuguese in the expedition, eight of them were invited into the tunnels. The ninth and last member, Raposo, was not invited inside. The other eight disappeared inside, never to be seen again, but not before they had signed the document. Raposo went on to Salvador and then back to Europe and to Rome, where he wrote the other document that is now, supposedly, in the Vatican. Raposo died in Rome, presumably never returning to the lost city.

Frankly, this latter story sounds suspicious. How did this "researcher" find out about this Vatican document? What happened to the remainder of the party of fourteen-hundred, the Negro slaves and Indian guides? Still, I know that Chabbert is telling the story as his researcher reported it. So, it is the researcher who is in question, not Chabbert.

§§§

I spent several days in Salvador, relaxing on the beaches and in the many cafés. One afternoon, while hanging up my laundry on the porch of the Hotel Central, I met another American. He had been living in Brazil for several years, and had come up to Salvador for Carnival. He was in his late thirties, with long, greying hair, and big tatoos on his arms. Both an army veteran and a former hippy, he had dropped out of the fast lane and was living in a sleepy village on an island off Brazil, just south of Salvador.

"Have you noticed how depressed everyone gets after Carnival?" he asked.

"I really hadn't thought about it much," I answered, hanging up some socks and underwear on the line, "but now that you mention it, people do seem a little glum."

"You're damn right!" he shouted. "Carnival is all that these people live for. For months they practice, save, dream of Carnival. Then it all happens. It's the climax of the year for them; their only escape from their dreary reality. When Carnival ends, they get depressed for months, until they start planning for the next Carnival. It's a whole vicious cycle."

Having voiced this particular grudge, he began to reminisce about his army days in Vietnam.

"Once, when I was in Thailand on a reconn mission, there was this big earthquake." He shuddered visibly, then continued, "Right in front of me, I saw mountains, small mountains, just rise out of the ground! I ran towards this big tree, but before I got to it, it disappeared, just sucked into the ground! Everywhere I ran, mountains popped out of the ground, or trees and rocks were sucked into cracks.

"Suddenly, it stopped, it was all quiet, and I was just standing there in the forest. The terrain was completely different than it was before, so I didn't even know the way back to my camp. It took me two days to get back. I just slept in the jungle until I found my outfit again. Man, I never want to go through that again!"

We looked out over the roof tops of Salvador silently for awhile. What he had described was quite frightening, but it was only a small earthquake compared with the sort of upheaval that would have destroyed the canal at Puma Punku.

For some reason, this story reminded me of the quake which had hit Santiago after I left. It was time to continue my quest.

Chapter Fourteen

The Matto Grosso:
The Search for Colonel Fawcett's
Lost City

Whether we get through, and emerge again,
or leave our bones to rot in there, one things for certain.
The answer to the enigma of Ancient South America-
and perhaps of the prehistoric world-
may be found when those old cities are located
and opened to up to scientific research.
That the cities exist, I know...
-Colonel Percy Fawcett

My recovery from Carnival took a few days, but I was soon restless, and lost cities beckoned. I caught a bus for Bela Horizonte, southwest of Salvador. The Lost Mines of Muribeca were certainly intriguing, but even more interesting was the city that the bandeiristas of 1753 had discovered. Many explorers had set out on the trail of that lost city. The most famous was my own, personal hero, perhaps the grand-daddy of all rogue archaeologists. If there was a model for "Indiana Jones," it was Colonel Percy Fawcett!

Though today he is virtually unremembered, he was well known and respected in the first quarter of this century. He was courageous, knowledgeable, and objective. His friends included such personalities as Sir Arthur Conan Doyle and H. Rider Haggard—he was the perfect hero for a rogue archaeologist. Looking back at my own life and various misadventures, I was ashamed. In many ways, I knew I did not match up to the quality of character of Colonel Fawcett.

Then again, it was possible I might be idealizing Fawcett too much. After all, heroes rarely exhibit all the virtues their followers imagine! Yet, even his end was romantic and true to legend. While on a much-heralded quest for the lost city of 1753, he disappeared in the jungles, never to be seen again. Such was his fame, that reports he was still alive persisted well into the 1940's. His memory lingers on still, especially among those who search for lost cities in the mysterious continent of South America.

Colonel Fawcett and his lost city, which never really had a name, became the essence of the lost expedition; the quest for the unknown; the romantic effort to solve the mysteries of the past. But the quest for the Colonel himself became an even bigger mystery. People all over the world became obsessed with solving the mystery of the disappearance of Colonel Fawcett and his party. Expedition after expedition entered the jungle in search of Fawcett. Interest ran so high, that more fame would probably have been won by the person who discovered the Colonel's fate, than by the one who found the lost city which was Fawcett's original goal!

In 1893, Percy Fawcett was a young British officer stationed at Trincomalee, Ceylon. He was keenly interested in archaeology and history, and would take long walks, often lasting days, into the remote jungle areas of the island. On one such trek, a storm overtook him, forcing him to seek shelter beneath some trees for the night. The next morning, as dawn broke into a new, sunny day, he discovered an immense rock, covered with strange inscriptions of quite unknown character and meaning.

He made a copy of the inscriptions, and showed them to a local Buddhist priest. This priest said that they were a form of writing used by the old Asoka-Buddhists, and in a cypher which only those ancient priests understood. This assertion was confirmed ten years later by a Ceylonese Oriental scholar at Oxford University, who claimed that he was the only man alive who could read the script. It was at this time that Fawcett became keenly interested in esoteric history and lost civilizations, eventually becoming one of the foremost authorities on ancient civilizations of his time.

He was quite successful in his army career, leading eight South American expeditions under contract with the Bolivian and Brazilian governments, to delimit the frontiers shared by these two countries with Peru and Ecuador. Between the years 1906 and 1922, he had made four arduous journeys in Bolivia and three in Brazil, as well as other expeditions into Peru and Ecuador.

At a lecture before the Royal Geographical Society in London in

1911, Fawcett described the "lost world" on the borders of Bolivia and Brazil, and told of gigantic footprints of primeval monsters he had seen. Sir Arthur Conan Doyle, the creator of Sherlock Holmes, was present at the lecture, later writing a book based on Fawcett's tales, *The Lost World: The Adventures of Professor Challenger.* You may have seen the movie version, made in the 1950's, on late-night TV.

Later, H. Rider Haggard, author of *King Solomon's Mines,* gave Fawcett a mysterious stone idol. Haggard had allegedly received it from the British Consul, O'Sullivan Beare, who had picked it up at a lost city in Brazil in 1913. This stone statue was in the procession of Colonel Fawcett when he disappeared in the jungle in 1925, but it's story didn't end there.

Fawcett, a believer in the paranormal, had several "sensitives" examine the statuette, in order to ascertain its origin. He wrote that they believed that the idol came from Atlantis. Fawcett himself was a great believer in Atlantis, and felt that the lost cities in the interior of Brazil had an Atlantean origin. He disagreed with one popular theory for the origin of Atlantis, which actually placed the lost civilization in Brazil, but believed that Brazil was once a colony of Atlantis.

Fawcett also believed that some of the writing copied at the end of the bandeirista's document was identical to the writing he had seen years earlier in Ceylon, and that both writings originated in Atlantis. He hoped to prove the existence of Atlantis by rediscovering this lost city.

Unfortunately, as you have undoubtedly guessed, several of Fawcett's assumptions were erroneous. Despite the psychics' opinions to the contrary, the idol originated in the Mediterranean area around 400 BC. According to Barry Fell, an author who has deciphered many ancient inscriptions, the foot-tall, basalt idol was made at or around Hallicarnassus before Hellenistic times. It is an image of a priest of Baal, advertising his temple, dedicated to Hercules (Melgart, son of Baal and Tanitte). The language is Creole Minoan-Hittite, according to Fell. It read, in two parts, "To ask the Gods for a lucky omen of the future, invoke Melgart and...bring a propriation for him."

In the ancient Mediterranean, an area of many diverse cultures, it was common for different countries to form alliances and work together for economic or political ventures. Therefore, it is not unusual that a combination of languages such as Minoan-Hittite would be used on a statuette left at one of the lost cities.

Furthermore, the inscriptions at the end of the bandeirista's document, which Fawcett felt were Atlantean, were actually nothing more than ancient Iberian "Firmas." These were a sort of fancy "X," used in the middle-ages by illiterate soldiers as their signature, according to Fell. Firmas were typically crosses, sometimes with little squiggles or embellishments added. Many illiterates developed their own distinct firma, especially if they werre requierd to sign papers often. All of the bandeiristas of the 1753 expedition were illiterate, and they all put their firma down at the end of Document 512. Ironically, Harold Wilkins also made a big case for these inscriptions in his books, believing the firmas to be Atlantean writing!

But the actual ancient writing found in the bandeirista's document, four inscriptions which they copied as closely as they were able, reveals a great deal about the origin of the city, though it is not Atlantean writing either. (Who's to say what Atlantean writing looks like, anyway?) According to Barry Fell, the four inscriptions are read and translated as follows:

1. *Kuphis* — corrupt Ptolemaic:
   "Fragrant Perfumes."
2. *Hedysmos* — corrupt Ptolemaic:
   "Aromatic Herbs & Spices."
3. *Khrys Phlkioun* — Alphabet of Scorpio:
   "Gold Treasury."
4. *Asem Ephedria* — corrupt Ptolemaic:
   "Guardhouse for Unstamped Ingots of Silver."

Ptolemaic Greek was a later form of Demotic script which replaced Egyptian hieroglyphics around 500 BC. With the rise of Crete, Carthage, Rome, and other Mediterranean cultures, and the decline of Egyptian civilization, Egypt "modernized" their language into a more phonetic script, adapting Greek letters to replace hieroglyphs. (This same thing is happening today in modern China, as they make a transition from pictographic characters into a phonetic alphabet.) These Ptolemaic Greek inscriptions on Document 512 insure its validity: no one, especially not illiterate Portuguese explorers, could have forged Ptolemaic Greek in the manner as written on the document.

The language of Halicarnassus was Dorian Greek, which was spoken in Crete and the Peloponnese. Halicarnassus was also bordered by the Persian Empire to the east and south, with Phoenicia further south in Lebanon, but a short trip in one of the large sailing vessels of the day. So here we see the connection with the gold coin found at the lost city, presumably a gold Daric. Halicarnassus would have been the ideal port for Persian goods to reach the Mediterranean at that time.

We now see, from the various evidence found by the bandeiristas and in Fawcett's possession, that Brazil was being exploited commercially by Mediterranean traders. Most probably, these ancient mines and trading centers were developed prior to 500 BC. by the Egyptians, possibly used by the Hebrews and Phoenicians, and later exploited by Ptolemaic Greeks. Indeed, evidence is mounting that the fabulous mines at Ophir may well have been King Solomon's mines, or the Lost Mines of Muribeca!

Colonel Fawcett reported just before his ill fated expedition that he had been told that a Nafaqua Indian chief, whose territory lay between the Xingu and Tabatinga Rivers, claimed to know of a "city" where strange temples could be found, and baptismal ceremonies were practiced. The Indians there spoke of houses with "stars to light them, which never went out."

Said Fawcett in his book, "This was the first but not the last time I heard of these permanent lights found occasionally in the ancient houses built by that forgotten civilization of old. I knew that certain Indians of Ecuador were reputed to light their huts at night by means of luminous plants, but that, I considered, must be a different thing all together. There was some secret means of illumination known to the ancients that remains to be rediscovered by the scientists of today—some method of harnessing forces unknown to us."[33]

Brian Fawcett then added a footnote to his father's book, "In view of recent developments in atomic research there is no reason to dismiss the 'lamps that never go out' as myth. The world was plunged into a state of barbarism by terrible cataclysms. Continents subsided into the oceans, and others emerged. Peoples were destroyed and the few survivors who escaped were able to exist only in a state of savagery. The ancient arts were all but forgotten, and it is not for us in our ignorance to say that the science of antediluvial days had not advanced beyond the level we have now reached."

I hate to dissappoint Brian in his fanciful speculation, but there is far simpler answer than atomic power to the mystery of these lights. There is today a method of growing a quartz crystal with phosphorous dispersed throughout it's interior. Such a crystal will absorb daylight and then emit that light at night. This would be a simple, yet ingenious device for creating a light that shines by itself, a light storage battery which could sit on the top of a pyramid or pillar for years, shining every night! The Mayans and Aztecs, as well as Tibetans and other cultures, used quartz crystals a great deal, leaving a famous crystal skull found in Mexico as evidence.

On May 29, 1925, Colonel Fawcett wrote a letter to his wife, Nina, from Dead Horse Camp, deep in the Matto Grosso. Fawcett had reached the same spot in 1920, but on that trip his horse had died, forcing him to turn back after giving the camp its name. This staging camp was the first outside Bacairy post, in turn the last outpost of civilization. In this letter to Nina, he expressed the belief that he would reach a waterfall, his first objective, in a week or ten days. "You need have no fear of any failure..." These were the last words that Colonel Fawcett wrote, in this letter sent back by Indian messenger to Cuyaba.

§§§

As I stared out the inevitable bus window on my way to Bela Horizonte, I wondered if Fawcett had ever reached his lost city. I decided to explore Cuyaba myself, to get a feel for Fawcett's environment in his last days. First, however, I wanted to see Ouro Preto, center of the booming mines in the 1700's, a town famous for its colonial charm and old churches.

My comfortable Mercedes bus pulled into Bela Horizonte after a night and a day. Colonel Fawcett would never have approved of rogue archaeologists traveling in such luxury, though I justified it to myself as preparation for the rigors ahead.

Bela Hoizonte is the third largest city in Brazil, but has the pleasant feel of a city far smaller than its two-and-a-half million people. The city has advertised its Carnival in the last few years, but most people still prefer to go to Rio, Salvador, or farther north to Belem or Recife. The city was declared a "nuclear safe zone" by atomic scientists recently, claiming that its prevailing wind and weather patterns promised relatively little fallout in case of a nuclear holocaust. Although Bela Horizonte is one the fastest growing cities in Latin America, its nuclear-free status is probably not the reason.

Should you spend the night here, you may stay in any one of several hotels around the bus station, including the Hotel Madrid, Hotel Minas Bahia, and the Hotel Sao Cristovao. However, I caught a bus straight out to Ouro Preto that afternoon, which was soon roaring over the beautiful green hills and past the small farms into the hilly valley surrounding the city.

Ouro Preto means "black gold" in Portuguese. The Brazilians revere this city the way Italians revere Venice or Florence; it is the artistic and architectural capital of Brazil. Founded in 1711, it soon became the center of the gold, diamond and semi-precious stone trading in the colonial era that followed. So much gold came from the surrounding hills, that the state became known as *Minas Gerais,* or General Mines.

In those days, the city was the "in" place to live, so many fine palaces, churches and houses were built on it's steep hills. Ouro Preto is so famous for its churches that architects come here from all over the world to study. Today, a town of 24,000, it is still small and easy to get around.

The bus station is just a short walk from town, but I didn't know that when I arrived. A taxi driver was waiting at the station, a run-down shack with a small café. For about a dollar each, the driver took an Australian couple and I into the center of town. It was about a two minute ride, and the taxi coasted most of the way. I almost felt like asking for my money back when we got to the cobblestone square in the center, but a deal is a deal. I said goodbye to the Australians, and shouldering my pack, started walking down the street looking for a pension or hotel.

Naturally, rain began to fall nearly the instant I stepped out of the taxi. Pulling my hat down tight, I stuck close to the buildings. The first place I found was the Hotel Tofolo, but it was too expensive ,at $5 for a single room. Nearby, the Pensione Aparecida was full. I finally found a small family-run pension, the Peseoa Tropicala, which had an open room at the top of the stairs. I gladly took it for $2 a night.

I hit the streets again just as the rain stopped. The steep, rain slicked cobblestone lanes wound around the buildings and hills in a labyrinth of passages. It is quite easy to get lost at night in Ouro Preto, something I verified by actually getting lost. My compass would not have helped much.

But Ouro Preto is a college town, and students were just returning from their Carnival vacation. The cafés and pizza joints were packed full, and more students crowded the streets and the main plaza. Lots of excited, young men and women were talking and laughing together everywhere, while spontaneous entertainment erupted in the cafés.

I had a beer at a café on the main square. After a few minutes, the people at the second table over pulled out a mandolin, saxophone and tambourine, and began to play. Their music began with the sound of unfamiliar musicians warming up together, but this soon evolved into lively Brazilian dance music. In moments, the entire café joined in by clapping their hands. After enthusiastically participating for over half an hour, I strutted out and walked across the square, stepping to the beat of the passionate tunes fading away behind me, and ending up at a New Wave place called the "Electric Janella Bar." The abrupt change in atmosphere caught me by surprise; inside an actor painted half in white and half in black did a monologue in Portuguese that I could barely follow. In place of the lively rhythm of the café, I now caught phrases in the monologue like, "What happened to the revolution? What happened to Bob Dylan? What happened to John Lennon?" I wondered about some of these questions myself, though I have to confess that Colonel Fawcett was more on my mind at the time than John Lennon.

I spent the next day walking around town, visiting the churches, where I met and had lunch with two Australian architects, Lucky and Bob. I regretfully took my leave this beautiful town of soon after to catch a bus back to Bela Horizonte, and then toward Brasília.

One of the world's newest cities, Brasília was laid out in the shape of an airplane by the Brazilian architect Lucio Costa in 1957, and in 1960 succeeded Rio de Janeiro as the capital of Brazil. Located in a sparsely settled region in the interior, the city has a strangely alien feel, dominated by ultramodern public buildings and wide avenues, in the middle of the Amazon. The roads linking Brasília with the rest of the country were not even completed until 1982. Government officials often fly out of the capital every weekend, to Rio or elsewhere on the coast, because there is really nothing to do in Brasília. The few tourists who do visit the city usually see all the sights (government buildings!) in one day.

Not really interested in exploring Brasília, I headed directly for Campo Grande in Matto Grosso do Sul state. The Mercedes bus again served as hotel room, and I woke up the next morning as we were leaving Minas Gerais state. That next day was one long bus trip through the scattered bush and rangeland of the Brazilian Highlands. Looking out the window, I watched for emus, the large flightless birds similar to ostriches. Often I saw fifteen or more, running about with the cattle on the ranches.

Stopping several times for meals during the day, I tried an excellent *churasquino* (steak sandwich) at one café. In this vast region of south-western Brazil, towns were few and far between. We would stop at a bus station for half an hour, then drive another endless three or four hours until we came to another small town.

Dusk had mercifully ended the long day when the bus arrived in Campo Grande, the capital of Matto Grosso do Sul. This exciting city has two sections: the area around the train station, and the area around the bus station. I spent a night at the Hotel Turis, paying two dollars for a bed in a dormitory, then left again for Cuyaba the next morning. The road here has no stops, and no other roads cross it to break the monotony of swamps and forest. I tried to keep my eye peeled as drove through this wild country, to catch a glimpse my own lost city, but the constant low hum of the bus caused me to keep dozing off. After ten hours of this never-ending jungle, we pulled into Cuyaba.

Cuyaba is the only town of any size in Matto Grosso state, with a population of about 85,000. Stepping out of the bus terminal, I said under my breath, "So, this is Cuyaba," It had probably changed a lot since 1925. Cuyaba was my Mecca, having been Colonel Fawcett's starting point on his last expedition. I was making a pilgrimage, to pay my last respects to that grand-daddy of rogue archaeologists.

I checked into the Hotel Santa Luzia for the night, then went out to eat. Besides the Santa Luzia, other hotels near th bus station are the Liboa, Miranda, Cristal, and Sao Francisco. About five blocks away and across the river, you will find the main plaza, the Praca da Republica, with its cathedral, post office, cafés and all that stuff that clusters around the center of town. Many good cafés are located along the Avenida Gal. Valle, where I had dinner before retiring.

I spent the next afternoon exploring the town and relaxing in one of the cafés, eating a slow lunch with tea. Naturally, my thoughts turned to Colonel Fawcett and his search. Had he ever found his lost city?

The first indication that Colonel Fawcett might still have been alive after his disappearance came in 1927, when a French civil engineer named Roger Courtville arrived in Lima after a long motor tour. He reported that he had talked with a sick and tattered old man whom he had found sitting at the roadside when he was passing through a remote area in the state of Minas Gerais. The old man had said his name was Fawcett. It happened that Courtville was ignorant Fawcett's reputation; but on learning of the mystery, he was anxious to organize an expedition in search of the old man.

One year later, an expedition in search of Fawcett was finally mounted by George Dyott, who knew the territory fairly well. They discovered a trunk which had belonged to Fawcett, though it proved to have been discarded during his 1920 expedition.

In 1930, a similar expedition set out under the leadership of a journalist named Albert de Winton, but, so far as is known, no member ever returned.

In 1932, a Swiss trapper named Rattin reported that that he had talked to "an English Colonel" who was prisoner of an Indian tribe north of the river Bomfin, a tributary of the Sao Manoel River. The man had refrained from giving his name.

In June, 1933, a theodolite compass belonging to Fawcett was sent to his wife by the Royal Geographical Society. It had been found near the camp of the Bacairy Indians in the region where Fawcett disappeared

299

by Colonel Aniceto Botelho, the deputy of Matto Grosso.

An explorer, Tom Roch, reported that sometime after 1931, he had met two white men called "Fawceth" who told him that they had been collecting stones for five years in the Matto Grosso area. One man was elderly, the other young.

Miguel Tucchi, another explorer, stated around 1932 that he had seen Fawcett in the region of the Rio das Mortes, and that the old man had told him that he had private reasons for remaining with the Indians.

During 1933, a British expedition left in search of Fawcett's party, starting at Belem at the mouth of the Amazon and heading south through portions of the Matto Grosso and Goyaz state. Accompanying the expedition was the British writer Peter Fleming, who later wrote a popular book about the journey, *Brazilian Adventure*.[64]

In July, 1933, the narrative of Virginio Pessione's expedition to the Kuluene River was sent to the President of the Royal Geographical Society by Monseigneur Couturon, Administrateur Apostoliqu of the Salesian Mission in Matto Grosso. This report stated that three white men, whose descriptions fit the members of the Fawcett party, had been living for some years with the Aruvudu Indians, and were known to have been alive in 1932. The youngest man had married an Indian woman, who had borne him a white, blue-eyed son.

In 1935, two brothers, Patrick and Gordon Ullyatt, said they came across rubber gatherers during their journeys through Matto Grosso, who seemed to know quite a bit about Colonel Fawcett, including his current location.

In 1937, American missionary Martha Moennich wrote a letter to Mrs. Fawcett, giving a very circumstantial account of her husband's movements, of the death of Rimell, of the marriage of Jack Fawcett to an Indian woman and the birth of a son. She also related the killing of both Fawcett men by the same Indians who held them captive. This lady claimed to have seen the child of Jack Fawcett as a baby, and later as a growing boy in 1934.

Later, she gave more details in her book, *Pioneering for Christ in Xingu Jungles*. To quote her rare book, "Certain it appears that none has ever descended the Rio das Mortes. Only the headwaters are known, and the part that empties into Rio Araguaya. About eight-hundred miles in between are barred by impassable rapids and savages, by Chavantes and Cayapos. Every expedition assaying this ascent has been driven back by attacks of savages who kill without warning, preferably by clubbing...This, then, is the region in which Colonel Fawcett, Jack, and Raleigh Rimell are thought by some to still survive."

"Later, word came out of the jungle through Indian channels that the Fawcetts had been restrained by the Kurikuros as virtual prisoners, and that Jack had been forced to accept marriage with the daughter of a chief, which would explain the child's parentage...At any rate, in the middle of the Rio Kurezeu was this group of Indians with an unusually blond infant.

"...the visiting Kurikuros related that Raleigh Rimell had died of fever and infected insect bites. The Colonel and his son, the Indians declared, had both gone overland towards the Rio das Mortes, and nothing had been heard of them since."

Miss Moennich relates that other Indians reported to her that Colonel Fawcett and his son had gone on to the Kalapalos Indian tribe from the Kurikuros, and desired to press on in the direction of their lost city, located still further to the east. "From the first the Kalapalos had tried to dissuade the explorers from their purpose, telling them that it would be impossible to traverse the dense forest and trackless land beyond without either food or water and in constant danger of the Cayapos." The Cayapos were an especially hostile and savage tribe, who would capture, torture, and eat trespassers.

"Yet in spite of their own advice, the Colonel had persuaded eight of the Kalapalos to accompany him for a short distance, at least, and the party set out. After four days of hard travel across the Kuluene and eastward toward the Dio das Mortes, their food supply gave out without hope of replenishment. All were too emaciated to proceed. The Kalapalos, recognizing the danger, begged the white men to return with them to their village. But the latter determined to go on, and turned their backs upon the Indians, three of whom followed and shot the explorers from behind.

"We gathered the impression that pity also had mingled in the thought of the assassins, since, by a sudden death from their great arrows, they were saving the Colonel and Jack from a more lingering and painful fate." The Indians in this area all live in a horrible fear of the Cayapos, which is evidently why, according to Moennich, they killed the Fawcett party—to save them from a far more horrible death.

Moennich also wrote that the name of the Indian boy fathered by Jack Fawcett was named Dulipe. In 1944, in Lima, Brian Fawcett, Colonel Fawcett's youngest son, received a telephone call from señor Edmar Morel of Sao Paulo. Morel said that he had with him an Indian boy named Dulipe, who he claimed was the son of Brain's brother Jack, and offered to send him to Brian. However, in Brian Fawcett's view, there was not enough evidence to support the claim that the boy was Jack's son. Seven years later, Brian Fawcett heard that it was established that the boy was an albino, with no white blood. In 1951, señor Morel published an account of his 1943 expedition which included a confession by a Kalapalos Indian chief, Izarari, that Fawcett and his two companions had been killed by the Indians.

In 1951, señor Orlando Vilas Boas of the Central Brazil foundation, published a confession by chief Izarari, that he had clubbed the two Fawcetts and Rimell to death. Izarari's successor, Comatzi, disclosed the alleged grave of Colonel Fawcett, where bones were subsequently dug up and sent to England for examination. After a team of experts from the Royal Anthropological Institute in London examined these remains, they declared that they could not be the bones of Colonel Fawcett. It is possible that they may have been those of Albert de Winton, however, who was lost searching for Colonel Fawcett in 1930.

From this evidence, much of which is undoubtably idle story-telling, it seems possible that Colonel Fawcett, Jack and Raleigh were still alive as late as 1935, an incredible ten years after they had begun their expedition! But Brian Fawcett, in the final chapter of his father's book, draws negative conclusions from the evidence, not believing that his brother fathered a child with an Indian girl, and questioning the story brought back by Rattin of the nameless English Colonel. Quoting Brian, "And why-why did the old man not tell his name?"[33]

Actually, there is a good reason why the real Colonel may have remained silent. Brian himself tells the reader in the prologue to *Exploration Fawcett* that his father, before setting out on this last journey, "...fearful of other lives being lost on his account, urged us to do everything possible to discourage rescue expeditions should his party fail to come back."[33] And there may have been other reasons Fawcett chose to not disclose his identity. He may actually have preferred to stay with the Indians, though certainly his son and wife could not have imagined this.

Kalapalos Indian chief Izarari's confession to the clubbing to death of the three explorers seems at least partially untrue, because the bones he asserted were Colonel Fawcett's proved not to be. Furthermore, Izarari also told Edmar Morel that the party had been shot with arrows.

Colonel Fawcett was a believer in psychic phenomena, as was his friend, Sir Arthur Conan Doyle. In 1955, an interesting book called *The Fate of Colonel Fawcett* was pubished by the Aquarian Press in London. This rare book is an investigation into the disappearance of Colonel Fawcett by psychic Geraldine Cummins, who allegedly "makes contact" with the Colonel on several successive instances.[57] As unconventional as its topic may be, the book makes fascinating and exciting reading. It reads, curiously enough, like an H. Rider Haggard novel, full of mystery, lost cities, savages, and evil priestesses.

According to *The Fate of Colonel Fawcett*, the Colonel was still alive in 1935, when the "contact" first started. Raleigh and Jack were killed, just as Miss Moennich had stated, by the Indian tribe that held them captive, when they insisted on continuing on to the lost city that they sought. Jack Fawcett was well liked by the Kalapalos, but the Indians felt that Rimell was devious, influencing Jack against them. As the two set off on their quest, the Indians who were supposedly escorting them shot both Jack and Rimell on the orders of chief Izariri. Jack was killed instantly with a dozen arrows in his back; Rimell was allowed to suffer for a few hours, as he was deemed the instigator in wanting to take Jack Fawcett away from the tribe.

The reason Izariri wanted to keep the explorers captive was that the chief had lived for some time among Europeans, and did not want the Whites' civilization to affect his tribe. He was afraid that if he let Fawcett's party loose, they would return with more Europeans. This is a common concern among natives; Tatunca Nara of Akakor expressed the same concern for his people. Izariri wanted the whites to believe that Colonel Fawcett was dead, and even provided proof so that they would discontinue the search. This could be why Albert de Winton was killed, then his remains passed off as those of Colonel Fawcett.

According to *The Fate of Colonel Fawcett*, the Colonel did eventually reach the lost city, after the death of Jack and Raleigh. Izariri had wanted Colonel Fawcett to marry his sister, a high priestess. This woman hated Fawcett, and vice versa. The union never took place, as before the marriage, Fawcett insisted he visit the lost city, finally being escorted there safely by an Indian servant. Fawcett eventually died back in the village of the Kalapalos, poisoned by the priestess. So ended the bizarre story of Colonel Fawcett and his ill fated expedition, as related through the medium Geraldine Cummins.

In the most bizarre part of this book, Fawcett says in the supposed communication that he could imagine Egyptians walking the city. It may be that the story is in fact a forgery, using Miss Moennich's story as a basis and elaborating on it. Yet it is curious that Cummins would call the city Egyptian, as Fawcett himself believed it to be Atlantean.

§§§

That was not the end of the incredible legacy of Colonel Fawcett and his lost city. In 1947, a New Zealand school teacher named Hugh McCarthy quit his job in Wellington, and flew to Rio de Janeiro, determined to find the lost city that Colonel Fawcett had sought.

Like a man posessed, the frail thirty-two year old, believed that he could find the city, which he presumed to be full of gold. In Rio, he rented a cheap flat near the Biblioteca National and poured over accounts of Colonel Fawcett the original eighteenth-century Portuguese explorers.[58]

Many months later, he made his way to the village of Peixoto, a small Indian settlement located on the eastern fringe of the unexplored Matto Grosso. Here he met the Reverend Jonathan Wells, a missionary who had lived in the area for many years. McCarthy stayed for some time, and the two became good friends.

Reverend Wells tried to convince McCarthy to abandon his search for the lost city, saying the area was unexplored and filled with hostile Indians. McCarthy could not be deterred, however. Not being able to dissuade the adventurer, the padre gave McCarthy a gift: seven carrier pigeons.

The two men worked out a system of communicating by shorthand. Hugh promised to send a report back to Wells of his solitary expedition, once a week or whenever possible. Into a small Indian canoe, he packed some meager supplies, food, an automatic pistol, a rifle, three hundred rounds of ammunition, and the seven carrier pigeons in a separate wicker baskets. Dissappearing upstream, he was never again seen alive.

His story, though, is nearly as fascinating as Fawcett's. He did manage to communicate with Reverend Wells, his shorthand letters sent via the carrier pigeons somehow seeming considerably more valid than the "psychic communication" of Geraldine Cummins.

The first carrier pigeon did not reach Reverend Wells until six weeks after McCarthy had left on his search. At the top of the strip of paper it indicated that it was the third letter sent; the first two had not reached the padre.

McCarthy wrote: "I am still quite ill from my accident, but the swelling in my left leg is gradually receding. Had it not been for these friendly Indians and especially the girl, Tana, my body would now be lying in an unmarked grave. The Indians have taken me into their hearts and I could be happy living here the rest of my life. When I regained consciousness, I found myself looking into the face of this beautiful girl. Her pale blue eyes made me think I had already died and gone to heaven. I have changed her name to Heather and am now teaching her English. (How incredibly British of him!) Tomorrow I leave to continue my mission. I am told that the mountains which I seek are only five days away. God keep you. Hugh."

So Hugh was alive, though he had had an accident. We will never know exactly what it was; perhaps a poisonous insect or snake bite. That the Indian woman had blue eyes is very interesting. Was she a member of one of the mysterious tribes of white Indians?

The fourth letter never reached the Padre, but six weeks later, the fifth carrier pigeon arrived at the mission. Reverend Wells' hands shook as he read the note:

"I have reached the snow-capped mountains, but am in dire circumstances. Long ago I abandoned my canoe and threw away my rifle as it is impractical in the jungle. My food supply has been exhausted and I am living on berries and wild fruits. The weather has turned cold, and at night I am unable to sleep. I could turn back, as I know Heather is waiting for me, but having come this far nothing can stop me from scaling these peaks to either final victory or merciful death. Somewhere in these snow-capped peaks, I hope to find Fawcett's Lost City of Gold. But should I fail, it was at least a glorious adventure. Pray for me."

Three weeks later, the seventh and final carrier pigeon returned, only the third to do so. The note it carried read:

"I know that the soft cold hand of death will touch me shortly, and in these last moments I can but pray that all of the pigeons I sent out arrived safely. Writing is difficult and my lucid moments are few. But what a glorious way I have chosen to leave this world. I hope my map arrived safely by carrier pigeon number six, so that you, of all people in the world will know the location of this City of Gold. It is magnificent and unbelievable, with a golden pyramid and exquisite temples. With God's help, you will soon be able to lead an expedition of archaeologists back to this most wonderful of all cities since the beginning of Time and its treasures can be preserved for generations to come. My work is over and I die happily, knowing that my belief in Fawcett and his lost City of Gold was not in vain. Hugh."

Hugh McCarthy had done the impossible! Excited, Wells ran down to the river with the three letters, and took a canoe down river to a nearby town where he could charter a plane. Four days later he was in Rio de Janeiro, hoping to interest the authorities in sending out an expedition to find McCarthy and save him, if that was still possible. However, the Matto Grosso is a vast region, and there are not one, but four mountain ranges in the area. Nor was there any historical or other evidence that such a lost city of gold existed.

They concluded that Hugh McCarthy had lost his mind, and delirious, wrote about his lost city of gold. Thus the courageous school teacher from New Zealand added a bit more mystery and frustration to the legends of lost cities and treasure. It is indeed unfortunate that his map did not reach the padre, yet, this lost city of gold may soon be discovered.

Even as you read this, it may have been. After years of pouring over satellite maps made using infrared photography of the Matto Grosso region, Rene Chabbert believes that he has found Colonel Fawcett's lost city. He has identified the plaza, river and archway on his satellite photo, just as described by the bandeiristas. He has applied for an exploration permit from the Brazilian government to go to the city sometime in the second half of 1986. A television crew will accompany him.

And what is the location of the city? Only Chabbert knows the exact whereabouts. And it is by no means easy to figure out! In Colonel Fawcett's book, he gives the location of "Raposo's City" as just east of the Rio San Francisco, which would position it in Bahia State. It most certainly is not there! Fawcett left Cuyaba heading north, and wrote that he intended to head to the east, toward Bahia. Chabbert says that the city that he has located on his satellite photo is actually west of Cuyaba, and he thinks Fawcett knew that. Lost cities full of gold are secrets to be kept!

Perhaps, the mystery of Colonel Fawcett's lost city will finally be solved in the near future. And maybe when Rene Chabbert enters it, he will find Hugh McCarthy's bones sitting near those of Colonel Fawcett, both skulls grinning wildly. Will the history books have to be rewritten? Will the experts finally have to give in to the rogue archaeologists?

A gold Daric, showing King Darius (521-486 B.C.) as an archer kneeling with bow, quiver and spear.

Carved from black basalt and believed to come from a lost city in Brazil, this idol was later given to Colonel Fawcett.

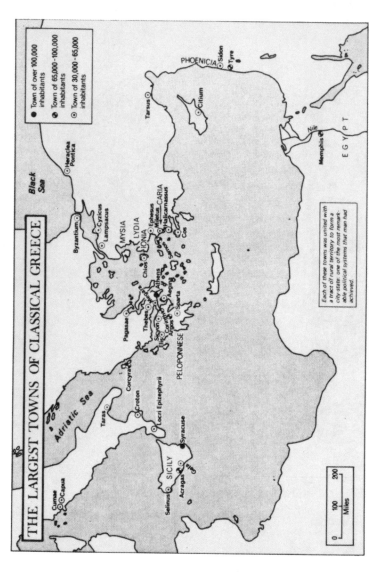

THE LARGEST TOWNS OF CLASSICAL GREECE

Legend:
- ● Town of over 100,000 inhabitants
- ❷ Town of 65,000–100,000 inhabitants
- ◎ Town of 30,000–65,000 inhabitants

Each of these towns was united with a tract of rural territory to form a city-state, one of the most remarkable political systems that man had achieved.

Black Sea

PHOENICIA   Sidon   Tyre

Tarsus

Citium

Heraclea Pontica

Byzantium

Cyzicus

Lampsacus

MYSIA

LYDIA

Chios   IONIA   Ephesus   CARIA   Halicarnassus

Athens   Samos   Miletus   Cos

Thebes   Argos

Pagasae

Sicyon   Corinth

Elis   Sparta

PELOPONNESE

Corcyra

Croton

Taras

Locri Epizephyrii

Adriatic Sea

Syracuse

SICILY   Gela

Selinus   Acragas

Cumae   Capua

Nile

Memphis

E G Y P T

0   100   200
Miles

Colonel Fawcett's idol probably came from Halicarnassus, an ancient
seaport. What was it doing in the Amazon?

Colonel Percy Fawcett.

Colonel Fawcett and a companion discover the tracks of a giant reptile on the border of Bolivia and Brazil. Fawcett believed that dinosaurs still lived in the forests.

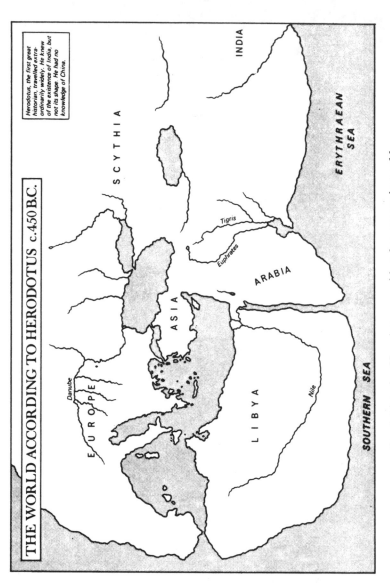

THE WORLD ACCORDING TO HERODOTUS c. 450 B.C.

Herodotus, the first great historian, travelled extraordinarily widely. He knew of the existence of India, but not its shape. He had no knowledge of China.

EUROPE

SCYTHIA

ASIA

INDIA

Danube

Tigris

Euphrates

ARABIA

ERYTHRAEAN SEA

LIBYA

Nile

SOUTHERN SEA

Greek historian Herodotus, considered an expert in world geography, nevertheless managed to leave a few details out of his maps.

Egyptian ship of the Punt Expedition.

Phoenician ship, C. 700 B.C.

Viking ship from Oseberg.

Colonel Percy Fawcett.

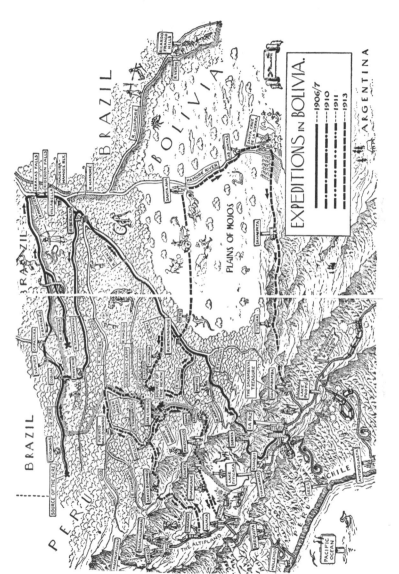

Fawcett's map of Bolivia.

Perhaps one of the reasons Fawcett's adventures captured the minds of so many was his illustrations.

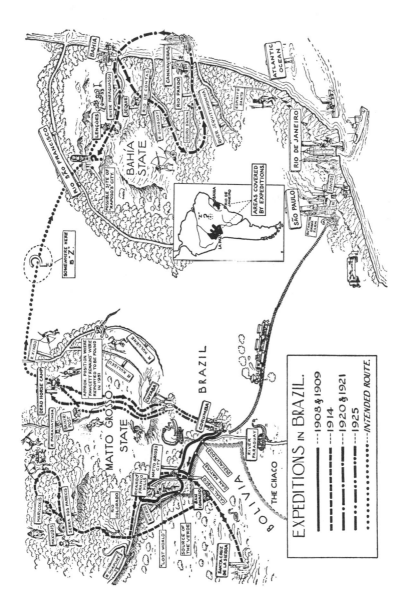

Fawcett's map of Brazil.

Greek galley, 4th century B.C.

The inscriptions from Document 512.

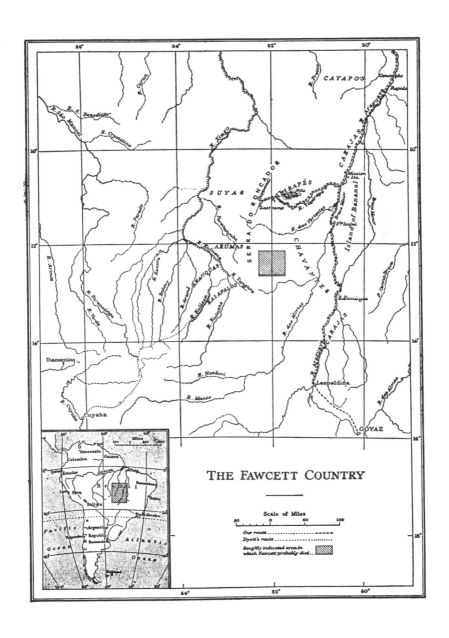

THE FAWCETT COUNTRY

Scale of Miles

50   0   50   100

Our route ....
Dyott's route ....
Roughly indicated area in
which Fawcett probably died..

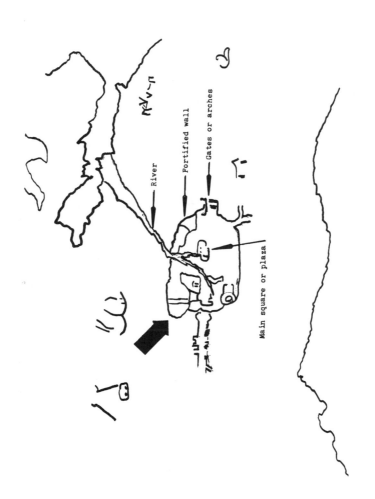

Rene Chabbert's drawing from his satellite photo, which he believes represents is the city of 1753 which Colonel Fawcett sought.

Chapter Fifteen

The Jungles of Bolivia:
Lost Cities, Tunnels, and the
Death Train

With Colonel Fawcett's lost city just a daydream behind me, I was back on the street in Campo Grande, buying a train ticket to Corumba on the Bolivian border. From Cuyaba, I could have traveled further into the Matto Grosso and the Amazon on the Trans-Amazonian highway, but there is no turning back from that decision. One can theoretically drive to Porto Velho, and from there to Manaus, or Boa Vista on the Venezuelan border, but travel is difficult and slow. Sometimes no vehicles will pass for days on end, which makes life difficult for a hitchhiker. With the money I had made selling my camera in Buenos Aires dwindling, I had to get back to Peru. That meant going through Bolivia, which would be tough enough.

If I kept on going northwest through the Amazon and up to Porto Velho, I would be getting close to Akakor country. This area is still mostly unexplored and it is virtually impossible to cross into Peru from there. So I had taken the bus back to Campo Grande, then decided to head west through the jungles. Besides, there was a lost city that I wanted to inspect. It would be easier to reach than Akakor, that much was certain.

Back in Campo Grande, I barely had time for dinner, since the train for Corumba left that evening. At the station, I met an Austrian traveler named Jorge. He drove a taxi in Vienna, presumably coming to South America to brush up on agressive driving techniques with the experts. He even looked the part of a Brazilian kamakazi driver, whith his wild curly hair and thick mustache. He had arrived in Rio a month before and, like me, was headed for Peru.

Around nine o'clock that night, while we were waiting for the train to leave, Jorge remembered he had run out of Brazilian currency. I had changed a few dollars earlier at a hotel, so I took him there. They did not want any more foreign currency, but suggested that he might try a liquor store down the street. Even banks in remote regions of Brazil sometimes will not change money for travelers! Travel agencies or hotels are usually your best bet, especially at night.

Entering the small, cramped liquor store, we observed a scene which somehow reminded me of an ancient pagan ritual. Half a dozen old men were crouched in a vague circle, playing cards as they tested a healthy sample of the store's wine. The owner, a fat, greasy man, said he would change five dollars for Jorge—at a pretty poor rate—but only if he bought a bottle of wine. Having little choice, Jorge agreed.

But just as they were striking the deal, the card players all jumped abruptly to their feet, startled by a rat the size of a house cat running across the floor from their corner. They began stamping at it with their boots as it dashed from shelf to shelf, searching for an exit from the deadly floor. The obese merchant watched casually as they finished their sacrifice, then went back to their cards, leaving the carcass lying dead in the middle of the store.

I turned away in disgust. Jorge took his money and his wine and we left. Once on board the train, which was only about half-full, we shared the wine and watched the flat swamps of the Matto Grosso sweep by under the light of the full moon. I leaned back, looking out the window, and fell asleep in the seat.

Waking at dawn, we found the train progressing through Pantanal Forest wilderness area, a Brazilian national park. A huge bluff rose out of the swamp in the dawn light, wisps of clouds swirling around its top, and green forests stretching up its sides. The Pantanal Forest swamp is full of these unusual butte formations, which hold the largest deposits of manganese in the world.

Soon, the birds began to stir, then the vast swamps came alive with a wealth of animal life: deer, ocelots, puma, boar, anteaters, tapirs, rheas, *capivaras* (giant aquatic guinea pigs), and *jacare* (large Brazilian alligators). Jacare swarmed the banks of the Paraguai River and its many tributaries, twisting waterways that wind through the immense swamp. Over 350 varieties of fish inhabit these waters, including the vicious piranha and the giant pintado, which can weigh over 150 pounds! The more than 600 native bird species include parrots, coots, herons, storks and ducks. This is one of the best places in Brazil to observe Amazon wildlife.

It was mid-morning when we arrived at Corumba. Collecting our packs, Jorge and I piled out of the train. After walking a mile or so from the train station, we caught a bus into town. Corumba is right on the border of Bolivia, across the river from the Bolivian town of Puerto Suarez. Small droplets of rain began to fall as we boarded the bus, continuing to fall steadily for the rest of the day. Since there isn't much to do in Corumba except visit the magnificent Pantanal Forest, we were eager to cross the river to Puerto Suarez in the Bolivian side, then catch a train to Santa Cruz. Unfortunately, this meant catching the "Death Train" from Puerto Suarez.

This train is got its name from the fate of some unfortunate passengers who cannot endure the grueling trip. Because there is no road for over 400 miles through the completely unpopulated swamps, mountains and jungle between Puerto Suarez and Santa Cruz, anyone travelling on this route must take the train. Most passengers ride packed into boxcars like sardines. Some suffocate on the twenty-hour trip, and it is not uncommon to find a frail man or woman lying dead on the boxcar floor, having expired during the course of the journey.

Jorge and I took a local bus out of Corumba straight to the border, where we got stamped by customs out of Brazil and into Bolivia. This is a pretty lax border crossing, where you can pretty much just come and go between Corumba and Puerto Suarez.

Puerto Suarez is a small town a few blocks long, with dirt streets, a small park, and a few shops and guest houses. Unfortunately, because . of delays due to the the rain, we had to wait a full day for the Death Train. Jorge and I killed the time sitting in Puerto Suarez's only café, drinking beer, eating lunch, and talking with a couple of Peace Corps volunteers who had been stationed in Ecuador. They had been waiting two days for the train, which was now a total of three days late, stuck in the wilderness somewhere between Santa Cruz and Puerto Suarez. Given the train's already grisly reputation, we wondered how many people would still be alive when it finally arrived. While it seemed unlikely that people would starve to death in just a few days, they would probably be getting rather hungry.

One of the Peace Corps volunteers was a bearded young man from Michigan named Harry. At the café, over our third beer of the afternoon, he told us about South American "snuff films." I hesitate to relate this story, but I feel that it may illustrate the low value with which human life is regarded in parts of South America. Snuff films are movies where people are actually tortured and killed on film. No special effects are used; everything is real. These movies are fortunately illegal in the United States, but I understand they are frequently shown in South American theaters. I have never seen a snuff movie, nor would I care to.

"I once read," I said, directing my comments to Harry, "that snuff movies do not really exist."

"Oh, they exist all right; I've seen them myself," he answered.

"What happens in snuff movies?," Jorge asked.

"Well, the first one I saw," Harry began to recount, "was done as a documentary. In it, a narrator is shown at the beginning explaining that what the viewer is about to see is actual footage of an expedition into the jungles of South America. The camera crew was killed, but the film was recovered.

"The story is about some journalists who go into a jungle area, then torture and kill a group of Indians. It was all very graphic and disgusting, and so believable, it hardly seemed possible it could be anything but real. The film ends with the Indians, in turn, torturing and killing the journalists. It was really horrible: very graphic, and undoubtedly real."

Harry went on to say that he had seen another movie like this, quite similar in content. "They were quite popular in the Ecuadorian town where I was stationed," he said. "I don't know how they could have made those movies without killing people. The only other explanation was that they used bodies that were already dead. But they didn't look dead at the beginning!"

Probably the inspiration for snuff movies was a real event in Ecuador in the 1950's. A camera crew which ventured into a remote area of the jungle was killed by Indians while filming their village. Their film was recovered the next year, and is often used today in documentaries on Amazon Indians.

I felt sick to my stomach hearing about these films. In some ways, the Amazonian Indians were still considered animals, low-life to be exterminated since they stood in the way of "progress"—the clearing of the Amazonian forests. It was no wonder that Tatunca Nara and the Ugha Mongulala called Europeans the "White Barbarians." The type of kidnapping and slavery portrayed in the 1985 film, *The Emerald Forest* hits very close to home. These atrocities against Indians have been commonplace in the frontier areas of Brazil.

The Death Train finally arrived in Puerto Suarez that night, so we were all able to leave for Santa Cruz the next morning. Jorge and I enjoyed the luxury of our own seats; the other options were second class benches and the economy class boxcars. Since the train had been delayed for several days, it was literally overflowing when it left Puerto Suarez, with passengers seemingly bursting out of every door and opening in the boxcars. But by late morning, we were chugging away through the densely forested Santiago Mountains toward Santa Cruz. The train occasionally stopped at tiny towns along the way, but otherwise made good time.

On the train, we met a group of beautiful Peruvian women, who had all been traveling in Brazil. They were all from the northern city Trujillo, the surfing capital of Peru. I was heading that direction soon, so was glad to meet them. One of the beauties, Charo, actually ran a hotel in Trujillo, and invited me to come visit. I could hardly resist.

We arrived in Santa Cruz that evening, amazingly on time and in one piece. On that journey, to my knowledge, the infamous Death Train failed to claim a single victim.

In Santa Cruz, Jorge and I shared a room at the Alojamiento 7 de Maio. There are a number of inexpensive hotels here, all known as Alojamientos. Most are located around the main plaza, the Plaza 2 de Septiembre. The more prominent are the Alojamientos Oriente, Excelcior, 24 de Septiembre, Santa Barbara, and the 7 de Maio.

At nearly 400,000 people, Santa Cruz is the major town in eastern Bolivia, with a healthy, active economy that is the best in the country. In fact, it does not seem like Bolivia at all, but more like a cross between New Mexico and Brazil. Because the economy in Santa Cruz is exploding, everyone seems to have plenty of money. Brand new jeeps, Toyota four-wheel drive wagons, and other expensive luxury goods from the States are common. Unmistakabe is the suave European feel of Santa Cruz, as opposed to the Aymara and Quechua Indian-look of most Bolivian towns on the Altiplano.

Why is Santa Cruz so prosperous and westernized compared to the rest of Bolivia? The answer is simple: it is the cocaine capitol of the world! Coca leaves are grown and processed here, then shipped as finished product to Columbia and the United States. The suitcases full of dollar bills used on *Miami Vice* to pay off diabolical drug dealers usually end up in Santa Cruz in real life.

The king of cocaine dealers, Roberto Suarez Gomez, owns a huge cattle ranch in the Beni region, just north of Santa Cruz. According to a *TIME Magazine* article, this wealthy cattle owner first realized the potentially huge profits to be made trafficking cocaine in the mid-1970's. As an expert pilot with a fleet of planes originally acquired to transport beef from his isolated ranches, he was able to become the main long-distance middleman between Bolivian coca growers and Colombian buyers.

By 1980, intelligence reports estimated that his cocaine operations were netting him $400 million a year. Now 55, and known simply as "Suarez," he lives his life like someone from a James Bond movie. He carries a gold-plated handgun, and keeps a pet leopard with a diamond-studded collar by his side at his remote Beni ranch. Complete with his own private air force of missile-carrying jets, he controls his own mini-kingdom, and has been known to boast of hiring Libyan "experts" to train his security force. Paradoxically, he is fond of buying newspaper space to lecture to his countrymen about corruption in their government.

Actually quite popular in Bolivia, Suarez has the reputation of a modern Bolivian "Robin Hood," who underwrites the entire education costs of the Beni and Santa Cruz districts, in addition to providing college and technical education abroad for local young people. He is, in short, a Bolivian Cocaine Hero, and quite possibly one of the richest men in the world. Ah, Bolivia.

We spent two days in Santa Cruz. For a town of such opulence, quite frankly, there is very little of interest, but we did meet a New Zealander named Paddy at our hotel. Paddy was a tall, athletic, young guy with short dark hair who had traveled all over the world. Like me, he was headed toward La Paz.

But my immediate destination was a small town just out of Santa Cruz called Samaipata. Here is located one of the least known, but most interesting archaeological sites in South America; a lost city of great mystery and wonder. Paddy wanted to go to Cochabamba, the next main town, and then on to La Paz. Jorge was headed south to Sucre and intended to fly. Since we were headed in the same direction, Paddy and I linked up together.

At four the next afternoon, we were off on the bus to Cochabamba. We only made it about 60 miles out of Santa Cruz, however, when we came to a stop behind a long line of trucks and buses. Getting out, Paddy and I walked forward along the traffic jam, discovering to our dismay that all the traffic in both directions was caught, trying to get across a very bad, muddy stretch in this mountainous road. We counted over 200 vehicles waiting in front of our bus alone.

The road wound precariously along a mountain river, roaring along a hundred feet below. At the blockage, the road turned into a sea of mud, three-feet deep. Trucks which tried to pass through it were in deep trouble, because if they slipped too much down the slight incline, they would take the long plunge into the roaring river below. Seeing all this, we realized that our bus was not going anywhere that night.

We stopped at a small, makeshift shelter standing by the roadside at a point overlooking the road, where several Indian women had set up an impromptu tea stall. They were heating a pot of coffee on an open campfire, with another pot of vicuna stew simmering slowly beside it. A rare cousin of the llama living in the Andes, the vicuna is a member of the camel family, with extremely fine fur. The animal was held sacred by the Incas, only royalty being allowed wear its fleece. Feeling guilty, yet ravenous, I hungrily devoured the strange stew.

Crouched in front of that fire, sucking on a vicuna bone, I felt strangely like some ancient, primitive native. Looking up across the fire, my eyes caught those of a real native Indian who squatted there. Her hair was long and black, her features sharp and proud. With dark eyes and a smile she stared back at me as she poured some Singani liquor into our coffee. I sensed that she relished life like I did; she too knew what it was like to sleep out in the open, to lay your head down on a flat rock to rest after after a hard day. She knew much better than I ever would.

Walking back to the bus, Paddy and I stared in wonder at the forest, the moon, the river, the fireflies that danced around us. Surrounding us with the sounds of a strangely-alien orchestra were the sounds of the abundant fauna. Frogs croaked nearby; one sounded like a World War Two dive-bomber. In the distance, a monkey howled like some jungle demon in search of prey.

The line of vehicles had not moved an inch by morning. Paddy, having bought a ticket to Cochabamba, was determined to stay with the bus until it could get through. I, on the other hand, was in no mood to let this little inconvenience stall me any longer. Smiling, I grabbed my pack from the top of the bus and handed it down to Paddy.

"Good luck on your trip," he said, helping me adjust the shoulder straps. "Maybe I'll see you in Cochabamba."

"Sure," I said. After picking the name of a hotel in my guidebook, I suggested that we try meeting there in a few days. With that, I set off down the road to the sounds of the river roaring below, the birds singing, and several hundred angry truck drivers cursing the mud slide.

When I got to the blockage, I took off my shoes, rolled up my pants, and waded through the knee-deep mud. It felt gushy and soft between my toes, like a good mud pie you made when you were three. I found it difficult to keep my balance, and several times almost fell over, narrowly avoiding a mud bath. Meanwhile, a bulldozer had arrived and was trying its best to clear the blockage, so that the rest of the world could get across.

After fording the sea of mud, I stopped at a small stream to wash my feet. As I was putting on my shoes, the first of the trucks from back on the other side made it through with a healthy shove from the bulldozer.

Jumping to my feet, I grabbed my pack and ran after it, like a prisoner escaping from a concentration camp, hell bent to catch the ride that would take him to freedom. With a last surge of energy, I leapt onto the back of the truck, my feet balancing narrowly on the bumper, my hands tightly gripping the wooden cage. I waved as we passed the hut where we had dined on vicuna stew the night before. The lady with long black hair smiled and waved back.

With that, the truck roared off through the mountains once again. Loaded with chickens in plastic cages, piled a good twenty feet high, I supposed it was headed for Cochabamba. My pack was pulling me back awkwardly, but I hung on for dear life, especially when the driver accelerated around curves. Maybe he was trying to throw me from the truck. After all, I hadn't asked him for a ride!

After awhile he stopped, coming up behind a few trucks stalled on a bend in the mountain road. I jumped off and walked up to him in the driver's seat. "May I have a ride on your truck to Cochabamba, señor?" I asked him politely in Spanish. He was a short man, with the marks of smallpox on his face, his black hair slicked back from his forehead.

He nodded without speaking. As I climbed up onto the chicken crates, he shifted into gear and started up the mountains. The chickens squawked and the engine roared as the sun began to climb higher in the sky, the mountains and jungles whizzing past us in the bright, South American morning. I grinned a mad grin; I had left behind the frustrating world of stalled buses and delays, and was on my way to explore the lost city of Samaipata. Life was good!

When we arrived at Samaipata three hours later, I was quite ready to disembark. Every time the truck had driven around a corner, which happened frequently in the steep mountains, the chickens let out a squawking that somehow seemed to make the truck shake. The effect was nerve-wracking.

I thanked both the driver and the chickens for the ride as I got off. Looking for refreshment, I staggered into the Touristas Hotel restaurant, one of two hotel cafés in the small village of Samaipata, and set my pack down on a chair. Samaipata is a small town of only a few thousand, so there is little reason for tourists to stop. At one time, the Bolivian government had hoped to develop Samaipata as a tourist center, along the same lines as Tiahuanaco. They even built a museum here in this sleepy little town, to accommodate the thousands of tourists they hoped would visit. Yet, Samaipata remains remote and without visitors.

I ordered some eggs and toast and ate them ravenously, since I had not eaten anything else that day. Wanting to head up to the ruins, wherever they were, I asked the waitress if she could give me directions.

She ran off and came back with a man named Martin. About thirty, of medium height, he appeared to be a friendly, honest person, even if a bit lethargic. Genuinely helpful, he spoke only fair English, but told me that *El Fuerte* (The Fort) was located on top of a mountain to the east of town. We talked over tea at one of the bare, wooden tables, about Samaipata, El Fuerte, and life in his little town. When I asked if any buses to Cochabamba left from here, he said no, but I knew that eventually the buses from Santa Cruz would have to pass by.

Martin took me outside and directed me down the road to El Fuerte. A number of rather scruffy men were hanging around across the street, eyeing me suspiciously as I came out of the café. Martin threw them a quick glance and put his hand on my shoulder. "The place you seek is down the road and to your right. You must climb that mountain there," he said, pointing to a brush-covered slope in the southeast. "Never mind those men, they do not like strangers in our town. Here, take this, you have a long trip ahead of you."

He handed me a bundle of coca leaves and a bit of hard lime to use as a catalyst while chewing them. With that, I headed down the road and began to slowly chew the astringent leaves. It was a two-hour walk to the site, winding up an old jeep road that lagged slowly up the mountains. By the time I reached the top, the road had become clearly impassable, even with a small jeep. I figured that it had been built ten or fifteen years ago, to accommodate the hoards of tourists who never came. It looked like no one had been over it since, except perhaps a rogue archaeologist or two.

Rounding a corner, I faced a small shack and a metal fence. From out of the building came the caretaker, a young man holding a small baby girl on his hip. He was surprised and pleased to see me. Literally beaming with happiness, he wrote me a ticket to the site, which cost about thirty cents. According to my ticket, I was the 153rd person to visit the site since it was opened in 1974!

El Fuerte, or "The Place of Giants" as it is also known, is a huge area of red sandstone rock on top of a grass-covered hill. The north face is a sheer cliff with a drop of about 100 feet. I entered the area

327

from the north-west side, just to the west of the cliffs, climbing up the steep hill to gain the summit.

At first glance I was quite disappointed. I looked around, but could not really see anything. "This is it?" I asked myself. "Where's the fort, the city? I want my money back!"

But my opinion changed dramatically as I wandered the site. Gazing at what was left of the "fort," I was filled with awe and wonder. The place was incredibly mysterious!

On top of this remote jungle mountain was a large, fairly level area of sandstone. Cut into the rock all along the top of the mountain were unmistakable carvings—extremely weathered, yet deep and ancient. There were channels, pools, rooms, stairs, seats, petroglyphs, and many odd grooves, all of which seemed quite out of place.

Toward the east side, cut directly into the rock, was a large pool ringed with seats, much like a modern whirlpool bath. Some of the seats were triangular, others square. The pool was well worn, but was probably two or three feet deep at one time. Had it been used for ritual bathing?

Like other pools on the rock, it had a drain, about six inches in diameter. These drains led through carved channels to another even stranger square pool, one-and-a-half feet in depth, with two deep, parallel grooves running 75 feet to the west. Alongside these parallel grooves were two smaller channels etched in a criss-crossing diamond pattern, apparently for the flow of some liquid. These channels ran into two other pools, which drained off down the hill.

On the south side, the hill formed a crescent shape of solid rock. The ancient builders had carved seats into the slope, reminding me of bleachers at a stadium. In fact, the entire south side had an uncanny resemblance to an amphitheatre.

Square, room-like niches had been dug out of the rock, like special box seats. The odd thing about some of these seats was their triangular shape, which would have made them quite uncomfortable to sit on. Yet, what else could they be, especially when some had square backs, like regular chairs?

Stairs cut up through the "grandstand seats" of the amphitheatre to the top of the mountain. On the north side was a large, twelve-by fifty-foot room, hewn from the solid rock above the cliffs. Petroglyphs and geometrical markings were etched into the rock in many places, some of which looked like ancient graffiti! I smiled as I pictured an Egyptian youth, to commemorate his team's victory over the Incas in a pre-Columbian World Cup match, spending days to carve a slogan into the rock. What he would have given for a can of spray paint!

All around the rock were round holes, some at least a foot deep. Their purpose wasn't obvious, though they might have held poles used to support walls. Near one of the pools, I noticed a carved figure resembling a leopard lying on its side with a gutter around it. Were the builders part of a South American leopard cult?

Great confusion surrounds the ruins of Samaipata, very little scholarly work having been done there. One estimate dates the ruins at about 1430 AD. Yet parts of the ruins, especially to the west, had a good three feet of hard-packed earth covering them. Stone staircases, cut into the rock, ascend the hill toward this area, then disappear into the hard earth. What could have caused this burying, especially in only the last 500 years? I could only imagine some volcanic explosion showering several feet of ash onto the rock structures, covering them. Yet no volcano existed in the vicinity. I sensed that the site was incredibly ancient, thousands of years old. Most of the rock was so worn, that it obviously had taken thousands of years to be eroded so extensively.

The ubiquitous Erich Von Daniken mentions Samaipata in one of his books, theorizing, of course, that El Fuerte was a spaceport in antiquity, replete with rockets taking off from the bowl into the depths of space. The mysterious channels by the pools were somehow proof of that.

I found it easy enough to shrug off that explanation, but more difficult to figure out a legitimate answer for this place! At some ancient time, there must have been much more here than now remains, since what remains today is only what was literally carved in stone. Any stones that could have been moved are gone—to where, I don't know. Still, what is left is very impressive, and equally mysterious.

I could not shake the impression of a giant amphitheatre with seats, grandstand boxes and bathing pools at the summit. Many of the seats were likewise very large and wide, as if designed for a person seven- to ten-feet tall. Perhaps this is why Samaipata is also known as the Place of Giants. Also, very large human femurs have been discovered in the surrounding area. Just how large, I could not find out, but I was assured that they were from people "well above six feet tall."

It also occurred to me that a later culture might have taken over the site, transforming the mountain into a jaguar cult sacrificial area, creating some of the channels and pools for animal, or even human sacrifices to their jaguar god. There was, indeed, some indication of later building, including a rather poorly constructed wall of small stones. Probably only a few hundred years old, it did not seem to be part of the overall city. It may have even post-dated the jaguar cult.

From the remains, it seemed that quite a large population could have inhabited the area. Had they built their city, El Fuerte, on top of this mountain for defense purposes? But defense from whom—wild Indians from the lower jungles? It would get a little too cool up here for naked Indians from the lowlands.

I scanned the horizon for likely sights of other cities. I did not think that this could be a solitary outpost of some isolated civilization. There must be more sites around here where these people lived. And if they built on top of mountains to defend themselves, any other cities they built would likely be on top of mountains.

Across the valley about ten miles away loomed a heavily-forested peak with an odd, natural bowl shape at its summit. Like El Fuerte, it was a high, easily defended "amphitheatre" with steep sides. If there was another city around here, I thought to myself, it would be in that bowl on top of that mountain.

As I stood there, gazing out at the surrounding mountains, the lonely young caretaker approached. Eager to to take care of me, his only visitor for months, he escorted me to a spot down in the natural bowl on the south side of the mountain. We walked down the rock stairs and into an area of brush at the bottom. There he showed me the *Camino de la Chinchana.*

This turned out to be a two-meter wide opening in the ground, widening into a cavern which headed down and to the north. Squatting at the entrance, I peered in amazement into the cavern. It was dark and mysterious, but neither of us had a flashlight. The caretaker told me that the collapsed tunnel had been excavated by Bolivian archaeologists for 100 feet down into the mountain.

"Where does it go?" I asked him in Spanish.

He escorted me back up to the top of the peak and pointed to the north, toward the mountain I had picked out earlier. "There," he said, his voice shaking. "There, to *La Muela el Diablo*, is where the archaeologists say it goes. On that mountain is another city, just as here!" he exclaimed. La Muela el Diablo, as I translated with help from my Spanish dictionary, meant "The Devil's Dimple."

I was shocked. Just where I had theorized another city could be located, there was one. But I had not expected a tunnel to lead there from El Fuerte! The possibility that a tunnel ran from the top of this mountain to the top of another mountain at least ten miles away, through a steep valley with a roaring river between, was quite incredible.

I knew all the strange tales of the tunnels around Cuzco and the Andes. But here, I was witnessing a lesser-known, more mysterious version. This was perhaps proof that the tunnel system pre-dated the Incas, built by an unknown civilization many thousands of years ago. Did the tunnel connecting "The Fort" with "The Devil's Dimple" also connect to the larger tunnel system?

As I walked down the mountain, I resolved to visit Le Muela El Diablo the next day. It appeared no one had been there for quite some time. In fact, no one even seemed to be aware that there was a city on that mountain any more. Le Muela el Diablo was truly a lost city!

When I got back down to the main road leading into the village, I caught a ride for a mile on the back of a truck. The driver dropped me off at a house next to the small museum. The museum opened in 1974, but fewer than a hundred people had ever visited it by the time I got there.

Nearby was *Cerro de las Rueditas*, an ancient circle of megalithic stones. Were they possibly the foundations of a tower? Iron and stone tools have been found in the area, but at San Juan de Josario, 15 miles from Samaipata, more Roman amphorae were discovered! Called *Cerro de los Contaros*, they are exactly like Roman or Carthaginian amphorae, used to hold wine. What were they doing in the mountains of Bolivia? Colonel Fawcett's lost city was supposedly located somewhere in the western Matto Grosso, not far from Samaipata. Could the Romans, Greeks, or other Mediterranean explorers have ventured this far inland from the Amazon?

Pottery with a particular diamond-style motif, similar to a design carved into one of the channels at Samaipata, has been unearthed north of La Paz at a site attributed to the *Mollo* Culture. These people lived in the area known as Iskanwaya, apparently around the fifteenth-century, constructing rock pueblos on the hillsides. One unique feature of their culture was their practice of manufacturing drinking cups with built-in straws. Could the Mollo people have discovered an abandoned Samaipata, using the ancient site for their rituals? Perhaps they cut the grooves and diamond markings in the rocks—the Mollo were known to worship the jaguar.

One of the first people to explore Samaipata was a Bohemian naturalist, Tadeo Haenke, in 1795. On October 24, 1832, a French naturalist, Alcides Dessalines D'Orbigny, visited the site. Erland Nordenskiold, a Swedish ethnographer, visited Samaipata in 1908, and Austrian archaeologist Leo Krull came in 1937. This is nearly the entire list of outside investigators of one of the strangest archaeological sites in South America. To this day, most of the "experts" have never even heard of the place!

§§§

I returned to the Turistas Hotel just after dark, where I wanted to ask Martin to help me make arrangements to go to the "Devil's Dimple" the next day, but he was no where to be found. I sat down and ordered a meal of ribs, rice, salad, fried banana, and a Ducal beer. But as I began to eat, Martin came running in, obviously excited.

"Gringo," he cried, out of breath. "Where have you been? I looked all over for you," he huffed in Spanish.

"Martin, I want to go to Le Muela el Diablo tomorrow," I informed him, taking a bite from the fried banana, and washing it down with a beer.

"Le Muela el Diablo!" he shouted, and then his voice got suddenly serious. "Are you loco? Look," he said seriously, now speaking his best English, "you must leave tonight! There is much cocaine business here. They do not like strangers in town. They say you are a 'Federale.' Gringo, your life is in great danger! If you stay here one more day…" His voice trailed off menacingly as he made a cutting motion across his throat.

The South American cocaine business is no joke. These people will kill you in seconds, with or without the slightest reason. I swallowed hard on the last of my fried banana, then asked, "All right, what should I do?"

"I have found a truck for you to leave Samaipata on tonight. The driver is eating dinner next door. He leaves to Cochabamba within the hour. You must go on that truck!"

I was convinced. Finishing my beer, I grabbed my pack and followed Martin next door, to a large truck with a huge payload of cotton and two cars tied to the top. Martin introduced me to the driver, a jolly-looking fellow of medium height with a baseball cap and a ready smile. He would take me to Cochabamba on his truck, but I would have to ride in back, on top of the load.

This was all right with me, except that it was starting to rain. However, a large tarp was tied over the whole truck. Grabbing hold of the large steel cage on the back, I hoisted myself aboard. Martin held up my pack and reaching down, I hauled it aboard.

As the truck driver got into the cab where his greasy, seventeen year-old mechanic was already waiting, Martin said to me, "Take care, gringo, this time you are lucky. The mountains of Samaipata have many dangers!"

332

"Thanks, Martin!" I called back as it began to pour. Out in the night, some frustrated cocaine manufacturers longed to "do in" this crazy rogue archaeologist, but I would not give them the satisfaction. As I pulled myself under the chassis of a brand new Dihatsu jeep—the only dry, comfortable place I could find—a chill of excitement ran up my spine. I had escaped Samaipata, yet I would return some day to find out the secret of Le Muela el Diablo. Just driving the mountain roads through Bolivia is dangerous enough for most people, but even more so when people want to hasten your transition through this lifetime. As the rain poured down outside, pounding hard on the protective tarp, I realized how lucky I was to be alive.

I spent that night with the jeep bouncing continuously a few inches above my head, tryinf to sleep on the cotton bales. The rain poured down all night, so I slept intermittently, dreaming of a strange variety of people: ancient architects and tunnel builders, and modern bandits and cocaine dealers.

When I awoke late the next morning, the rain had stopped, but the jeep was still bouncing back and forth, a few inches from my face. As I lay on my back, staring at the threatening axle, I decided that I did not like riding beneath cars on the back of trucks in the mountains of Bolivia.

The truck stopped about mid-morning, and I climbed down from my perch beneath the jeep. We had breakfast in a small roadside cantina, then headed on to Cochabamba. This time I rode up front with the driver, whose name was Miguel. He was from Santa Cruz, he said, and loved baseball and most things American. His mechanic rode in back, sleeping on the cotton.

We barrelled through the green, cloudy mountains of eastern Bolivia for the rest of the day, pulling into Cochabamba late that afternoon. He let me off right downtown, where I checked into the Alojamiento Cocacabana in the heart of downtown. Cochabamba is a medium-sized Bolivian town with a warm climate, located just off the cool Altiplano. There are a number of inexpensive hotels around the central plaza, including the Hotel Aroma, and the Residencials Pullman, Escobar, Bolivia, Oriental, and La Paz.

Cochabamba is a friendly place to spend some time. There are some ruins nearby, which I did not visit. Known as Sipi-Sipi, they are several hours from the city. Ask at the Tourist Office on the main plaza.

I discovered the next day that none of the trucks or buses from Santa Cruz had yet made it to Cochabamba. This meant that Paddy was still stuck at the mud slide, and might remain there for days. Hopefully, the

333

Indian women would not run out of stew! When I left early the next morning, they still had not arrived.

Waiting to depart that morning by ferrocar, a type of mini-train, I sat in a teashop across the street from the station. I noticed an Indian, obviously just down from the hills. He seemed fairly young, only in his late twenties, but his face was brown and wrinkled, his teeth filled with gold. He wore beautifully embroidered pants and a handwoven, multi-colored wool shirt emblazoned with flowers and stars. A colorful wool hat hung over his ears with an old, dirty cowboy hat piled on top of that. He held a bag of coca leaves in his hand, and on his feet were sandals made from an old rubber tire.

As I sipped my tea, he stopped to look at me, as strange a sight as himself. There was I, a scruffy, blond-haired American, carrying a large, well-worn pack, and wearing a wild look on my face. I gave him a nod and he smiled. We were two of a kind, it seemed. I wondered if he knew the secrets of the Andes: of the tunnels, the treasures, the lost cities, the ancient mysteries. He had gotten all that gold in his teeth somewhere.

Later, as I stood on the train platform, a shuttle car came down the tracks to load passengers for a short trip to a nearby town. I stared in wonder and amazement—this shuttle car was fantastic! It was a green Nash from the 1940's, the tires removed and the car placed on train wheels! The front was a set of four small wheels and springs from a train, and the back had two larger wheels. It was a taxi that ran on the tracks, taking passengers 35 miles down the line. Once he had a few passengers, the driver jumped in, started his car, and flew off down the tracks. I wanted to hitch a ride, just for the experience, but I already had a ticket to La Paz.

The train was late, so I continued to wander the station, which was full of interesting characters. The Cochabamba train station had its madman, a young fellow of questionable sanity and cleanliness, who helped park cars by directing what little traffic ran in front of the station. I watched him as he worked, wearing a silly grin on his face, until one of the women serving tea suddenly drenched him with a bucket of water. This put an end to his traffic directing, at least momentarily.

With the blast of a whistle, my ferrocar was finally ready to depart. Rather than a complete train, the ferrocar was actually three small green cars run by an electric engine. The cars were only half full, and I had the luxury of two seats to myself, dozing for a great deal of the journey.

Later that night on the Altiplano, while we waited outside Oruro for an engine to take us into La Paz, I looked up at the stars and the Southern Cross. A three-quarter moon was rising, and the snow-covered Andes on the horizon were silhouetted against the starry sky. The weather was cold and brisk.

Standing outside on the tracks, I wondered, would I ever untangle the bizarre history of this continent of mystery? Staring up at the Southern Cross, I knew I probably never would. I also knew that it didn't matter. Love and life were what mattered, and I was determined to experience them both to the fullest. It was the least I could do!

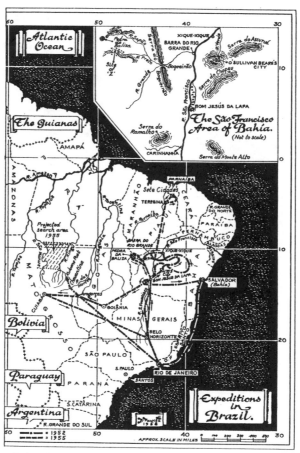

Colonel Fawcett's son Brian's 1955 map of his journeys
in search of his father.

Chapter Sixteen

Northern Peru Into Ecuador:
Pyramids and Gold Treasure

...of the gladest moments in human life,
methinks is the departure upon
a distant journey to unknown lands.
Shaking off with one mighty effort the fetters of Habit,
the leaden weight of Routine, the cloak of many Cares,
and the slavery of Home, man feels once more happy.
The blood flows with the fast circulation of childhood...
afresh dawns the morn of life...
-Sir Richard Burton
Journal entry December 2, 1856

The train finally arrived in La Paz at 3:30 AM, which seemed too late to go out looking for a hotel. Like most of the other people on the train, I slept in my seat until dawn. Then, as the first rays of the sun broke over the cold streets of the city, I headed out into the chilly Andean morning, pulling my hat tightly on over my head, and turning my collar up against the wind.

I checked into the Hotel Andes again, near the station, and spent the day walking about town. I was running out of money, and needed to get to Lima fast. I booked myself a ticket on a bus to Puno the next morning. I enjoyed the afternoon in the cafés and restaurants of La Paz and went to the Archaeological Museum again, in the hope of seeing the giant femurs found at Samaipata, but I was told that they were not on display. This seemed a strange; were they uninteresting, terribly delicate, or actually shocking?

I went to bed early that night, sleeping better knowing that neither the Bolivian police or cocaine smugglers were after me this time. I was up early, and caught the mini-bus to Puno. It drove up to the narrow Tiquina Straits, where we crossed by ferry and went by bus to Copacabana. Then we were off to Puno, arriving in the late afternoon, with just enough time to book a ticket on the evening train to Arequippa.

I had met a young man from Vancouver, Canada on the bus named Marvin, whose family were Mennonites. He had originally come from Poland to Paraguay as a child. His family then moved to Canada, where he now worked as a fire fighter. He was also on his way to Lima, and we teamed up, paying a ten-year-old to stand in line for us and purchase a ticket when the office opened at seven o'clock.

By ten o'clock, Marvin and I were rolling out of Puno in second-class, watching the moon's reflection in the water and reeds of Lake Titicaca. I fell asleep very quickly to the rumbling of the wheels, and when I awoke the next morning, we had arrived in Arequippa. We were on a roll, immediately catching a Mercedes coach down to the coast and north up the Pan-American Highway toward Lima.

Life spun by me in a whirl of desert sand and barren hills. I had seen all this before when I had first arrived in South America; it seemed like years ago, or was it only yesterday? Time seemed to have stopped, sped up and slowed down, throughout my journey. In a daze, I stared out the window, lost in thoughts of lost cities, tunnels, airships, Atlantis, Egyptian gold mines, and fantastic treasure. Was it all just fantasy? Some cruel hoax being pulled on the gullible masses, bored with their jobs in New York, London, Sydney, and San Francisco?

Yet, I knew deep inside that there was something behind the mysteries of South America—I had read, heard, and now seen too much not to believe that. Yet, how could I prove it to myself?

When we arrived in Lima the next morning, back where I had first arrived in South America, I had very little money left, less than one-hundred dollars. I wouldn't be seeing many lost cities with that budget, but I might still be able to get north to Ecuador, before I had to leave the continent.

Without even spending the night in Lima, I was off on another bus, north to Huaraz and the fantastic ruins of Chavin de Huantar. As my bus pulled out of the station in Lima, on yet another journey into the future and the past, I reviewed what I had heard about some interesting rock carvings, found in the mountains north-east of Lima.

The Marcahuasi Plateau is located near Marcapomacocha, a town in Junin province. It is difficult to visit this region today because of the

Sandero Luminoso (Shining Path) Revolutionaries who control this region of the mountains. In 1952, a Peruvian explorer, Daniel Ruzo, set out by mule-train to explore this remote, barren plateau, at an altitude of 12,500 feet, with an area of ove one square mile. Here, according the book, *The Morning of the Magicians*, Ruzo found "...rock carvings of animals and human faces which, owing to the play of light and shadow were visible at the summer solstice and at no other time. There were carved figures of prehistoric animals, such as the stegosaurus, and also lions, tortoises and also camels, which are unknown in South America. A hillside was carved to represent an old man's head; when it was photographed, however, the negative showed the image of a radiant youth."[59]

Dating of these ancient carved cliffs is nearly impossible, without some of organic remains. Ruzo believes them to be the remains of "the Masma culture, perhaps the oldest in the world."[59] Only a few years later, in 1957, writer George Hunt Williamson, mounted an expedition to the Marcahuasi Plateau. In his 1959 book, *Road in the Sky*, Williamson wote about leaving from the nearby town of San Pedro de Casta and journeying to the top of the plateau. He confirmed much of Ruzo's report, describing the well-worn carvings, some hardly recognizable, of animals, people, and what Williamson thought were even Egyptian gods, such as the Hippo god Thoueris.[60] Unfortunately, this book is one of the original "Gods from Outer Space" texts, making it difficult to separate the fact from the abundant fiction.

Williamson did however confirm that there was a carving resembling a stegasaurus on the plateau. Let us for a moment assume that the carving does depict a stegasaurus, and that it is genuine. The possibility that the carving was made at the time the dinosaurs died out, millions of years ago, seems remote. But, according to a radical new theory, the stegasaurus may have lived up until ten-thousand years ago, if not even more recently. Perhaps, according to this theory, the ancient reptiles which died more recently than millions of years ago did not leave any fossilized records. Why should they have? Fossils happen rarely, giving at best a spotty record of the past.

Everything that dies does not make a fossil. Literally millions of bison were slaughtered during the last century, their carcases left on the great plains of the United States, yet not one of them is likely to have become a fossil. If a stegasaurus staggered across the Marcahuasi Plateau ten-thousand years ago and died, we would never know it. Except perhaps if someone carved him in stone...

I reached Huaraz by nightfall, and checked into a hotel by the bus station, the San Isidro. The next morning I was off by bus to Chavin de

Huantar, a series of underground structures seven levels deep, dating back at least 2,500 years. These ruins might be compared to the underground cities at Derenkuyu in central Turkey. I was truly astounded as I descended underground into the ruins. Odd carvings decorated the walls, strange motifs which accompany the descent into catacombs that stretch hundreds of feet underground. Someone built here a giant city that extended well into the bowels of the earth. Did it connect with other tunnels in the Andes? Why did people build their cities underground anyway? Were they escaping some terrible war on the surface?

The ruins of Chavin are truly spectacular and bizarre. It's hard to imagine why humans would create such a strange abode. Today, after a major earthquake in 1970, only two of the seven levels can be visited, but it is still fantastic. Chavin is a good place to visit if you want to get an idea of what sort of culture existed in Peru prior to the Incas, sometime in the first millenium before Christ.

But my financial situation kept me from dallying. Once again, after three fast days exploring Huaraz and Chavin, I was on a bus for the coastal city Trujillo, founded by Francisco Pizarro.

Arriving in the late afternoon, I immediately called the Peruvian woman I had met on the train in Bolivia; a charming young lady of Japanese-Spanish descent named Charo. She managed the Huanchaco Hostel, a small place in the beach and surfing resort Huanchaco, a few miles from Trujillo.

Charo told me to take a taxi straight over to her place, which I did. She ran the small, yet comfortable hotel for her father, a Japanese immigrant to Peru, and her mother, a Spanish Peruvian. Charo was almost as thrilled to see me, as I was to see her again. After settling my things in a room in the family hacienda, she took me down to the beach, where we spent the rest of the afternoon, watching a volleyball game on the beach, gazing at the girls in bikinis (I did more of this than she did), checking out the few surfers, and mellowing out with the sunset. The entire experience reminded me of California, yet we were in Peru, part of the ancient Inca empire.

Trujillo was the center for the ancient culture of the Chimu, with their capital just to the south of Trujillo at Chan Chan. The valley of the Moche River has been home to civilization for thousands of years, with a number of successive civilizations coming and going. Between 900 and 1475 AD, one of the single largest and most successful of all pre-Columbian empires arose here—the Chimus.

The Chimus even constructed a great wall, much like the one in China, which ran some 60 miles inward from the coast, averaging some

340

ten-feet high, reaching twenty- to thirty-feet in spots. It was theoretically used to keep people like the Incas and other invaders out, although the Chimus were eventually conquered by the Incas in 1475, Chan Chan absorbed into the Inca Empire.

The Incas had their Great Wall too, which was in Bolivia, to keep out invaders from the south (who, one wonders? The giants of Patagonia?) The Inca wall was about 150-miles long, stretching along the altiplano at altitudes of 8,000 to 13,000 feet. It runs along ridges and is studded with stone forts at strategic intervals. Only a few sections of this wall still exist, and it does not appear to have been very high, about the height of the Chimu great wall. It is also conceivable that the Inca Great Wall was not built by the Incas at all, but by some earlier culture.

South American explorer Gene Savoy led several expeditions into the northern area of Peru, eventually showing that the Chimu Wall was part of a vast defensive system, running hundreds of miles along the coast to the south, and linked by hitherto unreported highways in the Andes. In fact, Savoy discovered that there was not one wall, but seven! Each started near the sea, crossed the coastal desert, and extended into the mountains.

Savoy learned that the system is served by a previously unknown "super-highway," that was an astonishing 100-feet wide. Compare this to the well-documented system of Inca roads, which were usually only about twenty-four-feet wide. This road was laid down for more than 125-miles through the deserts and over the mountain spurs between the coast and the crest of the Andes coastal range. The whole road system, in Savoy's opinion, was designed and built even better than that of the Incas. These roads were expertly laid out, run straight, and intersect each other at true right angles.

What is incredible, is that they are so wide, it is hard to imagine their original purpose. If they were designed for marching armies, those armies must have been staggering in size! This system of road works compares in physical size to that to the modern interstate highways in the United States, yet it was aparently built thousands of years ago. Once again, South America's mysterious past tosses up a tantalizing hint of great civilizations, vast armies, horrific wars, and the sudden collapse of an empire.

Are lost cities still hidden in the jungles, left over from this vanished empire which predates the Chimu? Once again, we have to return to the work of intrepid explorer Gene Savoy, who once said, "To be in my business, you either have to be crazy or rich. I'm both!"

In 1964 Savoy was credited with being the first explorer to reach the imposing ruins of Gran Pajaten.[39] An aerial survey showed that there were many ruins at Gran Pajaten, at least 3,000 structures scattered over seven hills, linked by a roadway which disappears into the forest. Where did this road lead? What other vast complexes are to be found in the jungles of the eastern slope of the Andes? All one would need to do, it seemed, was follow this ancient "Yellow-brick-road" to whatever lost cities it might lead to. This, naturally, is pretty much what Gene Savoy did.

Meanwhile, in early 1985, researchers at the University of Colorado announced that they had discovered a lost city in Northern Peru. The name? Gran Pajaten! How many times can you discover a city, especially one discussed in tourist guides? Actually, the archaeologists at the University of Colorado had made the discovery claim in order to justify an expedition to the trustees of the university. It sounded good at first, until journalists and other archaeologists caught on, and the real truth came out. In the end, the resulting archaeological scandal turned out to be great publicity for Savoy, who suddenly found that his early discoveries which had attracted only mild interest at the time, were now big news—twenty years later. Discovering lost cities in Peru in the mid-sixties was not fashionable. In the mid-eighties, it was suddenly the rage.

Another well known site in this same area are the ruins of Kuelap, probably built by the Chacapoyas. The construction of the walls of Kuelap is alarmingly similar to that of the Zimbabwe ruins in southern Africa, down to the same motif on the walls. Charles Berlitz claims that the construction is also similar to that of a giant, prehistoric stone fort in the Aran Islands off the west coast of Ireland. The capital of this area is Chachapoyas, and it is from here that expeditions usually embark for lost cities in the area. Other known ruins in the area include a city named Congona, and it has been suggested that hundreds of lost cities lie in the thousands of square miles of unexplored mountain-jungle of Amazonas and San Martin states.

In July of 1985, Savoy announced through his Andean Explorers Club of Reno, Nevada, that in May he and a group of twenty-five other explorers had discovered the largest complex of ancient buildings ever found in the Americas. The metropolis covered an astounding 120 square miles in the jungle-cloaked mountains of north-eastern Peru. Savoy describes the ruins as the most extensive of any ancient civilization found so far in the Americas. He named the ruins Gran Vilaya.

"The magnitude of the Gran Vilaya ruins, consisting of over 80 interconnected city-type layouts composed of some 23,950 structures to

342

date, makes this metropolis undoubtedly the largest ancient city in all the Americas," he said in an interview with the Associated Press printed in newspapers around the country on July 7, 1985.

Savoy said the city is located on mountainous plateaus 8,000 to 9,000 feet high, in an area "populated only by wild bears, monkeys, and puma." He theorized that the vast complex was the bastion of defense for the Chachapoyas, an empire dating back to 800 AD that was conquered by the Incas in 1480 AD.

Gran Vilaya is located in the remote regions of the upper east bank of the Maranon River in the state of Amazonas. It is about 400 miles to the north of Lima, and largely inaccessable. The city is built in the form of a citadel and looks down on the Maranon River gorge 6,000 feet below.

Most of the buildings were of a circular shape and were strung along a ridge for about 25 miles. The expedition calculated that there were 10,350 stone structures in the defensive network along the ridge, and another 13,600 stone buildings in the three major city layouts. The stone structures, some measuring 140 feet in length, were built atop terraces that go up the mountain slopes like stairs, Savoy said. He described them as "complex units of circular buildings with doorways, windows, and nitched walls...that soar up as high as a 15-story building."

Most mysterious about the city is its builders, the Chachapoyas. Savoy said that early Spanish reports, taken from the Incas, indicated that the Chachapoyas people were tall, fair-skinned and blue-eyed. These people were said by the Incas to be fierce warriors who used the Amazon River as their main highway. The Incas finally conquered the Chachapoyas by invading from the south just prior to the Spanish conquest of Peru. The people then vanished, and very little else is known about them today. The region, once the site of a huge city, is now uninhabited.

Savoy went on to say that there were stone highways leading in many directions from the city into the surrounding jungle. It was his intention to follow the roads to further cities...

§§§

Charo and I played volleyball on the beach, watched the sunset, then had dinner at her hotel with her parents. That night there was a party on the beach, but I was quite tired, and it got late fast. I left early

343

and slept well in their guest room.

Charo got me up early the next morning to explore pyramids found east of Trujillo. With her sister Nana and an Argentine law student named Bernard who was staying in the hotel, we drove out in Charo's Toyota Landcruiser to inspect the Pyramid of the Sun and the Pyramid of the Moon. They were both huge pyramids, constructed entirely out of adobe bricks, just like Chan Chan. Villagers had diverted a nearby river a hundred years ago, to wash away portions of one pyramid, hoping to uncover treasure buried inside. They found nothing, but destroyed half of the valuable, magnificent structure.

We hiked up to the top of the Pyramid of the Sun, where we got a great view of the surrounding countryside, a desert beautiful in its stark emptyness. One can gaze across the plain toward the Pyramid of the Moon and watch dust and sand swirling among the ruins. It was a bleak scene. "These were once great monuments, now turned to dust," I reflected to Charo. She nodded, looking out silently over the desert.

"You know, I've lived here all my life," she said suddenly, "but this is the first time I've ever come out here. The pyramids are beautiful!" Below us, the sands of time slowly eroded the ancient monuments. How much longer would they remain?

We dropped by the local museum, where I wanted to check out a stylized bird motif common on area pottery. I had seen that bird somewhere else, but couldn't quite think of where...suddenly I had it! Southern Africa, at the Zimbabwe Ruins. The motif was called the Zimbabwe Bird, and has even become the symbol of the country, largely because it was one of the few artifacts remaining at the ruins. And here was the same bird in Peru.

Charo drove us back to her hotel, and then took me to the bus station, where I would catch the bus to the Ecuadorian border. My money was running out fast, so I would have to get to Quito quickly.

Once again I was on one of the endless series of buses which had transported me across this continent, this time zooming north along the Pan-American Highway. Outside, the coastal desert of dust and barren hills faded in the distance like an endless brown carpet. In the morning I would be in Macara, an Ecuadorian border town where I could get a bus to Cuenca and Quito.

Ecuador is a small country, about the size of Nevada, yet has a population of nine million. Two high, parallel ranges of the Andes traverse the country from north to south, topped with volcanic peaks, the highest being Chimborazo at 20,577 feet. Quito, the capital of Ecuador, sits high in these mountains as the second highest captial city in the world, after La Paz.

Quito was once the capital of a collection of highland tribes who got together, according to historians, around 1000 AD. This civilization was called, cleverly, the Kingdom of Quito. Just prior to the Spanish conquest, the Incas subdued Quito and the surrounding highlands. Pizzaro landed in Ecuador in 1532 and turned it into a thriving Spanish colony built on exploitation of the Indians.

Ecuador became independant of Spain in 1809 under Simon Bolivar and joined the confederacy known as Greater Colombia. The confederacy collapsed in 1830, and modern Ecuador was born. Since then, its history has been one of revolt and dictatorships (not unusual in South America); but what of lost cities?

Ecuador is the location of lost cities and mysteries, but is most famous for its lost treasure, one of which is associated with the Volcano Sangay in eastern Ecuador near Riobamba. Since the Incas did not use writing, they kept their records on a knotted rope, called a *quipu*. By some accounts, when Atahualpa was being held captive by Pizarro, he forsaw his fate, and made a special golden quipu with instructions in it.

Atahualpa's quipu supposedly instructed his followers to stash much of the treasure in a secret place at the base of El Sangay, an active volcano towering out of the jungles at 17,000 feet. Gold statues, jewelry, and religious articles were all then supposedly placed in a chasm somewhere on the lower slopes of the volcano. Treasure hunters have searched the dangerous slopes for centuries, though no one has ever claimed to have discovered the treasure.

Jane Dolinger relates the story of one of the searchers for the treasure of Sangay in her book, *Inca Gold*. It is the story of Dr. Kurt Von Ritter, a Swiss-born archaeologist who lived in Quito back in the 1960's. He discovered an ancient trail that led from Cuzco in a north-easterly direction over snow-capped peaks and through great expanses of the Ecuadorian rain forest to the base of Sangay, and believed that this trail was used to transport some of the Inca treasure into hiding.[58]

Von Ritter followed this secret trail, he told Dolinger, from Cuzco along the highlands of Peru, through jungles where headhunting Jivaro Indians dwell, to the volcano Sangay. Along the way, he passed thirteen snow capped peaks, which was the same number of knots that Atahualpa had put on his quipu. Was there a connection? Von Ritter thought so, and spent weeks around the volcano searching for clues to the treasure. On the verge of giving up, he stayed in a small Indian village where a woman tended to the many cuts and bruises he had acquired on his search.

The woman's name was Ahana, and she was young, impressionable, and beautiful. Falling in love with Von Ritter, she told him that when the volcano slept, she would explore its slopes, and had once found a gold statue. One day she led him up the silent volcano, over narrow trails on the steep sides, past lava flows, cliffs and chasms. They spent the night in a cave high on the mountain, then reached the place where Ahana said she had found the statue.

Here Von Ritter discovered a skull that had been trepanned in the Inca fasion; the skull cut open and a piece of gold inserted into the hole. But as he started to search further, the volcano erupted! Turning, he found Ahana gone, having fled the impending danger.

Von Ritter looked up at the jagged cone still surrounded by a pall of gaseous smoke, standing transfixed while gigantic streaks of fire flared thousands of feet into the air. Horrified, he watched as the rivers of red molten lava came plunging down the mountainside toward him. He dashed wildly down the trail, the trepanned skull in his arms, impelled by fear to escape the approaching lava. For hours he ran down the mountain until he reached the relative safety of the jungle. Later he found a trail which took him back to civilization.

As an interesting epilogue, Dolinger says that Dr. Von Ritter disappeared from his home in Quito a few months after he told her his story, presumably on another expedition to Sangay. She reports that later, friends spotted him in Vienna, driving a new Rolls Royce and living at the best hotels. Dolinger suggests that he returned to Sangay, uncovered a small amount of the treasure and managed to smuggle it out of Ecuador. But as the author points out, "...those who are successful in finding buried treasures are the last to talk about it."[58]

I could use a little of that gold myself, I thought. I had about twenty dollars to my name. When the bus crossed the border into Ecuador, immigration had wanted to make sure that no destitute travelers, rogue archaeologist or otherwise, were trying to slip into their country.

"How much money do you have, gringo?" asked the officer. He was a tall man, of Spanish descent, with a thick mustache and a swarthy complextion.

"Uh...several hundred dollars," I answered politely, trying to look him straight in the face.

"Show me, *por favor*," he replied.

"Umm, I'll see if I can find it..." I answered, fishing around absently in my pack trying to stall him. There were other people behind me, so maybe he would get impatient.

Just then, another immigration officer called. "Hey, Francisco!" he shouted in Spanish, "Come here! I want you to see this!"

The officer glanced at me quickly and said, "Okay, go ahead." I sighed and swung my pack onto my back. I had made it into Ecuador, but would I make it out? Clutching my precious bus ticket to Quito, I boarded the bus and took my seat. My finances would not allow me to explore very many lost cities in Ecuador. It appeared I would have to head straight to the Quito airport to escape from South America without resorting to panhandling, or selling lottery tickets like my Peronista friend in Argintina.

One mystery in Ecuador that I was quite unhappy to miss was that of the tunnels rumoured to be found in the area of Gualaquiza on the Santiago river in southeastern Ecuador. In June 1965, Juan Moricz, an Argentine citizen born in Hungary, discovered the entrance to a tunnel system which may well link up with the mysterious tunnels in Peru and Bolivia. Moricz had an audience with the President of Ecuador in 1969 in which he was granted a concession to the tunnels and artifacts found within, under government supervision.

Moricz claimed to have found stone and metal objects "of various sizes and colors" and "metal plaques engraved with signs and writing." It seems that these tunnels genuinely exist; in fact, a British expedition explored the caves for several weeks a few years ago. A bit of a scandal was created when Erich Von Daniken wrote about them in his 1973 book, *Gold of the Gods*. Von Daniken claimed that Moricz took him to the tunnels, and showed him a fabulous gold treasure, secreted deep within. Moricz later denied having showed Von Daniken the treasure, though he did admit showing the Swiss author the tunnel system.

This entrance is located within a triangle formed by the towns Gualquiza, Yaupi, and General Plaza in the province of Morona-Santiago. The entrance is no longer a secret, but it is located in a rather remote area. Curiously, independent observers report the tunnels to be man-made, the passages set at right angles and leading deep underground. The walls are smooth and often seem to be polished. The ceilings are flat, at times looking as if they were covered with a kind of glaze. The description of these tunnels matches well with the descriptions of other tunnels in Peru.

Once again, we are faced with evidence of a vast tunnel network through the Andes. Von Daniken naturally would have us believe that these tunnels were built by extraterrestrials, possibly escaping from some interplanetary war. Tatunca Nara spoke of the tunnels in connection with Akakor. Other authors write of the tunnels and the lost treasure of the Incas. How were they built? Do they all connect? By this point in my South American journey, I had encountered nearly as many tunnel stories as buses!

§§§

It took a good day to get to Quito from the border, the bus winding through the green, rugged Andes, stopping in small towns along the way. I felt as if I had spent my whole life on a bus by the time it arrived Quito. In the early morning when I alighted at the central bus terminal in Quito, I had breakfast at a café then walked about the city for a bit. Low adobe houses with red-tiled roofs crowded the steep narrow streets. Indian street merchants in colorful costume walked the streets, selling their products in the small markets. This was a city I would have liked to have spent more time in, not to mention more money.

I checked at the Aero Peru office downtown for the next Miami flight. I couldn't even afford a hotel to spend the night.

By luck, there was a flight for Miami later that afternoon, with one seat left. I took it. My escape from South America was nearly complete, and I was leaving by the skin of my teeth. As I boarded the plane that would take me back to Miami, I opened my wallet to see how much money I had left. Five dollars. It would have been a waste to take home a lot more, rahter than using it to explore more of this fascinating continent. But this had been a great trip, one I would remember for many years to come.

What had I learned? What startling revelations had deepened my understanding of history, mankind, and myself? I thought about some of these things as the plane taxied down the runway and prepared itself for take off. At least this last seat wasn't on a damn bus!

Leaning back, I stared out the window at the Andes Mountains in the distance. How high they reached toward the heavens! How strong and unyielding they seemed! I had come to crack the mysteries of South America, to solve its riddles and put some misconceptions to rest. I now left knowing a great deal more than when I arrived. Perhaps I had unraveled a few mysteries, but beneath those solutions were yet more mysteries and riddles. Would anyone ever know the full story?

With a sudden roar of its engines, the Aero Peru jet flung itself forward down the tarmac. Within a few moments we would be airborne. I knew at that moment that I would be back. There was something about this continent of mystery which had attracted far too many explorers for me not to want to put in more time as well. I realized that I would never know everything, but I was strangely content with that realization. I was more mature now; South America had helped me grow up. This continent of lost cities and ancient mysterieswas going to give me a second chance, and I was grateful.

I have always loved a good mystery. If we solved them all, what would we do with our lives?

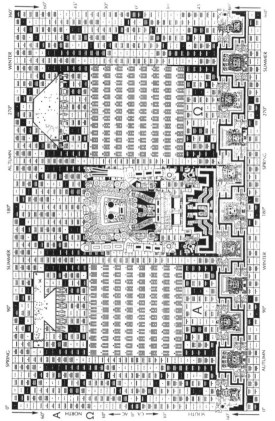

The figures from the Gate of the Sun at Tiahuanaco overlaid on the ancient Chinese I Ching by José Arguelles in his book, *Earth Ascending*.

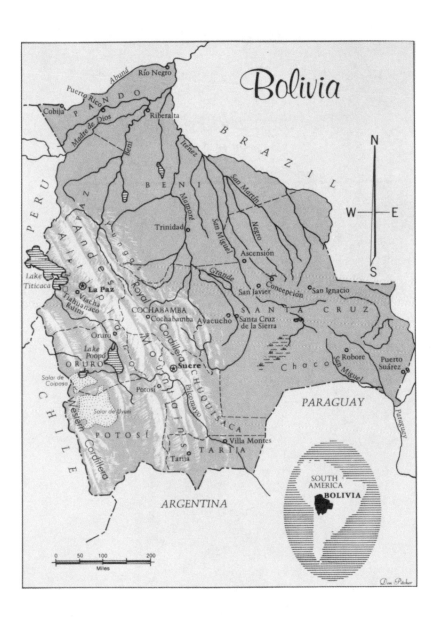

The alpaca, like the vicuna and the llama, belongs to the camel family.

Strange channels carved into the stone at the lost city of Samaipata.

El Fuerte, "The Fort," at Samaipata. What lost culture built this ancient complex, of which only foundations remain?

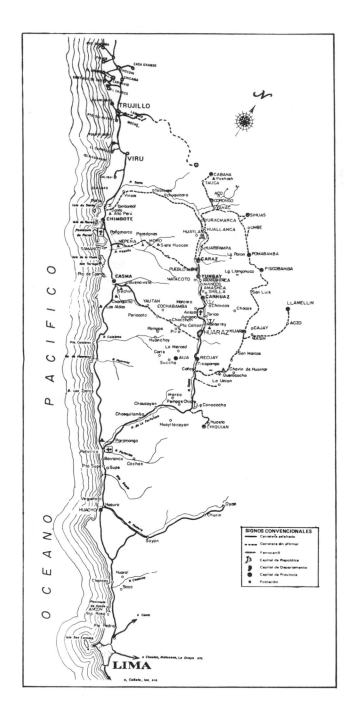

The Northern coast of Peru.

One of the huge rock carvings on the Marcahuasi Plateau.

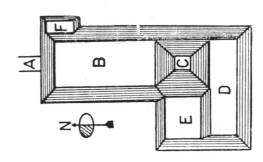

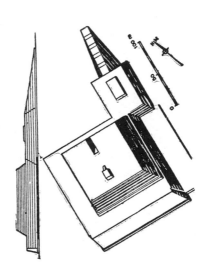

Pyramid of the Sun at Chan Chan.

A Chimu knife.

Two stylized warriors.

Chan Chan motif.

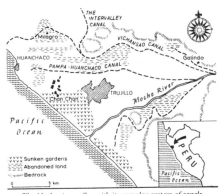

The Moche river valley with its complex system of canals

Pyramid of the Moon.

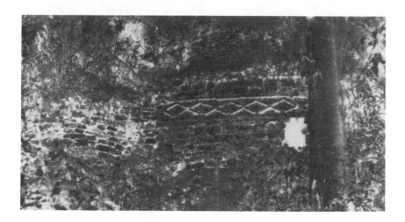

High wall at Kuelap. Its similarity to Zimbabwe is notable.

Aerial photo of the walled city of Chan Chan.

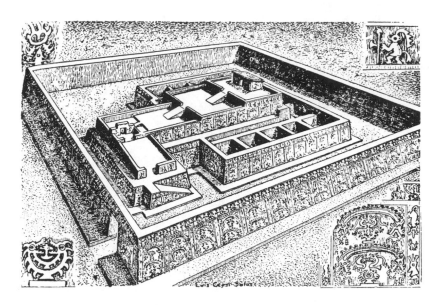

Courtyard at Chan Chan.

Mochica Warrior.

Carved stones at Chavin.

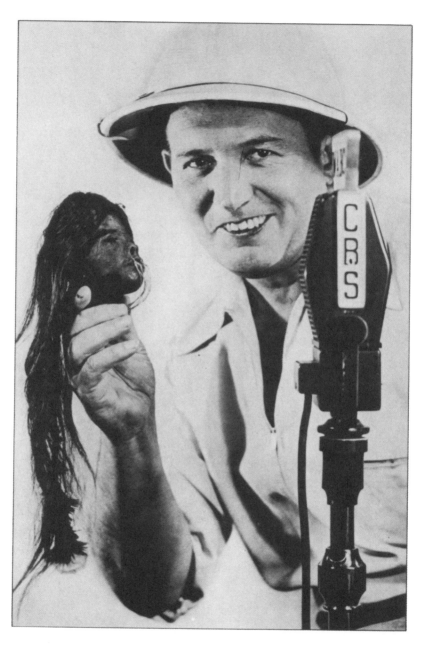

Robert Ripley holds the shrunken head of an Indian warrior.

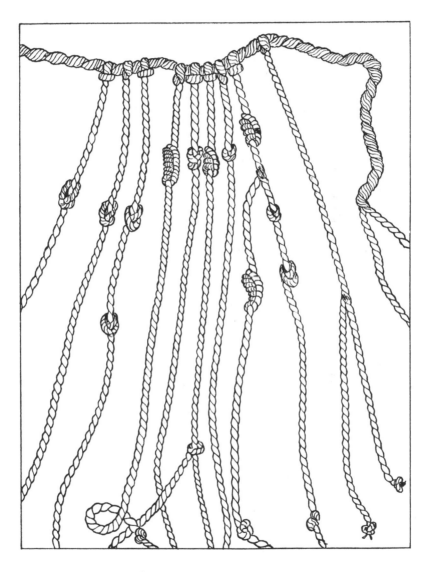

Portion of an Inca quipu.

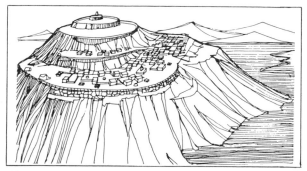

The mountain-top fortress of Cerro Pro
on the Rio Chillon near Lima.

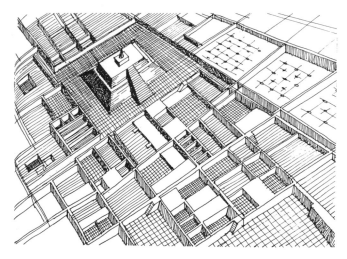

A portion of the city of Cajamarquilla

APPENDIX

Extract from the Revista Trimensal of the Instituto Historico e Geographico Brasileiro, Rio de Janeiro, July 21, 1865.

———◆———

Historical account of a large, hidden, and very ancient city, without inhabitants, discovered in the year 1753.

In America . . . .
in the interior . . . .
adjoining the . . . .
Master of *Can* . . . .
and his followers, having wandered over the desert country (Sertões) for ten years in the hopes of discovering the far-famed silver mines of the great explorer Moribeça, which through the fault of a certain governor were not made public, and to deprive him of this glory he was imprisoned in Bahia till death, and they remained again to be discovered. This news reached Rio de Janeiro in the beginning of the year 1754.

After a long and troublesome peregrination, incited by the insatiable greed of gold, and almost lost for many years in this vast Desert, we discovered a chain of mountains so high that they seemed to reach the ethereal regions, and that they served as a throne for the Wind or for the Stars themselves. The glittering thereof struck the beholder from afar, chiefly when the sun shone upon the crystal of which it was composed, forming a sight so grand and so agreeable that none could take eyes off these shining lights. Rain had set in before we had time to enter (in the itinerary) this crystalline marvel, and we saw the water running over the bare stone and precipitating itself from the high rocks, when it appeared to us like snow struck by the solar rays. The agreeable prospect of this . . . . (*uina*) shine
. . . .
. . . . of the waters and the tranquillity
. . . . . of the weather, we resolved to investigate this admirable prodigy of nature. Arriving at the foot of the ascent without any hindrance from forests or rivers, which might have barred our passage, but making a detour round the mountains, we did not find a free pass to carry out our resolution

* Translated by Mrs. Richard Burton, who begs indulgence, on account of this report having been written in old Portuguese by rude explorers, and therefore very difficult to render into English. All the lines that are not filled in, are illegible from the age and decayed state of the original MS.

to ascend these Alps and Brazilian Pyrenees, and we experienced an inexplicable sadness from this mistake.

We "ranched" ourselves with the design of retracing our steps the following day. A negro, however, going to fetch wood, happened to start a white stag which he saw, and by this chance discovered a road between two mountain chains, which seemed cut asunder by art rather than by nature. With the overjoy of this news we began the ascent, which consisted of loose stones piled up, whence we thought it had once been a paved road broken up by the injuries of time. The ascent occupied three good hours, pleasantly, on account of the crystals, at which we wondered. We halted at the top of the mountain, which commanded an extensive view, and we saw upon a level plain new motives to rouse our admiration.

We discerned about a league and a half from us a large settlement, whose extent convinced us that it must be some city dependent upon the capital of the Brazil. We descended soon to the valley, with the precaution . . . . it might be in such a case, sending explor . . . . gate the quality and . . . . that they should take good notice . . . . chimneys, this being one of the evident signs of settlements.

We waited for the explorers during two days, longing for news, and only waited to hear cocks crow to be certain that it was peopled. At last our men returned, undeceived as regards there being any inhabitants, which puzzled us greatly. An Indian of our company then resolved at all risks, but with precaution, to enter ; but he returned much frightened, affirming that he did not find nor could he discover the trail of any human being. This we would not believe, because we had seen the houses, and thus all the explorers took heart to follow the Indian's track.

They returned, confirming the above-mentioned deposition, namely, that there were no inhabitants, and so we determined all to enter this settlement well armed and at dawn, which we did without meeting any one to hinder our way, and without finding any other road save that which led directly to the great settlement. Its entrance is through three arches of great height, and the middle one is the largest, whilst the two side arches are less. Upon the largest and principal we discerned letters, which from their great height could not be copied.

There was one street the breadth of the three arches, with upper storeyed houses on either side ; the fronts of carved stone already blackened ; so . . . . inscriptions all open . . . . (d)oors are low of ma(ke) . . . . ·. . nas noting that by the regularity and symmetry with which they are constructed it appeared to be one long house, being in reality a great many. Some had open terraces, and all without tiles, the roofs being some of burnt bricks and others of freestone slabs.

We went through some of the houses with great fear, and nowhere could we find a vestige of personal goods or furniture which might by their use or fabric throw any light on the nature of the inhabitants. The houses are all dark in the interior ; there was scarcely a gleam of light ; and as they are vaulted, the voices of those who spoke re-echoed till our own accents frightened us.

Having examined and passed through the long street, we came to a regular square, and in the middle of it was a column of black stone of extraordinary height and size, and upon it was the statue of an average-sized man, with one hand upon his left haunch, and the right arm extended, pointing with his fore-finger to the North Pole. In each corner of the said square was a needle (obelisk ?), in imitation of that used by the Romans, but some had suffered ill-usage and were broken, as if struck by thunder-bolts.

On the right hand of this square was a superb edifice, as it were the principal house of some Lord of the land. There was an enormous saloon in the entrance, and still from fear we did not investigate all the hou(ses) . . . . . . being numerous and the *retret* . . . . *zerão* to form some . . . . *mara* we found o(ne) . . . . mass of extraordinary . . . . (per)sons had difficulty in raising it. . . . . The bats were so many that they attacked the people's faces, and made such a noise that it astonished them. Upon the principal portico of this street was a figure in demi-relief carved out of the same stone, and stripped from the waist upwards, crowned with laurels. It represented a young figure, and beardless. Beneath the shield of the figure were some characters, spoiled by time. How-ever, we made out the following. (See the Plate, inscription No. 1.)

On the left side of the said Square is another edifice, quite ruined ; but from the vestiges remaining, there is no doubt that it was once a temple, for part of its magnificent frontispiece still appears, and some naves and aisles of solid stone. It occupies a large space of ground, and on its ruined walls are seen carvings of superior workmanship, with some figures and pictures inlaid in the stone, with crosses and different emblems, crows and other minutiæ, which would take a long time to describe.

Follow this edifice—large portions of the city totally ruined and buried in large and frightful openings of the earth, and upon all this ground not a blade of grass, tree, or plant was produced by nature, but only heaps of stone and some coarse rough works, by which we judged . . . . *rerçao*, because still amongst . . . . *da* of corpses which . . . . is part of this unhappy . . . . *da*, and forsaken perhaps on account of some earthquake.

In front of the said square runs rapidly a mighty and broad river, which had spacious banks and was agreeable to the sight. It might be from 11 to 12 fathoms broad, without considerable turnings, and its banks were free from trees and timber which the inundations usually bring down. We sounded its depth and found in its deepest parts from 13 to 16 fathoms. On the further side of it are most flourishing plains, and with such a variety of flowers that it would appear as if nature was more bountiful to these parts, making them produce a perfect garden of Flora. We admired also some lagoons full of rice, of which we profited, and likewise innumerable flocks of ducks which breed in these fertile plains, and we found no difficulty in killing them without shot, but caught them in our hands.

We marched for three days down the river, and came upon a cataract which made a fearful noise from the force of the water and the obstacles in its bed, so that we thought the mouths of the far-famed Nile could not make more. Below this fall the river so spreads out that it appears to be the great ocean. It is full of peninsulas covered with green turf, with a sprinkling of trees, which make . . . . *davel.* Here we found . . . . in default of it if we . . . . (mu)ch variety of game . . . . . (o)ther many animals bred ; there being no huntsmen to chase and persecute them.

To the east of this waterfall we found several deep cuttings and frightful excavations, and tried its depth with many ropes, which, no matter how long they were, could not touch its bottom. We found also some loose stones, and, on the surface of the land some silver nails, as if they were drawn from mines and left at the moment.

Amongst these caverns we saw one covered with an enormous stone slab, and with the following figures carved on the same stone, which apparently contains some great mystery. (See the inscription No. 2.) Upon the portico of the temple we saw others also, of the following form. (Inscription No. 3.)

About a cannon-shot from the village was a building as it might be of a country-house, with a front 250 paces long. The entrance was by a large portico, and we ascended a staircase of many coloured stones which opened into an immense saloon, and afterwards into 15 small houses, each with a door opening into the said saloon, and each one bore its own water spout . . . . *a* which waters, and adjoining . . . . *mão* in the external courtyard . . . . colonnade in a cir . . . . *ra* squared by art, and hung with the following characters. (See the inscription No. 4.)

After this wonder we descended to the banks of the river hoping to discover gold, and without trouble we found rich " pay-dirt " upon the surface, promising great wealth of gold as well as of silver. We wondered at the inhabitants of this city having left such a place, not having found with all our zeal and diligence one person in these Deserts who could give any account of this deplorable marvel, as to whom this settlement might have belonged. The ruins well showed the size and grandeur which must have been there, and how populous and opulent it had been in the age when it flourished. But now it was inhabited by swallows, bats, rats and foxes, which fattened on the numerous breed of chickens and ducks, and grew bigger than a pointer-dog. The rats had such short legs they did not walk, but hopped like fleas ; nor did they run like those of an inhabited place.

From this spot a companion left us, who, with some others, after 9 days' good march, sighted at the mouth of a large bay formed by a river, a canoe carrying two white persons, with loose black hair, and dressed like Europeans, ... a shot as signal, in order to *ve* . . . . to fly or escape. . . To have . . . . hairy and wild . . . . *ga,* and they all curl up and invest . . . .

One of our companions, called João Antonio, found in the ruins of a house a gold coin, round, and larger than our pieces of 6$400. On one side was the

APPENDIX.

image or figure of a youth on his knees, and on the other side a bow, a crown and an arrow, of which sort (of money) we did not doubt there was plenty in the said settlement or deserted city, because if it had been destroyed by some earthquake, the people would not have had time suddenly to put their treasure in safety. But it would require a strong and powerful arm to examine that pile of ruins, buried for so many years, as we saw.

This intelligence I send to your Excellency from the Desert of Bahia, and from the rivers Para-oaçú (Paraguassú) and Unâ. We have resolved not to communicate it to any person, as we think whole towns and villages would be deserted ; but I impart to your Excellency tidings of the mines which we have discovered in remembrance of the much that I owe to you.

Supposing that, of our company, one has gone forth under a different understanding, I beg of your Excellency to drop these miseries, and to come and utilize these riches, and employ industry, and bribe this Indian to lose himself and conduct your Excellency to these treasures, etc. . .

. . . .
. . . . *charão* in the entrances
. . . . *bre* stone slabs . . .
. . . .

(Here follows in the manuscript what is found represented in the plate underneath, No. 5.)

1. K∪ΦI⟩⟩	Primeira.
2. ‡=∪ʒℋos	Secunda.
3. ‡‡‡⟩⟨∩ℑΛ⟨⟨†	Terceira.
4. A∪ᵛᵛƐ∩Ɛℚ‡◠---	Quarta.
	Quinta.
	Sexta.
	Setima.
	Oitava.
	Nona.

B.

Inscripçães encontradas na cidade abandonada de que trata o manuscripto, existente na Bibliothéca Publica do Rio de Janeiro.

Inscriptions found in the abandoned City, of which the MSS. to be seen in the Public Library of Rio de Janeiro, treats.

CHRONOLOGY OF EVENTS
AND EXPLORATIONS*

A.D. 1437 Chancas attack Cuzco.
1438 Chancas defeated by Inca Pachacutec.
1440 Antisuyo campaigns undertaken by Incas.
1466 Incas conquer Chimu.
1471 Death of Inca Pachacutec; Tupac Yupanqui assumes Inca Crown.
1480 Tupac Yupanqui conquers Chachapoyas.
1492 Columbus discovers America.
1493 Death of Inca Tupac Yupanqui; Huayna Capac assumes Inca Crown.
1500 Brazil discovered by Pedro Álvarez Cabral; mouth of Amazon discovered and explored by Vicente Yáñez Pinzón.
1500–11 Huayna Capac puts down Chachapoyas rebellion.
1518–20 Huayna Capac conquers Quito.
1522 Cortez conquers Mexico.
1526 Death of Inca Huayna Capac; Huáscar assumes Inca Crown at Cuzco; Portuguese launch expedition to colonize Brazil.
1527 Inca Empire reaches its zenith; Pizarro off coast of Peru; civil war begins between Huáscar and Atahualpa.
1530 Spaniards first hear rumors of El Dorado in Ecuador.
1531 Diego Ordaz looks for El Dorado; Pizarro launches full-scale expedition of conquest of Peru.
1532 Pizarro lands at Tumbes, marches to Cajamarca.
1533 Death of Huáscar by order of Atahualpa; Pizarro executes Atahualpa, marches on Cuzco; Sebastian Belalcazar conquers Quito.
1534 Manco II crowned Inca at Cuzco with approval of Francisco Pizarro.
1535 Antonio de Herrera looks for El Dorado; Pedro de Candia sent by Hernando Pizarro to investigate the Kingdom of Ambaya, eastern Bolivia.
1536 Manco revolts against Spanish, lays siege to Cuzco.
1537 Manco forces Chachapoyas from Amaybamba to Vilcabamba and beheads their chief at Urubamba; Manco retires into *montañas* of Vilcabamba with large host.

---

* Modern and Spanish dates used in the Chronology are as accurate as research permits. Inca dates must be considered tentative.

1538 Manco aids Antis Indians, visits Revanto; Spaniards found San Juan de la Frontera at Chachapoyas; Pedro Anzures leads expedition into Antisuyo east of Titicaca; civil war among conquistadores.
1539 Pedro Anzures contacts the Maguire nation on plains of Mojos and hears of a lost empire in the interior; Gonzalo Ximenes de Quesada fails to find El Dorado.
1540 Gonzalo Pizarro sets out for El Dorado and Forests of Cinnamon.
1541 Francisco Pizarro assassinated.
1541-42 Francisco de Orellana navigates the Amazon River.
1541-45 Philip Von Hutten hunts for El Dorado.
1542 Almagrists seek refuge with Manco in Vilcabamba.
1544 New Laws for the Indies issued by Spanish Crown.
1545 Manco assassinated in Vilcabamba; Sayri Tupac assumes crown of Vilcabamba line.
1550 Two hundred refugee Indians appear out of the forest at Chachapoyas.
1554 Huallaga region settled by Pedro de Ursúa.
1558 Lima receives word of El Dorado sighting.
1559 Spanish Crown sponsors El Dorado expedition under Pedro de Ursúa.
1560 Death of Sayri Tupac; Titu Cusi crowned Inca at Vilcabamba.
1565 Diego Rodriguez de Figueroa visits Titu Cusi in Vilcabamba.
1566 Marcos García enters Vilcabamba.
1568 Fray Diego Ortiz enters Vilcabamba.
1569 Viceroy Don Francisco de Toledo arrives in Peru.
1571 Death of Titu Cusi; Tupac Amaru crowned with Scarlet Fringe at Vilcabamba; Fray Ortiz martyred at Marcanay.
1572 Spanish army invades Vilcabamba under General Martín Hurtado de Arbieto; Vilcabamba the Old occupied by Spanish troops; San Francisco de la Victoria de Vilcabamba (Vilcabamba the New) founded by victorious Spanish; Tupac Amaru, last of the Vilcabamba kings, executed at Cuzco.
1581 Viceroy Toledo returns to Spain.
1584 Antonio de Berrio looks for El Dorado.
1595 Remains of Fray Diego Ortiz removed from Vilcabamba to Cuzco; Sir Walter Raleigh hunts for El Dorado, explores Orinoco.
1596 Lawrence Kemys sets out for El Dorado.
1597 Toribio Alonso de Mogrovejo missionizes Amazonas, Peru.
1613 Robert Harcourt looks for El Dorado in Guiana.
1619-21 Franciscans missionize jungles of eastern Peru.
1654 Fray Tomás Chavez claims to have contacted the Empire of the Musus after a 33-day journey from plains of Mojos. Paititi is said to be more densely populated than Peru and richer in gold than all the Indies.
1760 Apolinar Días de Fuente launches El Dorado expedition.
1764 Bodavilla expedition makes futile search for El Dorado.
1788 Fray Álvarez de Villanueva traverses The Pajatén.
1824 Eugene de Sartiques discovers Choquequirau.
1840 Sir Robert Hermann Schomburgk looks for El Dorado.
1843 Juan Crisóstomo Nieto discovers Kuelap.
1860 Arturo Wertheman explores Amazonas.
1865 Antonio Raimondi visits Spanish Vilcabamba in quest of Inca city.
1875 Charles Wiener travels over Pass of Panticalla, hears rumors of existence of Machu Picchu.

1877 Vidal Senéze reports existence of scattered remains in Rodriguez de Mendoza, Amazonas.
1892 Arturo Wertheman visits Kuelap.
1893 Adolph Bandelier explores Amazonas.
1895 Rubber planters explore fringe areas of Espíritu Pampa.
1901–07 Agriculturists first cultivate terraces of Machu Picchu.
1908 Theodor Koch-Grünberg looks for El Dorado.
1911 Hiram Bingham discovers Machu Picchu; makes unsuccessful attempt to explore Espíritu Pampa.
1916–28 Christian Bues maps Vilcabamba highlands.
1919 Augusto Weberbauer discovers scattered remains, roads leading to Pajatén country.
1925 Hamilton Rice looks for El Dorado; Colonel Percy H. Fawcett disappears in the Brazilian Mato Grosso.
1931–32 Shippee-Johnson Aerial Expedition discovers Santa Wall.
1933 General Louis Langlois explores Amazonas.
1942 Bertrand Flornoy explores upper Marañón.
1947 Arquimedes Toulier explores lower Urubamba.
1950–55 Henry Reichlen studies remains of Utcubamba.
1953 Malcolm Burke rafts down Urubamba, sights Inca terraces at Yavero; Victor von Hagen traces Inca roads of Peru; Julian Tennant explores for ruins in lower Urubamba.
1963 Brooks Baekeland and Peter Gimbel make first recorded traverse of Apurímac-Urubamba region; agriculturists from Huamachuco, Patáz and Pias observe archaeological remains in Pajatén territory.
1964 Carlos Neueschwander explores Pantiacolla for ancient remains; F. K. Paddock probes Urubamba.

Footnotes and Bibliography

1. *History's Timeline*, Fay Franklin, 1981, Crescent Books, NYC.

2. *American Genesis*, Jeffrey Goodman, Ph.D., 1981, Summit Books, NYC.

3. *The First American*, C.W. Ceram, 1971, New American Library, NYC.

4. "Ancient Roman Shipwreck Found In Brazil", Robert Marx, *Fate Magazine*, vol.36, no. 9, Sept. 1983.

5. *Voyagers to the New World*, Nigel Davies, 1979, William Morrow, NYC.

6. *Riddles in History*, Cyrus H. Gordon, 1974, Crown Publishers, NYC.

7. *6000 Years of Seafaring*, Orville L. Hope, 1983, Hope Associates, Gastonia, NC.

8. *America BC*, Barry Fell, 1976, Demeter Press, NYC.

9. *Mysteries of Forgotten Worlds*, Charles Berlitz, 1972, Doubleday, NYC.

10. *Lost Worlds,* Robert Charroux, 1973, Collins, Glasgow, Great Britain.

11. *Chariots of the Gods*, Erich Von Daniken, 1969, Putnam, NYC.

12. *Pathways to the Gods*, Tony Morrison, 1978, Andean Air Mail & Peruvian Times, Lima, Peru.

13. *The View Over Atlantis*, John Mitchell, 1969, Ballantine Books, NYC.

14. *The Bridge to Infinity*, Bruce Cathie, 1983, Quark Enterprises, Aukland, New Zealand.

15. *Investigating the Unexplained*, Ivan T. Sanderson, 1972, Prentice-Hall, Englewood Cliffs, NJ.

16. *Lost Cities of China, Central Asia & India*, D. H. Childress, 1985, AUP, Stelle, IL.

17. *Ancient Man: A Handbook of Puzzling Artifacts*, William Corliss, 1978, The Sourcebook Project, Glen Arm, MD.

18. *The Anti-Gravity Handbook*, ed. by D.H. Childress, 1985, AUP, Stelle, IL.

19. *Ice, The Ultimate Disaster*, R. Noone, 1982, Genesis Publishers, Dunwoody, GA.

20. *It's Still A Mystery*, Lee Gebhart & Walter Wagner, 1970, SBS, NYC.

21. *The Incas*, Garcilaso de la Vega, (first published 1608), 1961, Orion Press, NYC.

22. *Mysteries of Ancient South America*, Harold Wilkins, 1946, Citadel Press, NYC.

23. *Lost Cities of the Ancients-Uncovered!* Warren Smith, 1976, ZebraBooks, NYC.

24. *He Walked the Americas*, L. Taylor Hansen, 1963, Amherst Press, Amherst, WI

25. *Secret of the Andes*, Brother Philip, 1961, Neville Spearman, London

26. *The Subterranean Kingdom*, Nigel Pennick, 1981, Turnstone Press, Wellingborough, Northamptonshire, GB.

27. *The Ancient Atlantic*, L. Taylor Hansen, 1969, Amherst Press, Amherst, WI.

28. *Legends of the Lost*, Peter Brookesmith, ed., 1984, Orbis, London.

29. "Vilcabamba Revistited", G. Deyermenjian, *South American Explorer No. 12*, Sept. 1985.

30. *In Search of Lost Civilizations*, Alan Landsburg, 1976, Bantam, NYC.

31. *A New Search for Paititi*, Michael Mirecki, Lima Times, Feb. 15, 1985.

32. *The Search for El Dorado*, John Hemming, 1978, Michael Joseph, London.

33. *Exploration Fawcett*, Lt. Col. Percy H. Fawcett & Brian Fawcett, 1953, Hutchinson & Co., London. (U.S. title *Lost Trails, Lost Cities*)

34. *The Weaver and the Abbey*, Michael Brown, 1982, Corgi Books,London.

35. *Cataclysms of the Earth*, Hugh Auchincloss Brown, 1967, Twayne Pubs., NYC.

36. *The Path of the Pole*, Charles Hapgood, 1970, Chilton, Philadelphia.

37. *Pole Shift*, John White, 1980, Doubleday, NYC.

38. *Strange Artifacts*, William Corliss, 1974, The Sourcebook Project, Glen Arm, MD.

39. *The World's Last Mysteries*, Reader's Digest, 1976, Reader's Digest Association, Inc., Pleasantville, New York.

40. *The Ancient Stones Speak*, David Zink, 1979, E.P. Dutton, NYC.

41. *The Lost Continent of Mu*, James Churchward, 1931, Ives Washburn, NY.

42. *The Children of Mu*, James Churchward, 1931, Ives Washburn, NY.

43. *Secret Cities of Old South America*, Harold Wilkins, 1952, Library Publications, Inc., NYC.

44. "A Late Ice-Age Settlement in Southern Chile",Tom Dillehay,*Scientific American*, Oct.1984.

45. *Strange Life*, Richard Corliss, 1976, Sourcebook Project, Glen Arm, MD.

46. *Alien Animals*, Janet Bord, 1981, Stackpole Books, Harrisburg, PA.

47. *The Mysterious Past*, Robert Charroux,1973, Robert Laffont, NYC.

48. *Living Wonders*, John Mitchell & Robert Rickard, 1982, Thames & Hudson, NYC.

49. *Enigmas*, Rupert Gould,1945, University Books, NYC.

50. *More "Things"*, Ivan T. Sanderson, 1969, Pyramid Books, NYC.

51. *Strange World*, Frank Edwards, 1964, Bantam Books, NYC.

52. *Stranger Than Science*, Frank Edwards, 1959, Bantam Books, NYC.

53. *On the Track of Unknown Animals*, Bernard Heuvelmans, 1958, MIT Press, Cambridge, MA.

54. *The Chronicle of Akakor*, Karl Brugger,1977, Delacorte Press, NYC.

55. *The Queen of Sheba and Her Only Son Menyelek (Kebra Nagast)*, translated by Sir E.A. Wallis Budge, 1932, Dover, London.

56. *Hitler: The Survival Myth*, Donald McKale, 1981, Stein & Day, NYC.

57. *The Fate of Colonel Fawcett*, Geraldine Cummins, 1955, Aquarian Press, London.

58. *Inca Gold*, Jane Dolinger, 1967, Henry Regnery Co., Chicago.

59. *Morning of the Magicians*, L. Pauwels & J. Bergier, 1960, Stein & Day, NYC.

60. *The Road In the Sky*, G. H. Williamson,1959, Neville Spearman Ltd., London.

61. *Atlantis, The Lost Continent Revealed*, Charles Berlitz, 1984, Macmillan,London.

62. *Timeless Earth*, Peter Kolosimo, 1974, University Press Seacaucus, NJ.

63. *Highway of the Sun*, Victor von Hagen,1955, Little, Brown & Co., Boston.

64. *Brazilian Adventure*, Peter Fleming, 1934, Charles Scribner's Sons, NYC.

65. *Peru*, G. H. Bushnell,1957, Frederick Praeger, NYC.

66. *Conquest of Peru, Vol. One*, William Prescott, 1847, Harper, NYC.

67. *Conquest of Peru, Vol. Two*, William Prescott, 1847, Harper, NYC.

68. *The Incredible Incas & Their Timeless Land*, Loren McIntyre, 1975, The National Geographic Society, Washington D.C.

69. *Mysteries of the Ancient World*, National Geographic Society, 1979, Washington D.C.

70. *Atlas of Ancient Archaeology*, Jacquetta Hawkes,1974, McGraw Hill, NYC.

71. *Atlas of Ancient History*, Michael Grant, 1971, Macmillan, London.

72. *Antisuyo, The Search For the Lost Cities of the Amazon*, Gene Savoy, 1970, Simon and Shuster, NYC.

Who is Adventures Unlimited ?

Adventures Unlimited is an organization of *World Explorers* providing today's *Adventurer* a unique opportunity to experience the past and to uncover lost cities and ancient civilizations before they disappear forever. We specialize in the more remote destinations of the World, those skipped over by less committed guides, for it is our passion for discovery that drives us to seek out and find these undiscovered sites while others are content with the known.

Notice that nowhere in the descriptions of our expeditions do you find that unfortunate four letter word, "Tour". And for a very good reason: Our members abhor that form of travel. They often remember (as we do!) nightmarish experiences with bored guides, inarticulately reciting dull facts, while waving a flag over their head as if to alert all nearby to the unfortunate presence of tourists.

Picture yourself instead on one of Adventures Unlimited's expeditions. You, one of the explorers accompanied by two authors to the Egyptian Pyramids and Valley of the Kings, examining the most radical and exciting theories on the origin of this ancient civilization. Or one of the adventurers spending more than a week in search of a sunken stone city in the South Pacific, discovering and mapping for the first time ancient underwater columns. You could be one of the explorers reliving the Incas' final days, tracing their retreat from the Spanish Conquistadors through the high jungles of Peru, trying to answer the riddle, "Where was the final refuge of the Incas?"

Your expedition leader, David Hatcher Childress, is as unique as our members. As the author of seven adventure-travel books, he has been interviewed on the Today Show, in OMNI, Science Digest, National Geographic, People and a host of other international magazines. David is an exceptional and exciting personality to discover the world with.

Each of our expeditions is a personal journey of discovery. We travel because it is our joy and invite you to join us in our quests. Every departure is a new adventure, made more so by those who choose to join us. We have never failed to learn something new from expedition members, often sharing the excitement of their own discoveries made along the way.

Call us today to explore a unique opportunity; an expedition into the past.

Call Now!
For
Expedition Reservations and Information
815 253 6390

Explore the Past...

LOST CITIES OF CHINA, CENTRAL ASIA & INDIA

by David Hatcher Childress, 447 pp, 80 photos, maps & drawings, 6x9 tradepaper, $12.95.
Search for mysterious tunnels leading to supernatural realms, forgotten cities in the Gobi Desert, hidden monasteries high in the Himalayas while Childress spins amazing stories of travel, history and the mysteries of the past while searching for clues to the fabulous Rama Empire of India and other advanced, lost civilizations. Chronologically first in the Lost Cities series.

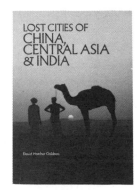

LOST CITIES OF ANCIENT LEMURIA & THE PACIFIC

by David Hatcher Childress, 382 pp, 120 maps, prints & photos, 6x9 tradepaper, $12.95.
Was there once a lost continent in the Pacific? Did ancient Egyptian, Peruvian, Chinese and other sailors continually cross the Pacific in ancient times? Who built the mysterious megaliths throughout the Pacific? In the forth book chronologically, in the Lost Cities Series, Maverick Archaeologist Childress searches the Indian Ocean, Australia and the Pacific in search of lost cities and ancient mysteries. Includes nearly every map drawn of lost civilizations & continents of the Pacific.

Forthcoming books in the Lost Cities series:

- **LOST CITIES OF NORTH & CENTRAL AMERICA**
- **LOST CITIES OF EUROPE & THE MEDITERRANEAN**

LOST CITIES & ANCIENT MYSTERIES OF SOUTH AMERICA

by David Hatcher Childress, 375 pp, 100 maps, prints and photos, 6x9 trade paper, $12.95.
Archaeologist/Adventurer Childress takes the reader on unforgettable journeys deep into windswept mountains in quest off cities of gold, deadly jungles searching for living dinosaurs, and scorching deserts on the track of Egyptian gold mines. Translated into both Spanish and Portuguese, and a top ten best seller in Brazil, (as well as Cuzco) this book is fast becoming a classic on the mysteries of South America.

LOST CITIES AND ANCIENT MYSTERIES OF SOUTH AMERICA

LOST CITIES & ANCIENT MYSTERIES OF AFRICA & ARABIA

by David Hatcher Childress, 400 pp, 110 rare photos, maps & drawings, 6x9 tradepaper, $12.95.
Chronologically the second book in the Lost Cities series, this book has been delayed for legal reasons. Now in production, we plan to release it sometime this summer. In this volume Childress travels through Africa and Arabia, to lost cities in the Empty Quarter, Atlantean ruins in Egypt, a port city in the Sahara, King Solomon's mines and antediluvian ruins in the Kalahari.

ICE: THE ULTIMATE DISASTER by Richard Noone, 380pp, 100's of photos and diagrams, 7x10 tradepaper, $12.95
Many books capture the imagination, but rarely does one capture the intellect. In a tour-de-force that starts with the Great Pyramid and takes us through secret societies and ancient mysteries, the author concludes that a massive cataclysm will take place on May 5, 2000. An incredible read, it also profiles the community of Stelle.

THE ULTIMATE FRONTIER by Eklal Kueshana. 300 pp, index, 6x9 tradepaper, $6.95.
This unusual book was first published in 1962 and was a cult classic in the late '60s. Written as a novel, it reveals esoteric information so startling and interest- ing, that two communities were started as a result. The book presents an inspiring philosophy of a brotherhood of scientist- philosophers dedicated to improving and preserving the best of civilization. The book predicts a global cataclysm in the year 2000, and a golden age to follow.

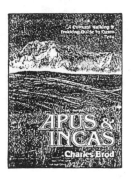

APUS & INCAS: *A Cultural Walking & Trekking Guide to Cuzco Peru* by Charles Brod. 150 pp, 15 maps & photos, 5x7 tradepaper, $9.95
This is a comprehensive guide to the trails and paths around the ancient Inca capital of Cuzco. It describes more than 16 treks and day walks. Want to hike an ancient Inca trail to a lost city? This guide is for you!

AMERICAN INDIAN MAGIC—*SACRED POW WOWS & HOPI PROPHECIES* by Brad Steiger. 200 pp, dozens of photos & illustrations, 6x9 tradepaper, $9.95
A compilation of interesting Amerindian material, there are chapters on Hopi Prophesy, Vision Quests, Coming Earth Changes, Indian prophets and more.

KAHUNA POWER by Timothy Green Beckley. 160 pp, dozens of photos & illustrations, 6x9 tradepaper, $9.95.
Kahuna means "Keeper of the Secret" in ancient Hawaiian, and this book explores some of the ancient mysteries of Hawaii, and even the very origins of Hawaiians themselves. Other chapters are on herbal remedies, Madame Pele, and ancient spells.

ANTI-GRAVITY AND THE WORLD GRID

edited by D.H. Childress. 267 pp, 100's of photos, drawings, 7x10 tradepaper, $12.95

Is the earth surrounded by an intricate electromagnetic grid network offering free energy? This complex pattern of the earth's energies, researchers believe, if properly understood, can shed light on the nature of gravity, UFO's, vortex areas, power spots, ley lines, and even the placement of ancient megalithic structures. One of our best selling books—fascinating and visual.

LOST SCIENCE SERIES

THE ANTI-GRAVITY HANDBOOK edited by D.

H. Childress, 195 pp, 100's of photo, drawings & diagrams, including patents, 7x10 tradepaper, $12.95.

Now into several printings, this fascinating compilation of material, some of it humorous, explores the theme of gravity control and the theoretical propulsion technique used by UFOs. Chapters include "How To Build a Flying Saucer", Quartz Crystals and Anti-Gravity, Arthur C. Clarke on Gravity Control, NASA, the Moon and Anti-Gravity, & flying saucer patents. There is also a rare article by Nikola Tesla entitled "A Machine to End All War".

MOONGATE: Suppressed Findings of the U.S. Space Program, by William Brian II

231 pp. 6x9, color photos, illustrations, trade paper, $12.95

Documented evidence, NASA photos and official government papers are used in this incredible book to expose the real nature, method and goal of the Apollo missions. Includes information on suppressed gravity research, secret discoveries on the moon by astronauts, "The Great Energy Cover-up", and more. A must for anyone interested in advanced technology, gravity control, NASA and the "Space Race". Profusely illustrated.

THE LOST MILLENIUM by

Walt & Leigh Richmond, 172 pp, 6x9 trade paper, $9.95.

How did the Atlanteans tap the free energy of the Universe?— asks the cover of this unusual book. Did Atlanteans have free energy? Did their science cause their destruction? Was the Great Pyramid of Egypt built as a "solar tap"? All this and more!

THE MANUAL OF FREE ENERGY DEVICES AND SYSTEMS compiled by D.A. Kelly. 123pp, 100's of photos, diagrams & patents, 9x11 tradepaper, $12.95.

In this manual, D.A. Kelly describes the viability and progress of each device from Nikola Tesla to present. Also mentioned are various spin-off inventions as a result of "free energy" research. Included are chapters on Joseph Newman, "N" Field Machines, Viktor Schauberger, Rudolf Steiner, Wilhelm Reich, John Searle, and more.

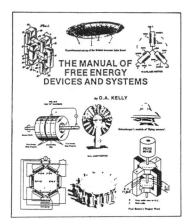

THE AWESOME LIFE FORCE by Joseph Cater. 472 pp, 30 diagrams & line drawings, 5x8, tradepaper. $15.95.

Here is a book that purports to solve all of the mysteries of life, including, but not limited to, UFO phenomena, gravity, Wilhelm Reich and orgone energy, teleportation, time travel, materializations, and just about every other strange occurance one can think of. A must for anyone seriously exploring the strange nature of reality.

ETHER TECHNOLOGY: A RATIONAL APROACH TO GRAVITY CONTROL by Rho Sigma. 108 pp, 20 photos and diagrams, 6x9 tradepaper. $9.95.

Written by a well-known American scientist under the pseudonym of Rho Sigma, this brief book discusses in detail international efforts at Gravity Control. Included are chapters on Searle Discs, T. Townsend Brown, Ether-Vortex-Turbines, and more. Forward by Astronaut Edgar Mitchell.

PYRAMID ENERGY: *THE PHILOSOPHY OF GOD, THE SCIEN OF MAN* by D & M Hardy and M & K Killick. 266 pp, hundreds of photos & diagrams, 6x9 tradepaper. $12.95.

This book is far more than the title proclaims. It is an exhaustive study of the many energy fields around us, including the purpose of ley lines, megaliths and pyramids, vortex energy, Nikola Tesla's coil energy, tachion energy, levitation, the meaning of the Ark of the Convenant, & more.

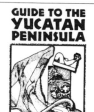

GUIDE TO THE YUCATAN PENINSULA by Chicki Mallan

Like a hitchhiking thumb jutting into the Caribbean, the Yucatan Peninsula is an invitation to adventure and discovery. Long isolated from the rest of Mexico, new roads through the rainforest make the Peninsula easily accessible at last.
4 color pages, 154 b/w photos, 55 illus., 53 maps, 68 charts, appendix, booklist, vocabulary, index, 300 pages.
ISBN 0-918373-11-5   US$10.95

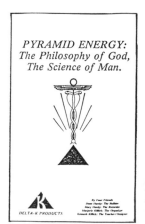

Now *YOU* Can Live and Work In Japan!

The Complete Guide to Living and Working in the Land of Rising Opportunity

John Wharton

- Helpful, friendly people — always kind to visitors.
- No need to speak Japanese.
- No special education or experience required.
- Earn US $30,000-40,000 in teaching, writing, entertainment and business — save ½ easily!
- Thousands of long and short-term jobs available now!

Jobs In Japan explains in detail:
- Making travel preparations.
- Dealing with Japanese culture.
- Setting up house.
- Negotiating with employers.
- Getting the right visas.
- Bringing along your children.

264 pp.
US $9.95
illustrated
ISBN 0-911285-00-8

Teaching Tactics for Japan's English Classrooms

explains in detail:
- How any native-speaker can teach English conversation.
- Current English-teaching methods.
- Popular classroom activities.
- Types of Japanese students and their needs.
- The history of English and how it works.
- Names and addresses of hundreds of English schools in Japan — most now hiring!

"Recommended to all"
    — Jean Pearce, *Japan Times*

"An inspired travel guide"
    — Julie Edgar, *Ann Arbor*

TEACHING TACTICS

for Japan's English Classrooms

John Wharton

JOBS IN JAPAN
TEACHING SUPPLEMENT

140 pp
US $6.95
ISBN 0-911285-02-4

VAGABONDING IN THE U.S.A.
Ed Buryn

A fascinating alternative to the ordinary books about our extraordinary country (plus Canada and Mexico), *Vagabonding* is packed with practical and humorous information, essays, maps, photos, and listings. It advises adventure-seekers on such means of transportation as freighthopping, hitchhiking, bicycling, automobile and motorcycle touring, and just plain hiking. . . . "Eating, sleeping, befriending, and staying in whatever United States, mental or geographical, that currently holds your fancy." —*CoEvolution Quarterly*

432 pp, illustrated, 5½ × 8½, $10.95

PUBLICATIONS

Blueprint for Paradise

How to live on a tropic island

Ross Norgrove

BLUEPRINT FOR PARADISE
By Ross Norgrove

Do you dream of living on a tropical island paradise? *Blueprint for Paradise* clearly and concisely explains how to make that dream a reality. Derived from his own and others' experiences, Norgrove covers: choosing an island, owning your own island, designing a house for tropical island living, transportation, getting settled, and successfully facing the natural elements. Breathtaking illustrations complete this remarkable guide, 202 pages.

ISBN 0-918373-15-8   US$14.95

JAPAN HANDBOOK
by J.D. Bisignani

Packed with practical money-saving tips on travel, food and accommodation. *Japan Handbook* is essentially a cultural and anthropological manual on every facet of Japanese life. 35 color photos, 200 b/w photos, 92 illustrations, 29 charts, 112 maps and town plans, an appendix on the Japanese language, booklist, glossary, index, 504 pages.
ISBN 0-9603322-2-7   US$12.95

JAPAN HANDBOOK

J.D. BISIGNANI

"*Japan Handbook* tells us more about out-of-the-way Japan than any of the other guides...As a guidebook his is clearly among the better.
    —Donald Richie, THE JAPAN TIMES

"If you have room to pack only one book on a trip to Japan, this is the one."
    —George Rosenblatt, HOUSTON CHRONICLE

INDONESIA HANDBOOK
Fourth Edition

Bill Dalton

A new edition of the first and only guide to the geography, flora and fauna, ethnology and culture of all the main island groups. The cheapest places to eat and sleep, antiquities, ". . . one of the best practical guides ever written about any country." —*The Sunday Times of London*

• **25,000 Copies in Print**

$12.95, Trade Paper ,
ISBN 0-918373-12-3, 600pp, 5¼ × 7¼

ORDERING INFORMATION

Fill in the Mail Order Form. Please **PRINT** all information.

Please do not send cash. All payments **MUST BE** in **$ US.**

Remit the amount due by check or money order.

When paying by Credit Card be sure to include your signature.

We accept telephone credit card orders. Call anytime   815 253 6390

We give a **10 % discount** when you **order 3 or more items.**

BACKORDERS:
We will backorder forthcoming and out-of stock titles unless otherwise requested.

RETAILERS:
Standard discounts available
Call or write for more information

SHIPPING CHARGES: United States
Postal Bookrate :
$1.25 for 1st book
50¢ each additional book.
Maximum you pay $5.00

United Parcel Service (UPS):
$2.75 for 1st Book
50¢ each additional item
Maximum you pay $5.00

Airmail:
$4.00 per item
Sorry , No C.O.D.

Residents of Illinois add 7% sales tax.

SHIPPING CHARGES:
Canada

Postal Bookrate :
$1.50 for 1st book
50¢ each additional book.
Maximum you pay $5.00

United Parcel Service (UPS):
$2.75 for 1st book
75$ each additional book
Maximum you pay $6.50
YOU MUST include your phone number for UPS deivery

Airmail:
$4.00 per item

SPECIAL PAYMENT NOTICE for Canadian customers
1. Remittance **MUST BE** $US
2. Canadian Postal Money Orders Accepted
3. Other Checks **MUST BE** drawn on a US Bank

Shipping Charges:
All other Countries

Surface Delivery:
$2.75 1st item
$1.00 each addition item

SPECIAL PAYMENT NOTICE for International customers
1. Remittance **MUST BE** $US
2. Checks **MUST BE** drawn on a US Bank

Adventures Unlimited
Welcomes correspondence from anyone • anywhere • anytime. Send us the names of your friends and we will send them a catalog.

Write or call for our latest catalogue
of unusual books and expeditions.

Our planetary Headquarters is 75 miles
from Chicago. Visitors are welcome.

Name _____

Address _____

City _____ State ____ Postal Code _____

Telephone Home (   ) _____ Work (   ) _____

Full Book Title	Price	Qty	$ Amount

Adventures Unlimited Press
Post Office Box 22
Stelle, IL USA   60919-9989
815 253 6390

Item Totals	
Less Discount	
Shipping	
Sales Tax	
Total Remit	

MasterCard VISA

☐ **Charge It** Credit Card Number _____
Expiration _____ Today's Date_____
Signature _____

☐ **Check Enclosed** (Drawn on US Bank in $US)

LOST CITIES & ANCIENT MYSTERIES OF SOUTH AMERICA

NOW ON VIDEO!

ANNOUNCING
THE FIRST
ADVENTURES UNLIMITED
VIDEO MAGAZINE

Adventures Unlimited has now completed the first volume of it's video magazine, a 60 minute visual magazine on the exciting and unusual topics explored in the popular Lost Cities and Lost Science Series. Hosted by author/explorer David Hatcher Childress, and produced by Karl Hart ,Adventures Unlimited presents presents some of the strangest and most fascinating stories presented in our books on video format. Volume One of the Adventures Unlimited's Video magazine includes these stories:

•LOST CITIES OF THE INCAS: Follow Maverick archaeologist & explorer David Hatcher Childress and Peruvian anthropologist Fernando Aparicio Bueno as they search for the final lost city of the Incas, Paititi. From the massive pre-Inca fortresses of Cuzco, to the mysterious tunnel systems beneath Sacsayhuaman to mysterious Machu Picchu to the vast and unexplored high jungles of the eastern Andes, Childress and Bueno search for the ancient sun disc from the Temple of the Sun in Cuzco, and the final lost cities of the Incas, Paititi and Yanantin Orco.

•DINOSAUR HUNTING IN THE CONGO: Do dinosaurs still survive in remote tropical regions of the world? While it is generally believed that dinosaurs became extinct 65 million years ago, this is not scientific fact at all, but merely a theory. It is a fact, however, that dinosaurs are reported around the world every year. Join us on a fascinating expedition into the central African country of The People's Democratic Republic of the Congo in search of Mokele Mbembe, a living brontosaurus said to be living in the remote Tele Swamps. The Walt Disney movie "Baby" was based on these expeditions.

•RADAR MEN FROM THE MOON: Are strange men from our hollow moon invading earth with the sinister intent of taking control of earth? Only Commando Cody and his lost planet airmen can stop them! This 40's serial features Anti-Gravity, particle-beam weapons, secret bases on the moon, strange technology ! It's so bizarre, it has to be true!

Available on VHS or BETA. $15.95 + 1.25 postage for your copy. Order with your book order, and save postage (also, we give a 10% discount with orders of 3 or more books and/or videos).

•Coming in Volume Two: At the massive crystal city of Nan Modal on the remote Micronesian Island of Ponape (Pohnpei) we explore an underwater city, and strange tales of levitation; Dr. Hatch's Anti-Gravity Tapes, Searching for Yeti & Sasquatch, Radar Men From the Moon, and more!